History of Buena Vista University

Third Edition

HISTORY OF
BUENA VISTA UNIVERSITY

THIRD EDITION

WILLIAM H. CUMBERLAND

Blackwell
Publishing

Blackwell Publishing Professional
2121 State Avenue, Ames, Iowa 50014, USA

Orders: 1-800-862-6657
Office: 1-515-292-0140
Fax: 1-515-292-3348
Web site: www.blackwellprofessional.com

Blackwell Publishing Ltd
9600 Garsington Road, Oxford OX4 2DQ, UK
Tel.: +44 (0)1865 776868

Blackwell Publishing Asia
550 Swanston Street, Carlton, Victoria 3053, Australia
Tel.: +61 (0)3 8359 1011

Authorization to photocopy items for internal or personal use, or the internal or personal use of spe-
cific clients, is granted by Blackwell Publishing, provided that the base fee is paid directly to the
Copyright Clearance Center, 222 Rosewood Drive, Danvers, MA 01923. For those organizations that
have been granted a photocopy license by CCC, a separate system of payments has been arranged.
The fee code for users of the Transactional Reporting Service is ISBN-13: 978-0-8138-0609-9; ISBN-
10: 0-8138-0609-7/2006 $.10.

First edition, ©1966 Iowa State University Press
Second edition, ©1992 Iowa State University Press
Third Edition, 2006

Library of Congress Cataloging-in-Publication Data

Cumberland, William H. (William Henry), 1929-
   History of Buena Vista University / William H. Cumberland.—3rd ed.
      p. cm.
   Includes bibliographical references and index.
   ISBN-13: 978-0-8138-0609-9 (alk. paper)
   ISBN-10: 0-8138-0609-7 (alk. paper)
   1. Buena Vista University—History.   I. Title.
   LD701.B32C8 2006
   378.777'18—dc22

                                                    2006008499

The last digit is the print number: 9 8 7 6 5 4 3 2 1

CONTENTS

v

PREFACE

The third edition of Buena Vista's history covers the era of the institution's emergence as a university. This edition details the last few years of the Briscoe Administration and the first decade of the presidency of Fred Moore. Undoubtedly, more changes have taken place at Buena Vista during the last fifteen years than in the entire preceding century as the University gained regional and national attention. This edition has sought to chronicle and to some extent interpret those changes that have altered the landscape, the facilities, the structure, and the emphasis of the University. Indeed, one of the major changes has been the achievement of university status as well as its implementation of technology as a major teaching and learning tool. The New American College concept, while not always understood, has freed the institution to spread its branches of learning in unprecedented directions. There are so many ways in which Buena Vista has truly become "a university without borders." There is little doubt that the faculty, administration, trustees, and student body are not only the best in the history of the school, but are competitive with similar institutions across the country.

Once again the task of the author was made easier by the assistance of many current and former colleagues, former students, administrators, and others. Special thanks goes to Donna Schoneboom, Assistant to the President. Donna was always on call, always dependable no matter how busy, never complained about interruptions or extra workload. Nancy Julich in University Communications and Jody Morin from the Information Technology Center always came to my assistance with good humor. This was actually their second time around because they also assisted in the preparation of the second edition. My special thanks to Cindy Bibler, Administrative Assistant to the Vice President at Buena Vista, who helped prepare the manuscript; Jennifer Felton, Buena Vista's

Director of Publications and Graphic Design, who designed the book cover; and Peggy Hazelwood, copyeditor at ISU Press, who detected and corrected the author's inconsistencies and errors. Ken Clipperton, the patient Managing Director of University Services, saved the manuscript from a possible computer disaster. Nick Huber, the ingenious Sports Information Director, helped correct some original errors in Chapter Ten, and provided valuable information. Chuck Offenburger, an outstanding Iowa author still remembered for his "Iowa Boy" column in the *Des Moines Register,* shed light on several aspects of college life. I am also indebted to current and past faculty, especially Carl Adkins, Mike Whitlatch, John and Sandra Madsen, and Bill Feis. I also thank President Moore for graciously letting me drill him during an interview and providing the necessary means for publication.

My deepest appreciation remains for Ingrid Cumberland, who joined me in 1959 departing her German homeland for unknown adventures, continued to live with me during my long tenure at Buena Vista, still sticks with me after more than 47 years of togetherness. She also provided invaluable assistance in researching much of the material. I repeat my promise of 1991 to dedicate to her my total attention as we continue our march through the valley of retirement.

I dedicate the third edition to the lengthening line of Buena Vista graduates, faculty, trustees, administrators, and friends who have supported the University through every adversity. Some have been around long enough to have witnessed the struggle and to have tasted the triumph. The others we honor in our collective memory.

As for me, I have had a great experience. I have made many friends, and I have felt disappointment at times but also the joy of success. It has been an honor to watch a college evolve from ashes into a citadel of learning. There will, someday, be a fourth edition. I know that author of the future will have an even greater story to tell.

HISTORY OF BUENA VISTA UNIVERSITY
THIRD EDITION

1

A LAND IS SETTLED

... a land almost flowing with milk and honey.
— NEWSPAPER CORRESPONDENT, 1891

Originally a part of the Louisiana Purchase, Iowa passed through a series of territorial phases before becoming a state on December 28, 1846. The population growth of Iowa was remarkable, jumping from 43,000 in 1840 to 675,000 in 1860. Meanwhile, the American Indian question had been solved in the usual frontier manner and the permanent capital had been located at Des Moines. Land was the great attraction — advertised by such early Iowa boosters as John P. Newhall in his *Glimpses into Iowa* — that drew both families from the East and European immigrants. Iowa, as historian Joe Wall wrote in his centennial history, was not only the land between two rivers but the Mesopotamia of America.

The first influx of immigrants into Iowa had a definite southern character, but by the 1850s and 1860s the majority of Iowans had New England origins. Many of them, however, migrated to Iowa from other midwestern states, particularly Ohio and Illinois, and not directly from the East. There were also many foreign-born settlers in the Hawkeye State — almost 11 percent in 1850 and nearly 17 percent by 1890.[1] In addition, Iowa was to have a variety of communal colonies ranging from the German Amanas to the French Icarian settlements. From the beginning Iowa was destined

3

to be an agricultural state with the corn-hog economy being dis-
cernible even in the 1840s. However, Iowa also had plentiful coal
deposits (although not of the best quality), and a number of coal-
mining communities blossomed in the central and southern parts
of the state. One such community, Buxton, was essentially black in
its composition and thrived until the mines gave out just prior to
World War I.

It did not take the adventurous Iowa settlers long to push into
the western regions of the state. Already by 1856 a small settlement
existed at Sioux Rapids, founded by a New Jersey bachelor, Abner
Bell, and the William Weaver and John W. Tucker families. Soon
other settlers joined the struggling group that in 1857 experienced
an unpleasant visit from Inkpaduta's raiders. Although the settlement was subjected to a variety of indignities, it escaped the fate
meted out to the pioneers near Spirit Lake.[2] Abner Bell was a
frontiersman who dressed himself with the skins of animals, wore
his hair long, grew a beard, and was described as "turbulent, restless, unlettered and uncouth."[3] He trapped the plentiful beaver,
otter, and mink along the Little Sioux and operated a store where
farmers could obtain groceries, powder, and other necessities.
Somehow he became sheriff, clerk of the district court, and ultimately a member of the board of supervisors. The name was firmly
enough established in local folklore that more than a century later
a Storm Lake entrepreneur named his stylish but short-lived cafe in
Bell's honor.

Buena Vista County was established by an act of the state
legislature in January 1851, deriving its name, like so many Iowa
counties, from the recent war with Mexico. Thus the rugged Battle
of Buena Vista, fought south of the Mexican town of Saltillo in
February 1847, was the inspiration for the name of an Iowa county
and an Iowa college. The English translation "beautiful view" was
not inappropriate. Iowans, however, corrupted the more poetic
Spanish pronunciation leaving domestic and foreign visitors con-
fused as to the correct way of saying *Bwayna Vista!*

However, Buena Vista County was not destined to share in the
general population growth of Iowa during the decade of 1850–
1860. A census taken by C. C. Smeltzer in 1860 revealed only fifty-

seven inhabitants in the county.[4] Among the early county officials were A. T. Reeves, county judge; William Weaver, treasurer and recorder; J. W. Tucker, clerk; and Abner Bell, sheriff. The county seat was about one mile southeast of the present site of Sioux Rapids and was called Prairieville.[5] No buildings were ever erected at the site and in 1869 the county seat was moved to Sioux Rapids and a courthouse constructed. The struggle between rival towns to become the county capital reopened with the growth of Newell and Storm Lake in the southern part of the county and intensified as a result of a disastrous fire that destroyed the courthouse and almost all of the county records at Sioux Rapids on New Year's Day, 1877. The following year Storm Lake emerged victorious in the "County Seat War," as the county electorate voted overwhelmingly to relocate the county capital at the young community on the lake.

The first settler on Storm Lake in the spring of 1867 had been Daniel B. Harrison. George Holt, the Harlans, John Ludington, and other families followed. The fact that the Dubuque and Sioux City Railroad was being constructed across Iowa enticed an increasing number of immigrants to the western sections of the state. The railroad would reach Storm Lake in the summer of 1870 and would coincide with the establishment of the city. Certainly the coming of the railroad helped spur the growth of the county's population, which jumped from 242 in 1869 to over 2,000 in 1871.[6]

Tales of the West inevitably involve struggles with prairie fires, high winds, blizzards, and grasshoppers. Ole Rölvaag describes the struggles in his novels set in the Dakotas. Western Iowans battled all these scourges, including the desperate war with the grasshoppers when the sky was darkened, the buzzing intense, and the land soon devastated. An old-timer wrote in the *Pilot-Tribune's* historical edition of 1931:

> Terrific blizzards during the winter and grasshoppers during the summer made trying times for everyone. The grasshoppers devoured all that was raised. Days of labor in the fields were lost in a few short hours when the pests came and settled over the entire county.[7]

Eventually the settlers won sway over the grasshoppers, but life remained primitive in the 1870s and early 1880s. Judge Gifford S. Robinson recalled that he had first seen Storm Lake in 1869 when "there was nothing on the site of the present town except a small amount of railroad grating." A temporary town existed somewhere east of the present Lake Avenue and "contained one frame unfinished building which was used as a hotel." There were also shacks and tents which served as the temporary dwellings of about fifty people.[8]

The railroad reached Storm Lake on July 7, 1870, during the same month the town was laid out into lots. On August 11, 1870, the lots — 35 by 100 feet — were placed on sale. The main street was 120 feet wide. This generous plotting meant that spacious residences, lawns, and the planting of shade trees were consistently encouraged.[9] The citizens of Storm Lake were civic minded from the beginning and worked energetically to keep their city in harmony with its beautiful natural setting. Land was selling between $3 and $10 an acre, business lots went for $50 to $200, and residential plots sold from $40 to $450 with one-fourth cash and the balance due within three years.[10] When in 1891 an eastern Iowa correspondent passed through Storm Lake, he remarked that "the streets are lined by trees but they have no fences. Lawns and flower gardens surround the elegant residences and viewing the whole from the cupolas of the courthouse . . . reminds one of a large flower garden set in the midst of a land almost flowing with milk and honey."[11]

The description did not seem extravagant to Storm Lakers who consistently maintained a city beautiful with expansive orchards and good schools. A century later, a widely celebrated Fourth of July, "Star-Spangled Spectacular" recognized the civic achievements of the city on the lake. The early 1970s witnessed a battle with Dutch elm disease which denuded the city of many luxurious trees, but by 1990 new foliage again lined the streets and parks.

By the fall of 1870 several businesses were being operated in the "new town" on the west side of the lake. The Smith brothers, James and August, and their father, T. S. Smith, moved their hotel and store to the new location. Among the early Storm Lake busi-

ness owners were: Barton and Hobbs, real estate agents; Jones &
Cass, druggists; W. H. McClure, hardware merchant; A. Eldred,
insurance agent; Carpenter & Turner, hardware merchants; Smith
& Bros., general merchants; Smith & Slutz, lumber merchants;
C. S. Green, lumber merchant; T. S. Selkirk, hotel owner.

Construction was rapid and by October 1870 there were
eighty-three buildings in Storm Lake. That was also the day that
Col. W. L. Vestal and S. W. Young started publication of the *Storm
Lake Pilot.*[12] Among the early Storm Lake bankers were John R.
Lemon, J. A. Dean, James Harker, and James F. Toy. It was James
Harker who organized the Storm Lake Bank (later the First National Bank) and who was still the bank's president at the time of
his death in July 1883. Harker's business interests were extensive
and his influence went far beyond the confines of the county. In
1875, he built the stately Harker House on the corner of Lake and
Third streets. The contractor was Jay M. Russell who received
$500 to "construct a sturdy brick residence."[13] The dwelling was to
outlast all other dwellings of that era. By the 1950s Harker House,
meticulously preserved by Mr. and Mrs. Bennett Marshall (directors of the Buena Vista County Historical Society) was one of the
historical monuments of the county. It continues to display the rich
heritage of the county following their retirement and death and is
now managed by the local historical society.

A concern for religion motivated the pioneers of the city to
construct houses of worship. The Baptists, 1871; Methodists, 1870;
Universalists, 1874; and Presbyterians, 1870 organized congrega-
tions and ultimately built churches. The Presbyterians and Congregationalists were to build Buena Vista College, but in 1870, when
the Reverend A. M. Darley first arrived in Storm Lake, members
of either faith were hard to find. When in August of that same year
the Reverend G. R. Carroll traveled to Storm Lake with Darley "to
look up Presbyterians," they found only a few names. At the end
of October they discovered five and on December 17, 1870, organized a church. Among the seven original members were Mr. and
Mrs. S. D. Eadie from the Presbyterian church of Toledo, Iowa.
By 1872, largely through the efforts of Mr. Darley, the Presbyte-

rians had secured a small church for a little less than $3,000.[14]

The Congregationalists organized a church in 1880 and erected a brick building on the corner of Third and Cayuga. By the 1890s the numbers of the Congregational and Presbyterian communicants were growing. When the Reverend John MacAllister became pastor of the Presbyterian church in 1892, a movement was under way to build a more substantial house of worship. About the same time someone proposed the two churches merge. It was a sensible proposal and not unusual for frontier Presbyterians and Congregationalists to join forces. The two groups were rational enough to see the logic and "after some negotiations it was agreed to enter the Congregational building, work in harmony for two years and then all become Presbyterians. . . ."[15]

There were social functions to occupy the leisure of Storm Lake's growing population during the 1870s. Surprise parties; the lyceum, which in December 1870 debated the question "Resolved More Pleasure in Anticipation Than in Possession"; a theater production of "Old Grimes" performed in the office of Barton and Hobbs followed by the Storm Lake string band; and the inauguration of a "ball" by Mr. and Mrs. Thomas Smith evidenced steady entertainment in a frontier community.[16]

By 1890 Buena Vista County was approaching 15,000 inhabitants and was one of the richest agricultural regions in the state. Its citizens formed a homogeneous, stable society. The English-Scottish strain seemed to predominate during the early 1870s, but there was later an influx of Germans and Scandinavians. The thirty-seven pioneers who formed the Old Settlers' Association in 1875 were essentially English and Scottish. Six were born outside the United States, but three of those six were born in Canada. Twelve were from the midwestern states of Ohio, Illinois, Indiana, and Iowa. One, Mr. Adolphus Bradford, was born in Virginia. The rest were from New York, New Hampshire, Vermont, and Maine.[17]

The political composition of the county and the city of Storm Lake was, like the rest of Iowa, essentially Republican. The GOP dominated state politics after the slavery controversy of the 1850s and would continue to do so most of the time until the Great Depression. Only an ex-Republican, Horace Boies, could briefly turn the tide for Iowa Democrats during the early 1890s. However,

Prohibitionists, Greenbackers, and Populists did have a scattered following. Iowa also had a small but vocal Socialist party and John M. Work, who was the party's national executive secretary from 1911 to 1913, was born in Washington, Iowa. Jay M. Russell, the future builder of Old Main, appears to have been a Democrat in 1871.[18]

The Puritan ethic with its components of frugality, sobriety, industry, temperance, and moderation survived in western Iowa long after the conservative economics into which it coalesced had elsewhere retreated. The conservatism was not, however, typical of the rampant greed that characterized the individualism and gaudy display of brassy tastes that is sometimes associated with the Gilded Age. The Puritan ethic played a role in building the stable communities of mid-America. There were strong values here that blended into the cult of Lincoln, the self-made, humane benefactor of the nation and two races. Many builders of the community and College—Sisson, Bailie, Edson—had recently moved from the land of Lincoln. One of these, Willis Edson, was born in Wilton Junction, Illinois, in September 1874. His father, whom he dearly loved, was a Civil War veteran who had fought in Grant's army. This was an era in history that forever remained close to Edson. Like Lincoln, Edson derived much of his humanity from the struggles encountered in life, and success never made him a victim of greed. A half-century of arduous and often unrewarding labor proved Edson was serious when he said, "When I graduated from law school in 1901 Judge Deemer advised that we sponsor some local project in the town where we located. I chose Buena Vista College."[19]

There were others like him, and while the ranks were sometimes thin and sometimes wavered, they remained in place. The people of northwest Iowa believed in individualism, self-discipline, and piety, but also in cooperative efforts necessary to promote civic progress. The inhabitants of Storm Lake in 1891 felt that on their magnificent lake they had founded a city with a future. Education was seen as the main pathway to progress, and so a college would take shape in the community. Thus in an era when few Americans advanced beyond high school, Storm Lakers and their northwest Iowa allies set out to build a college.

2

THE WORK OF SOWING

... plant here the seed of a college which . . . may bring a
harvest that the ages shall gather and garner.

—PRESIDENT LOYAL Y. HAYS

Within two decades of its establishment in 1870, the Storm
Lake community was ready to undertake the challenge of
supporting an institution of higher learning. The 1,682 citizens of
Storm Lake in 1890 entered the venture with enthusiasm. The Yale
of the Midwest that they set out to create was slow to materialize,
and it was not until after World War II that the College began to
progress at a steady pace. There were many shattered dreams along
the way. The history of Buena Vista College reveals a determined
effort to survive in spite of harsh economic times, wars, and often a
churchly indifference to its success and growth. Only a selfless
faculty, a few civic-minded trustees, and friends of the College kept
it alive during a long era of constant financial crisis. The founding
of Buena Vista College at Storm Lake evolved from a decade of
frustration on the part of western Iowa Presbyterians to establish a
stable Christian college. Among the initiators of a Presbyterian
institution of higher learning was the Reverend J. C. Gilkerson,
pastor of the Presbyterian church at Calliope (now Hawarden).
His efforts had led to the establishment of an academy at Calliope
in the fall of 1883, with Mrs. J. C. Nash as the first teacher. During
the second year of the academy's brief existence there were "about

sixteen students" enrolled.[1] Mr. Gilkerson urged the Fort Dodge presbytery to assume responsibility for the budding academy. The presbytery appointed a committee to consider the matter and to "visit the field and recommend to the Presbytery at its next stated meeting what action should be taken." In its session at Jefferson in April 1884 the presbytery recommended the founding of a Christian college. The committee, however, was reluctant to accept Calliope as the site of the proposed college. Acceptance of Calliope's offer to be the site of the new college was withheld until other localities "desiring such an institution of learning should have an opportunity to present their propositions."[2] The committee, adjourning, would meet again at Sanborn on September 17, 1884.

Calliope, Cherokee, and Fort Dodge all wished to be the site of a new church-related college. After much competition, Fort Dodge was chosen as the most desirable location. Fort Dodge had offered $10,000 and "grounds suitable and sufficient for the location of the Institute."[3] The Reverend F. L. Kenyon was selected as the first president, a building valued at $7,000 was purchased, and classes began on September 16, 1885.

One of the early instructors at the Fort Dodge Institute was E. A. Ross. Professor Ross would later gain recognition as a renowned scholar and sociologist at Stanford and the University of Wisconsin. Fort Dodge was a young, growing town of 6,000 when the twenty-year old Ross arrived in September 1886. His autobiography relates the crushing burden of teaching seven or eight classes a day. In two years at the Institute, Ross "taught English composition, American literature, German, physiology, physics, logic, psychology and commercial law."[4] Ross was a close friend of Will Kenyon, son of the Institute's president, and recalled that he "hobnobbed" with future Congressman Jonathan P. Dolliver.[5]

As a young faculty member Ross received $50 a month. Tuition in 1890 was $10 for the fall term, which opened on September 8 and closed on November 26. Board could be obtained for $1.50–$1.90 a week.[6] Ross had no college students to teach at Fort Dodge and he remained at the school only two years. By 1901 he was the highly acclaimed author of *Social Control*.

The Fort Dodge Collegiate Institute, however, was not destined to become a success. The lack of financial support from both the presbytery and the citizens of Fort Dodge was responsible for the resignation of President F. L. Kenyon in the spring of 1889. Kenyon was replaced by the Reverend Loyal Y. Hays, an able and dedicated pastor-scholar with wide experience, who did his best to salvage the Institute. Indeed, attendance held up relatively well during the years 1889–1891. The term that started on September 11, 1889, boasted fifty-four students between the ages of thirteen and twenty-six in attendance. The thirteen-year-old was Wesley Russell who gave an excellent account of himself except in the areas of United States history and deportment. A new high in attendance, eighty-five students, was reached during the term that started on December 1, 1890 and ended on March 13, 1891.[7] The low points were always the spring terms when many male students stayed home to help with the farm work.

Poor attendance did not kill the Institute, which lasted only six years. Upon coming to Storm Lake in the summer of 1891, President Hays remarked that the "preparatory school at Fort Dodge grew into such proportions and promise that new and larger accommodations were an immediate necessity."[8] While even the devout Hays may have been guilty of some propagandizing, he had other reasons, educational, social, and moral, for moving the Institute.

It is obvious that President Hays envisioned a liberal arts college rather than a preparatory school. The question was which western Iowa community could undertake the formidable task of supporting a liberal arts college? In April 1891, the presbyteries of Fort Dodge and Sioux City issued a statement to the effect that it was "useless for the Institute to carry on its work longer without increased facilities for doing so."[9] Soon Rolfe and Storm Lake entered the spirited bidding for the new college of northwest Iowa. The citizens of Rolfe, led by the Reverend A. C. Keeler, "offered nine acres of land and ten thousand dollars in cash." Rolfe also offered to assist the presbyteries to the "amount of seven thousand dollars in raising ten thousand dollars of the twenty needed for buildings."[10] The following month, Storm Lake indicated that if the presbyteries showed a real readiness to take action, they would present the most liberal offer yet.[11]

Meanwhile, the trustees of the Collegiate Institute at Fort Dodge made a desperate but futile effort to solicit the $30,000 deemed necessary to expand the school. The *Fort Dodge Messenger* was not eager to see the Institute removed from the city. The paper suggested that the citizens raise $10,000 and that the presbyteries raise between $10,000 and $15,000. Civic leaders like the Honorable L. S. Coffin urged the people of Fort Dodge to "keep the college in this populated county." Coffin felt that the Collegiate Institute not only would be a profitable investment but that it had advanced the community intellectually and morally.[12]

During the first week in May the trustees of the Institute decided to carry on if they could raise the necessary funds. By mid-May, however, the *Messenger* was becoming defeatist in its outlook, noting that "if the money could not be found the school would not be reopened. Students were being turned away . . . trustees were paying expenses out of their own pockets."[13] Meanwhile, Rolfe and Storm Lake were renewing their efforts to obtain the college.

On May 19, 1891, the presbyteries resolved not only to "enlarge the Fort Dodge Collegiate Institute and shape it as the foundations of a college," but also to locate "said Institute at some other point . . . if deemed wise to do so."[14] A subsequent meeting was scheduled for Storm Lake on June 10. The fact that the trustees of the Fort Dodge Institute had failed to raise the necessary funds by May 19 made it inevitable that the college move to a new site. The *Fort Dodge Messenger* naturally lamented the demise of the Collegiate Institute. In reporting the last Commencement, the *Messenger* asserted that "no effort would be spared to see that the school reopened in the fall." But in mid-July the *Messenger* finally reported that the college would be moved to Storm Lake.[15]

Meanwhile, the *Storm Lake Pilot* was jubilant. In its May 20, 1891 issue the *Pilot* assured its readers that Rolfe had given up the fight and Storm Lake would now secure the college. A college was desirable because it would mean that (1) many families of the best citizens would now become permanent residents, (2) a ready sale of real estate property would result, and (3) added sales and profits for every business would be realized.[16]

While the *Pilot*'s aspirations were obviously business oriented, those of President Hays were cultural and moral. He found Storm Lake a "classical little city" and remarked:

> Everything that can be done to care for the health and morals of the students is provided in this beautiful little lakeside city, far from the saloons and all the temptations of a big city. Here the quiet groves and parks, and the lake smiling in its purity, invites students to study and pure living.[17]

It would seem that President Hays's advocacy of Storm Lake as the site for the new college was partially due to the fact that, unlike Fort Dodge, Storm Lake had no saloons. In the new college's first announcement, Hays pointed out that Storm Lake did not have the "morally dangerous elements" of its predecessor, and that it was a community where the "sale of intoxicating liquors is not only prohibited, but any lot on which a Saloon should be set up, forfeits its title." The new college, the announcement continued, "invites young people to the pure, sweet influence of a small city of idyllic beauty, with no temptations such as are inevitable in a large city."[18]

The presbyteries, in their Storm Lake meeting on June 10, 1891, formally admitted that the attempt to maintain the Collegiate Institute at Fort Dodge had resulted in failure. The presbyteries further asserted that they deemed it "unwise to recommend to our Board of Aid any institution for such educational purposes which does not possess a good and eligible site, free from debt, and buildings or cash to the value of at least twenty-five thousand dollars." In addition, the curriculum offered by the new college was to be in advance of that of the neighboring high schools. The "resources and appliances" of the new college "were to be used first of all in the interests of those demanding the highest possible intellectual culture."[19] The attractive site and offer of Storm Lake was mentioned, and the presbyteries appointed a commission to meet in the lake city on July 8.

The meeting that formally brought the college to Storm Lake was held in the law office of E. E. Mack and James De Land on July 9, 1891. The failure of the Fort Dodge trustees to raise a substantial subscription, the withdrawal of the candidacy of Rolfe, and the offer of a suitable site by Storm Lake secured the college for the latter community. The Storm Lake Town Lot and Land Company through their representative, Zeph Charles Felt, offered to donate a campus of eight acres and to erect thereupon buildings of the value of $25,000 suitable for college purposes upon the following conditions:

    I. The title to said land and buildings shall be vested in a board of 17 trustees, 9 of whom shall be named by this company, 4 of the said 9 to be members of the Presbyterian Church.

   II. That the said Presbyteries of Fort Dodge and Sioux City shall agree to the satisfaction of the following named trustees viz: E. E. Mack, J. R. Lemon, Z. C. Felt, George Witter, A. D. Bailie, S. J. Rowell, W. C. Kinne, E. C. Cowles and J. P. Morey, known as the trustees of the college fund of this company, to equip and maintain in Storm Lake, Iowa, a college of liberal arts.

 III. That so long as the said property is used in accordance with the foregoing terms it shall be the property of and under the control of the said board of 17 trustees. But in the event of the failure on the part of said Presbyteries of Fort Dodge and Sioux City to successfully maintain in Storm Lake, Iowa, such an institution then the said property shall revert to the said Storm Lake Town Lot and Land Company.[20]

This proposal was accepted by the Fort Dodge and Sioux City presbyteries. Articles of incorporation were then adopted and a charter secured under the name, Buena Vista College. The name of the new College was selected in "grateful recognition of the substantial interest taken by the people of the County." The Storm Lake paper could now buoyantly proclaim that "what Fort Dodge with all its wealth could not accomplish, Storm Lake, nobly seconded by the citizens of the county, has done."[21]

It was already mid-July 1891, and teachers had to be hired, a curriculum set up, and plans made to construct a suitable College building. Much of the responsibility for this work fell upon President Loyal Hays, who not only handled numerous and difficult administrative duties but also served as professor of mental and moral science.[22] In the best late-nineteenth-century tradition, President Hays taught courses in psychology, logic, ethics, Christian sciences, political economy, and mental science. In a course called "Moral Philosophy" the students were expected to write themes on such topics as "The Nature of Virtue, Obligation and Its Various Theories, Moral Rights, Conscience, Restraints and Will."[23] These areas of instruction were assumed to be natural ones for the president of a denominational college, as such presidents were invariably clergymen.

Instruction in the collegiate department was essentially classical, with ancient history and languages being formidable obstacles for aspiring students. There was also a scientific course which led to the B.S. rather than to the B.A. degree. An examination of the classical curriculum of the collegiate department in 1892 reveals the nature of the intended academic program:

I. FRESHMAN CLASS

FIRST TERM—Cicero: *De Amicitia et De Senectute;* Xenophon's *Memorabilia;* Solid and Spherical Geometry.

SECOND TERM—Livy: Books XXI and XXII; Xenophon's *Memorabilia;* and *Novum Testamentum;* Plane and Spherical Trigonometry; Trench's Study of Words.

THIRD TERM—Tacitus: *Agricola et Germania;* Herodotus; Advanced Algebra; Botany: Plant Structure and Analysis.

THROUGHOUT THE YEAR—Latin Prose Composition; Roman History; Selections from English Literature; Bible Lessons.

II. SOPHOMORE CLASS

FIRST TERM—Horace: Odes and Epodes; Homer; Mensuration: Surveying and Navigation; Milton begun.

SECOND TERM—Horace: Satires and Epistles; Homer and *Novum Testamentum;* Milton; Analytical Geometry completed.

THIRD TERM — Cicero's Letters; Demosthenes; French, German or Calculus optional; Macaulay's Essays; Zoology.

THROUGHOUT THE YEAR — Rhetorical Exercises; Selections from English Literature; Bible Lessons.

III. JUNIOR CLASS

FIRST TERM — Whately's Rhetoric with Lectures; Chemistry; Mechanics and Hydrostatics with Lectures and Experiments; Practical Ethics; Elective: Greek and Latin Drama, French or German, Calculus.

SECOND TERM — Political Economy; Chemistry with Laboratory Practice; Pneumatics and Optics; Theoretical Ethics; Elective: Greek and Latin Drama, French or German.

THIRD TERM — Chemistry with Laboratory Practice; Acoustics; Electricity and Practice in the Physical Laboratory; Constitutional Law; Elective: Latin and Greek Drama, French or German.

THROUGHOUT THE YEAR — Rhetorical Exercises; Shaw's New English Literature with Selection; Bible Lessons.

IV. SENIOR CLASS

FIRST TERM — Psychology with Lectures on the History of Philosophy; Physiographic, Lithological and Historical Geology; Hebrew or German; Shakespeare.

SECOND TERM — Jevons' Logic; Dynamical Geology with Lectures; Astronomy begun; Hebrew or German; Shakespeare.

THIRD TERM — Jevons' Logic completed; Evidences of Christianity; Astronomy completed; Hebrew or German; Methods and Laws of Investigation.

THROUGHOUT THE YEAR — Rhetorical Exercises; Elocution; Bible Lessons.[24]

President Hays, who had a special interest in classical languages, devised both the curriculum and the College catalog. While the Buena Vista curriculum of 1892 appears alien to the contemporary student, it did produce disciplined and humanistic minds and was within the tradition of the liberal arts denominational college. However, it was the commercial, preparatory, normal, and music departments that sustained the institution during its early years.

An instructional staff had to be secured before the opening of the fall term. At the July meeting the Board of Trustees employed the Reverend George Herbert Fracker as professor of ancient languages for an annual salary of $800.[25] From 1891 until his retirement thirty-nine years later, Fracker's life was devoted to the welfare of Buena Vista College. A native of Zanesville, Ohio, Fracker was a graduate of Wooster College and Princeton Theological Seminary. Orphaned as a youngster, Fracker had been raised by an aunt. He worked his way through college and for a time was employed as a telegrapher and as a teacher. His wife was the daughter of the people who boarded him as a young teacher in Ohio. She had peered approvingly at the tall, thin, young man who had come to the door seeking lodging. After entering the ministry and obtaining his theological degree at Princeton, Fracker served pastorates at Ashton, Inwood, and Vail, Iowa, before beginning his long tenure at Buena Vista College. He mastered Latin, Greek, French, and German and possessed some expertise in physics and mathematics. Fracker organized the first College library collection. He was an avid reader and one of those universal scholars so vital to the struggling liberal arts college at the beginning of the twentieth century. Fracker perused scholarly journals in several fields and summers found him enrolled in graduate courses at the University of Wisconsin. No wonder Buena Vista students would proclaim in the 1920s, that "to know Buena Vista is to know Dr. Fracker, and to know Dr. Fracker is an inspiration."[26]

Other members of the original faculty were Dr. J. C. Hutchison, the founder of the College's natural science department, who was appointed professor of physics and chemistry for $25 a month and railroad fare; C. Ray Aurner, principal of the normal department at $65 per month for nine months; C. W. von Coelln, professor of mathematics; P. B. S. Peters and N. H. Tyson of the commercial department; Miss Ida Sisson, piano; Miss Mabel Marshall, vocal music; and Miss J. L. Bennett, drawing.

Because the construction of the main building was not yet under way, the first classes of Buena Vista College were held in the

Opera House on Main Street, which had been leased for $15 a
month.[27] The College announcement asserted that the main College building would be completed by January 1892. This report was
optimistic; the structure, built by the Russell brothers of Storm
Lake, was ready for classes by the autumn of 1892. The contractor,
Jay M. Russell, built much of early Storm Lake, and his careful
work added to his growing reputation as a "thoroughly reliable and
competent builder."[28] The Russell brothers manufactured their
own brick on a forty-six acre tract of land to the east of Storm
Lake.[29] The workmen employed in the construction of Old Main
were mostly Frenchmen. They occupied what was called the
"French colony" on Otsego Street.[30] Thirteen-year-old Stella Russell watched as her father directed the construction. She recalled
the building of the big arch over the front door:

> As the workmen lifted the stones in place according to father's
> directions, he explained to them just where they were to put
> them. I watched his hands reaching up and putting the stones just
> as they should be. I believe his hands must have touched every
> stone in the arch before he was through which was a sight I have
> never forgotten.[31]

However, until the main building could be constructed, the
Opera House, a large two-story frame building covered with sheet
iron, had to suffice. Its dreary atmosphere left a permanent imprint
on Buena Vista's pioneer students; one of them, the Reverend E. S.
Benjamin, described the now nearly forgotten structure:

> Going up the steps from the sidewalk you entered a hallway
> between two fairly large rooms, the one on your right being
> occupied by Dr. Hays, the President; the one on the left was used
> by instructors in shorthand and typewriting. At the end of the
> hall, double doors gave entrance to the auditorium, which at that
> time was the largest in Storm Lake. This auditorium was not
> used by the college.
> Just before you entered the auditorium you went up a flight
> of stairs, which took you into a large room running the full width
> of the building and perhaps 20 feet wide. This was the place
> where in the north end was a low platform with a desk and to one
> side of the desk a piano. And in front of the platform was an

array of loose chairs in which the student body sat for chapel.
Also, through the day this was the recitation place for the various
classes.[32]

Another student during that first year recalled playing "a
wheezy old organ for chapel" and having to dodge to "escape great
chunks of falling plaster." The falling plaster occasionally hit the
back of the organ and some of the students "also had some hard
cracks."[33] The venerable Dr. Fracker in later years recalled that
there were seven pupils and eight teachers at the first chapel service.[34]

The transition from Fort Dodge to Storm Lake was not an
easy one. The optimism of mid-July soured as the fall term got
under way. The preparatory course at Buena Vista attracted fewer
students than the similar course at the Fort Dodge Collegiate Institute. There were only five students enrolled in the well-planned
classical curriculum of the collegiate department. The charter
members of the collegiate department were Jennie Gordon Hutchison, a junior from Cherokee; S. A. Johnson, a Sioux Rapids
sophomore; and three freshmen—Bert A. Cowan of Paton, J. R.
Hitchings of Sutherland, and D. J. Mereness of Glidden.[35] The
four men students were known as the "big four" to the other students on campus. Miss Hutchison, the daughter of Professor J. C.
Hutchison, became the first liberal arts graduate of the College,
receiving her B. A. degree in 1893.[36]

The college year was divided into fall, winter, and spring
terms; tuition varying with each. The charges were $14 for fall, $12
for winter, and $10 for spring in the collegiate department, with
rates in other departments varying with the cost of instruction. The
commercial department (ancestor of the current School of Business) was the most expensive, charging $21 for the fall term.[37] A
student could secure board and room for between $2 and $3 per
week. Still, the cost of obtaining an education seemed high to
many students, who worked for wages of $1 a day, and to their
parents in rural Iowa, who in the farm depression years of the
1890s received 6 cents for a dozen eggs and $1.50 a hundredweight
for hogs.[38]

The difficulties of founding and supporting a college without solid financial backing became apparent almost immediately. The October 1891 meeting of the trustees was held in an atmosphere of depression, and the ensuing discussion centered on the survival of the institution. Finally the Board reluctantly resolved

> the necessity of a reduction of current expenses and [to] direct the executive committee [of the Board] to consult with members of the faculty with reference to the reduction of the teaching force and salary of those that remain and that said committee make such terms of compromise in settling with or discontinuing teachers now employed as in their judgement may seem for the best interest of the college.[39]

At the same time, the Board approved a motion that expressed its appreciation to the student body for the loyalty expressed to the College. The trustees asserted that they were determined "to spare no pains to give them all needed instruction according to the curriculum." The Board also elected E. R. Sisson to serve as financial agent of the College. Sisson was to receive as compensation for his services "ten percent of all funds raised by him together with one dollar for each student he would secure for the College."[40] Sisson was the first in a long line of financial agents whose expenses generally exceeded their collections. The depression of the early 1890s made the work of solicitors difficult, and the churches and the Presbyterian Board of Aid were sluggish in responding to the call for help. Furthermore, the Board of Aid felt Buena Vista was not yet in a position to claim status as a four-year college and refused to grant financial assistance unless the College would cease to offer the junior and senior years of instruction until academically equipped to do so.[41]

The salary cut, while imperative for the salvation of the College, was not pleasing to the faculty. C. Ray Aurner, principal of the normal department, refused to accept a $50 deduction in salary and resigned. After considerable haggling, the Board and Aurner agreed on a reduction of $42.25, and Aurner was "not to make any statements that might damage the college."[42] While most of the academic staff remained at the College, "back salaries" in the 1890s occupied a seemingly permanent place in the treasurer's reports.

President Hays spoke eloquently in behalf of the institution and its academic needs. The College needed books; and when Zeph Charles Felt presented the College with eleven volumes of *The Library of American Literature* by Stedman and Hutchison, Hays saw that it was front-page material for the *Storm Lake Pilot.* "It is the people's college," he said. "It belongs to no one man or denomination. Those who helped it to become great will have their names and deeds embalmed in the grateful remembrances of this and succeeding generations."[43] There is no doubt that President Hays loved both the Storm Lake community and the College he helped to create. One of the memorable events of his life was the day he turned the first spadeful of dirt for the construction of Old Main. In an address typical of the oratory of the age he told a large audience:

> The fame of this college will not come to it because of its building, however beautiful and commodious it may be. We never hear of the buildings of Princeton, or Yale or Harvard. The men and women who here shall build characters more durable than brass or granite will be the glory of this institution. . . . Let us hope that this spot may become the Mecca where pilgrims for generations will come in grateful memory for what they enjoyed as students here. We are now to break this soil in which there has never been a plow or spade, fresh as from the hand of God, and plant here the seed of a college which under God's care and our consecrated toil may bring a harvest that the ages shall gather and garner.[44]

Such was the spirit of a pioneer president of a denominational college. President Hays "struck the new spade" bought for the occasion and directed that it be kept in the College museum.[45]

Undoubtedly the fifty-four-year-old Hays looked forward to a decade or more of service as president of Buena Vista College. All contemporary accounts of Hays attest to his natural leadership, charm, and devout character. The president had grown up on his father's farm in Butler County, Pennsylvania. Graduating from Washington College and Chicago Theological Seminary, he had served pastorates at Malden and Ottawa, Illinois; Madison, Wisconsin; Springfield, Illinois; Crawfordsville, Indiana; and Mifflintown, Pennsylvania. Among the Hays's five children was a son George who in 1898 would serve in the war against Spain and a daughter who in the early 1890s was a missionary in Japan.[46]

The president's labors in the pastorate had always been somewhat diminished by the occasional loss of his voice, which once forced him to take a leave of absence from his ministerial duties. He traveled to Europe and then to California but finally returned to the Middle West when he discovered that changes in climate provided no cure for the illness. During the months when he was unable to preach, Hays busied himself with his studies and won at least local reputation as an outstanding scholar in Hebrew.[47]

His duties at Buena Vista were legion. In addition to being president of the institution, he had the task of preparing the catalog and soliciting funds. He was the professor of moral and mental science, which entailed teaching the courses of an entire division. His job also involved the building of an institution from the roots. The entire Storm Lake community realized that when President Hays fell before frustration, overwork, and the magnitude of his task that, Buena Vista College had lost her "best and truest friend."[48]

The end came on the evening of May 16, 1892. The crowds that visited the campus the first two Sundays in May, in order to see the progress of the College building, were not aware that Hays was suffering from a fatal illness. The president had been seized by severe cramps while preaching a sermon at the Presbyterian church ten days earlier. He had suffered similar attacks on previous occasions and apparently did not realize the seriousness of his illness. A postmortem examination conducted by Doctors Agnew, Kerlin, and Hornibrook revealed that gallstones that had ruptured the intestine had been the cause of death.[49]

The funeral was held Wednesday afternoon, May 18, at the Congregational church. The trustees served as pall bearers and the funeral oration was delivered by the Reverend George P. Folsom of Carroll, Iowa. The Reverend Mr. Folsom, who had been a close friend of the Hays family, spoke eloquently to the many mourners:

> The educational work of our church in Northwest Iowa, from which death has removed him, I think he looked upon with the

hope that it might be the crowning result of his life. . . . May his
Christian devotion and untiring zeal fall on those who shall carry
on this work.[50]

It was a slow, mournful trek to the Storm Lake cemetery. The
rains came in such torrents that those who witnessed the tragic
spectacle were to remember it for the rest of their lives. The body
of the deceased had to be taken to the cemetery on a railroad
handcar since the roads were "simply impassable." Another witness
recalled that after the burial party had waded through mud to the
grave they "found it full of water" and so "the casket was placed in
the sexton's little house and several weeks later, I believe, was buried there."[51] Since no gravestone or marker now exists in the Storm
Lake cemetery, the body of the deceased president must have been
removed by the Hays family. College officials had urged Mrs. Hays
to accept Storm Lake as the president's final resting place. Obviously, she decided otherwise and so the grave site of the first
president of the College remains unknown. For many years Hays's
picture adorned the south wall in Old Main where it most certainly
became a casualty of the great fire in 1956.

President Loyal Hays left a design. He would be remembered
as the "founding father" of the institution. At the memorial service
his successor noted:

> He is the connecting link between this College and the Fort
> Dodge Collegiate Institute. He is the recognized founder of this
> College. Its campus by the Lakeside adorned as it may be in
> future years and covered by stately buildings will not outgrow his
> name and fame will be his monument.[52]

The College, which had been launched the previous summer
with such optimism, now teetered on the brink of disaster. There
were no graduates in the spring of 1892. There was no endowment
and the captain of the ship had succumbed at the most critical
moment imaginable. However, the founders who had envisioned
the "Yale of the Midwest" would find that their travail was just
beginning. Crisis was to follow crisis, and years were to mushroom
into decades before Buena Vista College was destined to enjoy the
stability and prestige that its founders had intended.

THE FIRST FIFTY YEARS

1891–1941

1

2

1 Storm Lake around 1870. (State Historical Society of Iowa) **2** Fort Dodge Collegiate Institute, 1885–1891, predecessor of Buena Vista College. The Institute listed eighty-five students between the ages of thirteen and twenty-six in 1891, the year of the move to Storm Lake.

3

3 Margaret MacAllister, daughter of the Reverend John MacAllister who was pastor of the Lakeside Church, and a friend stroll on the board sidewalks behind a newly constructed Old Main in 1893. One hundred and twenty-one students enrolled in the new College, six of them in the collegiate department.

4   5

6

7

4 Zeph Charles Felt, president of the first Board of Trustees. Felt was a Princeton graduate and classmate of Woodrow Wilson.   **5**   Jennie G. Hutchison was the first graduate of the collegiate department in 1893. Daughter of original faculty member, J. C. Hutchison, she returned to Buena Vista as professor of Latin, 1909–1916   **6**   The *Tack* staff, 1895. (*Top row, from left*) F. O. Leonard, Nell Mack, Elizabeth Sohm, W. C. Edson; (*middle row*) Emma Anderson, Belle Ranney, editor in chief F. C. Aldinger, John Abels; (*front*) John Edson. The *Tack* was originally a monthly literary magazine.   **7**   College faculty in 1896, when there were nearly as many faculty members as students in the collegiate department. (*Back row, from left*) Professor P. B. S. Peters, President Willis Marshall; (*front*) Professor G. H. Fracker, Professor Campbell, Professor M. W. Cooper. Faculty were called on to teach any subject, often doing double work at half-pay, or less.

8

9

8 Graduating class of the commercial department, about 1900. (*Back row, from left*) Grace Johnston, Herbert Bowers, Walter Siebens—father of College benefactor H. W. Siebens, head of department Professor Ross, Kenny Walker, Daisy Bunn; (*middle row*) Orville Slater, Randa Enderson, Alfred Renshaw, Aline Corbett, Mary Huntly, E. R. Rhoades; (*front*) Essie Vine, Vesta Johnson.
9 Miller-Stuart House, acquired in 1901 as a home for the president of the College. It was demolished in 1974.

10

10 Interior of Old Main, 1905. **11** College campus, 1906. The buildings include (*from left*) Old Main, Miller-Stuart (the president's) House, Music Hall, Ladies' Dormitory. **12** Scott C. Bradford, Storm Lake banker, builder of the Bradford Hotel (torn down in the 1960s), and real estate investor. Elected president of the Board of Trustees in 1904, he was the "mystery man" who pledged a sizable sum for the first endowment fund. **13** Margaret Cummings, professor of education, 1906. **14** Alice Tozer, originator of the tree-planting ceremonies, 1906. **15** Alice Wilcox, 1907, dean of women and professor of English from 1902 to 1922. An early student remembers her as the best English teacher he ever had.

11

12   13

14   15

16   17

18

16 Bradford Debating Cup, presented to the Star and Franklin literary societies as a trophy for the annual debate. **17** Floyd Voris, professor of physical science from 1899 to 1905. As trustee, Professor Voris pleged generously to the first endowment fund, but later disagreed with the manner in which the principal was used. **18** Voris was curator of the College museum, a natural science collection that was typical of young colleges of the period.

19

20

21

19   E. F. Blayney, one of the few faculty at the time with a Ph.D. He taught Greek and mental science and canvassed for College funds during the summer months from 1903 to 1913.   **20** Forest Geisinger Ansley, 1913, a graduate of the College who also taught piano there from 1912 to 1914. The music conservatory in Dixon-Eilers Hall was named after her.   **21**   A music room, 1911.

34

22

WRITERPRESS

A Modern Machine on which Imitation Typewritten Letters are made

COLLEGE PRESS

The College is equipped with a complete job outfit and is prepared to do its own printing. Any job work received from outside sources will be appreciated. Let us figure on your next job and we assure you the price will be low enough to warrant you in giving us the work, which will be guaranteed in every respect. Job work done by the College will not extend into territory that competes with local printers.

WRITERPRESSING

Is a new departure in the printing business. We take jobs of circular letter work, run in names to match body of letter, direct envelopes, in fact get your letter ready to mail. Advanced students in our Typewriting department do this work for a reasonable wage.

Anyone in need of this kind of work will be helping some deserving student by letting us get out his letters. Prices and samples of work sent on application to the College Press.

PRINTERS

We can usually use student help in the printing office. If you know of a young man or woman who understands typesetting and job press work, have them write at once. We pay 20 cents per hour to those who understand the work. Press run by electric motor. This is an opportunity worth looking after.

23

22 Typing class, 1902. **23** The College Press, 1911.

24

25

24 The *Tack* staff, 1911. **25** Cleanup Day, 1919.

26

27

26 Storm Lake shoreline, 1911. **27** A faculty party, 1913–14. (*Back right*) President Linn.

28

29

28 The College library of 3,000 volumes was housed in Old Main — hard studies, hard seats, hard times. **29** Old Main, 1913.

30

31

30 Women's League, 1919–20. (*Front, from left*) Eva May, Ella McDermott, Mildred Rowe, Opal Kraemer, Maude Hoke; (*back*) unknown, Dewey Deal, Professor Alice Wilcox, Joyce Wake.
31 E. S. Benjamin, whose memories and letters have contributed to this book, was business manager of the *Tack* in 1897–98. He later became a Methodist minister.

32

33

32 A May Day celebration in the 1920s. **33** Maude H. Barnes of the class of 1909 submitted the drawing that was used for the College Seal. The rising sun symbolizes service and hope; the distance across the lake signifies time for preparation.

Extra
Buena Vista Tack
The Paper with a Point
Extra

VOLUME 42   SORM LAKE, IOWA, NOVEMBER 12, 1930   NUMBER THREE

Winners Never Quit!   Quitters Never Win!

Students Tell Facts of Interest

Interesting Facts are Revealed by the Answers

At a mass meeting held in the college chapel on Monday morning, and announced only an hour before time for the meeting about 150 students assembled. During the course of the meeting a questionaire was handed to the students and in answer to the question, 'Did your family choose to live in Storm Lake because the college is here?' 36 students answered yes. The college has brought about fifteen percent of the student body's families to Storm Lake to live.

In answer to the question, 'Have other members of your family attended Buena Vista?' 63 students answered yes. Buena Vista does report business. And it was discovered that the present student body has 256 younger brothers and sisters.

In estimating the amount of money spent in Storm Lake, it was found that the students who filled out the questionaire spend $12,371 for clothes, $13,532 for board, $8,689 for room rent, and $6,199 for incidentals during the college year. $40,800, according to the questionaire, are spent by 150 students, and out of this number were 46 students living in Storm Lake, most of whom did not estimate their expenses. Not only does Buena Vista make Storm Lake a cultural center, but it also contributes to Storm Lake's business.

Our College?

Supt. Farmer Writes Letter

Superintendent Fred Farmer expressed his regret to the editor of the Tack that because of the State Teachers Association Meeting in Des Moines it is impossible for him to be in town - for the mass meeting tonight. Superintendent Farmer is strong for Buena Vista College. He has not only encouraged the election of Buena Vista graduates to positions on the staff of public school teachers, but when his daughter was ready for college he ratified her choice of Buena Vista. Today he has sent us this special letter of encouragement.

Mr. Farmers' Letter

The old saying that "you never miss the water till the well runs dry" is evidencing
(Continued on last page)

Citizens Consider Problem

A mass meeting for citizens of Storm Lake and vicinity has been called by the Chamber of Commerce for the purpose of bringing to the attention of the public the situation at Buena Vista College. The meeting is to be held at the High School Auditorium tonight at 8 o'clock.

Let your supper dishes stand. Put on your hat and coat. Follow the drum corps and the band—

They will lead you to a jolly party. You will learn many things about which you have heard gossip, threats, and prophecies of dire disaster. You will hear the chapel choir. You will see all the green caps in a bunch.

You will hear some real speeches - -

You may hear some lively discussion - -

YOU WILL LEARN FACTS AND YOU WILL NOT BE ASKED FOR MONEY! GO!

Opportunity

By Dean A. C. Nielsen

America has long been heralded as the land of opportunity. We hope it may long be so. However, it is an undeniable fact that it is becoming increasingly difficult for the poor student to finance his way through college. It costs many hundred dollars a year if the student goes away to some distant institution for his education. Most of our students live near this college. Some attend here for as little as two hundred fifty dollars a year. More than 90% of our students earn their way entirely or in part. They want an education and are willing to struggle for it. This should be final proof that there is need for a college in Storm Lake. Furthermore, students who struggle there should not be turned out of a college in the middle of a year. For their sake and for others like them the college must go on.

"When we examine the literature of the past, we find that men invariably idealized some age, behind them. Rarely does a poet speak with full approval of his own age."—Dr. Frank Parker Day.

One advantage of telling the truth is that you don't have to remember what you said.

Quit talking about yourself for a while and see if anyone else will bring up the subject.

Here is the Situation in Nutshell

Meeting Tonight at High School For All

A mass-meeting of all friends and well-wishers of Buena Vista college has been called for tonight at 8 o'clock at the High School auditorium.

A reproduction of the letter distributed by the Chamber of Commerce, calling this mass-meeting is to be found in this issue of the Tack.

In order that you may understand just how matters stand at present this article presents briefly the situation.

A proposition to merge Buena Vista college with Coe college of Cedar Rapids was approved by the state synod of the Presbyterian church, meeting at Cedar Rapids, Wednesday, October 15.

Under the terms of the proposal, Buena Vista would become a junior college having only freshman and sophomore classes. The merger was to become effective September 1, 1931. President Gage of Coe would then be president of both schools, a dean having charge of the local institution. The faculty here would be completely reorganized.

Of the ten Presbyters in the state of Iowa, eight had approved the merger before it was even formally presented in the synod meeting.

After formal approval of the merger, the synod appointed a commission to work out the details of providing for the school's future. The commission is formed of representative men in the church and educational field, BUT THERE IS NOT ONE STORM LAKE MAN ON IT, NOR IS THERE ONE WHO IS INTIMATELY ACQUAINTED WITH THE TYPE OF FEELING THAT EXISTS IN THIS COMMUNITY TOWARDS BUENA VISTA. And this is the commission appointed to decide what shall become of this school!

Determined to save the institution if it is at all possible, the student body held a spirited and enthusiastic massmeeting Wednesday, October 22.

This student meeting accomplished four things. In the first place, it aroused student feeling on the question and brought about a determination to fight for the college to the last ditch.

Secondly, a ringing resolution, drawn up by the student council senator, Raymond Mansfield, was read and unanimously adopted. This
(Continued on page 3)

Prominent People Speak for Buena Vista College

Knowing that Buena Vista College is a real asset to Storm Lake and to Buena Vista County, I feel that I can heartily endorse the Mass meeting being called by this Chamber of Commerce. Every loyal citizen of our community should be present.

Bert Marchant, Mayor

The women of Buena Vista County acknowledged their faith in Buena Vista College by establishing the Bertha Knight Memorial Fund as a loan fund to be used by young women attending that institution. We have found that the girls who are taking advantage of this fund are earnest, worthwhile girls. The Club Women of the County have faith in our college and in the type of young women in attendance there.

Mrs. Geo. M. Pedersen, Custodian Bertha Knight Memorial Fund

I believe that Buena Vista College is an asset to the community, not only because of its inspirational leadership, but also because of
(Continued on last page)

the close-at-home, economical education it affords.

W. C. Skiff, County Treasurer

Buena Vista College undoubtedly swells the postal receipts of the Storm Lake Post Office. If for no other reason than this, I favor every activity towards retaining the college as a Storm Lake institution.

J. A. Schmitz, Postmaster

Storm Lake would miss Buena Vista College if its doors were to close. The gay joyousness of the young people and the youthful inspiration of two hundred purposeful young men and women would be missing. Can we afford this?

Elizabeth Rae, County Recorder

The Storm Lake Board of Education has employed many graduates of Buena Vista College as instructors in the public schools of the city. At present we have 8 on our faculty. In every case Buena Vista College graduates have averaged
(Continued on last page)

Fathers and Mothers of Buena Vista County:

Whether we like it or not, the trend of modern times has forced certain changes in the policy and operation of Buena Vista College. Unless these demands are met, your college cannot go on. That would be a calamity to your children!

No engagement is of greater importance than being present at the Citizens' meeting Wednesday evening. We urge you not to allow your absence to bring about a situation that you will regret as long as you live. Every Buena Vista County Parent is vitally concerned.

COME! GET THE FACTS! LET'S SETTLE THIS QUESTION!

—Storm Lake Chamber of Commerce

---

34 The *Tack* responds to the proposal to merge Buena Vista with Coe College.

3

THE NOT-SO-GAY NINETIES

Friends who question the value of the little western colleges
would be surprised and heartened. . . . Large salaries and
splendid equipment do not produce the best educational
results

—COLLEGE BOARD OF AID, 1896

The faculty and students, the Storm Lake community, and the
Fort Dodge and Sioux City presbyteries, were saddened and
dispirited by the death of President Hays, which had removed
from Buena Vista College her most competent and dedicated supporter. When in June 1892 the Reverend John M. Linn became the
hastily recruited second president of the College, he faced the unenviable challenge of replacing a man who had become something
of a martyr in the cause of Christian education.

The new president, however, was not a man to shirk a challenge. Students would remember President Linn as an aggressive
man with a "bristling red moustache, short stout figure and Irish
features."[1] Although his tenure as president was a brief one (1892–
1894), the Reverend Mr. Linn struggled valiantly to save the young
College during one of its most trying periods. Many years later he
recalled:

> It was a big, difficult place to fill. I had a much easier place
> offered me at the same time in Ann Arbor, Michigan, with a ten
> thousand dollar house to move my family into. What blunders
> we make! I accepted a pastorate and presidency without realizing
> the tremendous tasks before me. We are all heroes when we are
> young like David before Goliath and Daniel in the lion's den.[2]

41

In 1892 when Linn became president, Buena Vista College had no endowment and only a handful of students. Faculty salaries ranged from $30 to $104 a month, and sometimes faculty members labored for months with only partial or no pay.[3] While President Linn was employed at a salary of $1,250, the College still owed $820 to the estate of his predecessor.[4] Undaunted, Linn moved his talented family to Storm Lake and constructed a dwelling on College Street that became known as the "President's House." Linn's wife, Mary, was the sister of Jane Addams. The Linn's sixteen-year-old son, J. Weber, was an assistant in the commercial department and helped establish the first football program at Buena Vista College. Eventually, he became a professor of English at the University of Chicago and the author of three novels and two biographies.[5]

The one gala event during Linn's administration was the dedication of the main campus building, Central Hall, on October 4, 1892. The building had been constructed by Jay M. Russell and Brothers who had built most of the early business district of Storm Lake. The courthouse, the Bradford Hotel, the Catholic church, and North School were among the landmarks of the city erected by the Russell brothers.[6] Central Hall soon became known as "Old Main." This beloved building, until its destruction by fire after sixty-four years of service, was the rallying point and symbol of the institution.

"Storm Lake was in its heroic period," President Linn recalled. "We marched through all the streets with banners flying."[7] Actually, the line of march formed at the courthouse to begin the three-quarter-mile procession to the College by the lake. In the marching line were the faculty and officers of the College, students, high school teachers, and many citizens of the community. The College cornet band led the line of march. Joining the local citizens, friends of the College had arrived by special train from Des Moines and other towns.

The dedication address was delivered by the Reverend Dr. Howard Johnston, of Des Moines who spoke on the "Product of a Christian College." Following this address came the inauguration of President Linn. There were more speeches which, as the local paper noted, consumed more than two hours. But the enthusiastic audience "generously remained until the close." One of the highlights of the service was the presentation of the keys to the new building to President Linn by State Senator E. E. Mack, president of the Board of Trustees, who told the gathering that he performed the task on "behalf of the people of Storm Lake and vicinity."[8]

While the citizens of Storm Lake may have viewed their struggling institution as a college, the annual reports of the Presbyterian Church in the U.S.A. listed Buena Vista as an "Academy." The reports of the Boards of the General Assembly in May 1894 listed only three of the 140 students at Buena Vista as college students, with the remainder being classified as preparatory, normal, commercial, or music students. The catalog of 1895–1896 indicated eight in the collegiate, twelve in the preparatory, fifty-nine in the normal, and thirty-one in the commercial departments.[9] The Board of Aid may not have been entirely pleased that the Iowa presbyteries had removed the Institute from Fort Dodge and started a four-year college in Storm Lake. The Sioux City Presbytery maintained that the Board of Aid had been advised that the Iowa presbyteries considered the Collegiate Institute a failing venture. The Board of Aid had been invited to send a representative to advise the presbyteries, but no one had come and "no protest was made against removal of the Institute or the founding of the College."[10]

Meanwhile, on June 7, 1893, Miss Jennie Gordon Hutchison was granted the degree of B.A. as the first graduate of Buena Vista College.[11] Miss Hutchison was to know an anxious moment on that day, because just prior to the Commencement program it was discovered that the diploma had not arrived. As Miss Hutchison said:

> Not to have a sheepskin to present to the first graduate was indeed a calamity. What to do? Where to turn? At last Rev. Mr. MacAllister, in his desperation, offered his marriage certificate as a substitute, and the graduate, in her desperation, accepted it.[12]

She had been an excellent student with most of her marks in the mid- to high-nineties. The exception was German in which she received an eighty-four from Professor von Coelln.[13] At the Commencement ceremonies, Miss Hutchison delivered an appropriate

oration called "The Psychological Moment." President Linn gave
the baccalaureate sermon and the Reverend J. Milton Green of
Fort Dodge spoke at the Commencement exercises, which honored
the graduates of the commercial and preparatory as well as the
collegiate departments.[14] Jennie obviously enrolled at Buena Vista
because her father was on the faculty, but not only did Jennie
nearly miss receiving her diploma, in subsequent years a controversy developed over whether the name was Hutchison or
Hutchinson. The name has been spelled both ways in trustee minutes, college catalogs, yearbooks, and even census reports. However, the records of Monmouth College where Jennie was a student
until 1891 and where her father taught from 1858 to 1891 indicate
conclusively that it was Jennie Hutchison and not Hutchinson who
graduated from Buena Vista College in 1893.[15] Corroborating data
comes from the University of Northern Iowa where Miss Hutchison received the Master of Didactics in 1901 and taught English
and Latin from 1898 to 1909.

It appeared that Miss Hutchison might remain the only four-
year graduate in the history of the College. The financial panic was
in full swing by the summer of 1893; thousands of unemployed
Americans were roaming the countryside caught in a depression
that was far more severe than previous panics. These were the days
of Coxey's Army (the motley crew that marched on Washington
during the depression of the 1890s) and the Populist clamor for
"free silver" as a cure for the nation's economic ills. In agricultural
Iowa, corn was selling at 12 cents a bushel and hogs at $1.50 a
hundredweight. At those prices people who were dependent upon
farming or farm prosperity for their livelihood were not likely to
contribute financially to the support of a private, church-related,
liberal arts college. Even though the cost of an academic year at
Buena Vista was only $170,[16] not many felt able to take advantage
of it. The plea of President Linn that "there are enough young
people in Buena Vista County alone to fill our building if parents
will send them" met with small response. And his assertion that
Buena Vista will be to "western Iowa what Cornell or Grinnell are
to eastern Iowa" was not to be realized during his lifetime.[17]

Meanwhile, the College trustees and the Synod of Iowa turned again for assistance to the Presbyterian Board of Aid for Colleges. Earlier requests for aid in 1891 and 1892 had been rejected. The Board of Aid was reluctant to assist new, precarious institutions in waging seemingly futile and expensive battles for survival. Indeed, by the fall of 1893 the Board had made it clear that Buena Vista would receive no aid as long as it continued to offer the junior and senior years of instruction. Another argument the Board gave for denying financial assistance was that the College had no endowment. The policy of the Board of Aid was "to favor the starting of no more colleges without some endowment . . . and to push with all vigor the endowment of such institutions as have thoroughly proved their right to live."[18]

There was also a movement in Storm Lake to attach the College to the high school and convert it into a public junior college. While these plans had some local support, there was also adamant opposition to the thwarting of what once had been a grand educational design. The trustees at their annual meeting asserted that they had agreed "to maintain a college of liberal arts . . . we feel bound by our promises, and by our charter to maintain all the college grades." As for the endowment, the Synod pointed out that "in view of the financial condition of the country it is unwise for the Synod to attempt this at present."[19]

Unfortunately, the trickle of financial aid made the trustees more receptive to the pressures of the Board of Aid. The trustees were not even in a position to promise President Linn a definite salary. At that time the president's salary had to be paid out of funds raised by himself "unless there should be a surplus on hand from tuition and other sources to apply." The president also had to go out into the field to raise funds, eliminating his presence at the College except for the first two weeks of each term.[20] Not only was this disturbing to Linn's home life, but some members of the College community resented the lack of contact with students which this situation necessitated. Meanwhile, the Synod made the following proposal:

(A) Synod recommends Buena Vista College for aid from the Board to the amount of $800 on condition that the Synod raise for this College $1,200 making a total of $2,000 for the current college year.

(B) In case the Board of Aid declines to consider favorably this recommendation the Synod raise the amount of $2,000 for the current year.

(C) That Rev. J. M. Linn and Rev. John MacAllister with the Chairman of the Committee on Aid for Colleges in each Presbytery in this Synod be a committee to carry out the terms of this recommendation.

(D) That in view of the immediate needs of Buena Vista College and as an expression of the special interest of Synod now in session in Storm Lake, in the College located here, the churches represented in Synod and as many other churches as can be induced to do so be requested to take a special offering for the benefit of this College and this be done as soon as possible after the return of the delegates to their homes, and the amount forwarded directly to the College.[21]

The Synod then made a tour of College grounds and the buildings which consisted of Old Main and two dormitories known as Gentlemen's Hall and Ladies' Cottage. The dormitories had been erected by a Storm Lake syndicate "on the understanding that the college trustees should one day not far distant take them off their hands."[22] The value of the two dormitories was estimated at $9,600.

At the chapel an "impromptu meeting" was held, at which President Linn and the moderator of the Synod, Dr. Howard J. Johnston, spoke. Following the main orations, addresses were delivered by different members of the faculty—Senator Mack, the Reverend Mr. MacAllister, and Dr. McClintock of Burlington. The Synod and associates of the College had demonstrated not only their love of oration but also their determination to act. As the bulletin issued by the College stipulated: "Here is a plant worth $50,000. Last year there were all told 225 students in attendance . . . there are only four out of twenty-two colleges aided by our Board that have a larger attendance."[23]

The trustees met in December to consider the proposal that was now presented by the Board of Aid. The Board was willing to grant the $800 requested by the Synod but still insisted that the

College limit its instruction to the first two years in the collegiate program and that it restrict its canvassing to the presbyteries of Fort Dodge and Sioux City. A week later the secretary of the Board of Aid, Dr. E. C. Ray, visited and conducted an investigation of the College. The trustees, although still reluctant to diminish the offerings of the College, voted to accept the $800 if the Board would "grant us the offerings for colleges from Sioux City, Fort Dodge, Des Moines, and Waterloo presbyteries and that we be permitted to canvass the said presbyteries for personal gifts as well as contributions from the churches therein." The trustees would endeavor not to increase the indebtedness of the College and would not give instruction in the collegiate department beyond the freshman and sophomore years. Furthermore, the trustees would, with the assistance of the Board of Aid, seek an endowment so that full college work could be resumed "on a sound financial basis." In a joint meeting with the Board of Trustees, the College faculty agreed, "in view of the present financial difficulties . . . [to] accept decreased salaries for the year to such reasonable extent, as might be necessary in an effort to close the year without debt."[24]

The Board of Aid was endeavoring to place Presbyterian colleges on a firm financial and academic basis. The Board felt that "an endowment of $50,000 for a college or $25,000 for an academy will assure permanence and growing usefulness to the Church." The Board of Aid also insisted that "institutions aided by the Board keep current expenses within income, permitting no unsettled claims of teachers or of others." In the academic area the Board asserted that it would "favor institutions that promote classical study."[25]

As President Linn struggled to meet the requirements set forth by the Board of Aid, the Buena Vista faculty, led by the able classical scholar George H. Fracker, remained loyal to the institution. As in other denominational colleges, the Buena Vista faculty did "double work, often at half pay or less." Fracker not only served as professor of languages 1891–1930, during what still amounts to the longest active tenure of any Buena Vista professor, but also taught physics and mathematics when needed. Fracker was a true Renaissance man whose devotion to Christian education and the struggling College kept him occupied for nearly four decades at a salary that never exceeded (when paid in full) $1,700. As the depression neared its end in 1896, the College Board of Aid noted: "Eastern friends who question the value of the little western colleges would be surprised and heartened if they would examine the work done in our institutions. Large salaries and splendid equipment do not always produce the best educational results."[26]

On June 7, 1894, John M. Linn resigned as president of Buena Vista College. He had sacrificed much in the two years of his presidency. His salary had been uncertain; he had been forced to be absent from home on countless occasions; he had seen the College, due to pressure from the Board of Aid, reduced to the ranks of the two-year institutions and academies; and now he was faced with the serious illness of his wife. Five weeks after Linn's resignation Mrs. Linn, who had gone for treatment to the Pennoyer Sanitarium in Kenosha, Wisconsin, died.

Linn's resignation meant that the Board of Trustees had to search for a new president, the third in the four-year history of the College. In the meantime, the Reverend John MacAllister, pastor of the Lakeside Presbyterian Church and instructor in Bible study, was designated acting president. MacAllister was a capable Scotsman, with a noticeable Scottish burr in his pronunciation. He was small, dark-complexioned, and apparently an excellent preacher and pastor. He served the church in Storm Lake for eight years, 1892–1900, but had no desire to be more than the temporary chief executive of the floundering College, although he remained a trustee until 1904. His daughter Margaret was a student at Buena Vista during the mid-1890s.

Buena Vista had also lost the services of the able and energetic first president of the Board of Trustees, Zeph Charles Felt, when the Felts moved to Denver, Colorado, in September 1892.[27] The brilliant Felt, while at Princeton, had been a classmate of Woodrow Wilson. After graduating from Princeton in 1879, Felt had continued his studies at the Columbia University Law School. Young Zeph's father, B. F. Felt of Galena, Illinois, and Storm Lake banker James Harker had a friendship and business connection extending over some years. It must have been around 1881 that

Harker, one of the founders and first president of what became the First National Bank of Storm Lake, wired Zeph to come and assist in the management of his bank. The relationship of the Felts and the Harkers was such that Zeph immediately responded.

Thirteen-year old Nora Harker must have gone with her father to the station to greet Felt. Years later she recalled that Zeph was "wearing one of those skull caps" no doubt designed to thwart the drafts on the Pullman. An accomplished musician, the young bachelor moved easily into the social life of the bustling, but still frontier, community. There was a "musicale" at the home of Mr. and Mrs. J. Sampson on a late January evening, 1882. There Zeph played a flute solo and was part of the male quartet of Magoun, Cromwell, Felt, and French. Zeph was slightly above average height, slenderly built, quick, with intelligent eyes, and not only prominent but also well-to-do. He found Harker's daughter Nora increasingly attractive; and when she was only fifteen Zeph asked her to become his wife. "I was so amused," Nora recalled. "I was just a child, and he was ten years older than I."[28] Then Miss Harker went away to school—to Wells College at Aurora, New York. However, none of the young men she met compared with Felt, and on July 11, 1889, Nora Harker became Mrs. Zeph Charles Felt.[29] They went to Denver on their honeymoon and in the fall of 1892 returned to make the Colorado capital their permanent home.

Felt retained an interest in both his alma mater, Princeton University, and his Storm Lake project, Buena Vista College. He was to remain a trustee of the College for several years until pressing business demands forced him to resign from the Board. Felt had many friends in Storm Lake and before he departed for the West a reception was held in his honor at the First Congregational Church located at the intersection of Third and Cayuga. Attorney A. D. Bailie presented Felt with a "gold headed cane."[30] The College had benefited from Felt's presence. They had lost a progressive young businessman who knew firsthand the best management and educational techniques.

In the summer of 1895 the Board was at last able to find a successor to the Reverend Mr. Linn. This time Willis Marshall of

Springville, Utah, was selected by the trustees to serve as president of Buena Vista College. The *Pilot* described Marshall as "not a minister but a regular college man."[31] The new president had had charge of the Hungerport Academy in Springville, Utah. The academy was under the control of the Presbyterian church, and Marshall was well known and highly recommended. The new president would teach higher English and literature, while Mrs. Marshall would provide instruction in elocution.

After his brief tenure as president of Buena Vista College had come to a stormy conclusion, Willis Marshall must have wished that he had remained at his Utah academy. "E. S." Benjamin, a Buena Vista student in the mid-1890s, remembers Marshall as "a strict disciplinarian . . . but all the students thought a great deal of him . . . and he, too, was an excellent teacher."[32] Certainly, when unpleasantness arose between the Board of Trustees and the president in the spring of 1897, both students and faculty rallied to the side of the president. Marshall indicated during the winter of 1896–1897 that he would be willing to resign at the end of the school year. The trustees, however, decided that they could dispense with the president's services at the end of the winter term declaring that "the present relation of Willis Marshall as President or member of the faculty of the College is hereby declared to be at an end on March 19, 1897." After that date the trustees said that they would not recognize Marshall as president of the institution and he would receive no salary.[33]

The circumstances surrounding Marshall's resignation are vague. The fact that the College had incurred an indebtedness of $5,000, was on the verge of losing control of the two dormitories, and was being viewed unfavorably by the Board of Aid for Colleges are no doubt factors that contributed to Marshall's decision to quit at the end of the year. He must have felt that he was following an honorable course in announcing his intentions early. Marshall, the first lay person to fill the post as president of Buena Vista College, would find more secure employment as a mathematics teacher in a Sioux City high school. The trustees, faced with a declining enrollment and small receipts, apparently decided to cut out a salary they could not afford to pay anyway. They boldly asserted that "the engagement with the different members of the faculty including the President, is only during the pleasure of the Board."[34]

This was too much for the presbyteries and the Board of Aid who launched an investigation headed by the Reverend C. K. Hoyt of Des Moines. A joint report was submitted on April 23, 1897. The report noted that the College had been crippled due to the fact that the Board of Aid had withheld half of the $1,200 appropriated for the 1895–1896 academic year. The Board asserted, however, that Buena Vista College had violated the conditions upon which the grant had been made.[35] The Board of Aid demanded that the College (1) clear its indebtedness and (2) omit the outline of the junior and senior years in subsequent catalogs. Otherwise the investigation showed that the books of the institution were in good, if sometimes confusing, order and in general supported the trustees in the dispute that was ravaging the morale of the College.

Meanwhile the trustees reached a compromise with President Marshall. He could, the Board decided, continue as president of the College until June if he would agree "that his compensation shall be one-third of the church offerings assigned the College of the four Presbyteries during the period of said term and until June 15, 1897, and one-third of the tuition fees raised from the students of the classical and normal departments during and for the spring term."[36] However, his share from tuition fees was not to exceed $125. Marshall, somewhat reluctantly, continued as president of the College on these terms.

The trustees at the beginning of 1897 had succeeded in securing a $6,500 loan from P. Kinnie and Son of Dubuque for five years at 7 percent per annum. The trustees hoped to cover all their debts with this loan and to "make the $6,500 borrowed the only debt."[37] At the annual meeting held in the office of Mack and De Land the trustees voted to use part of the $1,000 expected from the Board of Aid to pay the interest on the loan and $500 of the $1,000 to meet the president's salary. In addition the trustees still had to select a man to succeed Willis Marshall.[38]

A number of trustees preferred the Reverend C. K. Hoyt of Des Moines to succeed Willis Marshall as president but other possibilities were the Reverend Harvey Hostetler, pastor of the Second Presbyterian Church in Sioux City; the Reverend A. Z. McGogney, a trustee from LeMars; and the Reverend Charles Carter of Fairfield. The Board balloted twice on June 2, the vote being close each time, with Hostetler having a slight 7 to 5 majority. The trustees decided to postpone balloting for two weeks while they further interviewed the two leading candidates. On June 17, the Board changed its mind and unanimously elected the Reverend Mr. Hoyt, only to have Hoyt write that after thorough consideration he had decided to decline. The Board then turned to Hostetler who accepted the none-too-coveted position as president of Buena Vista College.[39] While the Board was struggling to foist the dubious distinction of the presidency upon yet another candidate, the fledgling institution held its "first banquet of those interested in the college." Following a music recital on June 1, 1897 some 150 guests of the College sat down to "the supper at which Professor Fracker was the toastmaster."[40]

Originally a resident of Pittsburgh, Hostetler had moved to Iowa when he was eight years old. A graduate of Marshalltown High School, the University of Iowa, and Union Theological Seminary, he had served pastorates at Vail and Sioux City, Iowa. Now, at age forty, Hostetler was the fourth president of Buena Vista College. The *Pilot* noted that the new president had agreeable manners, sound health, and was very persistent in his endeavors, but student appraisal was not always so flattering. Although Hostetler possessed a likable personality, he gave the impression of being phlegmatic. Like his predecessors, Hostetler was professor of mental and moral philosophy. His duties apparently included a class in Latin in which the "prexy" as he was called, sometimes slept while the students recited. One student remembered him as being "very fleshy, always had a toothpick in his mouth."[41] Hostetler, however, was persistent in the service of Buena Vista, for after retiring from the presidency in 1900 he remained a trustee of the College until his death in 1939. Furthermore, it was Hostetler who planted the original trees around the campus.[42]

The year 1897 saw prosperity return to America. The cry for "free silver" faded into the background, and the nation began to drift toward war with Spain. Americans wanted to free Cuba from the Spanish yoke, to dismantle the concentration camps instituted by the infamous General "Butcher" Weyler, and to enter the world stage as a recognized political and economic power.

During the tense Caribbean crisis of the 1890s, Buena Vista College organized a military company of over seventy, including young men from the community as well as the College. The company commander was a Captain Carroll, who apparently was regarded as a bona fide member of the faculty as well as the squad drillmaster. Officers were elected by vote of the members of the company subject to approval by the captain, who was a fleshy fifty and wore a tremendous handlebar moustache. He was a good drillmaster but "would get badly out of breath if he tried to take an active part in the out-of-door drills. . . ." The company was never called into service but was alerted when war broke out between the United States and Spain in 1898. Several of the young men enlisted and "one or two died in camp in Florida."[43]

President Hostetler was determined to keep the doors of the College open and to restore its original promise of being one of the leading educational institutions in western Iowa if not the state. Hostetler was a capable, if somewhat plodding, executive and during his three-year tenure, 1897–1900, the prospects of the College appeared to be improving. Hardly had he settled in Storm Lake, however, when a report was circulated in several papers that Buena Vista had permanently closed its doors and would not open for the fall term in September 1897. President Hostetler determined to set the record straight and "the next morning saw him in company with Professor Cooper riding across the country to nail that lie."[44]

One of the problems that faced Hostetler was the maintenance of an adequate faculty. A flurry of faculty members had come and gone during the decade of the 1890s. While the College catalog of 1899–1900 listed some eleven positions, a total of thirty-seven teachers had been employed since the College opened in 1891.[45] Of these, only four—G. H. Fracker, 1891–1930; J. C. Hutchison, 1891–1896; C. W. von Coelln, 1892–1896; and Floyd T. Voris, 1899–1905—stayed any length of time. The rapid turnover in per-

sonnel was not due to incompetence in the faculty but occurred
because the College was unable to pay their salaries. A student at
Buena Vista during the 1890s remembered M. W. Cooper, principal
of the normal department, "as the finest teacher of them all unless
you except Professor Fracker." But Cooper left because "the pressure was too great financially." He later taught at a government
school and retired in California.[46]

What was true of Cooper was true of others. The former State
Superintendent of Public Instruction, C. W. von Coelln, came to
Buena Vista in 1892 as professor of higher mathematics. One day
the professor held an examination, and years later one of his students recalled:

> When I handed in my test Professor Von Coelln told me to wait
> until he had finished grading. He gave me a 98%. Then he fol-
> lowed me out into the hall. He said, "Your uncle has promised to
> give BV $50. Ask him to pay it to me. My salary has not been
> paid for six months."[47]

Professor von Coelln had been hired by the trustees for a
salary of $900 per annum. A treasurer's report for 1895 reveals that
the College owed the professor $1,412.50 in back salary and was
behind in meeting its payroll by $2,636.23.[48] No wonder that most
of the clergymen who served short terms as president in the midst
of such chaos were glad to return to the ministry at an early date.
Von Coelln was one of the great personalities on the faculty of the
1890s. He was described as a "solid old German" who

> wore a sandy colored beard heavily sprinkled with gray. He
> seemed to have no neck. His neck was so big—and the tremen-
> dous voice of a steam calliope! When he sang he did it with all his
> might and one could easily distinguish his voice as he sang bass,
> even in a large congregation.[49]

The von Coellns had come to America in the 1850s. While in
Germany, von Coelln had been a classmate of Carl Schurz (a German immigrant who became a Civil War general, a senator from

Missouri, and secretary of the interior during the Hayes adminis-
tration) at the University of Bonn. He was also a soldier in the
German army when it stormed through northern France during the
Franco-Prussian War of 1870–71. Apparently von Coelln's first
American experience was on a dairy farm in Ohio where he per-
fected his English. In 1863 he became professor of mathematics at
Grinnell College.[50] He was elected superintendent of public instruction in 1875 and served for six years. Among other things von
Coelln had taught in Missouri, founded an academy in Dubuque
County, and served as the editor of the Henry County *Times*.[51] He
died at New London, Iowa on April 20, 1913. A *Tack* writer commented that von Coelln was "A man of pronounced ability, whose
time, however, was so long ago that we fear there are few of his
active contemporaries to recall him."[52]

Professor von Coelln's daughter, Anna, was a student at
Buena Vista during the early 1890s. She completed the junior and
senior years of the preparatory school and then enrolled in the
scientific course as a freshman in 1893. She played the organ in the
first chapel services that were held, prior to the construction of the
main College building, amidst the crumbling plaster of the old
Storm Lake Opera House. In later years as Anna von Coelln
Stokes she retained a deep interest in the growth of Buena Vista
College.

Professor J. C. Hutchison continued to teach physics and
chemistry at Buena Vista between 1891 and 1896. Hutchison was
the superintendent of the Cherokee electric light plant and seems to
have performed a similar service for Storm Lake. He appears to
have earned a doctorate and taught for more than thirty years at
the college level. Dr. Hutchison taught the physical sciences,
mathematics, German, and Latin. He had presided as vice president and librarian at Monmouth College in Illinois before moving
to Cherokee County, Iowa, from where he made at least two trips a
week to the Storm Lake campus as he sought to contribute to the
success of a young college where his twenty-one-year-old daughter
became the first graduate in 1893.[53] Even after Professor Hutchison terminated formal employment with the College in 1896, he

expressed his "willingness to visit and teach once or twice a month if the trustees would accept the same as a contribution to the College."[54]

The dedicated Fracker continued to teach whatever courses no one else could teach. His primary field, of course, was language; but he proved so competent in the area of mathematics that Western Pennsylvania College once offered him a position as assistant professor of mathematics. Fracker's name was constantly among those to whom the College owed back salaries. When, toward the end of his life, someone mentioned this monetary sacrifice to him, he simply said, "I gave myself to the church years ago." Fracker's extensive learning did not prevent him from enjoying the laughter of young people, and the Fracker home was always open to Buena Vista students.[55] If it had not been for Professor Fracker, Buena Vista might well have been denied a powerful intellect and a spiritual force that spelled the difference between survival and death.

The battle to maintain a faculty continued throughout President Hostetler's brief sojourn. The capable head of the commercial department, P. B. S. Peters, departed to take a position in a Kansas City, Missouri, high school. Peters was destined to become the author or coauthor of a commercial law text, a business speller, a manual for business law teachers, and a shorthand outline.[56] He must have been in his eighties when he died in Kansas City in 1942. Peters was replaced in 1898 by J. A. Ross. Professor and Mrs. Ross apparently made a lasting impression on Buena Vista students during their two-year stay. Ada Whitted Edson in one of her homey columns for the *Pilot-Tribune* wrote, "Their home was my home during part of my college days. . . . A wonderful couple who exemplified the real meaning of home and home life, to whom religion was of vital importance in the family and community to which they gave liberally of their time and talent."[57] Professor Ross left Buena Vista in 1900 and enrolled as a student in Still College of Osteopathy at Des Moines. He completed his course work in 1902 and set up practice in Oklahoma City where he remained until his death in 1951 at the age of eighty-three.[58]

Perhaps the most notable addition to the faculty was Floyd T. Voris who arrived in 1899 to take charge of the Division of Natural

Science. Voris was a graduate of Highland Seminary in Des Moines and of McCormick Theological Seminary in Chicago. He was included among the members of the Board of Trustees and, ostensibly a man of substance, contributed financially as well as academically to the welfare of the College. Voris, along with Dr. Fracker, constructed the shelves for the first volumes in the College library. An able teacher, he seems to have possessed a Napoleonic complex. His pictures suggest a small man with a sandy moustache and elegant sideburns adding superficial maturity to a boyish face. Apparently, Professor Voris had been a close friend of the Hostetlers.[59] In any case, as we shall see later, his relationship with the College became somewhat turbulent during the administration of E. E. Reed, 1900–1906.

By 1899 attendance was up 50 percent, and the College realized $1,000 more in tuition than it had the previous year.[60] The one real disappointment was that Buena Vista College was still not able to give instruction in the junior and senior years. Until this situation was remedied, the institution could not think of itself as a bona fide liberal arts college—it remained a junior college with normal school, commercial, and preparatory segments.

Nevertheless, the Hostetler administration was laying the groundwork for a more progressive era. The thin line of books in what was generously called the College library began to grow— more through gifts than budget. A former pastor at Sanborn, Estherville, and Bancroft, the Reverend Daniel Williams, became College librarian, and for the first time that integral part of the College was handled in a professional manner. Williams prepared a card index of the subjects in the library "following the Dewey system of library classification." A significant number of new volumes were added, many as a result of appeals to regional clergymen. These additions included thirteen volumes of the *American Church History* series donated by the Reverend Samuel Ollerenshaw of Algona and a set of the *International Encyclopedia* presented by Professor Voris.[61] An exceptional gift came from the Galena Public Library, which in 1899 presented the College with ninety-one volumes of *The Official Records of the War of the Rebellion*. These important volumes that recorded every battle of the Civil War originally had been presented to the Galena library by Mr. Louis A. Rowley. Apparently Anna Felt (Zeph Felt's mother) had persuaded Rowley and the Galena library to donate them to Buena Vista. By 1900 the College library could boast some 3,000 volumes.[62]

Daniel Williams, a profound and sincere man, along with Professor Fracker was among the founders of the College library. In addition to his library duties, the Reverend Mr. Williams was professor of religion. A graduate of the University of Minnesota and Princeton Theological Seminary (1881), he had an avid interest in history and religion and was the author of several pamphlets, including *A History of the Lakeside Church* (1914). Williams moved to Storm Lake in the fall of 1898 and remained on the Buena Vista faculty until 1905, at which time he became a member of the Board of Trustees, a position which he held until 1917.[63]

Another interesting personality who served the College in a variety of ways was the Reverend R. E. Flickinger of Fonda, Iowa. Flickinger originated the College museum by providing the "first collection of specimens."[64] In 1896 we find him "soliciting funds for the relief of Buena Vista College."[65] Like others before and after him, Flickinger kindled enthusiasm but secured few funds. At the same time he was working the field, Flickinger was serving as a trustee from 1894 to 1905.

Flickinger, like Daniel Williams, enjoyed writing history. His most important work was *The Early History of Iowa and Pioneer History of Pocahontas County* (1898). An active leader of the temperance movement of the 1890s, Flickinger became the director of the Iowa State Temperance Alliance for the Tenth Congressional District, 1890–1895, and led the Pocahontas County Temperance Movement, 1888–1902. During the years 1886–1902 Flickinger was pastor of the Fonda Presbyterian Church. He was the stated clerk and treasurer of the Fort Dodge Presbytery, 1892–1904, and moderator 1901–1902.[66]

By 1898 Buena Vista College established a five-week summer session that was primarily for teachers or those preparing to teach. President Hostetler presented a course entitled "Methods and the General History of Education." Classes were organized in "Physics, Algebra, Civics, Economics, Didactics, Physiology, Geography, Grammar, Arithmetic, Orthography, Reading, and Penmanship." Students could also obtain special lessons in typewriting and shorthand from Professor Ross, and if demand were sufficient, it was announced that classes would be offered in Latin, Greek, French, and German.[67]

Tuition for the summer school was $4 and board could be had with private families for $2.50 a week and up. President Hostetler closed the announcement of the forthcoming summer school with a familiar ring:

> Storm Lake, with its well shaded walks and cool lake breezes, is a delightful place to spend the warm summer months. The well kept lawns of the citizens, and the spacious public parks are a delight to the eye. The lake with its facilities for boating, bathing and fishing is very attractive. It would be difficult to find a place offering better opportunities of rest and study than Storm Lake and our summer school.[68]

During Hostetler's third and final year as president of the College, church donations reached a new high of $2,494.30. There were now thirteen students in the collegiate department (first two years), and the total unduplicated attendance for the year 1899–1900 reached 204 students in the various departments.[69]

In the midst of this promising movement of the institution, President Hostetler resigned to return to the ministry. Being a pastor was more rewarding, more stable, and more conducive to family life than serving as president of Buena Vista College. Hostetler was a congenial, although not dynamic, president and was apparently held in high esteem by the trustees, faculty, and student body of the College. There was no pressure on Hostetler to relinquish the presidency and he would remain a loyal supporter of the College throughout his life. Certainly, Buena Vista College was a more stable institution in 1900 than it had been three years earlier. Now the trustees would have the task of selecting a president who could carry on the work started by Hostetler. They chose the Reverend E. E. Reed of Atlantic, Iowa, who was destined to provide the College with its most fruitful leadership yet.

4

A FIRM FOUNDATION: E. E. REED (1900–1906)

... great troubles, great struggles, and great successes.

—E. S. BENJAMIN

President E. E. Reed was born at Fairfield on New Year's Day, 1862. His boyhood was spent on an Iowa farm and he knew the state and its people. In the early 1880s young Reed left the farm and attended Parsons College where he received his B.A. in 1884. After Parsons, Reed took postgraduate work at Princeton University and McCormick Theological Seminary, graduating from the latter in 1888. While serving the Presbyterian church at Atlantic, Iowa, Reed earned a reputation as a successful pastor and a capable executive. Married to Margaret Murray on May 29, 1890, he was the father of five children.[1]

From the time of his ordination in 1888 until he became president of Buena Vista College in 1900, the Reverend Mr. Reed served the Presbyterian church as pastor in three communities—Kirksville, Missouri, 1888–1891; Griswold, 1891–1895; and Atlantic, 1895–1900. The remaining twenty-six years of his life would be devoted to presidencies of three Presbyterian colleges: Buena Vista, 1900–1906; Lenox College at Hopkinton, Iowa, 1906–1915; and Westminister at Fulton, Missouri, 1915–1926. Dr. Reed was an educator who served with energy and dedication wherever he went.[2] He was an outstanding speaker, a man of high standards, and a determined fund raiser. He staunchly faced the same problems at each institution—lack of endowment, faculty, and buildings. A successful administration at the older and more stable Westminster College was cut short by his death in 1926 at the age of sixty-two.[3] His nine-year tenure as president of Lenox College undoubtedly postponed that college's ultimate demise as a four-year institution. When Reed left Hopkinton in 1915, all but two of his faculty resigned.[4]

Two major tasks faced the new president of Buena Vista College. He had to raise a substantial endowment fund and he had to upgrade the academic status of the College so that Buena Vista would be able to offer the full liberal arts course and rejoin the ranks of the four-year colleges. An endowment and an indication of financial stability was essential if the original goal of the founders—a respected liberal arts college—was to be realized. Both trustees and community were adamant about having a four-year rather than a two-year institution.

The Presbyterian Board of Aid for Colleges insisted that Buena Vista show firm evidence of financial stability before becoming a four-year college. More than once the Board of Aid had chastised College officials for permitting instruction beyond the sophomore year and threatened to cut off aid (sparse as it was) to the College unless it ceased advertising course work for the junior and senior years. The trustees humbly declared their determination to "comply fully with all conditions in the future."[5]

The trustees, receiving trifling amounts of assistance from the churches as well as the Board, were faced with an impossible task. Trustee minutes between 1893 and 1896 weave a pathetic web. During those years the combined church collections totaled $1,812.92. Meanwhile, the Board of Aid contributed only $709.95 in 1894; $400 in 1895; $993 in 1896; and $1,000 in 1897.[6] The three years of the Hostetler regime witnessed only a slight improvement in the financial standing of the College.

When E. E. Reed arrived to take charge of the College in October, 1900, the decision to raise an endowment fund had already been made.[7] The ultimate goal was an endowment of $100,000. One-half of this amount was to be raised in Iowa and

one-half in the East. The Iowa quota had to be reached before the
Board of Aid would grant permission to solicit in the Ohio-Penn-
sylvania area. Buena Vista County's quota was $25,000.[8] This was
the challenge awaiting the new president and Reed did not take
long in getting his campaign under way. He set out to promote and
persuade, and neither frustration nor ill health could halt his endeavors. Soon, College and community were to embark upon the
first of many financial crusades in order to save Buena Vista College.

By February 1901 President Reed had his endowment drive
under way. In a speech at Lakeside Church the president informed
his audience that he had subscriptions amounting to more than
$7,000 from outside the city. Still, he said, "Storm Lake is to strike
the keynote for the future of this institution. I do not believe they
want a one-horse college. What is done must be done now and at
once; now or never."[9]

Buena Vista's new president pointed out the benefits that the
city derived from having a college: the saving of college costs for
parents, the enhanced real estate values, the trade and general
growth of the community. While the people of Storm Lake had
subscribed $11,000, considerably more was needed to meet the
goal. President Reed paraphrasing Shakespeare added:

> There is a tide in the affairs of men, which taken at the flood
> leads on to fortunes. We are now on the crest of such a tide. Let
> us ply the oars and pull together. Let every contributor become a
> solicitor and the work is done, and Buena Vista College with the
> best location in the state has been made a college of the first
> ranks.[10]

Others echoed the president's remarks. The College paper dramatically proclaimed that "Buena Vista has reached the turning
point of her history. The opportunity of her life may be seized or
neglected within the next few months."[11] All agreed that, as Board
member Dr. Chittenden of Sac City had pointed out, "if this movement should fail Storm Lake would have a dead college and an
empty building on her hands."[12]

There was, however, no thought of failure. President Reed;

Professor Floyd T. Voris; E. R. Sisson; attorneys E. E. Mack, A. D. Bailie, and Phil Schaller—who had come from Sac City to assist President Reed—all spoke earnestly and effectively on behalf of the College. It is true they spoke in a rather materialistic vein—a thriving college would raise the value of property. But this was a language any business-oriented community could understand. Occasionally, the deeper purpose of the institution penetrated some of the discussions; and E. R. Sisson was moved to say that people were "going to help build up a Christian college."[13]

Professor Floyd T. Voris pledged $5,000 if $25,000 could be raised in Buena Vista County. Scott C. Bradford, a prominent local speculator in real estate, pledged $1,500 and E. R. Sisson did the same. Sisson implied that he wanted to keep even with Bradford, but Bradford responded by raising his subscription to $2,500.[14] As it turned out, however, the pledging was made with more enthusiasm than the giving. The campaign, nevertheless, looked so promising that when the Synod made its report on President Reed's work at Buena Vista, it was moved to say that "in a year he has brought order out of chaos, he has given the institution local financial standing."[15] And at his inauguration on May 28, 1901, President Reed confidently asserted that "the day will come when Buena Vista College will be the pride of Iowa."[16]

Victory was farther away than Reed had anticipated. In April 1902, the president and the trustees were still struggling to raise the Iowa quota of $50,000. Only one month remained before the campaign was to close. A "mystery man" then pledged $5,000 if Reed could raise the $15,000 needed to meet the quota by May 16. In a meeting held in the office of Mack and De Land, the president and trustees pledged themselves to a renewed effort which the *Pilot-Tribune* said would make the foundation of the College "as lasting as the Rock of Ages."[17]

While the *Pilot-Tribune*'s optimism may have been premature, Buena Vista College was at last able to celebrate a notable achievement. Reed managed to raise the $15,000 and on June 10, 1902, a meeting was scheduled at the Lakeside Church. The mystery man was to be unmasked at the meeting, and a number of prominent associates of the College would speak, including Professor Voris,

Dr. Ray of Chicago (representing the Board of Aid), and the Reverend Samuel Callen of Waterloo.[18]

The mystery man was Scott C. Bradford who had already pledged $2,500 to the campaign. This meant that the combined pledges of Bradford and Voris totaled $12,500 or one-half the Storm Lake quota. The community viewed Bradford, Voris, and President Reed as responsible for the apparent success of the endowment drive.

Professor Voris, who like Bradford had a variety of business interests, spoke on the occasion. Having just returned from a quarter of graduate work at Columbia University, he could see the advantages of the small college over the large university where "there was no such thing as the possession of individuality by the students" and where none of them "could get acquainted with their instructors." Voris told the gathering in the Lakeside Church that he wanted to see Buena Vista College reach the academic plateau. He could see that the College needed a chemistry building, a library, and a gymnasium.[19] Some months earlier when Voris had delivered a similar speech, President Reed had remarked that a "Voris Science Hall" would "sound well."[20]

The crowd in the Lakeside Church could feel that this was the greatest day in the history of Buena Vista College. The success of the endowment campaign was a cause for rejoicing, and the church was gaily decorated with the College colors and wild flowers. The enthusiastic audience listened with approval to forecasts of future greatness (already a ritual) for the College. Perhaps the most realistic appraisal came from the young Methodist clergyman, E. S. Benjamin, who predicted "great troubles, great struggles and great successes."[21] Meanwhile, President Reed turned over the subscriptions to the treasurer of the College, and the trustees selected a three-person committee to take control of the endowment funds.

The success of the endowment campaign was not as complete as President Reed had believed. He was soon to clash with Professor Voris over the management of the funds. In June 1902, the trustees had agreed that "the permanent endowment fund of the College shall consist of such sums as are donated for that purpose and the principal thereof shall be kept intact, and only the income thereof used for current expenses of the College."[22] This was a traditional and certainly sensible approach. Unfortunately, while the endowment drive had succeeded, funds to meet current expenses were not forthcoming. Apparently upon the suggestion of the president, the Board decided to use some of the endowment in order to meet operating expenses:

> In view of an agreement signed by 12 members of the Board it was moved that the College loan from the endowment fund a sum not to exceed $2,500 to the current fund, and that as security for the same, the subscriptions for current expenses now on hand to the amount of $3,068 be collateral.[23]

Professor Voris felt that the principal in the endowment fund was untouchable. The fact that the College was now using $2,500 "in payment of its debts and current expenses,"[24] Voris felt relieved him of all liability concerning his pledge. President Reed and the Board of Trustees obviously did not agree and the case of *Buena Vista College* (plaintiff) v. *Floyd T. Voris* (defendant) was scheduled for the November 1904 term of district court. Voris was no ordinary professor to be intimidated by the preponderant power and status arrayed against him. He not only held academic rank but was a member of the Board of Trustees who had pledged a substantial sum of money to the College. He was in a position to pose a formidable challenge to both president and trustees.

Undoubtedly, the dispute had been festering for sometime, for in December 1903 Voris resigned from the College, claiming that "the principles that have controlled my work are that all the dealings of the institution with both students and public must be characterized by unflinching honesty and sincerity." If Buena Vista were to succeed, Voris said, it would do so only by "maintaining the highest standards of scholarship. I cannot degrade my work by submitting to other principles."[25]

It is difficult to see how Professor Voris could have attacked Reed for not maintaining high academic standards. The president had modernized the curriculum and had by 1904 returned Buena Vista to the ranks of the four-year colleges. Voris apparently felt that the president and trustees were about to squander the endow-

ment and so to submit his resignation was the only honorable option.

Actually, Voris had paid nothing on his pledge in either 1902
or 1903. The court record shows that Professor Voris gave his
promissory note to the plaintiff "for the sum of $5,000 dated May
20, 1902, with interest at 6% per annum from date and payable in
annual installments of $1,000 each." Voris was now preparing to
move to the west coast, and Buena Vista College asked for a "writ
of attachment against the lands and tenements, goods and chattels,
rights and credits of the defendant."[26] While Voris admitted the
note, he said that it was entirely without consideration and that the
"note is merely a naked promise to give and is therefore void."[27] He
also said that the College had never collected the full amount of the
endowment and that the use of a portion of the endowment fund
to pay current expenses had released him from his obligations.

The case was finally settled in January 1905 when Voris acknowledged that the note was a "just, legal and binding obligation
against him as to principal and interest . . . the defendant will pay
the interest that was due upon said note in May, 1904, together
with interest upon that sum from the day it was due until paid at
the rate of 6% per annum." The attachment against the defendant's
property was released, and the defendant and plaintiff agreed "each
to pay one-half the damages."[28]

While Voris's resignation in December 1903 created no re-
morse in President Reed or the trustees, it was disheartening to the
faculty. Indications are that the professor was popular among his
colleagues. On December 22, 1903, the faculty adopted a resolution lauding Professor Voris for having stood for "truth and justice" and praising his "devotion, work, and Christian character."[29]
There is no denying that Voris and his mother, Mrs. C. A. Voris of
Des Moines, were people of considerable means who had contributed much to the growth of Buena Vista College. Voris may have
envisioned himself as Reed's successor as president of Buena Vista
College.[30] Voris also endeavored to improve himself academically,
spending a summer session at the University of Minnesota as well
as a quarter at Columbia University.[31] In 1901 he became a member
of the American Association for the Advancement of Science.[32] At

the same time, Voris was noticeably absent from the College while he looked after his real estate interests in various parts of the country. As the College paper noted, the professor returned "just in time to alight upon us with the examinations which he had to take a month's vacation to forge."[33] Voris's term as a trustee of the College officially terminated in 1907. By this time he was in Tacoma, Washington, and apparently his once warm connections with Buena Vista College had ended.

Meanwhile, mystery man Scott C. Bradford had been unanimously elected president of the Board.[34] He was serving in this capacity at the time the College was bringing suit to collect Professor Voris's pledge. Scott Bradford had graduated from the Iowa Agricultural College at Ames in 1888 and had taught school at Sioux Rapids for one year. In 1892 he was elected clerk for the district court and served in this capacity for six years. He became a banker, invested in real estate in Minnesota and Iowa, built the Bradford Hotel, and as the *Storm Lake Pilot-Tribune* remarked when Bradford moved to Des Moines in 1915, "took an active part in furthering practically every forward movement in the community."[35] His endowment pledge of $5,000 had evidently served to elevate the thirty-eight-year-old Bradford to the presidency of the Board of Trustees.

However, Bradford was slow in making good his own pledge; and not until 1914 did he fulfill his obligation to the College by donating twenty-two lots lying south of the campus.[36] The tale surrounding Bradford's belated fulfillment of his pledge may have involved the resignation of then President James Patterson Linn. Bradford agreed to donate the lots if Linn would resign — which he did in October 1913. The trustees, in accepting the president's resignation, praised him for his "Christian spirit and loyalty to the school (which involved the sacrifice of his job) . . . and our confidence in him as a gentleman and a Christian man."[37]

While the endowment campaign presented a major obstacle, President Reed faced another struggle in moving Buena Vista College back into the ranks of the four-year colleges. One of the first steps in this direction was the modernization of the curriculum; in April 1903 the faculty approved the division of the College year into semesters and the adoption of the group system of courses.[38]

The group system was then in effect at most liberal arts colleges. The studies were arranged in different groups, in each of which were three leading subjects called majors. Twelve units of work had to be completed in each major. This meant that the subject had to be pursued "for two years with three recitations per week." Here are two representative groups (actually there were seven):[39]

GROUP I		GROUP 2	
Latin	12	German	12
Greek	12	Mental Science	12
English	12	History	12
Mathematics	6	English	6
Laboratory Science	6	Mathematics	6
Mental Science	6	Laboratory Science	6
Electives	66	Electives	60
Bible	4	Bible	4

Different combinations of majors could be selected within the seven groups. This arrangement was more modern than the old classical curriculum, although it was, according to the trend at the time, heavy on the electives. The College catalog informed prospective students:

> The Group system gives the student the opportunity of emphasizing the studies in which he afterwards intends to specialize, and gives to all the advantages of the rigid course system with those of the free elective system and to maintain a proper balance between educational control on the one side and individual freedom of choice and self-direction on the other.[40]

Costs remained relatively stable at Buena Vista during the first decade of its existence. Tuition per semester in the collegiate department was $18.50 or $37 per year. This was only one dollar more than it had been for the three terms in 1891–92. Candidates for the ministry and children of ministers still had their tuition fees reduced by one-half.[41]

The library collection, which had begun to grow during the Hostetler administration, now took on increasing importance. In his annual report in 1903, President Reed maintained that "the library was never used so much by the students as during the past few months. The number of volumes has now passed beyond the four thousand mark."[42] The College catalog of 1904–5 claimed 5,000 volumes and that "one thousand dollars has been expended for books during the past two years." One donor, Mrs. Nettie M. Adams, had sent a check for $500.[43] In addition to books and reference materials, the library subscribed to a number of magazines. These included the *Literary Digest, Harper's Weekly, Century, North American Review, Review of Reviews,* and the *Journal of American Sociology.*[44]

One of the desperate needs of Buena Vista College, President Reed believed, was the construction of a new library building. When he undertook a campaign in 1902 to secure the building, he succeeded primarily in launching an effort that was to frustrate every Buena Vista College president for more than sixty years. Reed's idea seems to have been to secure a library on the College campus that the Storm Lake public could use at will. With this in mind, he sought out the steel magnate and philanthropist Andrew Carnegie. After two years Reed was informed that Carnegie was unwilling to fund a grant of this nature. He proposed only the grant of $10,000 to construct a public library for community purposes. President Reed, though greatly disappointed, encouraged the city fathers to accept Carnegie's offer.[45]

Meanwhile, the College library, now totaling over 5,000 volumes, remained in the main building. When Reed assumed the presidency there were only 2,333 volumes in the collection and no systematic cataloging. In 1927 the library, now named in honor of Professor George H. Fracker, was moved into the newly constructed Science Hall. After World War II it was transferred into a remodeled brick structure that had once been an army barracks. By then the collection had grown to 30,000 volumes. Reed at least had achieved something for the city; the new library would remain a College project until 1965.[46]

While Reed had his problems with the endowment fund and

the library project, he did succeed in obtaining the house directly
east of the main building for the president. The house had been
built by the Reverend J. M. Linn, the second president of the
College, 1892–1894. Linn had constructed the house with the intention that it would be used by the president and would eventually
become the property of the College. The two-story structure originally cost "nearly $4,000 aside from the 120 feet of ground on
which it stands."[47] Due to the terminal illness of his wife, Linn
resigned in 1894 and no longer made his residence in Storm Lake.
He later remarried and served a church at Inwood, Iowa.

The trustee minutes reveal that in the winter of 1900–1901
Buena Vista College had the opportunity to "purchase lots 15, 16 in
block 35 in the College Addition to Storm Lake, from the heirs at
law of Mary C. A. Linn deceased, for the sum of $2,500 in cash."[48]
Certainly the property was worth far more than the $2,500 asked,
but the problem was to find a benefactor who would provide the
money for the necessary purchase. The Reverend William Miller of
Des Moines offered $2,000, and Mrs. Lois G. Stuart of Audubon
came forward to donate the remaining $500.[49] The grateful trustees
resolved that the property

> shall be known as the Miller-Stuart House, and that a door plate
> bearing such inscription be placed thereon. And be it further
> resolved, that the Secretary of the Board be [sic], and he is
> hereby instructed to furnish each of said donors a copy of these
> resolutions, and that they be spread at length upon the records of
> the college, and furnished to the local papers for publication.[50]

Miller-Stuart House served every president through Wendell
Halverson. However, by the arrival of the Briscoes in 1974, the
aging structure needed major repairs. A gift from Paul and Vivian
McCorkle enabled the College to obtain a modern, more elegant
presidential home on the west edge of Storm Lake. The Miller-
Stuart house was demolished without fanfare in 1974, and the only
reminders of its once-proud existence are a few nails salvaged and
given to the author by a 1938 graduate, Dr. Harold Wood.

Perhaps the most serious challenge that faced President Reed
was the attempt to build a competent faculty—this, with inade-

quate salaries. Salaries had never been munificent at Buena Vista, and back salaries remained a budget item. Those who worked for Buena Vista College did not participate in the prosperous decade of 1896–1906. President Hays was employed at an annual salary of $1,200 in 1891. Reed had come to Buena Vista at the same salary, and after four years of service the trustees had boosted his wages to only $1,600. On one occasion it was noted that Reed had donated $400 of his salary to the College.[51] Salaries for the regular members of the faculty ranged from $550 to $850 during the early years of the new century. At best, this compensation would provide a bare living for members of the College faculty. Unfortunately, current income was so uncertain that members of the faculty often went months without being paid. The young Storm Lake attorney, Willis C. Edson, discovered the financial problems of the College in a hurry when he became a trustee in 1904. The desperate trustees immediately thrust upon Edson the task of being College treasurer. At that time the College had only $1.89 in the bank, according to Edson, while the "faculty had given notice they would resign unless they got $1,500 by Saturday night." Edson recalled:

> I asked them if I was to raise the $1500. They said, 'Yes.' Then I said [to trustees Bailie and M. O. Miller], 'If you will each put up $100 I will too, if the Bank will loan it to me.' I went downstairs and the first man I met was W. L. Geisinger, a Methodist. I told him what I was doing. Without asking him for it, he gave me $100. I went into the bank and the first man I saw there was Connell, a Catholic. He asked me what I was doing and I told him. He said, 'Here is a check for $100,' so in about 10 minutes I had $500. I got the rest by Saturday and paid it to the faculty.[52]

For Buena Vista College this was to be the story for many decades. Even during the Reed administration faculty members who had taught in the 1890s were still trying to collect their back salaries. One of these was the former head of the commercial department, P. B. S. Peters, who was now teaching in the Manual Training High School in Kansas City, Missouri.[53] He desired settlement of a note for $128 at 8 percent per annum which had been given him by the College in 1895. In the summer of 1903 Peters "offered to accept one hundred dollars cash as full payment of his claim."[54]

After ten years of service, in 1901, Dr. George H. Fracker was receiving an annual salary of $750. This was less than his original contract in 1891 had stipulated. Fracker's long career at Buena Vista was, of course, one of deliberate sacrifice. He served the College in almost every conceivable capacity, and during the early struggles it was Fracker and Willis Edson who undoubtedly saved the College from extinction. Fracker was a universal scholar who, as one student recalled, "was able to take over about any subject in the curriculum."

> I never took work under him until my last year when I enrolled in Physics. Since there was no other person qualified to teach that subject that year, Dr. Fracker taught it and I remember him as being a most precise teacher—just such a one as is needed in science. I had high regard for him. He had great devotion for the College and I suspect there were times when he went without a salary for months.[55]

Surprisingly, President Reed was able to induce a number of competent faculty to join the high-risk venture that was then Buena Vista College. Some were young and beginning their professional careers, while others stressed the service aspect of their work. Among these were Professor J. E. Delmarter, the new director of the musical department, and Miss Edna Armilda Appleby, the principal of piano instruction. Delmarter had studied in New York and Chicago and had wide experience in teaching classes and conducting choirs, choruses, and cantatas. Miss Appleby was a graduate of the State Normal School in Winona, Minnesota, graduated in advanced piano and harmony from Frances Shimer Academy of the University of Chicago, and had studied harmony with Dr. Gustaf Schreck and Professor Hizey of Leipzig, Germany.[56] By 1903, when these two talented instructors departed, there were 191 students enrolled in the musical department.

One of the most noble spirits to come to the Buena Vista campus was Miss Alice Wilcox, a native of New York, who arrived in 1902 and was professor of English for twenty years. Her father had been killed at Gettysburg during the Civil War, and one gets the impression that Mrs. Wilcox was a possessive and dependent mother. Alice Wilcox studied in New York, Michigan, and Wisconsin. Mother and daughter lived together until Mrs. Wilcox's death at the age of eighty-five in 1922.[57]

Alice Wilcox was strict and exacting and not everyone loved her. Russell Anderson, a student during the early 1920s, had the task of firing the furnace in Old Main. It was no easy job and Anderson often stayed up until midnight and rose again at 4 A.M. On a January morning when it was $-22°F$, Anderson walked into Professor Wilcox's office and observed that she was attired in a "light lace dress." "Mr. Anderson, I am cold," she remarked. Anderson, no doubt tired from his long night vigil at the furnace, told her "Dress right and you will not be so cold." Anderson's impertinence led to a chilly relationship for Professor Wilcox not only refused to correct his papers but failed him in the course. Anderson was saved by the efforts of Dean Saylor and Dewey Deal after Wilcox's departure.[58] When students turned in their written essays Miss Wilcox had a rule that "if we misspelled a word, we would have to return to her room and write it ten times." For each additional essay the penalty went up by ten. But C. M. Drury, one of Buena Vista's most distinguished graduates, remembered her as "the first good English teacher I ever had."[59] Miss Wilcox served Buena Vista in many ways. She was the chairperson of the library committee, chairperson of the Commencement committee, the pioneer organizer of the Student Council, faculty member on the *Tack* staff, freshman class and YWCA advisor.[60] When Miss Wilcox left Buena Vista in 1922 to become the librarian of the Aldrich Public Library in Gouverneur, New York, she was awarded an honorary M.A. degree by the College.[61] Alice Wilcox returned to Storm Lake on several occasions including the 50th anniversary of the College in May 1942.

In 1903 Professor E. F. Blayney became professor of Greek and mental science at a salary of $700, plus an additional $200 for the summer session. President Reed expected more from the talented Blayney than work in the classroom. In a report to the trustees, Reed recommended "that our new professor in Greek and

Philosophy be sent into the field the first of July, for a continued
canvass from that time until the opening of school."[62] Blayney, one
of the few members of the faculty to have a Ph.D., taught at
Buena Vista from 1903 to 1913. He became acting president following the resignation of Edward Campbell in 1911. During this
time Blayney played an important part in raising $17,000 to reduce
the continued indebtedness of the College. In July 1912 Professor
Blayney obtained a leave of absence to serve a year as high school
principal in Orosi, California. Blayney found the West enticing
enough that he tendered his resignation from the Buena Vista faculty at the end of February 1913. The handsome, youthful-looking
Blayney died prematurely in October 1920.[63]

There was no wide differentiation in the salary scale. Professor
Voris in 1902–1903 received $700, as did Professor Merton L.
Fuller, principal of the normal department, while Professor George
A. Parker, principal of the commercial and shorthand department,
received $650. Miss Alice Tozer, the very competent professor of
Latin, was employed at a salary of $550. Miss Cora Thompson and
Miss Edna A. Appleby, two teachers in the music department, had
a different arrangement. They received 90 percent of the tuitions in
their department.[64]

The salaries were so low and uncertain that when Professor
Fuller resigned suddenly in July 1902 to accept a post with the
government as a weather observer, the *Storm Lake Pilot-Tribune*
reported that "friends rejoice at his good fortune." In those days
Buena Vista had a small weather-instrument house and Professor
Fuller used "to make readings for his weather reports to the U.S.
Weather Bureau and then hoist the weather flags on the pole atop
the College main building."[65] Apparently, Professor Fuller did his
work well, for the government snatched him from the frail arms of
Buena Vista College. But no doubt Fuller's marriage in August
1901 to Miss Nan Golden of Underwood, Iowa, prompted his decision to find more certain and lucrative employment than as head of
Buena Vista's normal department. Furthermore, Fuller's new position, as the *Pilot-Tribune* suggested, gave him "unlimited opportunities for scientific research." Fuller had been a valuable teacher.
Such losses were not easy to overcome.

President Reed desired a good faculty and he wanted to pay them adequate salaries, but campaigns to meet current expenses often ended in frustration. In 1905 trustee Willis Edson sent an urgent message to each of the churches in the Fort Dodge and Sioux City presbyteries, but only Schaller and Alta responded. Edson then undertook a personal campaign among the downtown businesses, where he found much criticism and little encouragement. However:

> Three men . . . gave generous contributions and also words of encouragement. A Greek, who operated a candy store, a Jew, Louis Kaplin, who fled from Russia when most of his family were killed in a massacre of the Jews, and a Chinese, J. T. Fong, who operated a laundry. They told the same story. In their home country, no one could get a college education except members of Royalty or the Ruling class.[66]

On another occasion Mrs. Reed, unknown to the president, endeavored to raise money for the unpaid faculty. She wrote to one of the College's early benefactors, Mrs. Flora S. Mather of Cleveland, Ohio, telling her of the serious financial plight of the institution. Mrs. Mather responded with a check for $5,000 which, temporarily at least alleviated the crisis.[67]

Meanwhile, President Reed continued his effort to enlarge the endowment and to place Buena Vista College on a more secure financial basis. In his annual report to the trustees in June 1904, Reed said:

> At my suggestion the Synod of Iowa in their meeting last Fall recommended that Buena Vista College should have $250,000 more to meet the immediate needs of the school. This was the footing of a careful estimate made and would be none too much for what I have in mind on a most conservative basis. And permit me to say I do not consider this an impossible undertaking.[68]

The goal that Reed envisioned was still a long way off, but between 1901 and 1907 the endowment fund moved beyond $61,000, with additional notes unsecured totaling $37,000.[69] And throughout his administration, President Reed sought funds both locally and nationally. In 1906 a noted Fort Dodge temperance leader, the Honorable L. S. Coffin, offered the College $10,000 to endow a chair of political science for the purpose of instructing the "youth of the land touching the enormous waste to the state, growing out of the sale and use of intoxicating liquors as a beverage."[70] This, of course, was an era when the great push for national prohibition was gaining momentum, and so Reed and the trustees were willing to meet Coffin's terms. Reed also endeavored to gain support from the "General Education Board, founded and endowed with ten million dollars by John D. Rockefeller and the Carnegie Foundation for the advancement of teaching."[71] These efforts were to be continued during the administration of Reed's successor, Robert L. Campbell.

One of President Reed's foremost dreams was that the College should "acquire all the land between the . . . campus and the lake, most of which land was used as a cow pasture." Unfortunately, the College was too poor to finance such a venture and Reed watched the first two houses built on the lake side with considerable dismay. Yet he remained enthusiastic and hopeful and saw Buena Vista as a "great if not large educational institution."[72] Ironically, the College in order to meet housing needs for students during the boom years of the 1980s eventually acquired adjacent property at inflated prices, and one of the "cottages" would be christened Reed House.

Reed's most significant achievement as president of Buena Vista College was to move the institution back into the ranks of the four-year colleges. The citizens of Storm Lake wanted a college, not a preparatory school nor a junior college, for their community. Between 1895 and 1901 this dream was on the verge of vanishing. Reed revived it and during his administration the College was again able to offer the last two years of instruction, and in 1904 presented its first B.A. degrees since 1893. The Commencement of 1904, the *Pilot-Tribune* said, had President Reed preparing for "one of the greatest days in the history of the institution . . . the graduation of the first class from the collegiate department."[73]

The graduates were four young ladies: Margaret McLean, Aura Garberson, Ethellyn Bailie, and Agnes King. President Reed proudly affirmed to the trustees that "Buena Vista is now a college. . . . She makes her bow to the public at this commencement with her first class graduating from the collegiate department."[74] It had been a long and treacherous road since the first B.A. degree had been granted to Jennie G. Hutchison back in 1893. From this time forward, however, Buena Vista would always have a Commencement and a growing line of graduates. During the last year of the Reed administration there were 220 students in all departments, and twenty-three of them were taking college work. By 1908 the number of students taking collegiate work totaled fifty-two.[75]

The fact that the four graduates of the class of 1904 were young women led President Reed to stress coeducation. Already in his annual report to the trustees in June 1903 he had urged the board to make greater efforts on behalf of coeducation. He urged the trustees to appoint an advisory board of women whose duty would be to "arouse an interest in Buena Vista College, to secure a more generous support of the school in any way that they may be able, and especially to look after the interest of the young women who are attending the College."[76] Six women were to make up the advisory board, and Reed especially recommended that one of the College's early benefactors, Mrs. Flora S. Mather, "be made an honorary member of this board." The Mathers were among the pioneers who developed the iron mines of Minnesota, and they had been active in the development of Western Reserve University in Ohio.[77]

President Reed was not a robust man and early in 1905 he suffered a prolonged illness that greatly hampered his work. Dr. Reed had undertaken an extensive eastern tour in an effort to add to the endowment fund of the College. This, and the many other trips that he undertook on behalf of the College, gave him little rest and little time for his young family. The president "worked so hard and the job was so frustrating that he came home . . . in a state of severe nervous exhaustion."[78] The trustees, who seem to have admired the president, voted him a lengthy vacation hoping that he would be able to resume his full duties in the fall of 1905.

Reed was able to return for the academic year 1905–1906 and renew the fight for a better Buena Vista. However, the constant battles to raise funds, to collect unpaid pledges, and to move the College into the ranks of the academically respectable institutions of higher learning took their toll. No doubt feeling he had done as much as was possible for Buena Vista, the president submitted his resignation in July 1906.

Reed would go to Lenox College, and then would end a long career of distinguished service at Westminster College, Fulton, Missouri. Reed, always a determined fund raiser, launched financial drives at Lenox College that secured pledges of $200,000 in a five-year period 1907–1912. As at Buena Vista, it proved easier to obtain pledges than collections, which were often impossible to secure. Reed, however, retained his enthusiasm for campaign drives during his eleven years at Westminster. Indeed, his administration "was marked by his incessant, persistent, appeals for money." He was always regarded as a strenuous and able leader.[79]

The trustees of Buena Vista College were not eager to lose a man of Reed's stature and urged him to remain at his post. Reed agreed to remain only until September 1906. There is nothing in Reed's resignation to suggest other than an amiable and regrettable severing of ties. The president had the respect of trustees, faculty, and the people of Storm Lake during his six years as president of the College. In his resignation Reed thanked the trustees for their "hearty support during the six years that I have served as President of this institution." The trustees hastened to acknowledge Reed as a man of "high ideals, of perfect fidelity, of uncommon ability in finances and of sincere devotion and trusts God in His Providence may spare him to many years of service and increasing influence in the cause of Christian education."[80]

Professor Reed had given Buena Vista College its most efficient and successful administration to date. He had secured two new structures, Miller-Stuart House and the Music Conservatory; he had raised the first endowment fund; he had modernized the curriculum; he had, in restoring Buena Vista to the status of a four-year college, reasserted the intention of the institution's founders. Reed's six-year tenure was the longest in the history of the College until the term of the Reverend E. L. Jones 1924–1931. Reed's achievements in an era when the College might well have succumbed to junior college status or folded have merited him a place among the institution's foremost builders. Noting that President Reed had secured $30,718.49 for the College since September 1, 1905, the *Storm Lake Pilot-Tribune* said he had achieved, "a great and good work . . . sometimes under adverse circumstances."[81]

5

Bright Promises and Deep Frustrations

I could hear the footsteps of the students of Buena Vista College
coming for a thousand years.

—THE REVEREND DAVID MACKINTOSH

When Robert Lincoln Campbell became president of Buena
Vista College in 1906, only two of the original seventeen
trustees remained. These were E. R. Sisson, a prominent real estate
man, and J. B. McKibben, whose long years of service to the
College were topped only by W. C. Edson. McKibben acted as the
treasurer of the institution until he resigned that difficult post in
June 1906. He remained a trustee of the College, however, until his
death in the early 1940s.

Eugene R. Sisson, the College's first financial agent, was also
a trustee from 1891–1910. The Sissons had moved from Indiana to
Illinois and finally to northwest Iowa. While living at Mason, Illinois, Eugene was a boyhood companion of A. D. Bailie who was
also to be a trustee. He married May Carroll in 1886 when he was
twenty-eight years old. Enticing "whole train loads of prospective
land buyers" to northwest Iowa, in one year he supposedly "sold
21,000 acres in Buena Vista County."[1] Sisson was also an accomplished cornet soloist whose family appears to have possessed considerable talent in music. Miss Ida Sisson, Eugene's sister, was instructor in piano at the College, 1892–1895, and his daughter Alice
E. Sisson was an assistant in piano during the Reed administration.

Sisson retired from business in 1920 and later moved to Minneapolis where he died in October 1938.

J. P. Morey, original trustee and influential booster of the College during the 1890s, became a well-known Storm Lake druggist and mayor of the growing community. Morey's family had followed a not unusual pattern of migration. Born in New York in 1850, young Morey had moved with his parents to Illinois in 1864. From Illinois, Morey migrated to Lafayette County, Wisconsin, and finally to Storm Lake in 1878. Morey remained a trustee of the College until 1896 when he resigned and moved to Des Moines.[2]

Another of the original trustees of the College was Samuel D. Eadie, in whose home the earliest Presbyterian service in Storm Lake may have been held. The Reverend A. M. Darley was the minister at this November 1871 service. Eadie was to serve the Lakeside Church in every conceivable way until his death in 1910: as elder, Sunday school superintendent, clerk of session, and janitor. He was already elderly in the 1890s when he labored briefly as a trustee. Mr. and Mrs. Eadie's long romance ended on the same day in October 1910. They died a few months after having celebrated their sixty-fifth wedding anniversary.[3]

Clergymen among the original trustees were the Reverends William Evans, John MacAllister, S. W. Stophlet, William Robinson, and H. D. Jenkins. The Reverend W. M. Evans, an early leader among western Iowa Presbyterians, retired from the Board of Trustees in 1893. The Reverend John MacAllister, pastor of the Lakeside Church, 1892–1900, moved to Missouri Valley, Iowa, after leaving Storm Lake. The Reverend S. W. Stophlet also retired from the Board in 1893 but later returned as one of the financial agents of the College.

Senator Edgar E. Mack joined the Board in 1891. When the Felts departed for Denver, Mack succeeded Zeph Felt as president of the Board. The senator's ancestors had been among the large number of Scottish-Irish immigrants who made their way to America during the eighteenth century. A fierce love of liberty and considerable mobility were among the characteristics of these people, and the Macks seem to have been no exception. The family was represented in the Revolution on the colonial side. James M.

Mack, father of Edgar, was a member of the New Hampshire legislature just prior to the Civil War. In 1861 the Macks moved to
Illinois and two years later moved again—this time to Alden, Iowa.
In the spring of 1870 the Macks arrived in Buena Vista County
where young Edgar Mack became active in business and politics.
He was instrumental in organizing the Storm Lake Electric Light
and Power Company and in 1890 entered into a real estate and law
partnership with James De Land. Politically, he was clerk of court
and in 1889 was elected to the state senate from the Fiftieth District. In 1890 he was a member of the Republican State Central
Committee and in 1892 became the chairman of the Iowa delegation at the Republican National Convention in Minneapolis.[4]
Edgar Mack was president of the Buena Vista College Board of
Trustees from 1892 to 1897 and was a member of the Board for
many years. He was killed in an automobile accident in August
1918.[5] The Mack tradition was carried on by his son Guy, who
served on the Board of Trustees during the troubled decades from
the 1920s to the 1950s, and his grandson Edgar, a 1935 graduate,
who as president of the Board in the 1980s would see Buena Vista
achieve a prestige and affluence that his distinguished forebears
and their associates would scarcely have envisioned in their wildest
dreams.

Three district court judges were for many years trustees of the
College: Lot Thomas, 1898–1905; A. D. Bailie, 1898–1936; and
F. F. Faville, 1896–1946. Judge Thomas's daughter, Cora, was a
student in the department of music in 1896, while Ethelyn Bailie
was one of the four graduates in the class of 1904. Bailie's son-in-
law, Willis C. Edson, first became a member of the Board of
Trustees in 1904. Young Edson was thirty years old at the time and
making his reputation as an attorney. He would be a member of the
state legislature, 1919–1927 and Speaker of the House in 1925. In
1936 he was the unsuccessful GOP candidate for Lieutenant Governor.[6] Successful farmer and businessman John T. Edson, Willis's
brother, was also a trustee in 1907. Still another trustee of the
College was the Reverend William Miller whose gift helped secure
the Miller-Stuart House, which served as the president's residence
until its demolition in 1974.

To discuss all of the trustees selected from the Storm Lake community and surrounding area would be impractical. Yet, obviously, many prominent citizens believed in the potential of Buena Vista College. In Robert Lincoln Campbell (perhaps because of his middle name) they were certain that they had a new College president who could enable Buena Vista to scale the ladder of noteworthy institutions of higher learning in America. Campbell not only was an experienced pastor but was serving as one of the trustees of Coe College, Cedar Rapids, Iowa.[7] Born in Pennsylvania, he was forty-two years of age, had received B.A. and M.A degrees from Wooster College, and his seminary training had been completed at McCormick in 1894. While in college he reportedly made a reputation as an orator, was business manager of the college annual, and maintained an interest in athletics.[8]

Unfortunately, Campbell stepped into a nest of problems. While Buena Vista had secured an endowment, not all of it was collectible, and the College still had to manage current expenses. The hard-pressed faculty continued to live on promises and unpaid notes bearing 7 percent annual interest.[9] In the summer of 1907, the treasurer's report revealed an indebtedness of $21,795. The albatross became heavier as the College sought to own, rather than rent, dormitory space. Ladies' Hall was finally purchased by sacrificing some of the endowment fund during the summer of 1907. Of the $61,839.87 remaining in the endowment fund, some $37,000 was in "notes unsecured."[10]

Campbell and his supporters remained optimistic during 1906–7. The *Storm Lake Pilot-Tribune* expressed confidence in the new president. Certainly, Campbell appears to have been a congenial man who felt his place was among the student body teaching and socializing as well as in the field soliciting funds. The president's addresses were reported as being "masterful." He organized a "booster" club among the students, which was to encourage support for the College during the summer months.[11]

When Commencement rolled around in 1907, the *Pilot-Tribune* announced that the year completed had been the most successful in the school's history with "brighter prospects for the future than ever before."[12] In his report to the trustees President Campbell also sounded optimistic, noting that attendance had reached 211 full-time students. Furthermore, the collegiate department had five graduates, there had been an absence of friction in the management of the affairs of the College, and there had been a 23 percent increase in the use of the library. Nevertheless, Campbell remarked that "the manifest need of Buena Vista at the present time is a sufficient endowment so that the income from it shall come somewhere near meeting the current expenses of the College."[13] There were other needs:

> We need to enlarge the work done by the college, especially along the line of History and Mathematics. In the library we need additional room to properly arrange the volumes coming to us. . . . On the campus we need a house for young men, a Science Hall and at least a temporary provision for Athletic work of various kinds.[14]

The needs that President Campbell cited were pressing and many of them would remain so until well into the twentieth century. He was also aware that the College needed a "master" fund raiser and that this task would require much time on the road away from the College and home. Campbell did not enjoy this part of a college president's life and it was a factor in his decision to resign in June 1908. In his resignation to the trustees he said:

> I do not wish to be interpreted in any way as being discouraged with the outlook for the college or that the work has not been congenial to me . . . to accomplish what needs to be done requires a man to sacrifice largely his home life and takes him away so much of the time from the college that his influence as head of the institution amounts to little with the student body, and makes it practically impossible for him to have the intimate insight into the internal affairs of the college which a president should have.[15]

The trustees urged Campbell to stay. No doubt they realized that it would not be easy to persuade anyone to take command of a small and struggling denominational college. President Campbell finally withdrew his resignation after spelling out several conditions, all of which the trustees accepted. The conditions included

(1) the raising of sufficient funds to meet the current expense deficit by September 1908, (2) the securing of a field secretary, and (3) allowing the president some time in the intimate work of the College.[16]

The trustees no doubt did their best to meet Campbell's conditions. They did secure Dr. S. W. Stophlet, Presbyterian pastor at Rockwell City, as financial secretary.[17] Furthermore, in September 1908 Buena Vista launched a fund-raising campaign that caused the *Pilot-Tribune* to assert "this has been the greatest week in the history of Buena Vista College." The presbyteries of Fort Dodge and Sioux City met in Storm Lake where the sessions concluded with a banquet in a tent pitched across from Ladies' Hall. Some three hundred friends of the College attended and pledged $10,000 toward meeting the deficit. Most of this sum apparently was given by Storm Lake people who by 1908 had contributed "$90,000 for the support of the College and the endowment." The presbyters, during their visit, "were given a ride around the lake on the steamer and were shown the city and nearby cities from automobiles."[18]

The effort was not sufficient to retain Campbell, for at the end of October 1908 he again announced his resignation. This time, in spite of the efforts of the trustees, he remained firm. Perhaps his greatest failing was that he did not like the "raising support" part of his job. He once said that he tried to interest people in the College rather than "constantly preaching about money."[19] This congenial man might have been an outstanding executive of an established college, but he was not adapted to the work of a struggling institution still unable to meet current expenses. Campbell appears to have been well liked and the *Pilot-Tribune* praised his brief tenure by noting that "things are in better condition than when he came here."[20]

But the struggle was not over. One president was to follow another, and each was to face the seemingly insurmountable tasks of raising the meager endowment, meeting current expenses, and paying off the rising institutional debt. The battle that Buena Vista College waged between 1908 and 1917 involved life or death for the institution. On several occasions the people of Storm Lake listened to exuberant forecasts. Each time the predictions proved illusory, and the citizens of the community found themselves participating in a new drive to see the College through yet another crisis. The College grew, but so did the debt. If Buena Vista were to survive as a full-fledged college, a new library, a new science hall, and a new gymnasium were musts. Other colleges were launching successful endowment campaigns. Reports (somewhat exaggerated) were that former president E. E. Reed had raised an endowment of $350,000 for Lenox College.[21] Buena Vista should do no less!

Meanwhile, Dr. George H. Fracker reigned as acting president. The years 1908–1910, while not stagnant intellectually, showed the need for a president who could move the College toward financial solvency. Buena Vista still had to win the hearts and pocketbooks of the Presbyterians of Iowa. The Synod, struggling for ways to provide assistance, passed a resolution vowing fifty cents per member for the support of the College. As financial secretary S. W. Stophlet noted, pledges and resolutions were easier to make than to honor; and he often had to make two or three trips in order to get people to pay their subscriptions. He did succeed in obtaining thirty subscriptions of $100 each for which, no doubt, he labored heroically in the field. About the same time, the Board treasurer gloomily predicted that of the subscriptions due "probably one-half cannot be collected."[22]

Disturbing news arrived from the University of Wisconsin that a former Buena Vista professor, Irwin Billman had "confessed to abuse of the mails in sending obscene literature and other matter and will be sent to a federal prison."[23] Billman had been a popular professor in the natural sciences and there was no hint of scandal during his stay at Buena Vista. However, he had engaged in extensive correspondence while attempting to form clandestine circles modeled on a creation of French fiction. Literature, pictures, and lists of names of people throughout the country were discovered in the Billman home. The former professor faced up to five years in federal prison for his criminal activity.[24]

In April 1910, another Campbell—the Reverend Edward Campbell of Estherville—consented to become the seventh president of Buena Vista College. The second Campbell seemed a promising choice; he was a graduate of Marietta and McCormick seminary and had been awarded a medal as the "best all around man in his class."[25] His salary was $2,000 and the free use of the Miller-Stuart House. The hearth was barely warm before Mrs. Campbell became seriously ill and the Campbells departed for the more moderate climate of California. The Board expected them to return by May 1911, but Mrs. Campbell's illness was severe enough that the still untested president resigned. The trustees had expected Campbell to launch a new endowment campaign, master current expenses, and rid the College of a debt which by June 1911 had reached $32,000.[26]

During Campbell's absence, the acting president, Professor E. F. Blayney, along with Willis Edson, Dr. Nusbaum, A. D. Bailie, and W. L. Geisinger, managed to ease the debt with a campaign that netted $17,000. Of this amount, some $5,000 was provided by the Board of Aid. The College still needed $13,000 to meet current expenses. W. C. Edson insisted that the Presbyterians would have to make good their pledge of 50 cents per member if the goal was to be reached. Edson was pessimistic, asserting that "less than one-half of that amount was realized during the past year."[27] Not long after submitting his report Edson resigned as treasurer although he remained on the Board as trustee. Having already won distinction in a number of ways in the Storm Lake community, Edson was to serve the College mightily for half a century. His dedication involved a loyalty that was uncompromising and unflinching in moments of triumph and in moments of misunderstanding and criticism. A few months later, at the time of his marriage to Miss Ethelyn Bailie, a 1904 Buena Vista graduate and the daughter of Judge A. D. Bailie, the *Storm Lake Pilot-Tribune* referred to Edson as "a substantial man who enjoys a peculiar degree of confidence, and has long been prominent in every good and progressive activity of the community."[28]

Willis Edson had seen all of the presidents of Buena Vista College. He had been a boy of seventeen when Loyal Y. Hays, the founding president, had died in 1892. He had seen two Campbells come and go and now he was on hand for the arrival of a second Linn (no relation) in Storm Lake in August 1911. Like several other Buena Vista presidents, the Reverend James Patterson Linn had been born in Pennsylvania. He was a graduate of Washington and Jefferson College and had taken postgraduate work at Western and McCormick Theological seminaries. He had served churches in Iowa at Early, Ireton, and Creston. The *Storm Lake Pilot-Tribune* with typical enthusiasm described the forty-one year-old Linn as a "man of high mental attainments, of indomitable will and perseverance."[29]

Certainly, there was something about Linn's reports that smacked of detached honesty. Few, if any, of the other presidents had reported a "mixed view" about the institution's progress. Linn also showed an uncommon concern for the welfare of his faculty, noting that it "will be a glorious day and a money saving day when we can arrange to pay our teachers and our bills as they come due."[30]

Nor was he blind to the needs of the College. The boilers in Old Main needed repairing, but the institution had not yet embarked on its badly needed building program. No doubt the trustees blinked when Linn forecast that an endowment fund of $350,000 would have to be raised in order to put Buena Vista permanently on its feet.[31] Linn also pointed out that the twenty-fifth anniversary of the College would be observed in 1916. Before that gala date, however, the Reverend Mr. Linn would again be engaged in pastoral work. He resigned in October 1913, receiving commendation from the Board for his loyalty and Christian spirit.[32] It is possible that not all Board members were supportive of Linn for this was the time that trustee Scott Bradford offered the College twenty-two lots on the condition that Linn would resign.[33]

Linn's successor in the growing procession of presidents was the Reverend R. D. Echlin, pastor of the Knox Presbyterian Church in Sioux City and a member of the Buena Vista College Board of Trustees. He held degrees from McMasters University in Toronto and from the University of Chicago. College officials had asked Echlin to accept the presidency in 1909, but he had declined. Now he accepted the challenge, which included an indebtedness of $40,000 haunting the College.[34]

Echlin's term of service, lasting from November 1913 until April 1917, was the second longest in the string of eight presidents.

When Echlin took office there were six Presbyterian colleges in Iowa, with Parsons, Buena Vista, and Lenox more tightly controlled than Coe, Highland Park in Des Moines, and the German Presbyterians in Dubuque. The Boards of all six colleges consisted of a majority of Presbyterians and were regarded as Presbyterian colleges.[35] The location of the Presbyterian seminary at Dubuque naturally strengthened that institution's ties with the church. Buena Vista was directly controlled by the Synod, which approved or rejected (early statements say elected) designated trustees and retained an influential hand in policy making into the 1960s.

Echlin was highly regarded as a speaker and clergyman in Presbyterian circles; and it was hoped that this handsome, dynamic man possessed the qualities that would make Buena Vista the institution that its founders had envisioned. While his administration was hardly a failure, Echlin was unable to build the endowment fund and in April 1917 he, too, resigned. His successor was Dr. Stanton Olinger of Lawrence, Kansas.

Still, Echlin's three-and-one-half-year administration was an exciting one. It was an era in the history of the College that was filled with accomplishment as well as tragedy. There were bright promises and deep frustrations. The twenty-fifth anniversary of the College was a critical one. Either the College would conduct a successful endowment campaign with a minimum goal of $100,000 or it would close its doors.

Meanwhile, the new Lakeside Presbyterian Church was dedicated on January 18, 1914. The history of the College and the church were entwined. Many members of the Lakeside congregation had served on the College Board of Trustees and many others had attended Buena Vista as students. All of the pastors of the Lakeside Church—MacAllister, Sloane, Comin, Mackintosh, and T. A. Ambler—had believed in the future of Buena Vista College. The admired John MacAllister had served as acting president of the College from 1894 to 1895. And now the Reverend David Mackintosh wrote to Daniel Williams of the College trustees: "I could hear the footsteps of the students of Buena Vista College coming for a thousand years. I could see that even twenty-five years hence if the right man was in charge of the affairs of the

College, five hundred students, perhaps one thousand would be in attendance."[36]

As Buena Vista moved through those difficult years, it seemed for a time that the footsteps might fade to an echo. And yet Mackintosh had retained the vision of 1891 and so had others. It was the task of President Echlin to turn the twenty-fifth anniversary celebration into a crusade for funds. Before he resigned, a new endowment campaign would be under way as Buena Vista College continued to wage its battle for survival. Unfortunately, battles on a larger stage—America's entry into World War I—prolonged the College's struggle for financial stability.

The friends and sponsors of the College were aware that Buena Vista needed not only a productive endowment but also ways to meet current expenses and finance new buildings. The goal of the campaign was $150,000, with $100,000 regarded as the absolute minimum. Unless they could collect $100,000, College officials asserted that "no contribution will be accepted."[37] The campaign, which had originally been set for March 1915 to March 1916, was delayed until May 1916. Between May and August 1916, Buena Vista College was determined to raise the minimum amount or consider closing its doors. Many friends of the institution empathized with Trustee F. F. Faville when he said:

> I love Buena Vista College. But I would rather see it close than to have it go on without sufficient support to insure its permanency. The hand-to-mouth policy which has been pursued during the last 10 or 15 years is not good for the College and is not good for the community. If we are deserving of such an institution as Buena Vista College is and should be, it will not be difficult for us to raise this endowment fund. The College should not continue unless it is to have proper support, and if it is to close I would just as soon see it close now as to see it continue for another year or two and then go out of existence.[38]

These were harsh but affectionate words. Faville said that he would do all that he could in the campaign that saw Storm Lake's portion placed at $50,000. Supposedly, the new campaign for funds would remove the impediments to progress; and Buena Vista, free from its fetters, would move into a "class by itself among the accredited colleges of the West."[39]

The ever-confident Storm Lake newspaper sounded optimistic in May, a little less buoyant in late June, and enshrouded in gloom in mid-July, when it finally posed the question, "Is Buena Vista College to continue stronger and better than ever before or is it to close its doors forever?" The *Pilot-Tribune* had carried a weekly report on the progress of the campaign, and in some of the weeks the mercury climbed slowly. The newspaper felt that the future of the city and the future of the College went hand in hand. If the College was lost, the prestige of the city would suffer a mortal blow. "There will be," said the *Pilot-Tribune,* "plenty of houses with signs ready to let on them."[40]

Due to the release of the conditional pledges, the campaign succeeded at the last moment. Some 750 pledges, the *Pilot-Tribune* announced, had totaled $101,738.07.[41] Fred and George Schaller, George H. Cummings, and James F. Toy of Sioux City had all made major contributions toward making the campaign at least a minimal success. Buena Vista did not intend to stop with the raising of the $100,000 but continued efforts to secure an amount that would enable the College to construct its badly needed buildings.

An endowment of $100,000 was not the only thing that the College netted. A 160-acre farm in South Dakota was deeded to the College, a lot in the College Addition, a lot at Casino, and "two four-year-old broken to harness mules." There was some dispute concerning the correct name for the beasts. Some referred to them as Jax and Ajax, others as Buena and Vista, while still others thought Give and Take more appropriate. In any case the *Pilot-Tribune* pointed out that Storm Lakers would be given an opportunity to see the mules, since it was more than probable that they would "be sold at public auction with the bidding lively and interesting."[42]

President Echlin's administration had reached its first milestone and expected to launch another drive for funds in 1917. Meanwhile, Buena Vista was advancing on other fronts. In November 1916 the State Board of Educational Examiners recognized Buena Vista College work. This meant state accreditation (although Buena Vista was not then a member of the North Central Association of Colleges and Secondary Schools) according to the standards of that era. In January 1917 Dean Seashore of the University of Iowa notified Dr. Parkhill of the College that the State University "would admit graduates of Buena Vista College to the graduate school on the Dean's recommendation." Furthermore, the College Board of the General Assembly of the Presbyterian Church had now reclassified Buena Vista and placed it in the ranks of the Class A institutions in "Curriculum, faculty and equipment." It seemed that the trustees had every right to be optimistic about obtaining a second $100,000 by the end of 1917, and that the necessary funds to construct a gymnasium could be realized in the not too distant future.[43]

However, the focus on the successful struggle for the survival of the College could not offset the personal tragedies that seemed to plague Buena Vista with unusual frequency during the years 1913–1918. While a larger tragedy was occurring abroad as a result of the Great War, a series of unhappy and unrelated events started in the midst of the Echlin administration and continued after Dr. Stanton Olinger had taken office. On a damp Monday morning, the first day of summer in 1915, Ladies' Hall burned. Since Commencement had been a short time before, there were only four residents in the dormitory and all escaped injury. Young Harvey Hood dashed to the Stuart-Miller House in his nightclothes, and President Echlin turned in the alarm. There was little that anyone could do. The streets were muddy from the recent rains, and the primitive horse carts could hardly make their way to the scene of the disaster. When they finally arrived, "it was twenty minutes or more before there was pressure enough to do any good." The *Storm Lake Pilot-Tribune* informed its readers that "had there been pressure, three-fourths or more of the loss could have been avoided."[44]

For the College it meant a loss of $10,000. Ladies' Hall was one of the few buildings owned by the College. Purchased during the administration of President Robert Campbell, it had been built in the 1890s by the so-called Storm Lake Syndicate, apparently headed by trustee and businessman George Eastman.[45] The building was capable of lodging more than twenty students — its loss meant new dormitory facilities would have to be found. During the three decades that passed before the College could construct a modern residential hall it also lost the two lots upon which Ladies' Hall stood.

This was not the only disastrous fire in Storm Lake during these years. In October 1917 an overheated chimney caused more than $1,000 damage to Mather Hall. As far as the city was concerned, the most costly fire, occurring on Thanksgiving Day, 1917, was the one that destroyed the Masonic Temple and severely damaged the Storm Lake Lumber Company, the L. S. Dlugosch building, the E. L. O'Banion building, and the Commercial National Bank.[46]

There was still stately Old Main, however, which would continue to serve as the focal point for College activity. Upon entering the front door, one faced a wide flight of stairs leading to the second or main floor and "flanked on either side by stairways leading to the basement where the furnace, men's toilets and classrooms for the commercial department and bookstore were built into a corner of the hall." In 1915 the second floor contained the administrative offices, a library of about 8,000 volumes, plus the women's toilet and classrooms. The third floor housed the chapel, the chemical and biological laboratories, and three small classrooms. The top floor had two large rooms that were used by the Franklin and Star literary societies. The floors of Old Main were bare boards without carpets or linoleum.[47] One can imagine the noise — resounding even into the library. Old Main was the citadel of the campus. There were no other brick structures for more than twenty-five years. Because the College lacked dormitories it remained the focal point of all College gatherings and events. The memories of all those who attended Buena Vista were centered there. There was a certain grandeur in its exit as a result of the great fire of 1956. Perhaps the memory and the myths that Old Main evokes make the building far more stately than warranted by the facts. Nevertheless, it appears certain that Old Main calls forth a special reverence in the hearts of all those associated with Buena Vista College.

The fires of 1915 and 1917 did not take any lives, but the winter of 1915–16 was less kind. As the holiday season approached, many young people desired to take advantage of the frozen lake. Buena Vista's young football coach, Edward G. Ball, was no exception. The coach was a solidly built, athletic man who had played on Purdue University's Western Conference teams of 1910–1912. In 1911 he had been selected as an end on the all-conference squad. In Ball's first season at Buena Vista in 1915, he had given the school its most successful gridiron team since 1907.

In early December Ball and twenty-two-year-old Fern Benedict were skating on the lake when the ice gave way. They were about a quarter of a mile from the shore, but their frantic calls attracted help. Two students, Russell Ensign and C. M. Drury, realizing that the ice had broken, rushed to the spot and "soon saw a hole in the ice, her muff and his hat." Help came, but it was too late. Some men pushed a boat over the ice and "one had a grappling hook."[48] All efforts to revive the couple failed. Coach Ball, the *Pilot-Tribune* said, could have saved himself but would not abandon Miss Benedict. President Echlin had the sad duty of accompanying the deceased coach to his home in Lafayette, Indiana, where final services were held. That same month the Reverend David Mackintosh, former pastor of the Lakeside Church and devoted friend of the College, died of appendicitis.[49]

It seemed for a time in 1917 and 1918 that the founders of Buena Vista College were being summoned by a higher authority. Two early benefactors of the institution, E. E. Mack and George Cummings, were killed in automobile accidents. Cummings had been a member of the Board for fifteen years. "He is the hardest man on the Board to lose," Willis Edson remarked. "He did more than any other then on the Board."[50] Dr. L. M. Nussbaum, a former Board president and highly respected Storm Lake physician, died of erysipelas in May 1917. Another member of the Board, S. A. Ensign, was an early victim of the influenza epidemic that struck during the winter of 1918–19. Miss Shirley Harper, a graduate of the class of 1917, also fell victim to the flu.[51]

The long and heroic struggle of the College for survival was made palatable by the success of the graduates. Attorneys, teachers, medical doctors, and ministers came from the ranks of those who passed through the collegiate department and the hard tutelage of Dr. George H. Fracker, Dr. E. F. Blayney, and professors M. W. Cooper and Alice Wilcox. There were ninety-four four-year graduates of the collegiate program offered by Buena Vista College between 1893 and 1918. In addition, there were thirteen two-year graduates during the years 1896–1901 (when Buena Vista was prohibited from offering the baccalaureate) whom the College included in its directories because they took all the work offered. From this entire group came four Ph.D.'s, fourteen attorneys, and fifteen clergymen. There were successful entrepreneurs, such as Joseph Sohm (class of 1916) who became superintendent of the California Packing Corporation, and many young women who, in an era when family was stressed over career, became successful homemakers.[52]

The Ph.D.'s were Homer C. Newton, 1897; J. E. Spencer, 1898; Stanley Black Fracker, 1910; O. W. Chapman, 1915; and C. M. Drury, 1918. Newton received his Ph.D. from Cornell University in 1902 and launched a successful teaching career at New York University. Professor Fracker's son, Stanley, received his Ph.D. in biology in 1914 from the University of Illinois and soon became the state entomologist of Wisconsin. He holds the distinction of being the first four-year Buena Vista graduate to obtain the doctorate in any field. C. M. Drury was to have a brilliant career as author, missionary, chaplain, and finally professor at San Anselmo Theological Seminary. O. W. Chapman received his Ph.D. from Iowa State College and became a professor at Kansas State Teacher's College in Pittsburg, Kansas. Buena Vista graduates were able to hold their own from Illinois to Edinburgh.

Among the large number of Buena Vista's graduates to choose the legal profession were Willis Edson (a two-year graduate), 1896; Peter Balkema, 1907; and Z. Z. White, 1914. All three were to become trustees of Buena Vista College, with Edson as president of the Board from 1918 to 1954. Z. Z. White was on the Board from 1928 until his death in 1980 — a fifty-two year stint that is not likely to be surpassed.

Six of Buena Vista's graduates during this era served as missionaries—Frank Senska, 1906; Victor Hanson, 1909; Bernice Gregg Cochran, 1912; Ellery M. Smith, 1913; C. M. Drury, 1918; and Florence Mitchell Wylie, 1918. Frank Senska of the class of 1906 attended the University of Iowa Medical College and went to Cameroun, Africa, as a medical missionary. While in College Senska had been president of the Student Volunteer Band formed at Buena Vista in 1906. The Volunteer Band, whose members were young men and women who were preparing to enter the mission field, had come about as the result of efforts made by Carl A. Felt, secretary of the Student Volunteer Movement. Bimonthly meetings were held, during which the Volunteer Band studied the life works of missionaries in foreign fields.[53]

Other students who attended Buena Vista during this early period also achieved eminence. Among them were Dr. Ira Lockwood, a member of the 1904 football eleven, and Tom Fairweather, 1898–99. Lockwood eventually became president of the American College of Radiology, which honored him in 1955 by bestowing on him its gold medal. This was a rare distinction because only twelve such medals had been awarded in thirty-one years.[54]

Tom Fairweather, an earlier gold-medal winner, received his honor at Buena Vista during the oratorical contests of 1899. Fairweather's life was an active one—teacher, farmer, banker, and baseball team owner. Moving to Des Moines, he served on the city council and eventually became mayor. Between 1912 and 1920, he was co-owner of the Des Moines baseball team. Later, 1934–1949, he became president of the Western Association and the Three-I League. When Fairweather died in January 1951, Sec Taylor of the *Des Moines Register* commented on the great assistance he had given to young men, "expecting nothing in return but the satisfaction of seeing them become solid citizens."[55]

Two of Buena Vista's early students, Margaret Cummings Harrison, 1905, and Jennie Gordon Hutchison, 1893, returned to the College as instructors. Miss Cummings was professor of education, 1908–1914 and became the College's first registrar. In 1911 Frank A. Harrison arrived to act as professor of mathematics. It was one of the arrangements of Providence. Harrison and the attractive Miss Cummings, "gowned in white crepe de chene trimmed in point lace," were married in the summer of 1914 by the Reverend T. A. Ambler.[56]

Miss Jennie Gordon Hutchison was professor of Latin and Greek, 1909–1915. She was also the resident head of Ladies' Hall. Jennie had known some anxious moments in June 1893 when her diploma had not arrived, but the infrequency of her paychecks caused Jennie even greater anxiety during her professorial years. Back salary owed Jennie in 1913 and 1914 accumulated 6 percent interest, until by 1915 it had reached $720. Professor Hutchison finally took her case to court in order to collect, ultimately gaining satisfaction in August 1917.[57] By 1916 Jennie had obviously endured enough and with her aging father (Buena Vista's first professor of the natural sciences) departed for Monmouth, Illinois. One suspects burn-out and ill health had taken their toll, for in 1920 we find Jennie in California working for a real estate agency. The transition and the climate aided her recuperation so that she soon abandoned the business world and apparently spent the rest of her life as a teacher in California.

Buena Vista's first graduate did make a notable contribution to her alma mater. Hutchison and Elyse M. Wallace produced Buena Vista's first opera, *On a Tropical Isle,* which was presented at the Storm Lake Opera House on December 16 and 17, 1910. The setting was Havana, Cuba, and her favorite song was the *Cubanole Glide.*[58] Professor Hutchison also fitted into the religious life of the College, attending chapel services and lecturing to the YWCA on the topic, "The Value of the Christian Life." She attended state conferences for Latin teachers and appears to have made a determined effort to convince students and colleagues of the importance of the classics. Jennie was the toastmistress for the traditional color ceremony (an annual banquet when the classes exchanged their class colors) in November 1911, pointing out during her speech, "how ideally our education here was indeed for service."[59]

The Reverend R. D. Echlin had the distinction of being at the helm in 1916–1917 as the College celebrated its twenty-fifth anniversary. The silver anniversary was not a festive occasion—it was not even a temporary lull in the long survival struggle. There were fifty-one students enrolled in the collegiate department in the fall

of 1916. Nine B.A.'s had been granted at the June 1916 Commencement. The commercial, music, and preparatory departments, however, raised the total attendance above the two-hundred
mark.[60] But the struggle to meet current expenses was becoming
more difficult each year.

Still Echlin's administration could point to some notable
triumphs, particularly the raising of the sum of $100,000 during
the hectic summer months of 1916. The August evening when the
College officials had announced that the goal had been reached and
the College saved to fight for survival on yet another day, the
student body attending summer school headed for the streets to
celebrate the victory. They sang College songs and chanted the
College yells that ordinarily rent the air during football season.[61]

Echlin and the trustees were undoubtedly aware that it would
take much more to save Buena Vista. An even greater drive would
have to take place almost at once. Indeed, within a few years,
College officials would be talking in terms of $1 million. Perhaps
the knowledge of the extensive needs taxed Echlin's strength beyond endurance. He was a fine man and his kindly disposition
made him a beloved figure among the students. Being president of
Buena Vista College was unremitting and often unrewarding toil.
As the College seemed permanently on the edge of bankruptcy, the
trustees felt that a better fund raiser was needed.[62] Finally, in April
1917 Echlin and his field secretary, I. G. Smith, resigned. "The
imperative necessities of the program seemed to leave no other
course open," was the *Pilot*'s comment. Like other Buena Vista
presidents before him, Echlin retreated into the ministry accepting
the pastorate at Perry, Iowa. He also served as one of the editors of
the Synod magazine *The Iowa Presbyterian*.[63]

6

FROM WAR TO DEPRESSION

The quality of an institution's faculty and students determines its destiny.

— PRESIDENT HENRY OLSON

S tudents at Buena Vista College, like many Americans, moved blithely through the early war years, 1914–1917; even the sinking of the Lusitania made only a minimal impression. However, the decision of the German empire to renew unrestricted submarine warfare — a direct challenge to President Wilson — brought a sudden awareness that war was imminent. Soon Buena Vista students were drilling on the lawn in front of Old Main using broomsticks for rifles. Harvey Hood was the first Buena Vista student to be drafted, and as others followed enrollment dropped by 30 percent. Because of the decline in male students, enrollment in the collegiate department dipped to forty-one during 1917–18. Only fifteen under-draft-age men were out for football in the fall of 1917.[1]

While America's entry into World War I posed a challenge to the work of the College, it did not threaten its existence. The reasons for the relatively smooth progress through the war were threefold: (1) While the male enrollment in the collegiate department was substantially reduced in 1917–18, the numbers of students in the other programs of the institution held their own; (2) the conflict after American entry was so brief that basically only one academic year was disturbed; and (3) Buena Vista was fortunate in having an extremely able president at this critical moment. Dr. Stanton Olinger, who came to the College as president in 1917, had earned a Ph.D. from Kansas State University, kept a modernized curriculum in operation, and in the fall of 1918 secured a Student Army Training Corps (SATC) on the campus. Had the European conflagration continued, the presence of the SATC would have been a vital factor in preserving the institution.

Buena Vistans were, nevertheless, well aware that a war was raging on the other side of the Atlantic. The catalog of 1918–19 lists well over one hundred former Buena Vista College students who had entered the armed forces. Among the enlistees was Merrill Drury, 1914–1918. Drury was also destined to be a participant in World War II, serving as a Navy chaplain between 1941 and 1946. Edmund L. Marousek, later a Presbyterian minister in Des Moines and stated clerk of the Synod of Iowa, entered military service during the summer of 1918.[2] Other well-known Buena Vista students or alumni listed in service were Lt. John Fulton, 1915–1917, a football star before and after the war; Lt. John Parkhill, 1915–1918, who was killed in a flying accident in 1929; Sgt. Basil Rice, 1916–1917, who returned after the war to become president of the class of 1921; and Zeno Z. White, 1910–1914, ultimately a distinguished trustee of the College.[3]

The roles of Buena Vista's many representatives in the services varied. Merrill Drury, still under draft age when America entered the war, was one of the first of the class of 1918 to enlist. He served as a private in the Chemical Warfare Service (probably because he had taken chemistry in College) and spent about eight months at Yale Medical School working with phosgene gas in an effort to find a cure for gassed men.[4] Private Drury was one of several to write the *Storm Lake Pilot-Tribune* concerning his wartime experience. In a letter written shortly after the signing of the Armistice, he said:

> I was a little disappointed in that I didn't get across to take part in the big parade over there but as long as it was my lot to stay in this country I certainly couldn't ask for more interesting work than that I have been enjoying here. My life has been entirely different than that usually ascribed to a soldier. I have never

drilled a day and K.P. has little significance to me. But now if you want to talk about gas, its effect on the body, I might stop and talk with you.[5]

Drury's classmate, Edmund Marousek, was stationed at Austin, Texas, in the summer of 1918. He noted that the arrival of an Iowa contingent was so unexpected that "they were given sky barracks with the ground for the floor, the sun for light and heat, and a lot of good advice by the old soldiers in camp."[6]

While Drury and Marousek were becoming inured to army life, Lt. John Beard (a student in 1904) was part of the Argonne Forest drive in late September 1918. For his bravery in caring for wounded men during the action he received the Croix de Guerre and a promotion to captain. A year later he was serving as the pastor of the First Presbyterian Church in Hoquain, Washington.[7]

Arthur Riedesel, 1915–1918, was in the regimental band. He had played all across the United States prior to his unit's departure for France. Like many other Americans from Franklin to Pershing, Riedesel fell in love with "dreamy, picturesque old France." He wrote the *Pilot-Tribune:*

> I have gone through a most forbidding doorway of hewn stone and often passing through a dirty dark alley way found myself in a delightful restaurant where I had no hesitation in demolishing "deux omelettes ou deux oeufs" with coffee and rye bread and fresh strawberries.[8]

This combination, which so delighted Riedesel, had cost him only ninety cents. He also wrote that he found the French language difficult to master although he was "picking it up and manage to get along pretty well. I expect to be a confirmed Frenchman in a few months."

Patriotic zeal sometimes spilled over into the intolerance that President Woodrow Wilson feared. The German language, German place-names, German culinary delights, German artists, and people with too German-sounding names were all victims. A German artist, Marie Mayer, who had played the part of Mary Magdelene in the 1910 Oberammergau Passion Play had signed an agreement to appear at the College prior to the declaration of war. She arrived in Storm Lake on December 6, 1917, in the midst of what C. Merrill Drury described as an "amazing amount of opposition." There were College and community threats of boycotting the program and widely expressed fears that she would send her honorarium back to Germany. Drury met her at the train station, visited with her for an hour in the hotel, and found her a charming person who spoke excellent English. The program was held in Lakeside Presbyterian Church before an audience too small to meet the necessary expenses incurred by the student body for the program. However, the Redpath Bureau, which provided such artists for colleges, sent another speaker at no cost to help make up the losses incurred.[9]

Meanwhile, the Olinger administration did not forget the growing ranks of former students who had entered the armed forces. The library staff, headed by popular librarian Edith Cooke, prepared a *Scrap Book for Soldiers and Sailors* that they sent to the servicemen who had been in the class of 1918. It contained pictures of familiar campus scenes, some sage advice, cartoons, and two caustic ditties referring to the Kaiser—altogether a great deal of humor and much sentiment.

On June 4, 1918, the College Service Flag, made by the faculty, was dedicated in the farewell chapel service for the year, and many Buena Vista College students now in the military service were honored. Dean J. W. Parkhill, Dr. George H. Fracker, Miss Edith Cooke, and Mayor W. C. Edson were the main participants during the ceremony. Edson spoke of the part that the United States must play in the war. The audience joined in singing "Onward Christian Soldiers," "Battle Hymn of the Republic," and "America." Miss Norma Siebens, a student in the commercial department of the College, sang a solo "America for Me." There was at this time one gold star on the flag, representing Ilo Taylor, 1905–6, who had died in January 1918. After leaving Buena Vista, Taylor completed a degree in civil engineering at Iowa State University.[10]

The SATC unit, obtained for the College during the summer of 1918 by President Olinger, consisted of ninety-six young men under the command of Captain Robert Shaw.[11] The unit got under way in October 1918 and functioned during the year 1918–19. It was only a temporary addition to the life of the campus and although it aroused a few questions regarding absences and credits its effect was not far-reaching.

While the war was too short to threaten the College's existence, it certainly did not alleviate the long-standing problems. Buena Vista needed an endowment, needed to standardize its offerings, and needed to launch a vast building program. If Buena Vista could not keep up with the progress of American education during the postwar years, then it would have to close its doors. Institutional needs were now urgent if the College were to continue to function. While the 1920s were politically conservative, they were socially liberating. More young people would be entering colleges seeking professional and business careers, and colleges would become increasingly coeducational. They were also likely to be more selective.

Edith Cooke, who had done so much for Buena Vista's servicemen, had also modernized the registrar's office and streamlined the reference and cataloging facilities of the library. Miss Cooke had arrived in 1912 as an instructor in English but in 1914 became the second registrar of the College (Margaret Cummings Harrison was the first). By 1920 she had worked out a new office system providing more efficient and complete student and alumni records. As head librarian, she reorganized the entire library including the card catalog, sheet list file, and gift book file. The 1915 *Rudder* was dedicated to her, and when she departed for a position with the Burlington Public Library in 1922 the students lamented, "What shall we ever do without her?" Cooke's departure ended her plan of writing a history of the College library.[12]

Buena Vista had three presidents during the 1918–1931 period that marked the end of World War I and the deepening of a depression inaugurated by the stock market panic of October 1929. Dr. Stanton Olinger was an able executive but left the College for a position on the Presbyterian Board of Education in 1920.[13] He was succeeded by Dr. Arthur Boyd, the second Ph.D. in succession to become Buena Vista's president. Boyd's presidency was also brief, for in the summer of 1923 he, too, resigned to accept a position

with the General Board of the Presbyterian Church.[14] During his
brief tenure Boyd donated over three hundred volumes to the College library and temporarily relinquished the presidential house so
that it could be used as a residence for students.

Early in 1924 a new president, Evert Leon Jones, moved into
Miller-Stuart House. The Reverend Mr. Jones received a salary of
$3,600, which made him (at that point) the highest paid president
in the history of the College.[15] He was destined to face the difficult
task of guiding the school through the early years of the Depression. The ordeal proved too much, and Jones resigned in 1930 as
Buena Vista prepared to give up the long fight for existence. All
three presidents who guided the College during the years 1917–
1931 were devoted and capable men. They were abreast of the
times, tolerant, and dedicated to the liberal arts ideal within the
framework of the church-related college. However, the obstacles
they faced seemed insurmountable.

The 1920s seem prosperous when compared with the Depression-ridden 1930s. Nevertheless, agriculture's share in the general
prosperity lagged throughout the period. For a college located in
the midst of the nation's farm belt this was critical. It meant that
the student body, drawn mostly from a radius of a hundred miles,
would be unable to pay tuition fees; and it meant that fund-raising
drives would face an uphill battle.

Old Main was the College's first brick structure, and for more
than twenty-five years it appeared that it might be the last. College
officials had often discussed the need for a new library and a new
gymnasium, but the pressing problem had always been how to
cover current expenses and forestall the growing indebtedness. Disaster piled on disaster — not the least of which had been the destruction of Ladies' Hall by fire in 1915.

When the trustees met on June 10, 1919, two new resolutions
were passed. The first provided for a pension at half-pay for professors who had taught at Buena Vista College for twenty-five
years. This meagre measure would likely benefit only Dr. Fracker
and Alice Wilcox. Furthermore, the years of service had to be
consecutive and the pension applied "only to all such persons who
have reached the age of 66 years, and thereafter retire from teach-

ing." It also included those who had taught twenty-five consecutive years but were forced to retire because of disability. It was still a decade before social security triumphed over rugged individualism. The imperative need in the 1920s was still to meet the monthly payroll. Professors might labor as long as they were useful and then retire on their own resources. There was no real concept of institutional or societal obligation.

The second resolution of the trustees involved the construction of a badly needed gymnasium. Buena Vista students had only the outdoors or the basement of Old Main. The trustees thought a gymnasium could be constructed for $50,000, and decided to name it Victory Hall "in honor of our soldiers, sailors, and marines."[16] The *Storm Lake Pilot-Tribune,* with its usual booster spirit, called the plans for Victory Hall the "last word in gymnasium construction." The architectural style was to be pure collegiate Gothic and was to have a running track, swimming pool, locker room, and the capacity to seat more than 1,000 people.[17]

The construction of Victory Hall was more of a struggle than the trustees anticipated and the original plans were scaled down. As a result, the new structure was outdated before two decades of fast-break basketball had sped by. It was too small for players and for the crowds who virtually sat on the playing floor. Inflation had boosted the cost to $70,000, of which only $55,000 had been raised by the time of the dedication ceremonies on November 14, 1920. The rejoicing that day featured religious and patriotic songs and the usual speeches by local and church dignitaries. The stage was replete with the American flag and Buena Vista pennants. Willis Edson, one of many speakers, told the audience that the new gym would be a "place where young men and women prepared for life." The building, said the *Pilot-Tribune,* was "more of a community building than a College building."[18] Indeed, the high school, the American Legion, and various community groups did utilize the new structure.

With improved practice and playing facilities, the College expected to upgrade its basketball program and schedule better teams. However, Buena Vista lost 20–18 to Western Union in the first intercollegiate game played in the new gymnasium. It was not until the 1921–22 season that Buena Vista won its first victories on the new floor.

In 1962 Victory Hall was renamed in honor of W. C. Edson in recognition of Edson's athletic prowess and to honor him for the unparalleled devotion he had given to the College for over half a century. It was, however, an empty gesture because the building was in dire need of refurbishing and had become obsolete as a sports center. The building would eventually be used by the YMCA and finally be turned into a storage area for the College. By 1990 a major renovation was underway as the structurally sound edifice was transformed into a center for the College's expanding music program.

The gymnasium had been conceived by the Olinger administration, but Stanton Olinger was far away at the time of the dedication. He had left Storm Lake during the summer of 1920 to take a new post in the East as secretary of the Presbyterian Board of Education. The trustees, now used to the early departure of capable executives, acknowledged the quality of Olinger's presidency: "We desire at this time to gratefully acknowledge the debt which this institution owes him for his accomplishments in the advancement of Buena Vista College and of Christian Education throughout this section during his tenure of office."[19] Dr. Olinger, the Board said, had brought Buena Vista College "out of the slough of despondency and set it upon a rock." The people of Storm Lake, and especially the College community, were shocked a few months after the dedication of Victory Hall to learn that Dr. Olinger, while at the zenith of his career, had died in a New York hospital. Olinger's health had been failing and he had undergone surgery several times for an undisclosed ailment.[20]

A third major building was added during the administration of Dr. Evert Leon Jones. Originally Dr. Jones had planned to construct a new dormitory, but in November 1924 this plan gave way to the proposals for a science hall. Jones had no intention of abandoning the construction of a new dormitory but felt the science building must have priority. He believed the building could be paid for in 1925 and assured everyone that it was "the policy of the present administration to operate on a cash basis. The college is paying its way as it goes and paying off the old indebtedness as rapidly as possible." The new president also asserted, "It shall be my purpose to maintain the Christian emphasis with increasing vigor."[21] Increasing vigor would be more likely when the College had an endowment of $500,000 and was able to balance its budget on an annual basis.

In the summer of 1925 the cornerstone for the new Science Hall was laid. There were the usual marching bands and speeches. Board president Willis Edson, who had already fought Buena Vista's battles for twenty years and would do so for thirty more, in a moment of unguarded optimism announced that prospects were good for a new library building and a new dormitory. Aging Jay Russell, the builder of Old Main, attended the ceremonies as the oldest member of the Grand Lodge. The Reverend R. H. Brown, pastor of Central Presbyterian Church in Des Moines, spoke on the relation of science to religion. "I am glad," he said, "that this new structure is in enlightened Iowa and not in medieval Tennessee."[22] This, perhaps, illustrated the attitude of the Presbyterian College toward the Tennessee courtroom spectacle of 1925. Brown was alluding to the Scopes trial that tested a Tennessee law forbidding the teaching of evolution. Two years earlier Arthur M. Boyd, then president of Buena Vista College, had attended the Presbyterian General Assembly at Indianapolis and noted with dismay that W. J. Bryan (a fundamentalist Presbyterian) was there endeavoring to get the church to deny support to any college that taught evolution. Boyd expressed satisfaction that Bryan's effort had lost. "Bryan," he said, "is making a fight on a subject that was alive twenty-five years ago."[23] While the issue was not as dead as Boyd imagined, it had never caused controversy at Buena Vista.

On May 25, 1926, Science Hall was dedicated. Ideally the new structure could have been dedicated free of debt, but more than $6,000 was still needed.[24] Nevertheless, the College had built its second major structure in seven years, and the future looked brighter than at any time since 1891. The College still needed a new library, however. In the summer of 1923, Willis Edson had said that "Buena Vista College needs a new library building most of all."[25] He had reiterated this need at the laying of the cornerstone

for Science Hall. The achievements of the 1920s, considerable as
they were in respect to the building program, nonetheless stopped
short of a modern library building.

There were, however, two positive steps taken in the direction
of future library plans and current library service. The library was
named Fracker Library in honor of the much revered Dr. George
H. Fracker and it was moved from Old Main to the new Science
Hall. While it required considerable physical effort to transport the
14,000 volumes of the 1928 library from one end of the campus to
another, every knowledgeable person realized how small and inadequate Buena Vista's library remained.[26] Miss Florence McFadden,
a 1927 Buena Vista graduate, became the first librarian to oversee
the "new" library, holding that position until after her marriage to
Paul Edwards in 1932. Miss McFadden, who also served as registrar (the two positions were then combined), had been a member of
Phi Alpha Pi, Alpha Psi Omega (drama), Pi Kappa Delta (forensics), and the Women's Athletic Association.[27] Still an active Presbyterian, she continued to maintain an interest in the progress of
Buena Vista College in 1990.

As the number of buildings increased, so did the students.
Buena Vista was becoming a contemporary liberal arts college as
the collegiate department began to dwarf the other areas of instruction. The academy disappeared in the early 1920s; and by the end
of the decade President E. L. Jones was speaking in terms of five
hundred students, and he meant five hundred college students. In
the fall of 1928 there were nearly two hundred such students including eighty-eight freshmen. Seven years earlier the total enrollment in the collegiate department had been ninety-four, including
forty-nine freshmen. There were twenty-five graduates in 1929
compared to seven in 1921 and twelve in 1924. Tuition during the
same span of years had jumped from $36 to $65.[28]

Buena Vista College officials expressed at least a surface optimism concerning the future of the institution on the eve of the
stock market crash in the fall of 1929. The University of Iowa,
Iowa State College, and the Teacher's College in Cedar Falls all
accepted Buena Vista credits without question. The superintendent
of public instruction and the Board of Education of the Presbyte-

rian church also recognized Buena Vista as a fully accredited institution.[29] Victory Hall and Science Hall had joined Old Main as parts of the campus scene. The Board of Education exhibited a greater willingness to support the institution than it had in the past, and pledges from the churches increased during the golden decade of the 1920s. Public pronouncements seemed to indicate that the future of the College was assured. The *Tack,* at Commencement 1929 proclaimed that 1928–29 had been a banner year!

> We will graduate the largest class in the history of the College; the loyalty and character of the students and faculty is unquestionably the best; the prospects for summer school and next fall enrollment promise a big increase and now, if you will pull or push or pray, nothing can hold us back.[30]

Unfortunately, while the external picture was bright there were rumblings underneath. The Depression and World War II were to come close to delivering the knockout blow that forty years of uncertain financial support had not been able to do. Perhaps the fact that Buena Vistans were so long accustomed to austere rations enabled them to weather the crisis that was in store.

The Reverend Evert Leon Jones became president in 1924. His tenure of six and one-half years was the longest that anyone had yet remained at the helm of the institution. Jones had started his career as a lawyer, serving as deputy district attorney in Portland, Oregon, 1913–14. He was ordained in 1917 and served churches in Chicago and Philadelphia in addition to doing field work for the Presbyterian Board of Education.[31] Always vacillating between the ministry and politics, Jones was a talented man who had difficulty deciding which career he desired to pursue. Born in December 1883 in Wharton, Ohio, Jones knew poverty as a youth and in many ways was a self-made man. At the age of four, Jones's family moved to Culver, Indiana, where he worked on a farm and attended country school. An often told story related how young Jones earned his first money selling grasshoppers to the fishermen on Lake Maxinkuckee, before Mr. and Mrs. D. W. Gardner of Terre Haute (wealthy patrons) gave him a home.[32] Beginning his cross-country travels at seventeen, he received his B.A. degree from Albany College in Oregon. Then followed years of travel and study from Columbia University to the University of California.

President Jones seemed to be the man that Buena Vista needed in order to achieve her purpose during the twilight days of the heroic age of individualism. There was something brilliant about Jones. He was an intellectual; he was an outstanding speaker; he had a superior education; and he knew how to turn a phrase. But his business acumen fell short of mastering the challenge of the nation's deepest depression, which blocked all paths to financial success and stability for Buena Vista College.

But for a while in the 1920s the administration of the handsome, fortyish President Jones would seem to prosper. Both the College and the nation were enjoying the bubbles of illusion. While they did, Evert Leon Jones spoke eloquently for the College and dabbled in politics on the side. He was an avowed Republican and an avid supporter of President Hoover in 1928. After surrendering the presidency in 1930, Jones remained temporarily in Storm Lake and announced his intention of becoming a practicing attorney and legislator. However, Republican party politics offered few opportunities, and Jones accepted a parish at Pipestone, Minnesota, in 1932, where he preached four years. In 1936 Jones left for Rapid City, South Dakota, where he still "hoped to take an interest in politics."[33] He died at Glendale, Oregon, on July 26, 1957, at the age of seventy-four. He was a man for the good times — had they continued he might have been a superior college president.

As it was, the Jones administration completed the construction of Science Hall and started laying plans for the oft-discussed endowment campaign that was to net the College $500,000. No administration had ever attempted an endowment drive of this magnitude, and far more modest campaigns had known small success. Stanton Olinger had successfully concluded a drive in 1918 for an endowment of $200,000, which in view of World War I and the influenza epidemic had been an outstanding achievement. But, as in previous drives, the success of the campaign was stunted by fact that many of the pledges proved uncollectible. Twenty percent of the endowment of $200,000 had been written off by 1923. Growing critics of the College were saying that Buena Vista College was not an asset to the community. The *Pilot-Tribune* again rose to the defense of the institution, showing the amount of money employees of Buena Vista spent in Storm Lake, the savings to the people of Storm Lake who could send their children to a local college, and the prestige a community gained from having a college in its midst.[34]

Meanwhile, some of the stalwarts of the College were being forced to the sidelines. In October 1929 appendicitis claimed forty-year-old Fred Reusser, head of the mathematics department.[35] A stroke forced the retirement of former Dean John F. Saylor in 1930. Dean Saylor had come to Buena Vista College at the age of sixty-seven in 1921. He had received his first degree from Iowa State Agricultural College at Ames in 1880, beginning a long career in public school and college work.[36] But it was the retirement of Professor George Fracker at the age of seventy-seven in 1930 that marked the end of an era. For thirty-nine years Fracker had given his complete loyalty to an institution involved in an annual struggle for survival. The *Tack* sincerely and honestly noted:

> What he has done for the college can never be repaid and the appreciation felt by all connected with the Alma Mater can never be adequately expressed. There were lean years with meager salaries when a large part of his went back into the school; there was work done for which there was never any salary. There were summers spent in doing odd jobs of repair work in order that Old Main might be in good condition for the fall term; and there were subjects taught that the others could not or would not teach.[37]

All of this indicates that the College often depended upon seasoned faculty who under ordinary circumstances would have been retired or who had retired elsewhere and found refuge at Buena Vista for a few more years of service and work. This geriatric brigade would have made Claude Pepper proud. For this band of dedicated professors was instrumental in providing not only superior instruction and counsel, but the moral power of their presence was an important factor in keeping the College afloat.

Now the Jones administration prepared for the greatest financial campaign the College and community had yet undertaken. The great push for the half-million dollars in endowment funds was scheduled to begin on January 1, 1929. There were good reasons, the administration announced, for launching the endowment drive at this time: (1) The College was moving in the direction of an enrollment of three hundred students, which was certainly an indication of increased esteem in the public mind. (2) The College was performing an outstanding service within the state of Iowa. State institutions were becoming increasingly crowded—a factor that illustrated the need for private, favorably located colleges like Buena Vista. (3) To meet the opportunities latent in education, Buena Vista would have to have an adequate endowment. (4) The year 1929 was a prosperous one. Business and farm conditions were improving throughout the nation.

An adequate endowment, the Jones administration had said, "was the only salvation for the Christian college."[38] The big drive started on January 29, 1929. Storm Lake's quota was $75,000 and the county quota was $100,000. Such an amount must have sounded incredible to old Buena Vistans like Harvey Hostetler who, until his death in 1939, continued to serve both the church and the College. Hostetler's presidency had seen the Board of Aid frown on the College's junior and senior years of instruction. Now Storm Lake's quota was greater than the total amount of endowment that Hostetler's successor, E. E. Reed, had been able to raise during the campaign of 1902–3.

At the start of the big drive, the *Pilot-Tribune* was sanguine. The undergraduates and the faculty pledged $15,000 at the very outset, which left only $60,000 for the Storm Lake community to raise. Certainly, the community and the Presbyterians of Iowa would be able to meet the challenge. "Now is the supreme time. Today is the day of salvation," cried the Storm Lake paper. However, as in other campaigns, it soon became apparent that the day of salvation would be postponed. The campaign moved slowly. Even the usual early optimism of such drives was lacking. President Jones spoke in somber tones when he said, "We have been leading up to this campaign for the past five years. Unless this College obtains a substantial endowment fund it can not continue. I can see no hope for the future if this campaign fails."[39]

Other College officials sounded equally pessimistic notes. Trustee president, Willis Edson, spoke of the repeated financial worries of the College during the entire course of its troubled history and concluded that "loyal friends could not and would not again go through the experiences of the last ten years."[40] In mid-February the *Pilot-Tribune* told the public that the goal was far from being reached and that "indifference and criticism are far too prevalent."[41] The campaign was extended on into the spring and summer as the goal of $500,000 seemed increasingly beyond reach. Then in October 1929 came the stock market crash. The seriousness of the financial events of the fall of 1929 were not at first realized; there had been other "panics," and the College had weathered them. This time, however, the effects of the American Depression were to be global, and the spirit of capitalistic enterprise that had built the industrial structure of the nation was to be seriously challenged.

While the local endowment campaign was withering, the Jones administration still hoped for substantial aid from the churches and for support from the Iowa Synod. In February 1930 it was announced that the Synodical Council of the Iowa Synod was preparing to take action relative to the financial needs of Buena Vista College. Also, Buena Vista was to be provided the services of an eastern representative, Edward W. Vose of New York City. Vose was to devote six weeks each year to canvassing for the College. Furthermore, sacrificial church offerings from May to July were to be turned over to Buena Vista.[42] These were destined to be futile efforts that never really got under way.

President Jones had inherited financial and managerial problems that defied solution. Jones and the trustees sought to put the College on firmer grounds by refinancing. In short, the College sold bonds to the value of $170,000 in order to cover its indebtedness. The First Trust Company of Lincoln, Nebraska, acted as trustee between 1926 and 1932. After 1932, Ralph Sheffield of the Citizens First National Bank was named trustee.[43]

In 1926 the property value of the College was estimated to be $450,000. The institution owed the Board of Education $36,000 and had total liabilities in excess of $160,000. The *Pilot-Tribune* in

1926 had optimistically asserted that the bond issue "will clean up odds and ends of indebtedness and permit President Jones and his field force to work unhampered in building for the future."[44] Far from enabling the institution to work unhampered, the bonded indebtedness proved to be a legacy that nearly undermined the existence of the College. At the time, however, College officials felt it was the only course open to them. Unfortunately, the superficial prosperity and upward surge of the stock market of the 1920s led many to assume that economic panics belonged to history. Certainly, the College was growing during the twenties. The growth, however, was more surface than substance and the Depression soon rocked the institution.

As early as the fall of 1930 the question was not one of continued growth but whether or not the College could be saved. The people of Storm Lake were stunned in October 1930 when Dr. Harry M. Gage of Coe College visited the campus, and the rumor spread that Buena Vista College would be merged with the Cedar Rapids institution. The proposed merger was to be discussed at the mid-October meeting of the state Synod in Cedar Rapids. Upon his return to Cedar Rapids, Gage intimated that the Storm Lake directors of Buena Vista wanted Coe "to take over the management of the school, making Buena Vista College a junior college with executive offices being located at Coe."[45] Eight of the ten presbyteries in existence in Iowa at that time approved the merger before it came to the Synod.

This was not the first discussion of the possibility of merging Buena Vista with another collegiate institution. In 1927, when old Des Moines University was breathing its dying gasps, the possibility was broached of joining that Baptist institution with Buena Vista.[46] The Augustana Lutheran church also expressed an interest in taking over the administration of Buena Vista College. The Lutherans even sent a delegation to visit the campus and apparently even during the panic-ridden years of the early thirties desired to establish an educational institution in northwest Iowa.[47]

Both the Baptist and Lutheran discussions of merger fizzled out, but the union with Coe was a definite possibility. The Synod met in Cedar Rapids and on October 16 the *Pilot-Tribune* announced that the merger had been approved. There was a somber, almost catastrophic, note about the announcement — Buena Vista College for the second time in its history was to be reduced to the ranks of a junior college. Dr. Gage would be president of both institutions, with the management of Buena Vista left to a resident dean. Students who enrolled for two years of study at Buena Vista would be encouraged to complete their education at Coe. The presbyteries were unanimous in approving the new educational setup. There seemed to be no alternative if Buena Vista was to survive the economic hazards induced by the Depression. Coe, it was believed, had a sufficiently large endowment to carry on and would become the Presbyterian University for Iowa.[48]

The new arrangement would involve a complete reorganization of the College and the faculty. It also meant that Evert Leon Jones's reign as president of the College was over. A few days after returning from Cedar Rapids where he had been one of the Storm Lake delegates, President Jones sent a letter of resignation to the Board of Trustees in which he said:

> I present herewith my resignation as President of Buena Vista College to take effect January 31, 1931. In so doing I wish to express my sincere thanks to you and all the members of the Board of Trustees for their loyalty, support, and cooperation and to assure you of my continued interest in and support of the College and the cause of Christian Education.[49]

After his resignation took effect, Jones returned to the practice of law and on one occasion even sought to be elected to the state legislature. In the meantime, the running of the College was in the hands of the capable dean, A. C. Nielsen.

The decision of the Synod did not mean the extinction of Buena Vista as an educational force in northwest Iowa but certainly meant diminution in its prestige and the stifling forever of its aspirations of becoming a recognized liberal arts college. The choice, however, seemed to be either a truncated existence or death. It seemed best to bow to the inevitable and become a junior college rather than to continue with the uncertainties that had plagued the school since its founding. Further struggle in the midst of critical times seemed impractical, unwise, suicidal.

Nevertheless, the student body and many members of the faculty were determined to make one last effort to save the College. A mass meeting was held in the chapel in Old Main where a stirring plea was made to forestall closing the foundering institution. Student Council president, Raymond Mansfield, was instrumental in drafting and sending to the Synod, on behalf of the Buena Vista student body, a message that they hoped would assist in keeping the College's doors open for another generation of students:

> We offer our faith, our courage, and our clean student life, together with the unselfish devotion of our faculty, as an active, living evidence of the Christian character of our College. . . . We beg of you, to come over to Macedonia and help us in a very definite way. It is not only the fate of our College as an institution, the Alma Mater of all those worthy men and women who have earned their degrees from this College, but with many of us it is the deciding factor in the acute trend of our lives which has been given over to your earnest deliberation and wise judgement.[50]

Faculty members, including Dean Nielsen, Grace Russell, and Dewey Deal all spoke in behalf of the salvation of the College. Reverent hymns and College cheers rent the air of the historic building. The student body and the faculty wanted to save the College. Did the community? The people of Storm Lake were aware that the merger with Coe had been approved and that Buena Vista was destined to be reduced to the ranks of the junior colleges. Some were upset that no Storm Lake person had been appointed to the commission appointed by the Synod to work out the details.[51]

A meeting sponsored by the Chamber of Commerce at the high school in mid-November revealed that Buena Vista's life might be as short as two weeks unless drastic action was undertaken. The "College is without funds, the faculty is unpaid, there are debts to meet, in brief the College has reached a crisis." College students paraded to the auditorium behind the Legion drum and bugle corps and the College band. They carried with them placards urging the citizen body to "SAVE THE COLLEGE FOR THE TOWN." Dean A. C. Nielsen was the principal speaker and pleaded for an all-out effort. Many students in northwest Iowa would not be able to obtain an education, Nielsen said, if Buena Vista College folded. Nielsen strongly intimated that the long-suffering faculty merited some consideration for its attachment and loyalty to the College. Loyalty, however, "does not pay coal bills. It does not buy clothing. It does not provide groceries. We have reached the point where we cannot continue longer under the present conditions." He also pointed out the fact that the College owed the faculty $40,000 in back salaries and $26,000 of this amount was due the present faculty. Scattered throughout Iowa were some $200,000 in pledges to the College that were apparently uncollectible. Willis Edson spoke of the financial conditions that made it impossible to collect these pledges, but at the same time he noted, "People spend thousands on autos . . . they should be willing to pay at least a small part of that amount for education." He concluded that it "has been worth all it cost to carry on this College." Perhaps the most sentimental moment of the rally was when Grace Russell, the head of the English department, stood up and told how as a little girl she had carried a tiny tin shovel while Old Main was being built by her father, Jay M. Russell.[52]

Buena Vista students volunteered to solicit the unpaid $200,000 in pledges. It was also pointed out that eighty-one students, or approximately two-fifths of the current student body, would be unable to attend college anywhere should Buena Vista go under. Students could attend Buena Vista for as little as $250, 90 percent earned their own way. The loss of the College would remove many desirable people from the community and mean, in addition to the loss of prestige and culture, a reduction of $100,000 in business revenues.[53]

The Storm Lake community did make an effort to retain the College. A committee of fifteen was formed to work out emergency measures that would assist the College in carrying on the battle. The committee consisted of the pastors of the four major Protestant denominations in town, Carl Whitted, business manager of the College; Mayor Bert Marchant; and other prominent citizens. By November 20 the committee had managed to raise only $4,225, which included substantial gifts from George J. Schaller and the Commercial Trust and Savings Bank. The money raised was designated to pay faculty salaries and was to be disbursed only at the direction of three trustees who had been appointed to handle the funds.[54]

Meanwhile, a fourfold plan was worked out for the "emergency" period of operation. Faculty, students, trustees, and citizens all had responsibilities to meet. The faculty was to guarantee the College that it would finish out the academic year. The student body was to guarantee an enrollment of 180 for the second semester. The trustees were to meet the interest on the bonded indebtedness, current expenses, and to take care of unexpected emergencies. The citizens of Storm Lake and Buena Vista County were to guarantee, for the balance of the school year, a monthly budget that would be used to meet faculty salaries.[55] Grace Russell, in a plea for contributions, informed the Missouri Valley Presbytery in the spring of 1931 that the College owed the faculty over $45,000. Meanwhile, F. F. Smith, who had replaced the retired Fracker as the most respected member of the faculty, was designated as faculty trustee to "receive and properly distribute any money intended for faculty salaries."[56]

During the hectic days of 1930 and 1931 a number of benefit performances were held for the College. In December 1930 the managers of the Empire Theatre held a special performance for the benefit of the Buena Vista College faculty. The picture *Maybe It's Love* netted $275, which was turned over to the College fund.[57] Similar benefits were to be held on behalf of the College during the Depression years by theater managers, the Chamber of Commerce, and the music department of the College. Indeed, Myrna Loy and George Brent would never know that *Stambul Quest* helped a small liberal arts college retain its dignity and sense of direction.

By the spring of 1931 the merger with Coe seemed less a possibility than it had a few months earlier. President of the trustees, Willis C. Edson, was more positive about the prospects of maintaining Buena Vista as a four-year college. "We have never had a better or more loyal faculty. The student body ranks high in both scholarship and character. If the alumni and local supporters of the College will remain loyal the College can succeed."[58]

Buena Vista's continued existence owes much to Willis Edson. In May 1931 the Storm Lake lawyer was a delegate to the General Assembly of the Presbyterian church at Pittsburgh where he pleaded for an increased budget to meet the educational needs of the church. The budget of the church, Edson pointed out, "is over 18 million dollars, but only one and a quarter million is apportioned for educational purposes."[59] While Edson's success at the General Assembly may have been minimal, the battle he waged to preserve Buena Vista would be successful.

At the June Commencement 1931 it seemed certain that Buena Vista College would maintain its standing as a four-year college. The presbyteries of Fort Dodge, Sioux City, and now Council Bluffs pledged a renewed effort on behalf of the College. The national Board also agreed to give the College $2,100, if by July 1 the trustees would adopt a budget that "will not exceed the income of the school."[60] Hard times were a long way from being over—in fact, they were just beginning. The future of Buena Vista College would depend upon its ability to meet its expenses and reduce its debt. In more prosperous times the College had continuously run up a deficit. It hardly seemed possible that it could ride out the despair into which an entire nation had sunk.

In the summer of 1931 Willis C. Edson set out to find a man who could administer and bring order to the desperate financial plight of the College. In better times men had accepted the presidency of Buena Vista College with misgiving. Now the College was on the verge of bankruptcy and its existence precarious. The man whom Edson found was Henry Olson, the school superintendent at Greenfield, Iowa. He had served in this capacity for eight years and was earning $3,400. Edson in his desperation had turned to Agnes Samuelson the superintendent of Public Instruction who recommended Olson as having the "best record of any man under her jurisdiction in the State of Iowa for business administration of his office."[61] Edson related that all he had to offer was the presidency of a bankrupt college and a salary of $2,400.

In fact, Olson labored during the first year of his administration not as president but as acting president. Furthermore, anyone accepting the presidency of Buena Vista College was running the risk that his salary might not be paid. Perhaps Edson's quote from the Italian patriot Garibaldi helped Olson decide:

> Let those who wish to continue the war come with me. I offer you fatigue, danger, struggle and death, the chill of the cold night in the open air and the heat under the burning sun, no lodgings, no munitions, no provisions, forced marches, dangerous outposts and continual struggle with the bayonet against batteries. Those who love freedom and their country follow me.[62]

Henry Olson, a graduate of Saint Olaf College and the University of Iowa, was not yet forty years of age when he moved to Storm Lake in the late summer of 1931. In addition to the superintendency at Greenfield he had served the schools of Shannon City and Lake Mills. The new president was a veteran of World War I, a Lutheran, and a dedicated family man with three sons and one daughter.[63] He also possessed a steel-like determination with which he would lead Buena Vista through the Depression and World War II. Olson was devoted to the cause of the small liberal arts college and the purpose of his life would merge with Buena Vista College.

A few years later President Olson reported to the meeting of the Presbyterian Synod at Red Oak that when he accepted the reins of office on September 1, 1931, Buena Vista had twenty-six cents in cash and a debt of $300,000.[64] It seemed to observers, he said, that the College was dead.

Many people believed that the death knell of the institution had already sounded early in 1931 when the historical edition of the *Storm Lake Pilot-Tribune* came out. One of the contributors was Anna von Coelln Stokes. Mrs. Stokes had attended Buena Vista College during the mid-1890s when her father had been a professor of mathematics. She recalled how all who had attended Buena Vista had been ardent boosters of the College:

> If loyalty were all that was needed to run a college then old BV would be sitting on top of the world, for never did citizens of any

community do better than have the residents of that great city lying in about Storm Lake towards an educational institution.[65]

The new acting president of the College had a peculiar ability to command the loyalty of his faculty. Perhaps he sensed that the desire for academic and professional excellence transcends all else among educated people. Perhaps the humanitarian instinct that motivated Olson to keep tuition costs low was appealing to the faculty in an era when money was scarce everywhere and great riches seemed far away. Perhaps some wanted to stay to see if this zealot, who rode freight trains to professional meetings and settled the accounts of the College by resorting to barter, could actually succeed.

In the midst of a sea of poverty, President Olson was to take command and give Buena Vista College a stability it had never known before.

7

Work of Salvation: Henry Olson (1931–1941)

Our prospects are good. Our ideals and standards
we submit to the inspection of all men.

—TRUSTEE WILLIS EDSON

When thirty-nine-year-old Henry Olson came to Buena Vista as acting president and business manager it seemed likely that he would preside over the liquidation of the institution, as the desperate struggle for survival reached its climax. Three hundred Buena Vistans would have graduated from a defunct liberal arts college and forty years of educational service would have come to an end. Even if Olson could hold the school together during the academic year 1931–32, there was no guarantee that the trustees would select the former superintendent as permanent president. The only nonclergyman the trustees had seen fit to elect had been Willis Marshall back in 1895. Furthermore, Olson was a Lutheran. While Presbyterians have never been narrowly dogmatic, this was still a break with tradition.

Apparently Olson liked the challenge. Buena Vista in 1931 had a bond debt of $170,000 and two years' interest, plus $50,000 in unpaid faculty salaries and past-due notes in several banks.[1] The total indebtedness ranged over the $250,000 mark, and some believed actual indebtedness to be as much as $325,000. The College also lacked dormitory space even for its limited enrollment of 150 students; library and science facilities were obviously deficient; the main building was in desperate need of renovation; and the endowment was a meagre $112,000.[2] The College did have $200,000 in small pledges, but as Trustee Willis Edson recalled:

> These obligations were in small amounts from over widely scattered areas. We employed men to collect these claims but the amount they got in cash was not enough to pay their salaries and expenses. Nearly all the banks in Western Iowa were closed. The only income the College had that amounted to anything was tuition paid by students.[3]

Many students were unable to pay cash and "gave notes instead." A girl from Marathon struck upon an ingenious way to "depression finance" her way through college. She brought butter and eggs from the farm and presented them to Olson as partial payment for her tuition. Olson accepted the barter and an unpaid and underfed professor received the produce in lieu of his salary.[4] One student of the 1930s recalls her father, "having butchered homegrown beef, placing large portions in the trunk of the car, and B.V. professors were happy to show him how much to cut off & weigh."[5] The cash value was credited to the student's tuition. The mother of another student did laundry for two professors resulting in a reduction of tuition for laundry service.[6] Barter was a way of life at Buena Vista during the Depression years.

Meanwhile, the institution's creditors were closing in as the bondholders threatened the foreclosure of their mortgage. Banks, desperate to stay alive, presented to the trustees notes that had been endorsed by them.[7] When Edson's father-in-law, Judge A. D. Bailie, died in 1936, a claim for $170,000 and interest was filed against his estate. And Willis Edson, now in his sixties, gave up his last chance for political success, surrendering plans to campaign for the senate nomination in order to pour $3,000 of savings into the battle to save Buena Vista College. It seemed a long time since the January 1904 day when Edson had been invited by Bailie and M. O. Miller to become a trustee. Years later he was to say with some bitterness, "I try to forget what it has cost me in money and what it has cost me in countless hours and sleepless nights, in broken health, and in political dreams destroyed." In Henry Olson,

Edson found a man not unlike himself — a man talented, optimistic, and hard — a man who saw nothing bizarre in a college president riding a cattle-train caboose to Chicago with a sandwich in his pocket in order to attend a professional meeting. And when Olson traveled to speak, he paid his own expenses and turned the fee into the College treasury.[8]

The ninety Buena Vista freshmen got their first look at the new president when Olson spoke in chapel on September 16, 1931. His welcome speech was undoubtedly in the same vein as one he gave a few years later when he said, "I value my work done in the small school [Saint Olaf], and treasure my memories of the time spent there as much, or more than I do the years spent in the University."[9]

Somehow, Olson was able to see the College through the difficult year 1931–32. The staff was cut back, salaries reduced, and the strictest economy practiced. Indeed, Olson became the first Buena Vista College president in history to balance the budget. The trustee minutes in the spring of 1932 noted with astonishment and gratitude:

> To balance the budget for the first time in our history in the face of the most adverse conditions is an achievement that did not seem possible, and we most heartily commend Mr. Olson for his administration of the business office and pledge our untiring support for the completion of the budget plan by August 31st.[10]

The trustees also praised the loyalty of the student body and delivered the usual platitudes to the faculty, which they said was "the equal of any in any previous year," and that "they have carried on the work of the school in a spirit of self-sacrificing devotion, meriting a far greater pecuniary reward than they have received, and deserving the heartfelt appreciation of all who believe in the value of a Christian education." The brilliant F. F. Smith received a salary of $1,800; Professor Crawford, now close to his Ph.D. at the University of Chicago, $1,800; and the able Dean A. C. Nielsen, $2,400. The total budgeted for salaries was running about $6,100 under what had been allocated during the last "prosperous" year 1928–29. Faculty actually accepted salary reductions during the academic year 1931–32 so the institution could continue. Salaries were further reduced for the term 1933–34. Salaries increased only marginally during the remaining years of the 1930s and the early 1940s. As late as 1942, most salaries hovered between $1,500 and $1,700. Pleas continued to go out to the national church for assistance.[11]

Meanwhile, there were those demands that make the era seem so narrow in retrospect. In the fall of 1939, Olson requested "all unmarried faculty to refrain from dating Buena Vista College students."[12] Faculty were asked to turn off radiators when they opened windows in order to conserve coal. Faculty were expected to cooperate "100 percent" when the Kiwanians and Rotarians threw a "party for the public school teachers and college professors." Furthermore, both institution and faculty were to give sixty-day notices in case of dismissal or decision to leave the institution. Failure to do so could result in a deduction of $100 from the faculty member's paycheck.[13] This was where Buena Vista College stood in 1940 when the American Association of University Professors (AAUP) adopted its statement of principles and procedures governing academic tenure and freedom. Yet there seemed to be no feeling of being circumscribed as faculty and students joined forces to save something they believed to be larger than themselves.

In spite of his initial success, Olson remained acting president during 1932–33. When others were questioning the feasibility of the small college in an era of economic crisis, Olson was proclaiming that the Depression proved the "need for small colleges." The quality of a college, he asserted, "depends no longer on the splendor of buildings. The quality of an institution's faculty and students determines its destiny." Olson boasted that the tuition at Buena Vista was the lowest in the state of Iowa and that board and room costs were the lowest since 1914.[14] The College catalog, 1931–32, listed tuition costs up to sixteen hours at $65 per semester, with minimum room and board combined at $66 per semester. Minimum semester costs were listed at $166 and maximum at $270.[15] With low-cost education of this type, President Olson expected an enrollment of around three hundred for the academic

year 1932–33. "We'll beat them [the students] out from under the
bushes," he forecast.[16] While this goal was not reached, enrollment
moved well beyond the two hundred mark.[17] Meanwhile, the College was tackling the problem of its indebtedness. The endowment
was used to meet the obligations to creditors, and the bonds were
paid at the rate of 40 to 50 percent of value. Trustee President
Edson recalled:

> Many of the $170,000 bonds we issued were sold in Missouri.
> One day we had a letter from a person who had a $500 bond. He
> was desperately in need of money. He would sell his bond for
> $200. We sent the money. . . . Soon we were besieged with simi-
> lar offers. Most of the bonds we paid 40 per cent up to 50 per
> cent.[18]

Perhaps it was not the most desirable solution, but as the
secretary of the Presbyterian Board of Education noted, the College could do one of two things. It could use its resources, including what little endowment there was, to satisfy the creditors; or it
could foreclose the school and liquidate the debt. Harold McAfee
Robinson, recommended the former. "We paid," noted Willis Edson, "a larger percentage of our obligations than banks paid under
receivership and saved the College from bankruptcy."[19] Meanwhile,
President Olson, still using for his office "the small room west of
the stairway on the first floor in which room the ceiling had partly
fallen off,"[20] had managed to balance the budget for the second
consecutive year. Indeed, by June 1933 it appeared that the College
might survive the Depression. The trustees praised Olson for having increased the enrollment, for reducing the debt, and for making the 1932 summer session the most successful in the school's
history. The trustees now followed the obvious course of electing
Henry Olson as the full-fledged president of the institution.[21]

President Olson managed to keep costs level in 1933–34 and
pushed the regular enrollment closer to the desired three hundred
mark. The *Tack* noted that Buena Vista had the biggest increase in
enrollment in the history of the College. There were 267 regular
students with a freshman class of 137. Olson proclaimed:

I am certain Buena Vista College, in the academic year 1933–34, will meet the high standards of the most exacting student, and will be highly successful in her great mission of being of the greatest service to all those having the privilege of coming into contact with her positive influence.[22]

In late June 1934 President Olson read a report of the College work to the Synod meeting at Red Oak, Iowa. During his three-year administration, Olson said, the College had "pulled out of a hole a mile deep." He noted that the College had been able to pay faculty salaries in full since 1931, was making substantial progress in reducing the burden of debt, and had balanced the budget each year. Furthermore, Olson intimated that there was a surplus of $19,000 during the academic year 1933–34. In addition, the College had processed sixty-four graduates and had registered a total of 1,081 students for the academic year including summer school. Among the faculty, Dr. Lyman White had published a book entitled *The Structure of Private International Organizations,* and Dean A. C. Nielsen was writing a newspaper column called "Foreign Shores" which was utilized by several weeklies in northern Iowa. In conclusion, Olson reminded the Synod:

When I look back on the accomplishments, the efforts expended and the results achieved the past year, I cannot help but feel optimistic regarding the future usefulness of the institution. Providence, we are justified in stating, certainly has done well by us. We have come through a hard and trying time with results that should cause us to be encouraged at the great possibilities evident at Buena Vista College.[23]

The bells tolling the College's anticipated death sounded fainter after 1934, but the struggle was by no means over. The yearly battle to balance the budget and to secure students continued. There was still a large debt that had to be reduced. It was an arduous task to secure first-rate students and competent faculty members for an institution whose academic status was occasionally questioned. Able faculty members came to Buena Vista to receive their baptism of experience and then departed to give their loyalty to institutions that could offer more lucrative positions. For example, the brilliant Dr. Lyman White left for the West Coast; the able and dedicated Dean A. C. Nielsen left for Fort Dodge (he eventually became president of Grandview College); and the College lost the services of its stellar coach, Frank Casey, who moved to Simpson College in 1935.[24] And yet it was during this era that professors Luman Sampson and George Reynolds gave three decades of service. Professor Maryanna (Anna) Hamer and talented poet J. Luke Creel provided the nucleus for an outstanding English department. Professor Hamer was also a poet and the author of two children's books that served as second and third grade readers. She was the organizer in 1933 of the Entre Nous Club (another casualty of the 1960s) composed of nonsorority women, faculty advisor of the YWCA, and she wrote the words to the College's alma mater. After sixteen years, 1931–1947, Professor Hamer moved to Central College at Pella, where she finished her career.

George Reynolds became an endearing permanent fixture — the man who did a little of everything, ranging from professor to counselor to wartime basketball coach. He was short and pudgy, with round weathered features, a squeaky voice, and a shuffling gait. His head was capped with bushy, unruly hair through which he constantly ran his hand in a futile attempt to perform some act of grooming. He wore shirts with frayed cuffs and his collars often curled because they lacked the necessary stays. During his later years, Reynolds became a legend, and the tales of his idiosyncratic behavior abounded as they were passed from one generation to another. "Did he really drive to Sioux City and, forgetting how he got there, take the train home? Is it possible he actually gave a baseball player an "A" on a crib sheet to average with an "F" on an exam?"[25] Students claimed that Reynolds lectured with his eyes closed and that he dropped the blue books crammed with long essays down the stairs to determine exam grades. He never used notes in any class whether a fifty-minute or a three-hour period. Some complained that his love of sports occasionally blinded him to the deficiencies of athletes. You could hear him above all others at the basketball games.

Professor Reynolds was an ardent and conservative Republican who once denounced FDR's New Deal as "a form of social-ism"[26] and yet found it possible to contribute to George Mc-Govern's senatorial campaign in South Dakota. George Reynolds (and Florence) might have fit into a Dickens novel—there was that inherent puckish quality. He probed and darted at the issues until he hit them dead center. He possessed a fiesty, fertile mind, the brightness and creativity of which was sometimes lost in the lab-yrinths of a unique logic. George helped care for an aged mother-in-law, and a chronically ill brother-in-law. He owned a house in Waterloo often rented to poor families whom he rarely pressed for payments. He was the Mr. Chips at Buena Vista and, along with Dr. Hirsch, the most beloved of teachers. For thirty-five—mostly lean—years he taught at Buena Vista College. Professor Reynolds served willingly on all committees; he sponsored the Young Re-publicans; he was the law advisor; the catalyst of the model UN; and cofounder of the campus chapter of Phi Alpha Theta. Some-times the butt of good-natured humor, there were few who could rival this man for his steadfast loyalty, keen intelligence, or depth of humanity. It was a memorable sight to see him in action in the classroom, and perceptive students, although somewhat amused by his antics, soon understood the extent of his knowledge and his mastery of detail.[27] As one distinguished graduate recalled, "George Reynolds ran law classes with as rigorous a Socratic dia-logue as I have seen in any law school in the country."[28] Students, faculty, administration, and local citizens from the academic low tides of the 1930s to the brighter prospects of the 1970s mourned his death in the summer of 1977. In 1980 W. H. Cumberland and the School of Social Science, Philosophy and Religion inaugurated the first of the George F. Reynolds lectures that continued through-out the decade of the 1980s. The Alumni Association granted Rey-nolds honorary membership and the College honored him during a chapel service prior to his retirement. The long line of Buena Vista College alumni who successfully completed law school owed much to the influence of George Reynolds.

Buena Vista's enrollment continued to grow during the diffi-cult 1930s. The freshman class passed beyond the two hundred mark in September 1936 and along with forty-three seniors, constituted a class record. The College now had a faculty of twenty-two and could offer majors in ten fields.[29] The trustees could note with pride that the College debt had been reduced by $100,000 and "that we have met every cent of our operating expense except about $5,000 and now hold student tuition notes aggregating over $20,000 accrued during that time and on which we are realizing returns almost daily." The jubilant trustees maintained that Buena Vista College had grown during the previous half-decade more than any of the colleges under the control of the Presbyterian Board of Education. As Willis Edson pointed out in a letter to Dr. Robinson:

> Our tradition is written in the College Motto, "Education for Service." Our service is a standard education leading to Bachelor's degrees in arts, sciences and music. Our financial condition is improving. Our prospects are good. Our ideals and standards we submit to the inspection of all men.[30]

In spite of the encouraging progress, the struggle continued. The Depression of the 1930s was far deeper than the panic of 1893 or the recession of 1921. Thirteen million unemployed haunted the nation. Collegians could find a temporary refuge, but there was scant assurance that they would be able to sell their skills upon graduation. Buena Vista continued to train an increasing number of teachers, but as the student paper noted, there were "teachers, teachers everywhere and not a school to teach."[31] Realizing the daily struggle most students faced in pursuing their education, President Olson appeared at chapel service pleading that no one would "quit college without coming to see him first." Furthermore, the College enticed a number of good students by offering one-half tuition to class valedictorians.[32]

Still, there were bright spots for the entire College community such as the performances of music director John Bloom's choir on radio station WHO in Des Moines. Bloom had come to Buena Vista in the fall of 1934, pulled something of a coup by marrying Eleanor Olson, a 1935 Buena Vista graduate who happened to be the president's secretary and sister.[33] All expenses were paid and the

choir was heard across the state and the nation, and three ships at
sea even picked up the broadcasts. These were the days when an
amiable young sportscaster, Ronald Reagan, was working at
WHO.[34] Bloom eventually became professor of voice and director
of choirs at the University of Arizona where he taught from 1951 to
1976.

Meanwhile, the needs of the College continued to grow.
Treasured Old Main was becoming a fire hazard but remained one
of the two brick structures on the campus. The College budget
moved steadily upward from $46,000 in 1932–33 to almost $70,000
in 1936–37. Olson prophesied that it would soon take $100,000 a
year to operate the College. Furthermore, Buena Vista College was
approaching the fifty-year mark of service to education. President
Olson knew that Buena Vista would have to make a major effort to
improve its facilities. "At that time," he said, "we have set as our
goal to have our debts paid, and at least one-half million dollars in
endowment and four substantial buildings on campus such as a
men's dormitory, a chapel, and a conservatory."[35]

President Olson was certain that all this was within the realm
of possibility, even though it would take the unprecedented sum of
a million dollars to bring it about. Already preparations were under way to push through what seemed a gigantic campaign during
the 1936–37 year. Vice President W. A. Stevenson undertook a
development program intended to secure a quarter of a million
dollars, $45,000 of it from Storm Lake. The consistently loyal
College faculty pledged the surprising total of $5,220.[36] "Buena
Vista College in the last five years has outgrown its clothes," said
Willis Edson. The drive, according to Edson, was the first general
campaign for finances made by the College in seventeen years.[37]
The College had to finance needed equipment and library facilities
or face accreditation problems. The campaign, however, seemed to
move slowly in spite of the usual proclamations of success. The
Storm Lake Pilot-Tribune noted in July 1936 that the drive "was
well over the half way point," which was another way of saying
that the Storm Lake drive scheduled for May 11–22 had not fared
too well.[38] By late fall the College trustees stipulated that it was
"not advisable to continue the financial drive because of uncertain

economic conditions in Western Iowa."[39] Conditions would not improve during the recession years of 1937 and 1938.

No crisis could deter the heroic team of Edson and Olson who were determined to ride out the Depression and build a better Buena Vista College. Neither man was accustomed to bending before personal or public frustration. Their capacity for hard work and personal sacrifice seemed unlimited, and when cash was not available they resorted to barter and trade. But nothing could keep the physical plant from deteriorating, and eggs from the farm could not substitute for money in the bank.

Meanwhile, Buena Vista College students continued to climb the oily stairs of Old Main and shiver in the classrooms that old-timers remembered as "airy" in the 1890s. The chapel floor was beginning to break, and the plywood chairs posed a distinct hazard to suits and dresses. The students had to attend services in shifts, and the editor of the *Tack* — as the fiftieth-year anniversary approached — stoutly remarked that the "present chapel is a disgrace to the institution."[40]

Although Willis Edson was not in a position to construct a new building, he did set out to improve the chapel situation. He later recalled with some humor that:

> I wangled the Lane Moore Lumber Company, one of my clients, to let me have enough flooring. I got a good carpenter to do the job with the help of the janitor and some students. We then varnished it. It was a fine job thus far. But it wouldn't do to put those old seats back again. The manager of the Vista Theatre told me of a company in New York that bought up old seats, reupholstered them as good as new. I wired them that I wanted 256 chairs. They wired back that they had just finished 260 and that they were as good as new. I wired we would take them. They wired that a trucker from Omaha was in their office looking for a return cargo. I told them to ship at once. There wasn't time to talk with President Olson and other members of the Board.[41]

Edson finally cornered Olson and got his approval. As Olson gave his assent, he looked out of the window and saw the truck arriving with the chairs. "Good heavens," he said, "here comes the truck now." Edson had obtained the chairs for one-half the price of new ones, repainted the walls, and solicited contributions sufficient to pay the bills. When investigation showed that the chapel floor was giving way and collapsing into the large classroom east of the business office, Edson "bought the lumber, laid the floor and painted the walls at my own expense."[42] This was the spirit that saved Buena Vista College during the years of famine.

When Henry Olson assumed the temporary presidency of Buena Vista College in 1931, he was determined to (1) keep the institution functioning in spite of the worst financial crisis in the nation's history, (2) remove the debt and keep the budget balanced, and (3) improve faculty and facilities. Certainly the president had achieved the first of his goals by 1935. As long as Olson was at the helm, there was confidence that the College could outlive the Depression. Furthermore, during the decade 1931–1941 Olson and his trustees were gradually able to reduce the burden of debt, pay back salaries, and keep the operation of the institution out of the red. Olson's goal — to retire the last bond before the fiftieth anniversary year began in the fall of 1941 — was achieved when, at the end of July, Walter Stock presented the College with its last outstanding bond. This meant that the last of the bond issue floated almost a generation earlier had been retired. "The lifting of this mortgage," Olson proclaimed, "is the beginning of a new era for Buena Vista College. All her resources can now be utilized to provide the equipment and instruction necessary for the proper development of any individual on a college level."[43] This had been done in an era when most Buena Vista students enrolled for two years and transferred. As one graduate recalled, his entering class of one hundred had dwindled to twenty by graduation, but he felt the faculty did an excellent job, the classes were small, and a strong learning atmosphere prevailed. Like most Buena Vista graduates he encountered no problems in graduate school.[44]

A decade of Olson's tenure had removed the debt and saved the College. Estimates of the 1931 deficit vary, but Olson maintained on several occasions that it had been $325,000.[45] With the liquidation of the crippling debt, Buena Vista College could look forward to a period of consolidation and expansion. Now it could develop the blueprints for a new library, dormitories, and work towards the acquisition of a million dollar endowment over a ten-year period.[46] These goals seemed possible in 1940 and 1941 as the nation moved out of the throes of the Depression into a new prosperity.

Indeed, the College was in a festive mood as the fiftieth anniversary got under way in the spring of 1941. Professor Grace Russell, daughter of the builder of Old Main, presented her historical pageant at the high school auditorium. Alice Wilcox returned to the campus after a long absence and invoked memories of her two decades of service.[47] A special tribute was paid to the unforgettable "Grand Old Gentleman," Dr. Fracker. The long-established Buena Vista traditions—the Senior Swing Out, Tree Day, the Pipe of Peace—were performed. At Commencement honorary degrees were conferred upon two of Buena Vista's most distinguished graduates, Dr. Clifford M. Drury (1918) and Dr. Stanley Black Fracker (1910).[48]

Olson's first decade as president had been the work of salvation. He had revived the institution by rescuing it from bankruptcy. On the other hand he had constructed no new buildings, he had raised no endowment, and he could not yet be credited with having appreciably raised the academic standards of the institution. Buena Vista's enrollment had reached new heights, but relatively few of her graduates continued into areas of professional study, though some of those who did achieved considerable distinction. Carl Reng, (1932) was the president of Arkansas State College for twenty-four years. Robert K. Meinhard (1940) became a distinguished professor of history at Winona State College in Minnesota. Edgar Mack (1935) graduated from the University of Iowa College of Law, and eventually returned to Storm Lake as a prominent attorney and as the chairperson of the College Board of Trustees during the 1980s, John Kircheis (1939) served as chairman of the board and chief executive officer of Mobil Oil, Ltd., in London, and V. Elizabeth Coffin-Kwart (1944) became the first woman to be accepted in the surgical residency program at the University of Iowa School of Medicine.

By the autumn of 1941 Olson had been at his post longer than any college president in the state,[49] and no other Buena Vista College president would come close to Olson in length of service. He seemed to be an invaluable and permanent fixture. The first phase of his work had been completed. The second — the period of consolidation and expansion — was about to begin.

Unfortunately, the world crisis continued to deepen in 1940 and 1941. As the spring of 1940 approached, President Olson became increasingly aware that an American involvement in the global conflagration was a definite possibility. This would mean that colleges like Buena Vista, which had emerged scarred from the Depression, would now face the depletion of their student body through the call to war. Nevertheless, the nature of the struggle and the role that education must play were both equally clear to President Olson when he remarked, "If American democracy is to be saved from the revolutionary and destructive forces now at work in the world, it will be done through a program of Christian education."[50]

The blast that many Americans had come to regard as inevitable came on December 7, 1941, when the Japanese war lords launched their devastating attack on Pearl Harbor. President Olson cautioned the College community against panic:

The burden of mobilizing the spiritual and social resources must, in large measures, be borne by the teachers of America . . . the teachers must be leaders in taking a sane rather than an emotional or hysterical view of the present crisis . . . teachers must remember they are training citizens to live in a future where justice, tolerance and good will must prevail.[51]

Plans for expansion would have to be delayed. Buena Vista had weathered a decade of Depression. Could it survive four years of war?

8

CONSOLIDATION AND EXPANSION: HENRY OLSON (1942–1954)

> I had an ambition to make Buena Vista College a highly accredited and outstanding institution of higher learning in the realm of Christian education.
>
> —PRESIDENT HENRY OLSON

By 1942 Buena Vista, like other colleges across the nation, began to feel the squeeze of full-scale national mobilization. Never short on patriotism, Buena Vista faculty, students, and alumni began to report for military service. The first faculty member to enter military service was the chairperson of the physics department, Professor Robert Cushman Wyckoff who departed in mid-January 1942 to become an inspector in ballistics at the Ankeny small-arms plant.[1] By 1944 he was a full lieutenant in the United States Navy.[2] Professor Wyckoff had been at Buena Vista since 1938 and would return to the campus following his discharge in 1946 but would remain only one year before departing for the University of Oklahoma. Business Manager Marion Nelson left in 1942 and saw considerable service in the Eighth Air Force, participating in a number of bombing raids over Germany. The popular journalism instructor, Kermit Buntrock, entered the army in February 1944 and was part of the push into Germany. By November 1944 Willis Edson estimated that Buena Vista College had more than six hundred former students and faculty members in military service.[3]

Perhaps there was not quite the same zip and zest in 1941–1945 that there had been in 1918. If this generation brooked no quarter for tyrants, it had no illusions about crusades either. The nation had matured. Buena Vista's service men and women in 1941–1945 were as concerned about the nation's freedom and honor as their fathers and uncles had been. They were no less heroic, but they were less flamboyant. In World War I the only Buena Vista collegian to die in service had been Ilo Taylor. This time the price of service was much greater. By January 1945 eighteen former Buena Vista students or graduates had been killed in action.[4] Among former students who would not return were Bruce Heflin, Bill Brinkman, Eugene Butler, Dick Moses, Don Jones, Phil Bertness, and Darrell Lindsay. Lindsay's courage in a dangerous mission over Germany merited him the Medal of Honor. In August 1944 Captain Lindsay, a Buena Vista student 1939–40, stayed with his doomed B-26 bomber on a fatal mission over France enabling the rest of his crew to escape.[5] An oil portrait of the captain along with that of Ralph G. Neppel, one of the nation's most celebrated heroes, was given an honored place in Siebens Forum.[6]

Neppel, a sergeant from Glidden, Iowa, won distinction on December 14, 1944. Horribly wounded (both legs would be amputated), Neppel "pulled himself up by his elbows" to his machine gun and forced the attacking Nazis and their solitary tank to retreat. Neppel held his position until rescued eight hours later, at his insistence, only after his wounded sergeant had been evacuated. For his heroism (he always denied he was a hero — "the heroes don't live.") he was awarded the Medal of Honor in 1945.[7] He would complete a business major at Buena Vista, receive his degree in 1952, and spend much of his life working for the Veterans' Administration helping veterans and their families overcome the red tape of bureaucracy. Between 1970 and 1978 he served on the Governor's Committee for the Employment of the Handicapped and in 1986 represented Iowa at a D day celebration in Caen, France. Neppel married and fathered four children. His accomplishments never led him to hold himself in awe, "It was just a question of fighting on and doing what a fellow could or get killed. I don't know why people are being so wonderful to me. I'm just a small-town boy. I've never known anything but simple things, and that's sort of the way I'd like to have it."[8] Neppel died at Iowa City in 1988.

Among the wounded were former basketball stars, Jay Beekmann and Harold Simmons, who were both serving in the European theater in 1944. One of Buena Vista's most decorated heroes was young Don McKenna, a P-47 veteran of 131 missions. McKenna received the Distinguished Flying Cross and "air medal with seventeen oak-leaf clusters, presidential unit citation and five stars on his E.T.O. ribbon." The *Tack* noted some 260 awards and decorations among the seventy-three veterans who had returned to campus by February 1946.[9]

Kermit Buntrock came through without serious incident and during the postwar era abandoned teaching for photography. Buntrock, a 1929 graduate of Waukon High School in the dipping hills of picturesque northeast Iowa, began writing sports and features for Storm Lake newspapers in 1936. His sports commentaries for the *Buena Vista County Herald* were hidden under the enticing pseudonym, Kay Looey, leaving a later generation wondering if rugged feminism had originated on the sports pages and in the locker rooms of northwest Iowa. "Tis a great old world," Kay had remarked, "where you can have more fun than anybody."[10] President Olson knew what to do with the bright young man who was soon handling the public relations department and teaching courses in journalism. World War II found him in military service and in the campaign across Germany. His horizons broadened and he joined forces with Duane Salie to establish the Buntrock-Salie Studio in 1947. The partnership lasted twenty-seven years until retirement in 1974. Meanwhile, Buntrock had served as president of the American Society of Photographers (1969) and as a member of the Buena Vista College Board of Trustees since 1954. He became a Buena Vista College and Storm Lake booster, established a forty-seven-year mark of perfect attendance as a Kiwanian, and was chairperson of the Committee of 100 for a new Buena Vista County courthouse. As witty as he was dedicated, Buntrock would remain a trustee for more than thirty years, become an honored figure, and be awarded in 1983 the Founders' Citation of Excellence. He was fond of saying, "If any institution deserves to live it's Buena Vista College." The well-to-do Buntrock of the 1980s, his walls studded with honorary plaques and medals for his professional photography and for his work with Kiwanians, and for the Iowa Hawkeyes, could still recall the sterner days of the 1930s when "there would be frequent times when I'd wait six months to cash my paycheck."[11]

Although Buena Vista College was approved for the Navy's V-I and other reserve programs, the College secured no training unit on campus during the war. Naturally, as a result of the large draft calls, enrollment dropped. The effect of the war on College attendance is illustrated by Table 8.1. These statistics indicate that by 1944–45 the regular student body had declined to 132 students. In that year there were only sixteen upperclassmen. Football was curtailed in 1942 and dropped altogether during the years 1943 to 1946. Jake LaFoy kept basketball alive in 1942 and 1943 but then moved to Storm Lake High School where he produced a state tournament team in 1945. The situation in basketball was so critical that the College had to draft history professor George Reynolds as coach. Reynolds had practiced law in Waterloo and had taught a year at Colgate before coming to Buena Vista in 1937. Calm and wise in the classroom, he was a vocal and frantic spectator at the athletic contests. For years he was Buena Vista's representative on the Conference Athletic Commission and was twice president of the Iowa Conference. The cage games were played with colleges in western Iowa and with independent teams. Although he lost two-thirds of the games played under his direction, including six in two years to arch rival Western Union (now Teikyo Westmar), Reynolds silenced his critics for the duration early in 1945 by upsetting Morningside 41–32.

TABLE 8.1. Buena Vista College enrollment, 1941–1945

	1941–42	1942–43	1943–44	1944–45
Seniors	22	19	9	10
Juniors	21	29	6	6
Sophomores	103	74	51	43
Freshman	123	126	71	73

Source: *Buena Vista College Bulletin,* Aug. 1945, p. 58.

Athletics was not the only area to suffer a previously unknown nadir during the war years. Editorials in the *Tack* deplored the intellectual depression that had inevitably hit the campus with most of the young men in service. The 1942–43 Buena Vista Players were called the poorest in the school's history, the YMCA consisted solely of officers, and the International Relations Club had held no meetings. Old traditions like Hobo Day became a more serene and patriotic Cleanup Day.[12]

While the war impeded the growth of the College, it did not destroy the impetus already established by the Olson administration. With Professor Luman W. Sampson as dean, 1941–1947, Olson was certain that the academic structure of the College was in strong hands. Sampson's ability and integrity as chairperson of the Division of Social Sciences during the 1930s and as dean of the College in the 1940s helped prepare the foundation for the College's later stability. George F. Reynolds, F. F. Smith, and J. Luke Creel helped carry the College through lean years. They were the pillars of strength. When Bob McKenna arrived back on campus in September 1945, he eloquently expressed the sentiments of other returning veterans as he noted the old reliables of the faculty:

> Dr. Sampson with a more mellow pessimism; Prof. Creel—his curly hair grown grayer now; Dr. Reynolds knowing more history because there has been more history; Prof. Smith who remembers the names, characters, and capabilities of uncles, aunts, parents and older brothers and sisters of his present pupils; and Miss Hamer, who continues to write children's literature and textbooks. Indeed, finding something exactly the same as when he left is a joy perhaps no one can know in such complete fullness as a returning veteran after having been long where he saw everything constantly changing and where nothing seemed certain or secure.[13]

But the sameness was only a surface sameness. The GI bill brought an influx of veterans who would change American education forever. They would give Buena Vista College its largest enrollment in history and demand additional well-qualified faculty and new residence halls. The returning veterans like McKenna had also changed. They were not quite the same people returning to the same home. Older than their years, they were serious about their degrees and thirsted for an education that would set their course in a volatile world. They had had experiences that were not in the books and that they could not erase; they were married and had children; they studied in makeshift college housing popularly dubbed "chicken coops"; they went on to graduate school; their wives worked. The quiet isolationism of the 1920s and 1930s was no longer possible in this new world. In the nuclear age the ocean was no longer a pocket of safety. For good or ill, and short-lived as it would be, this was the American century and the sense of change pierced the smallest hamlets.

For colleges like Buena Vista it was move with the flux or perish. The fact that Buena Vista College had been accredited by the Iowa State Department of Education was no longer satisfactory, as the state's role was limited to approving teacher certification. Furthermore, the Presbyterian Board of Education in a meeting with College representatives in Cincinnati in 1944 insisted that the College gain regional accreditation, which meant approval by the North Central Association (NCA).[14] Such approval was impossible to obtain during the war years, because the NCA had ceased granting accreditation but it would be a priority project once the war ended. If Buena Vista were to take advantage of the postwar emphasis on education and attract the wave of veterans enrolling in colleges under the GI Bill of Rights, the College would have to improve its academic rating and plant facilities. As Willis Edson asserted in 1944, "We know that a large number of ex-servicemen will return to college after the war and at the expense of the government. This for us will be a great privilege as well as a great opportunity. The question is, are we going to meet it?"[15]

The College trustees in 1944 had adopted a five-year program for expansion—a program that ostensibly had the support of the national Board headed by Dr. Fay Campbell. Similar plans had been advertised before but had fallen prey to Depression, war, or had been filled with more oratory than substance. The 1944 campaign was the College's first multimillion dollar fund-raising drive. The goal was to raise (1) $500,000 for permanent endowment, (2)

$500,000 for the construction of vitally needed men's and women's dormitories, (3) $100,000 for a new library, and (4) $100,000 for general building improvement.[16] It seemed to President Olson and the trustees that Buena Vista College could count on a postwar enrollment of around five hundred students. If so, the million-dollar campaign would meet only the minimum needs of the postwar years. The College, now in its sixth decade, still lacked dormitory facilities, and the Fracker Library was but a collection of books isolated in aging Science Hall. Every Buena Vista president from E. E. Reed on had endeavored to secure adequate library facilities and had been frustrated by constant financial exigencies. Designs and plans vanished into the limbo of cherished dreams. The nearest that Olson got to the dream library was an artist's sketch that appeared in the August 1944 *Tack*.[17]

Still, Olson did secure a makeshift library that served the College for almost two decades. In October 1946 it was announced that Buena Vista College had secured a building from the Federal Works Agency of Kansas City.[18] The building, which had originally been a frame mess hall at the Sioux City air base, was now dismantled and moved to Storm Lake. The College gave it a brick covering and converted it into a new Fracker Library. While later students found the shelves cramped and the floor arrangement anything but commodious, the postwar students rejoiced that the Fracker collection had at last found a home. The 1948 *Beaver Log*, feeling the change marked an improvement, proclaimed that the College books had been transferred "from the dingy crowded quarters in the basement of Science across the street to the cheerful, sunny, spacious new location in a building all its own."[19] The College hired Alberta Dwelle, who held a master's degree in library science from the University of Minnesota, to manage the collection. One of her tasks was to exterminate the dozens of mice who sneaked into the less-than-compact structure (she caught fifty in one month).[20] Professor Fracker's portrait was to hang in the anteroom—the thin, sad, intelligent face seeming to mourn the still-rustic accommodations for 30,000 volumes.

It was easier to lodge books than students. And though Buena Vista's needs were legion, none was so imperative as the construction of new dormitories. Lack of dormitory space had plagued the College since the Storm Lake syndicate had constructed two frame halls during the 1890s. One of the buildings had been transformed into a music hall and the other had been destroyed by fire in 1915. In 1942 the College had leased the Lakeshore Hotel for use as a girls' dormitory. The hotel, on the banks of Storm Lake, accommodated thirty students at a cost of $30–$35 a month.[21] While the lakefront location was attractive the building was not, and it was far from the campus. The trustees, in order to house the influx of married GIs, purchased a plot of land along the lake southwest of the main campus, where the field house is now located. Government-owned army barracks were secured to house the former servicemen and their families. Trustee and pastor of the Lakeside Presbyterian Church, Dr. Clarence Richardson, quickly countered downtown rumors of a shanty town going up at the College by recommending the area be named "Vista Park."[22]

While the usual struggle to raise funds continued, a major break came when H. E. Swope, a Minneapolis businessman, contributed $40,000 to the cause. Now past eighty, Swope had resided in the lake city some years before and was the father of Storm Lake resident Mrs. Lurene DeLand. Swope's benevolence, President Olson said, would enable "the College to break ground on Senior Swing Out Day, May 26, 1949."[23] The College gratefully named the new structure Swope Hall. Swope came to Storm Lake to turn the first spadeful of dirt that signified the beginning of construction and was scheduled to come again in May 1950 when the cornerstone was laid. Unfortunately, Swope died one week before the formal dedication of the building that bears his name, but the completion of Swope Hall marked the first major campus construction in a generation. The total cost of the structure, however, was estimated at $200,000 with $50,000 of that sum still needed in the summer of 1949.[24]

The converted library and Swope Hall were the only buildings constructed during the twenty-three years of the Olson administration. The absence of brick and mortar was the fault of neither Olson nor the trustees. Both the Depression and World War II had frustrated expansion plans between 1931 and 1946. The effort made from 1946 to 1953 was modest in view of needs, but again trustees and administrators faced circumstances beyond their control. The College now had to focus upon securing North Central accreditation and hiring a competent postwar faculty with a strong sprinkling of Ph.D.'s. In September 1946 with 480 students at Buena Vista College the prediction of 500 students was becoming a reality, and it was necessary to increase and improve the faculty and administrative staff. A rigorous self-study was undertaken as the College prepared for the North Central investigation. The academic disciplines were moved into a six-division setup with a chairperson appointed by the president over each division. The divisions were:

1. Language and Literature
2. Natural Science
3. Social Science
4. Bible
5. Fine Arts
6. Vocational and Professional Training (Education)

Furthermore, a substantial building program required the participation of influential and wealthy donors. During the Olson administration only two substantial bequests were made to the College. One was the Swope gift in 1949. The other gift was a pledge of $50,000 in 1952 for a new music conservatory. The donor was Mrs. Forest Geisinger Ansley of Tampa, Florida. Mrs. Ansley had been a member of the college faculty, 1912–1914, serving as professor of piano. Her parents, Mr. and Mrs. H. V. Geisinger of Sioux Rapids and Storm Lake, were regarded as prominent citizens of the community and College. Remembering her years at Buena Vista Mrs. Ansley noted:

> The influence of Buena Vista is far reaching. The clean, wholesomeness of its college life, the personal contact of faculty and students, only possible in smaller schools, the beauty of Storm Lake expressed in its environment, churches, homes, gardens and many other factors contribute to the happiness and security of those enrolled.[25]

Still, the great challenge and achievement of the Olson administration was the victorious climax of the long struggle to gain NCA accreditation. Although Buena Vista's credits were acceptable to most graduate institutions within and without the state, there was an increasing stigma because the College remained unaccredited by the NCA. The North Central Association had been in existence since 1895, and by 1915 ten Iowa colleges and universities including Morningside, Penn, Parsons, Simpson, and Upper Iowa were members. By 1945 North Central covered a twenty-state area, and with 312 member institutions was the most prestigious accrediting body in the nation. Loss of accreditation, as Parsons College would discover in 1967, could result in the demise of an institution.[26] Regional accreditation became an added component of survival in postwar America. Furthermore, the Presbyterian Board of Education continuously pressured trustees to gain approval by regional accreditors. Unless Buena Vista College improved her academic image, she was likely to lose out in the postwar rush for students. Acceptance by the NCA involved a herculean effort that began as early as the spring of 1944 and, after the agony of an initial rejection, succeeded in April 1952.

Dean Luman Sampson headed the committee on accreditation. Coming to Buena Vista in 1935, Sampson, along with F. F. Smith, had filled the gap left by Professor Fracker as the intellectual and spiritual leader of the College. Always concise, alert, and with impeccable integrity, Sampson could move quickly to the core of any problem. Sampson's somewhat sober judgement of the universe was tempered by his lively humor and his deep humanity and concern for the welfare of others. He motivated many Buena Vista students to tap their unrealized potential and pursue professional careers. Sampson, who as a relentless and determined conservative stressed self-reliance and the work ethic, pursued his own career until retiring as a "lively elder" at age seventy-seven in 1964. Not yet finished with life, Sampson's house across the street from Swope Hall became a mecca for faculty who knew and loved him until his death at age ninety-nine.

In his report to the faculty Sampson suggested better faculty organization; higher entrance requirements; increased funds for the library; better personnel records; and more attention to social, religious, and guidance programs of the College.[27] These would be some of the internal aspects of the College that the accreditors would investigate. When a preliminary report of North Central was presented to the faculty a year later, Sampson's prognosis was borne out. The report pinpointed a number of needs: (1) Additional books should be purchased and put in the library as soon as possible, (2) magazines should be bound, (3) leniency of the grading system should be questioned, (4) better systems for selecting students should be found, (5) more frequent and regular faculty meetings should be held, (6) the College should have a cultural program, (7) members of the faculty should belong to their respective learned societies, (8) the Church and the College should be more closely united, and (9) a study of the College curriculum should be made.[28]

And so the struggle to gain North Central approval had begun. There were more reports and investigations. Faculty members were interviewed, and a study of the College plant completed. New fund drives were undertaken, for an increased budget was required if accreditation requirements were to be met. From the reports Buena Vista College learned much about itself. In a study presented in 1950, the provincial atmosphere of the institution was noted. Of the 539 students in attendance during the 1949–50 academic year, 517 were from Iowa. Seventy-four percent of the student body lived within fifty miles of Storm Lake and 88 percent within a radius of a hundred miles. While this may have indicated that Buena Vista was providing an important regional educational service, it also gave the College a rural character that it sought to circumvent. There were "crudities in living accommodations," which the College had started to correct with the construction of Swope Hall in 1950. The report also illustrated the excessive teaching load of the faculty, the lack of an insurance program, and the glaring inadequacy of the library which was "well below the median situation in colleges accredited by the North Central Association." The report was critical of the financial administration of the institution, but at the same time acknowledged that the nineteen years of the Olson era had built the resources of the College from "less than nothing to $1,103,668." Athletic scholarships, however, seemed to dominate, and it was pointed out that "athletes receive considerably larger scholarships than other recipients of scholarship." Furthermore, the College stood at the lowest possible percentile regarding employment of Ph.D.'s and only in the nineth percentile for educational experience. The report found the College "at the fourteenth percentile on the criterion of median instructional salary, which probably explains the employment of teachers with limited experience."[29] Buena Vista faced the challenge of demonstrating progress in overcoming these deficiencies before accreditation could be granted.

The Association report indicated that there were some outstanding members of the faculty. Two of these were teachers "with mature scholarship and thorough European training in the fields of languages and economics."[30] The report was speaking of Professor George Brozaitis of the department of economics and Professor Albert Hirsch of the Division of Languages and Literature.

Dark-haired George Brozaitis had studied in Germany, England, and in his homeland of Lithuania where he obtained his doctorate in 1940. For three years he had been assistant price administrator for the Lithuanian government and later was a member of the Lithuanian Board of Trade. Following World War II, Brozaitis entered the U.S. Occupation Zone and worked for the United States army as a lecturer and English language instructor. Eventually, he fell into President Olson's procurement net and became a mainstay of the Buena Vista faculty for several years.[31]

But Albert Hirsch came to Buena Vista to stay. A native of Frankfurt, Hirsch had gone to Munich to study and had received his Ph.D. in 1912 and served in the German army during World War I. Subsequently, he taught in Frankfurt, published a widely used German reader and German grammar book, and received academic tenure and apparent security. Then came the Nazi regime. Professor Hirsch lost his tenured position. For a time he survived as the headmaster of a prestigious Jewish school in Frankfurt; but when the Nazi persecution intensified in 1938, he and his wife Lilly were incarcerated in the horror camp at Buchenwald. The Hirsch children had been sent to England in a special children's transport. In August 1939 the Hirsches were among the last permitted to emigrate to England, where they managed a hostel in Birmingham during the height of the Battle of Britain. Later, Professor Hirsch taught at an English grammar school, and in 1946 fulfilled his long intention of coming to the United States. War and persecution may have made Hirsch more sensitive to the frailties of human nature but did not dull his intellect or wit. The Hirsches arrived in New York City on a sweltering day in July 1946. When the inevitable American question of first impressions came, Hirsch replied, "Hot and noisy." The ways of democracy sometimes proved perplexing. When Lilly Hirsch spotted President Fisher shoveling his driveway one cold winter morning, she shook her head and muttered, "Only in America." In Europe no professional would engage in such menial tasks.[32]

Albert and Lilly Hirsch joined a faculty of twenty-eight full-time teachers and an administrative staff of five when they started the 1946–47 academic year in a tranquil Storm Lake that seemed far removed from the suffering Europe of that fall and winter. The academic dean doubled as registrar and taught sociology. The dean of women taught commercial courses and did secretarial work for the president, and the wife of the business manager occasionally helped in that office.[33] In two decades of devoted service the brilliant and cultured Hirsch was to become one of the legends of Buena Vista College. Along with G. H. Fracker, F. F. Smith, L. W. Sampson, and George Reynolds, he was one of the most beloved of professors. The Hirsches entered into the life of College and city and became active citizens of their adopted country.

Personal tragedy produced no lasting bitterness in the Hirsches. They returned to Germany in 1962 and again in 1963 as Dr. Hirsch helped in the preparation of a book on the Nazi persecution of the Frankfurt Jews. They met old friends and former students. Young Germans coming to America were welcomed in their home. When Ingrid Cumberland arrived from Germany as a young wife in 1959, she was soon invited to Dr. Hirsch's German class. After initial probing, a warm relationship soon developed with Lilly Hirsch. Invited to dinner at the Cumberland home, Lilly Hirsch rubbed her finger across the counter and proclaimed, "Ah, a German kitchen." The Hirsches would accompany the Cumberlands to Sioux City when Mrs. Cumberland received her citizenship.

Nor did the Hirsches feel isolated in the vast plains of mid-America. With his usual simplicity and sincerity, Hirsch informed the Storm Lake Rotarians in 1946, "Personally, I am glad that I have reached this part of America, a small city in the Middle West, where I can see the real heart of America at close perspective."[34] The services that Hirsch was to perform for Buena Vista College were legion. He was the leader of those who stood for academic excellence; a mature scholar and a mellow human being who could deflate sham gently but effectively, wink at the minor follies, and pursue his goals with a wise tolerance and quiet dedication. As one student recalled:

> He was an early morning person, so he taught German at 7:30 A.M. For two years I struggled to stay awake, and only the fact that this remarkable personality was at the front of the room enabled me to present a semblance of life in his classroom. His was not simply a course in the German language, but one in which he shared with us his profound insights into the culture of that country and people. His knowledge of opera was also interspersed into the course. I'll always remember his commentaries concerning opera when he and his wife invited me into their home to listen to the Metropolitan Opera broadcasts with them.[35]

The Hirsches enjoyed social relationships. Lilly Hirsch was active in the Faculty Dames and the Hirsch residence, a small, well-kept bungalow on Fourth Street, was a frequent gathering place of friends and guests. Rudy Hirsch, the son, became a successful business executive and a member of the Board of Trustees, serving from 1978 until his death in 1984. Dr. Hirsch was seventy-six when he retired in 1964 (the College was just beginning to enforce mandatory retirement at sixty-five). Albert and Lilly Hirsch maintained an active interest in Buena Vista College throughout their long and rich lives, which ended within a few months of one another in 1977.

As the battle for accreditation continued, President Olson

sought to attract other competent scholars to the Buena Vista campus. In 1947 and 1948 Gladys and Theodore Kuehl were added to the Buena Vista faculty. Gladys recalled:

> It was in 1947 that I received a notice from the Speech Association of America Placement Bureau, indicating a vacancy in the Speech Department of a "liberal arts college in the midwest" — not even the name of the institution and location of the college were listed, but the description of the college sounded good.[36]

The Kuehls, looking for moorings and seeking good schools for their two children, found the setting of the city and College campus impressive. They were even more impressed by the "cordial greeting" of the administrative staff. The interview with President Olson went well, and before the afternoon was over Gladys had been signed to a position in the speech department where she "was expected to build an entire curriculum — with various extra-curricular activities to direct," and Ted was to assume the entire burden of the education and psychology courses for the summer session, because of the illness of the professor of education. That summer the Kuehls resided at the Willows Motel across from the city park close to the lake, ate their meals in downtown restaurants, and partook of summer activities at the College.[37] It was the beginning of a career that would ultimately place Dr. Kuehl among the top half-dozen teachers in the life of the College as she built a speech program acclaimed throughout the Middle West.

Ted Kuehl spent the summer of 1947 teaching at Buena Vista and the following year as principal at Aurelia High School. He then joined the College faculty as chairperson of the Division of Education and Business Administration, where he remained until his premature death in 1962. Kuehl, tall and dark, with dancing, mischievous eyes, came from a varied background in the business and educational world. There was a pungent yet gentle sarcasm about him, and he had a way of exposing the hyperbole that occasionally crept into faculty meetings. He revitalized the education program at Buena Vista; he directed the Placement Bureau; and he sponsored the Circle K organization. Circle K members provided the funds for the flagpole erected in Professor Kuehl's memory and served as pall bearers at his funeral.[38] Another able faculty member who arrived on campus in 1948 was Dr. Donald Graham, professor of history and government. In his six years at Buena Vista, before leaving for the Wisconsin State University system, Professor Graham left a reputation of excellent scholarship.

When Dr. Sampson expressed the desire to return to full-time teaching in 1947, President Olson selected thirty-four-year-old William D. Wesselink as dean of the College. At this time Wesselink, an air force veteran, was chief of the veterans' guidance center at Buena Vista. An outstanding athlete at Central College where he had received the B.A. degree in 1931, Wesselink pursued graduate work at the universities of Iowa (M.A., 1932) and Minnesota. There followed years of high school teaching at Pierpont, South Dakota, and Hawarden, Iowa, before he became an instructor in mathematics at Emmetsburg Junior College in 1936. Two years later Wesselink became the dean of Webster City Junior College and served in this capacity until he entered military service in 1942.[39] Wesselink was already well known and well liked in Storm Lake, and the *Pilot-Tribune* hailed his selection as "another step forward" in the progress of Buena Vista College.[40] Wesselink combined the duties of registrar and student counselor with the deanship. A sympathetic understanding of human difficulties and a steadfast loyalty to the College were his trademarks for nearly three decades. Twice, at critical moments in the College's history, Wesselink would be asked to serve as interim president.

The first effort to gain acceptance by the North Central Association failed. The blow of rejection was not softened by the kind words of Dean Wesselink who informed the faculty that only one college had ever been accepted on the first application.[41] There was, of course, much work to be done and neither Olson nor his staff nor the trustees had any intention of turning back.

During the long years of struggle, President Olson may at times have seemed like a hard trail boss as he warned the faculty that "we must do more research and there must be a greater contribution by the faculty to the general welfare of the College." The divisional structure also needed additional clarification and plans had to be made "to secure an annuity and pension system for every faculty member."[42]

The year 1951–52 saw the College enter a whirlwind campaign in order to gain the coveted accreditation. Failure to gain approval from North Central meant the State of Iowa would no longer extend accreditation to Buena Vista education graduates. Since 90 percent of Buena Vista graduates entered the profession of teaching, the loss of state accreditation would threaten survival.[43] A new financial campaign to net more than $100,000 was launched and completed, new books were added to the library, courses of study were added, and new Ph.D.'s were lured to the campus. Then on April 2, 1952, President Olson and Dean Wesselink left the decisive NCA meeting in Chicago and telegraphed the College that Buena Vista had been admitted into the North Central Association. The next day President Olson arrived in Storm Lake on the Illinois Central. As he looked out the window, he could see a large crowd on the station platform—the entire faculty and student body, hundreds of townspeople, and the College band playing "Hail, Hail, the Gang's All Here." As Olson stepped from the platform the band played the "Alma Mater" written years before by Professor Maryanna Hamer. Then Olson in his greatest moment walked through a wildly cheering throng to a waiting automobile. He would proclaim for all to hear that acceptance into North Central "is the greatest victory the College has won in its sixty-one years."[44] A few weeks later Olson was honored by a recognition banquet in Swope Hall and presented with a "beautiful Scottish Rite Masonic Ring" as a gift from the faculty. Willis Edson and the trustees gave Olson an electric clock. Edson and Olson received standing ovations from the guests present at the recognition banquet.[45]

Neither President Olson nor Willis Edson were cognizant that this was the zenith of their long services to Buena Vista College. From this point the descent from the mountaintop would be rapid. Both Willis Edson and President Olson had carried Buena Vista College through seemingly impossible times. They had literally resurrected the institution and given it life. And yet in little more than a year Willis Edson could say with no little bitterness, "The Chamber of Commerce presented Henry with the keys to the city. They spread their garments and palm leaves in his path. A year and a half later the High Priests crucified him."[46]

There were, however, still to be some happy days at Buena Vista College in 1952. In one of the most noble actions yet undertaken by the College, Professor F. F. Smith was given appropriate and deserved honor. Born in Walpole, Massachusetts, in 1874, Frederic F. Smith had received his academic training at Tufts and later at the University of Iowa.[47] He was a curious, energetic man who had been a world traveler and teacher—living in England, Canada, and Africa for extended periods. He reached Buena Vista during the administration of President Stanton Olinger in 1919. An avid collector of specimens (he kept a skeleton in the closet of his classroom), Smith was a profound scholar and inspiring teacher who steered numerous students into the fields of medicine and science. Even though Buena Vista paid him little or not at all, this frugal man rode a bicycle and saved and invested through the years. Some were surprised and even found it distasteful (feeling a teacher should accumulate little of this world's goods) that when the old man died in 1961 he possessed an estate of $186,000. He was probably unaware of the extent of his holdings. His character was beyond question and he was devoted to both profession and College. He left a vast collection of lecture and research notes written in several languages, which revealed a wide acquaintance with international journals and a detailed knowledge of a variety of scientific fields.

Buena Vista's 1952 Homecoming was dedicated to Professor Smith. The "Grand Old Man" of the College was honored at a silver tea at the president's home. He rode in a new convertible during the Saturday morning parade and sat in a place of honor during the football game with Upper Iowa.[48] As the College band, directed by guest conductor Karl King, performed the half-time salute, the old man stepped onto the playing field and gazed into the throng in the stadium. At that moment the card section came to life and spelled out SMITH HALL.[49] It dawned on Dr. Smith that the building in which he had labored for a generation would from that moment on bear his name. When the inscription was finally emblazoned across the old Science Building, Professor Smith, perhaps groping for an appropriate remark murmured, "Well, it is quite undeserved, but very nice."[50] Until his death in November 1961, Professor Smith would continue to march in all the academic processions and to attend all the College banquets. In a brief eulogy Professor Sampson could truly say, "His was a life devoted to the cause of education in the truest sense. His was a character of integrity. He was a scholar in the best sense of the term. His life was an inspiration to all who came under his influence."[51]

World War II had brought Rosie the Riveter into national focus, expanded the number of women in the work force, opened up new professions. Despite these important milestones along the brush-infested path towards true equality between the sexes, academic historians can illustrate how difficult it has been to break established patterns in the educational world. Buena Vista College was no exception. After World War II the beginning salary for men teachers was low enough, $2,600, but for women it was only $1,900.[52] Professors were paid on the basis of a nine-month contract. Men were paid extra for summer teaching but women, although expected to teach if asked, were not. The conventional view was that women teachers were either married (so their husbands were responsible for living expenses) or were single without family (and therefore did not need the money). This seemed "barbaric" to Gladys Kuehl who headed a delegation to President Olson to remedy the obvious injustice. By the time the delegation reached Olson's office only Gladys remained, for the others had reasoned loss of courage preferable to what they feared might mean loss of jobs. However, the following year the policy was changed.[53]

When Willis Edson attended a meeting of the Presbyterian Synod at Ames on July 7, 1953, he was given a standing ovation by the delegates. The reason for the acclaim was the splendid work that Edson, as president of the College trustees, had accomplished at Buena Vista.[54] The Synod took note that Edson had been connected with the College for sixty-three years either as a student or as a trustee.

He has had faith through the years that the college was needed in its place, that the church should support it, and that it has had something to offer to young people. In that faith, he has stood firm in many a crisis, given money and asked it from other people, and never permitted a thought to come that the college could close or cease to go forward.[55]

The College had weathered both the Depression and World War II. It had been accredited by the North Central Association. The prospects for Buena Vista's future were the brightest in history. Edson could feel that a half-century of arduous labor had resulted in a final triumph. It would not be long until he would have completed a golden anniversary of service that dated back to 1904.

Then in October 1953 the College and community were stunned when President Olson suddenly announced his resignation. The *Des Moines Register* reported that Olson was the oldest president in the state in length of service, that he had eliminated the College debt and balanced the budget for seventeen years, achieved North Central accreditation, and that enrollment for the 1953–54 academic year was up by 20 percent.[56] And yet in a move the causes of which remain vague after half-a-century, the Olson administration had been toppled. The proceedings had the air of a coup engineered by the Synod and the Board of Education of the Presbyterian Church. At the age of sixty-two and after almost twenty-three years as president, Olson prepared to relinquish his post. In one of his final statements Olson said:

I had an ambition to make Buena Vista College a highly accredited and outstanding institution of higher learning in the realm of Christian education. I wished to lay a foundation that would insure its future security and educational service. In my humble opinion this has been accomplished.[57]

Actually, the action of the Synod and the Board of Education appears to have been encouraged by a number of trustees who felt that Buena Vista must make more radical changes than Olson and Edson were willing to endorse if it was going to remain competitive. Clandestine breakfast meetings were held in cafes to discuss how to change the image of the College without damaging Olson and Edson whom they genuinely respected and readily acknowledged had done so much to save the institution from extinction, but whom they felt had not caught the vision of future possibilities.[58] The trustees consulted with the Board of Christian Education and the Synod. Recommendations came from the Board of Christian Education, which led the Synod Council, and the Committee on Christian Education to appoint a committee of seven headed by Dr. Charles E. Friley, president of Iowa State University. The committee undertook several investigations during the summer and fall of 1953 as it "studied the situation in detail." There was now a determination emanating from the highest governing bodies of the Presbyterian church "to place Buena Vista College on such a sound educational basis as will insure its proper development as an acceptable Presbyterian College."[59]

Thus the impetus for the removal of Olson and the resignation of the incumbent Board of Trustees appeared to come from the Board of Christian Education and Synod as they reviewed conditions at Buena Vista and probably came to share the concerns of a significant number of Board members. The Synod Council met in Des Moines on October 13, 1953, and recommended the resignation of both Olson and the Board of Trustees and the selection of a qualified new Board that would appoint William Wesselink as acting president while it sought a replacement for Olson. The Synod then decided to undertake a study of the other Presbyterian colleges in Iowa in an effort to see which institutions the church should support.[60] The actual order appears to have come from the Board of Christian Education and was carried out by the Synod of Iowa. The Synod had the right to dismiss the trustees because it had elected them.[61]

Trustee president, Willis Edson, called the Board together on Monday, November 2. Olson's resignation was not his idea. The Board met jointly with the Board of Visitors, and H. E. Stalcup convened and presided over the joint meeting. Stalcup had been to Philadelphia to meet with the National Board of Christian Education and had returned with a check for more than $12,000.[62] In fact, the Synod suggested the rather large body of trustees, forty in all, also resign by December 31. Apparently the Synod, in an action that Edson felt violated the constitution and bylaws of the

College, wanted a complete reorganization.[63] Three reasons for demanding Olson's resignation were presented to the perplexed Edson: (1) opposition of at least half of Storm Lake businessmen to the Olson administration, (2) opposition of a large number of churches and pastors, (3) an apparent lack of "religious penetration in the student body."[64]

To the Synod the present administration seemed archaic and the Board too large to be effective. The demands of accreditation and new buildings had resulted in a new overall deficit of $141,132.97 on December 1, 1953. Of this, $74,500 were outstanding First Serial Mortgage Bonds, and more than $66,000 in current debt.[65] One reason for the Synod's steamroller action may have been that Olson and his unwieldy board lacked fund-raising expertise. A debt once cleared was now re-emerging—the full extent of which the Board would discover later.[66] While the Synod no doubt appreciated the long service that Olson had rendered the institution, it possibly concluded that the affluent era of the 1950s called for younger and more dynamic leadership. Olson's economy-minded administration had saved Buena Vista from extinction, but new buildings would have to be constructed and the faculty rescued from poverty. The survival mentality still occupied President Olson—it was too entrenched for him to embark upon new ventures. The Synod questioned not his dedication, but his acclimation to the new age of education in the American century. A change in pilots was necessary to reclaim Buena Vista College for the Presbyterian church and impose new standards of academic progress.

Olson's Lutheran upbringing was not a factor in his forced resignation. The practical Olson not only joined but became an elder in Storm Lake's Lakeside Presbyterian Church. What bothered Olson's critics was that Olson did not seem to realize that he could not improve Buena Vista's standing among midwestern colleges by riding the cattle train to Chicago for conventions, that the "cheapest" professors did not bring professional excellence, and that modern management required a certain elegance that the president had out of necessity placed on the back burner. There were hundreds of returning GIs, there was government money to

be had, and it would take a new and dynamic vision to maintain
the hard-won accreditation. Nor was a college president so long
established prone to listen to suggestions.[67] Nevertheless, the dismissal was sudden and brutal. There was no prior notice and Olson
was not able to finish the semester let alone the year.

The suddenness of Olson's departure was disconcerting to
many of the faculty and staff whose loyalty to Olson was exceeded
only by their loyalty to the College. They, too, had known the pain
of the struggle to relieve the College from stifling debt, to gain
accreditation, to use makeshift quarters, to recruit qualified students. Like Olson, the faculty believed the corner had been turned
and Buena Vista was on its way. Of course he could be blunt, he
sometimes wounded the pride of area businessmen and clergy, and
he had no national sources of support. As Lilly Hirsch vividly
recalled, "Whatever he did, thought, lived for, it was meant for the
progress and for the good of the College. He had no other outside
interests. If he hurt a number of people, and he did, nobody was
ever hurt as he was, with the sudden dismissal at the height of his
success." Mrs. Hirsch remained adamant in her conviction that
Olson had that "special gift" of demanding and creating loyalty
from his faculty and that "never again was there the same cooperation and unity of purpose."[68] Olson had been kind to the Hirsches.
He had the wisdom to realize the contribution to the College these
German-Jewish refugees could make, thus he extended an offer of
employment and was helpful in every way possible. He received
their steadfast loyalty in return.

Meanwhile the Synod hierarchy endeavored to maintain faculty morale and ease fears that a general purge was under way. Dr.
Charles B. Friley, chairperson of the Board of Visitors, informed
the faculty that while the Synod had requested the resignations it
"did not consider itself a policy-forming body and would cease to
function with the inauguration of a new Board of Trustees to be
chosen by the Synod." Any changes in College personnel would be
the responsibility of the new administration. The Synod's goal was
to assure adequate financial support that would enable the College
to build a future enrollment of 600–800 students.[69]

Certainly, Henry Olson merits a position at the top of the

Buena Vista legend. He brought the College through the most trying era imaginable and carried burdens that in retrospect seem
incredible. Along with Willis Edson he revived the heartbeat of an
institution near death. The team of Edson and Olson had battled
and liquidated debt, won admission into North Central, increased
the enrollment, and added two new buildings to the College campus. Now more buildings, an expanded curriculum and faculty,
higher salaries, and fringe benefits were mandatory if Buena Vista
College was to be competitive and maintain her accreditation.
While only Henry Olson could have lifted Buena Vista from the
doldrums of the Depression, the Synod felt the nuclear age required a new vision.

Naturally, the severing of relations was painful for the Moses
who had led the flock to Canaan. The incumbent Board, upset by
their own as well as the president's impending dismissal, voted that
Olson be paid full salary until August 31, 1954, and a monthly
pension of $200 after that. Then bowing to Synod pressure, the
Board voted to resign at the end of the year.[70] However, the new
Board rescinded the generous pension provisions, initially reducing
the monthly amount to $81.92, and finally getting Olson to agree
to a lump sum settlement. The Board seemed to act with unusual
pique, raising F. F. Smith's pension from $50 to $75 a month while
reducing Olson's.[71] The Board found Olson's life annuity a vexing
problem because of the lean financial conditions of the College.
Meanwhile, the Board of Visitors maintained that the only promise
made to Olson at the time of his resignation was "that his salary
would be continued to June 30, 1954." The Board actually continued Olson's salary until the end of August, and a small settlement
appears to have been made beyond that. Olson's salary as president, which never exceeded $6,500, along with the less-than-gener-
ous final settlement did not enable the deposed president to retire
in comfort.[72] Olson, who had never accumulated great wealth, sold
stocks and bonds in Minneapolis "until his death one cold winter
morning waiting for the street car to take him to work."[73] Somehow the new Board deemed Olson wealthier than perhaps he was,
that he would be eligible for social security at age sixty-five, that
according to actuary tables the $200 pension would add a burden-

some institutional debt of $30,000, and that there was no legal or binding obligation to Olson for such a pension.[74] The still precarious financial condition of the College was heightened by the discovery that the College had an excess of $60,000 in unpaid debts. Although no fault of Olson's, this influenced the new Board in their seemingly tight-fisted approach to Olson's pension. It was now asserted that the obligation of the Board was a moral one — to recognize Olson for his twenty-three years of service, during which he helped "carry the institution through the perilous years of the depression."[75] Such was the exit of Henry Olson!

It was a heart-rending moment for Willis Edson, who believed that neither the Board of Education nor the area churches had ever given Buena Vista the support it deserved. He had grown old in the service of Buena Vista College. It had been his project and he had loved it. If "age is but a quality of mind," as Edson had once said, then Buena Vista had kept him young. Certainly it had kept him active. He had been hurt beyond words, but he remained loyal to the institution during the twilight of his life. He had given the College part of his fortune and of his heart. He had persuaded others to do the same, and was sure now that Buena Vista would succeed. Edson was convinced that the expertise of the poorly paid faculty rivaled that of most institutions of similar size.

Edson would sometimes feel forgotten and neglected by the younger men who replaced him — those who wore expensive, tailored suits and traveled in jets and built monuments fitting for a new age. The lines of graduates and faculty would continue to grow, but the men Edson had known would fade from memory. In late November 1961, Lakeshore Drive would be the scene of the Edsons's fiftieth wedding anniversary. Sometime later there came a note from Henry Olson with words that could not help but reduce the sting of being left behind:

> I could not help but reflect about the tremendous accomplishments which you and your wife have made in the last half century. Of all your accomplishments, I believe the struggle you put forth in saving Buena Vista College stands out as a monumental achievement.[76]

THE MIDDLE YEARS

1940–1960

1

2

3

1   George H. Fracker, a brilliant self-taught universal scholar, devoted a lifetime to the welfare of the College. One of the first professors employed by Buena Vista, Fracker arrived to teach ancient languages in 1891. From then until he retired in 1929 Fracker was the strength of the College.   **2** Fracker Library, 1946. The converted army surplus brick-covered barrack was named in honor of Professor George Fracker, who left his collection of classics to the library. It housed a collection of over 35,000 volumes for twenty years, until the completion of the Ballou Library.   **3**   Interior of the Fracker Library in the late 1940s.

4

5

4 Science Hall, built in 1925. It was renamed Smith Hall in 1952 in honor of Professor F. F. Smith, the "Grand Old Man" of Buena Vista. **5** The great F. F. "Bugs" Smith, long-time head of the Division of Natural Sciences, taught at the College from 1919 to 1952.

6   7

8   9

At the fiftieth Commencement of the College in 1941, honorary degrees were conferred upon two of Buena Vista's most distinguished graduates, Dr. Stanley R. Fracker and Dr. Clifford M. Dury. **6** Stanley Fracker, president of the class of 1910. As a USDA scientist in 1959 he was awarded the German Order of Merit for outstanding work in promoting the exchange of German and American scientists. (USDA photo) **7** C. M. Dury, class of 1918, served in the Chemical Warfare Service in World War I and as navy chaplain in World War II. He received his Ph.D. at the University of Edinburgh and was the author of *A History of the Chaplain Corps* and other works. **8** Dr. Luman W. Sampson, chair of the Division of Social Sciences and dean of the College in the 1940s, in a characteristic pose of "mellow pessimism." Sampson was always interested in academic achievement and inaugurated the Buena Vista Honor Society in 1936. **9** Jake LaFoy, director of admissions (1954–1969), persuaded many students to attend Buena Vista.

10

11

10 Kermit Buntrock, a witty, dedicated, articulate, and well-liked trustee and member of the faculty.   **11** Homecoming parade, 1952.

12

13

12 President and Mrs. Halverson in a Homecoming parade, 1960s. Marian Halverson was a great lady with a strong social conscience. **13** Bill Green, director of bands and fine arts chairperson from 1950s to 1970s.

14   **15**

16

14 Professor Gladys Kuehl, architect of Buena Vista's prestigious forensics program from the 1940s to the 1960s. One of the all-time great teachers at Buena Vista.   **15** Professor Ted Kuehl, head of the department of education during the Olson and Fisher eras, 1947–1962.   **16** Gladys Kuehl leads the forensics team on a trip in the early 1950s.

17

18

19

17 Dr. Albert Hirsch in German class. One of the legends of Buena Vista, Hirsch escaped from Nazi Germany in 1939. He became chair of the Division of Languages and Literature in 1946. For two decades the brilliant and cultured Hirsch taught with tolerance and dedication.　**18** Faculty gathering of Hirsches, Grahams, Reeds, Landises, and Marhags in early 1950s. Lilly Hirsch is at the right.　**19** President Henry Olson in the 1940s. Most long-time Storm Lake residents insist that Olson, who guided Buena Vista to North Central Association accreditation in 1952, saved the College from extinction during a decade of economic depression.

20

20 Men's residence halls completed in 1956 and 1962, named after trustees Z. Z. White (*left*) and H. A. Pierce. An addition to Pierce Hall in 1965 increased the capacity of the complex to 366.

21

22

21 Freshman mixer during the more tranquil 1950s when coke was Coke.   **22** A Neanderthal brigade emerges triumphant with loot taken during a panty raid in the 1950s.

23

24

23 Ruth Ann and Jack Fisher at the beginning of his presidency, 1954.   **24** Graduation Day in the 1950s. (*From left*) Dean Wesselink, speaker, President Fisher, trustee president Dixon.

25

25 Old Main was the symbol and rallying point of Buena Vista College for sixty-four years. The trees surrounding it were planted during the traditional planting ceremonies of Senior Tree Day. (Photo by Buntrock-Salie, Storm Lake)

26

27

26 Old Main burning. In 1956 the entire community aided in salvaging irreplaceable contents and mourned its loss.   **27** The shell of Old Main following the 1956 fire. The destruction was the end of an era, but it was also the beginning of the "New Buena Vista." (Photos by Arthur N. Hough, Storm Lake)

28

29

28 A new building rose on the ashes of Old Main, named for veteran trustees Paul Dixon and Tom Eilers. The building houses administrative and faculty offices, twenty classrooms, the Grace Memorial Little Theatre, and the Forest Geisinger Ansley Department of Music.   **29** The Victory Arch, reassembled from the stone entrance to Old Main, became a symbol of the strength and continuity of Buena Vista College.

30

31

30 Willis Edson, from his days as a student athlete in the 1890s, through forty years as a trustee and chairman of the Board, never wavered in his devotion and service to the College. **31** New faculty members arrived during the Fisher regime of the 1950s to strengthen the academic program of the College. (*Top row from left*) Professor Ronald Smith, biology, initiated a yearly marine biology trip to Jamaica. Dr. James Christiansen, chemistry, came from a career in industry. The Reverend Henry Eggink. (*Second row*) Dr. Robert Tollefson, an outstanding teacher who became one of the real consciences of the College, and the Reverend Lester Williams strengthened the department of Bible and philosophy with their respective interests in teaching, academics, logic, and archaeology. Professor Donald Cox became chair of the Division of Education before leaving to accept a position with the Department of Education in 1967. Dr. Felix Cruz, formerly dean of the University of Havana Business College, was appointed to the business administration and economics department where he served with distinction 1961–1969.

32

32 A scene in Sunset Park depicts the natural beauty of the College setting.

9

THE BEAVER HERITAGE

That Stone Arch is also a symbol of the future of the
College. It is a symbol of the determination . . . to build
. . . an institution of Christian higher education which
will more effectively serve . . . the youth of today and
tomorrow.

—PRESIDENT WENDELL HALVERSON

The struggle for survival did not keep Buena Vista College students from creating an enviable line of traditions. Some of
these perished with time or were discarded by the changing priorities of new generations of students who had come to regard them
as immature. Nevertheless, each tradition was meaningful to the
class that originated it. These were the symbols that united the
classes long after graduation. And a few of the traditions born during the formative years of the College have achieved a permanency
that time will not easily uproot.

Student activity in the 1890s revolved around the literary and
debating societies, which fall more into the category of organizations than traditions. Two early literary societies were the L.Y.H.
Society, named in honor of President Loyal Y. Hays, and the Jane
Addams Society, named in honor of the famous progressive and
founder of Hull House. Jane Addams was the sister-in-law of John
M. Linn, Buena Vista president, 1892–94. There is no record, however, of Miss Addams ever having visited the Buena Vista College
campus. Both societies died before the turn of the century and were
replaced by the Star Society, founded in 1896, and the Franklin
Society, founded in 1898.[1] These literary and debating societies

flourished until the early 1920s when the rise of campus organizations and social fraternities and sororities brought about their demise. For several decades, however, the rivalry between the Stars
and Franklins was intense. Both societies were interested in stimulating the intellect and in developing oratorical style. Numerous in-
tersociety debates were held, and in 1902 the two societies wrestled
with the question, "Resolved. That the policy of the United States
with regard to the Philippines subsequent to the Spanish-American
War should be approved."[2] The Franklins won the debate and
emerged with the Bradford Silver Cup, which was to become the
permanent possession of the society that won three of the debates.
After their initial loss to the Franklins, the Stars won three consecutive debates and retired the Silver Cup.[3] There was also the Faville
and Whitney Debating Cup retired by the Franklins, the Blayney-
Ross Debating Cup permanently won by the Stars, and the S. A.
Ensign Debating Cup offered by Mr. S. A. Ensign in 1915–16. As
late as 1915, the Stars and Franklins were still providing a major
portion of the social life of the College.[4] Every serious-minded student aspired to belong to one of the two organizations. The meetings, which were held twice a month on Friday evenings, ended
with games and refreshments.

During those Victorian days both smoking and dancing (not to
mention drinking) were forbidden on campus. Possibly interesting
things happened at the meetings, because in November 1902 the
faculty passed a rule providing for the segregation of the sexes at
the meetings of the literary societies—a rule that was quickly rescinded because of its unpopularity.[5] While World War I cast off the
aura of American innocence and certainly promoted the use of to-
bacco as a sophisticated and relaxing, even healthful fad, Buena
Vista did not alter its restrictions. Indeed, as late as 1928 new students were reminded that "it has always been a tradition that
Beavers do not smoke on campus."[6]

The intellectual life of the College also revolved around the
College newspaper, the *Tack,* preceded by several other papers. One
of these was the *College Yell,* which was the continuation of an earlier paper known as the *Commercial Review,* published by P. B. S.
Peters of the commercial department. A paper was also published

by another literary society, the Philomatheans, which flourished briefly during the 1890s. This paper, which was the forerunner of the *Tack*, was edited by a determined Irishman, J. P. Mullen.[7] Mullen, born in Ireland, had settled on a farm near Fonda. After a brief stint in public school teaching, he became a livestock dealer, the co-owner of a farm implement business, and the owner of 1,300 acres of choice Iowa farmland.[8] Because of his leadership qualities Mullen was designated as the "head of the *Tack*," while the editor of local news, Miss Emma Anderson, was known as the "point of the *Tack*." Supposedly, the decision of the Philomatheans to publish the *Tack* as a regular paper was made while the society was completing one of its "expeditions to Alta."[9]

Mullen, who became the father of nine children, left Buena Vista College in 1895. However, with F. C. Aldinger as editor, the *Tack* was to become the permanent College paper. Emma Anderson, J. C. Abels, Belle Ranney, Nellie Mack, F. O. Leonard, Elizabeth Sohm, W. C. Edson, and John T. Edson were other members of the staff.[10] Another story concerning the origins of the *Tack* was carried in the October 1905 edition.

> As a society paper it was not called the *Tack* until in January of 1895 when an exceptionally good paper was produced. In the course of the preparation of this number a box of tacks was accidentally upset and spilled. Thus the name "Tack" suggested itself and that number was so called. Before this each number had a different name which was chosen by those preparing it.[11]

During these years the *Tack* was a monthly magazine publishing literary and historical articles written by students. Articles ranged from "The Land Where Lost Things Go" to "The Women of Shakespeare's Principal Comedies."[12] The somewhat rigid but very competent advisor of the *Tack* staff 1902–22 was Miss Alice Wilcox, professor of English.

Elizabeth Sohm became editor of the *Tack* in the fall of 1896. This was the beginning of a long newspaper career for Miss Sohm. After her departure from Buena Vista College, Miss Sohm went to work for the *Storm Lake Vidette*, the *Pilot-Tribune's* Democratic rival. By 1905 she was the owner of the paper. Although the *Vidette* had its problems, Miss Sohm impressed Joseph Morcombe of the *Cedar Rapids Gazette*.[13] The two were married in 1908, and in 1923 the Morcombes departed for California. Six years earlier, Mrs. Morcombe had sold her interest in the *Vidette* to J. R. Bell of Alta, but she long maintained an interest in the Storm Lake community and in Buena Vista College.[14] Nor did the death of her husband in 1942 halt a life filled with activity—past eighty years of age in 1954, Mrs. Morcombe was the manager of a printing shop in California. Her brother Joseph Sohm, also a Buena Vista College graduate, had become the manager of the California Packing Corporation.[15]

Other members of the original *Tack* staff moved successfully into the professional and business world. The Edson brothers, Willis and John, graduated from the University of Iowa Law School and began a lifetime of community service around Storm Lake and Schaller. F. O. Leonard, J. C. Abels, and editor F. C. Aldinger all entered the ministry. In 1918 Abels, after an absence of two decades, wrote the *Tack* that he had traveled in twenty countries and circumnavigated the globe.[16] Nell Mack had attended Northwestern University in 1896 and in 1900 married Van Wagenen. Emma Anderson enrolled in Moody Bible Institute and in 1906 married the Reverend B. B. Sutcliffe. In 1897 Belle Ranney had married Robert Bleakley of Storm Lake who was for many years a trustee of the College.[17] One of the early business managers of the *Tack* was E. S. Benjamin, who served in that capacity in 1897–98. Benjamin had been the *Tack's* literary editor the previous year when it was still a monthly literary magazine. It cost $12.50 plus postage to get each issue printed (it cost $124 in 1990) and some of the early issues "went into the red." Benjamin recalled that he was able to put out every issue "promptly and pay all the bills."[18]

The *Tack*—in some years its point sharper than in others—was to continue to be an important training ground for a variety of careers. It was also a sounding board for student proposals as well as frustrations, and wise administrations read the student paper with care. By 1911 the paper devoted its pages to campus news and had ceased to be primarily a literary magazine. By the mid-1920s the *Tack* had become a full-fledged student newspaper. The 1930 *Tack* received an honor rating from the National Press Association.[19] During the late 1930s Louise Flynn Zerschling (class of 1938) became editor. This marked the beginning of a long career in journalism, for Zerschling became a distinguished feature writer for the *Sioux City Journal* and the recipient of numerous awards from the Iowa Associated Press, the Managing Editors Association, and the Iowa and National Press Women. In 1982 she received the Distinguished Service Award from the Buena Vista College Alumni Association.[20]

Unfortunately, the *Tack* had neither a steady existence nor complete preservation. Consequently, there are some gaps. Some issues during the 1930s and 1940s are missing, and the paper became more of an administrative than student organ in the late 1960s and early 1970s. For years the *Tack* was a bimonthly publication, but was printed weekly in 1969, then reduced to ten issues a year in 1972. No issues at all were published from the winter of 1973 to April 1974. Ingeborg Stolee, a respected professor of English (the Stolee lecture is named in her honor), oversaw a quality paper in the early 1960s. During this era, Koy Sheets, Maryann Nitzke, and Denise Benna served as editors and Dave Lampe (1958–62) produced a controversial column in which he invented a bizarre, fictional character known as Wolfgang von Nutbread and championed the elimination of Monday.[21]

A colorful Austrian, Dr. Karl Lichtenecker, served as *Tack* advisor for a year during the late 1960s. A gifted linguist with a Ph.D. from the University of Vienna, Lichtenecker had once been press attaché at the Austrian embassy in Washington and had worked in the government press service in Vienna. He was accepted as a gifted scholar who brought his attractive wife and infant son with him to the Buena Vista campus. He was also a romantic, an intellectual mountebank dashing hither and thither, often without much purpose. Back in his home country, Lichtenecker was later apprehended and convicted (of establishing an information service for the benefit of a foreign power) as a minor spy assisting the Czech government. Lichtenecker had accepted a temporary appointment at Buena Vista in the hope that he could escape his double role as spy and diplomat. He was in too deep, feared for the reputation of his family, and insisted that he had never meant to betray Austria. However, upon returning to Austria the peripatetic Lichtenecker found himself once again in the clutches of Janku, his Czech contact. His apprehension came when a colleague accidentally knocked a portfolio from Lichtenecker's desk, spilling the contents and the secrets. In fact, not much damage was done to Austrian national security and Lichtenecker was recognized for what he was, "a blunderer completely wrapped up in his thoughts, who had to pay the price of his unsurpassable disorderliness."[22] Fortunately, Lichtenecker's time in jail was brief; the forgiving Austrians released him on Christmas Eve after some months of confinement. He was soon employed by the Translation Institute of the University of Vienna.

The more sedate hands, faculty advisor John Madsen and editor Doug Laird, rescued the *Tack* from several years of oblivion in April 1974,[23] and mass communication professor, Bruce Ellingson, oversaw the paper's transformation during the age of technology in the 1980s. By the late 1980s the *Tack* had an unprecedented staff of forty and held the distinction of being "one of the first college newspapers in the nation to use Apple Macintosh computers and laser writers for writing, editing, and production" and was fearlessly reporting campus news and winning journalism awards for excellence.[24]

Bruce Ellingson became faculty advisor in 1984 and held that position until he took a leave of absence in order to complete his doctorate at the University of Iowa. He was replaced by Andrea Frantz during the years 1989–92. Ellingson resumed his duties as *Tack* advisor from 1992–99. Ellingson, a 1993 Wythe Award winner, then became advisor to Buena Vista's television station, KBVU. Chuck Offenburger, a popular author known throughout the state as the "Iowa Boy" columnist for the *Des Moines Register*, became a member of the Buena Vista faculty as writer-in-residence and served as *Tack* advisor from 1999–2001. Offenburger, a professional with high standards, worked his staff hard as he acquainted them with his own experiences as a journalist, and produced a first-class student paper. Eventually, Offenburger and Vice President of Academic Affairs (VPAA) Karen Halbersleben came to have serious budget disagreements and Offenburger resigned as *Tack* advisor and left the University in 2001. He envisioned an enlarged and increasingly professional journalistic endeavor. Consequently, Offenburger increased the size of the staff and sought to publish more editions. Prominent regional journalists such as the *Des Moines Register's* John Carlson visited his classes. His students had e-mail contact with Carlson, Mike Kelly of the *Omaha World-Herald,* and Dave Barry of the *Miami Herald.* He was able to send the two top editors of the paper to the national editors' conventions in Seattle (2000) and Washington, D.C. (2001). Students were able to visit and get a rare inside look at the *Chicago Tribune.* He assisted staff members in obtaining internships at several Midwestern papers including the *Des Moines Register.* The *Tack* also won a number of regional and national awards during this period. Offenburger's effort to build a still more professional university paper meant more funds than Buena Vista was willing to designate. Offenburger, no doubt, expected support from *Tack* journalists. However, when VPAA Karen Halbersleben discussed the issue with several members of the *Tack* staff she discovered that they felt already pushed to the maximum and none of them supported increasing the number of issues. Offenburger in spite of his obvious success had lost the battle and so submitted his resignation.[25] The "Iowa Boy" creator, although disappointed, held no grudge and continued to be a staunch Buena Vista supporter as he moved back into full-time journalism. He eventually relocated on a farm in Greene County, Iowa, and wrote biographies of Buena Vista graduates and current trustees E. Wayne Cooley, who for many decades headed the Iowa Girls' High School Athletic Union, and Bernie Saggau, the long-time CEO of the Iowa Boys' High School Athletic Association.

From the mid-1980s on the *Tack* possessed a number of able student editors and writers such as Teri Kramer, Deb Houghtaling, Leah Haverhals, Courtney Weller, Sally Rezabek, and Jamii Claiborne and by 2005 Kristen Waggener and Amy Best. Offenburger remembers Kramer and Weller as two of his best journalists. Another favorite was Sally Rezabek, a Glidden, Iowa native and a starter on the Buena Vista women's basketball team who became the paper's editor-in chief for the year 2000–01. She was "a real cool hand under pressure, gutty when tough decisions had to be made, a strong sense of right and wrong in her editorial/column decisions" recalls Offenburger.[26] Jamii Claiborne, a 1996 graduate and the author of short stories and a novel, returned to Buena Vista in 2001 as an instructor of Media Studies. The new professor had completed her graduate work at Old Dominion University and in August 2001 became another very competent advisor to the *Tack*. The paper also established a reputation as being somewhat socially and politically progressive in a conservative environment. This on occasion resulted in strong commentary from those who disagreed with the editorial or who feared excessive criticism. The Buena Vista Administration was consistent in upholding the "freedom of the press" tradition. The *Tack* during the 1990s and early years of the twenty-first century won numerous awards including five consecutive first place "with special merit awards," from the American Scholastic Press. Columnist and future editor Teri Kramer won the "outstanding service to the community award" for her weekly column dealing with Buena Vista's impact upon the community. Under Jamii Claiborne's supervision the paper has won "several Iowa Media Association awards and an American Scholastic Press Association Award."[27] These awards further enhanced the paper's reputation as a journalistic endeavor of distinction.[28] Kermit Buntrock (some called him "Old Plain Vanilla"), professor of journalism during the 1930s and 1940s and an early advisor, found the *Tack* of the 1990s, "a quality paper."[29] During Buntrock's years on the faculty the future mass communications area was a one-man department that Buntrock wryly noted he headed.[30] In February 1999, Buntrock then a resident in the Methodist Manor, and a life trustee, donated $218,000 to Buena Vista University to provide a journalism laboratory. It was one of many contributions, financial and personal, that Buntrock made during his half century of association with Buena Vista. He was fond of quoting a former professor who told him, "You have to lock yourself into something that is bigger than you are."[31] Senior Andy Offenburger, operating on a $500 budget, produced a lively 1998 musical based on love letters exchanged between Kermit and Lucille Buntrock at the time of their forced separation during World War II. The Buntrocks married in

1939, and their union remained a real love match until Lucille's death sixty years later. The war-time separation was difficult but nothing could sever the bond between them. Offenburger composed several of the songs himself including "Sometimes" and "Were You There." The musical was a hit and a tribute, and Buntrock praised the production and announced that he was "proud as punch."[32] Kermit Buntrock died in January 2001, and was a stalwart Buena Vista supporter until the end. He was a man of great inner strength, had a gentle sense of humor, had a deep love of his favorite cause (Buena Vista), and was one who never let the world stand in his way.

Not until 1907 did the junior class produce a College yearbook. Previously, a special edition of the *Tack* had been devoted to the College organizations and main events of the academic year. Yearbooks were printed annually except in 1908, 1934, 1935, 1936, and a gap that stretched from 1938 to 1947, until a new apathy set in during the 1980s. Once again a valuable source of the social history of the College was reduced and eliminated. The junior class of 1907, which had sponsored the first yearbook was known as "A Species Not Yet Classified."[33] The custom of naming classes started in 1906 and was discontinued sometime during the 1930s. The 1919 freshmen suffered through four years of being called the Bolsheviki.[34]

That first yearbook, christened the *Rudder*, was dedicated to President Robert Lincoln Campbell. Several pages were in memoriam to Miss Grace Garberson who had died during the school year. Miss Garberson, only twenty years old, was the daughter of Mr. and Mrs. Calvin W. Garberson of Storm Lake. The well-to-do Garbersons were landowners on a large scale and very proud of their three daughters, Grace, Aura, and Rena. Rena married Buena Vista graduate Felix Ross. The Rosses and Aura Garberson sponsored the Grace Memorial Theatre when the new administration building was constructed following the great fire.

The *Rudder* gave way in 1946 to the *Beaver Log*. However, the purpose and structure of the yearbook remained the same. Many of the annuals were dedicated to faculty or members of the administration. It seemed to be a tradition to dedicate an annual to a new president, and during the most hazardous days of the struggle for

survival there was a steady supply of fresh faces. Several of the annuals were dedicated to the esteemed Fracker. The 1911 and 1923
Rudders honored Miss Alice Wilcox. In 1930 Professor George
Crawford was given well-deserved recognition by the *Rudder* staff.
Professor Crawford served Buena Vista in a variety of ways during
his association with the College from 1925 until 1944. Professor
Crawford, who earned a Ph.D. from the University of Chicago in
1944, headed the Division of Education and also served as dean of
the College. During the last decade of his life he taught at Oakland
City, Indiana. Crawford was an able and considerate teacher who
possessed that rare quality of being able to remember everyone's
name.[35] Kermit Buntrock ranked Crawford as one of the most colorful individuals he had known in his more than fifty years of association with the College. The Crawfords drove a Model A in
which a huge police dog rode in the back seat.[36] Annuals were also
dedicated to F. F. Smith, George Reynolds, Luman W. Sampson,
and Albert Hirsch. These four men totaled 110 years of service to
Buena Vista College. The author of the 1951 dedication page of the
Beaver Log succinctly caught the meaning of these men to the
College when he said, "Dr. Sampson is not only the chairman of the
Division of Social Sciences on this campus, but he is the permanent
chairman so to speak, of the concepts and ideals so necessary in
modern times for a responsible democratic society."[37] The 1966 edition was dedicated to William Cumberland, recognizing his account
of the first seventy-five years of *The History of Buena Vista College;*
the 1971 *Log* to long-time admissions director Jake LaFoy; and the
1974 *Log* to retiring president Wendell Halverson. By the mid-1980s
the *Log* was no longer published. Finally, in 2004 an effort was
made to revive the publication.

However, it was the *Beaver Log* of 1947 that achieved an un-
realized coup when the editors obtained the services of movie actor
Ronald Reagan to judge the first annual Beaver Beauty Contest.
The candidates were chosen by the student body, and Reagan (from
his California home) made the final selections. Pat Stafford,
LoRaine Devereaux, and Lenora Hopkins were among those cho-
sen. This highlighted the first College yearbook in over a decade.[38]
Columnist Billy Rose (at that time a greater celebrity than Reagan)

accepted the challenge of judging the second Beaver Beauty Contest in 1948. After that, and for reasons unknown, the contest seems to have died.

The original College colors, adopted during the 1890s, were salmon and black. By 1919, however, the switch was made to dark blue and old gold. Apparently salmon was a difficult color to obtain and it faded easily.[39] The problem became acute in the fall of 1919 when the College was unable to secure football sweaters in the College colors.

One event, unfortunately almost unnoticed, was the adoption of the College Seal sometime between April and October 1909. The Seal first appeared on the October 1909 issue of the *Tack*. Many years later in answer to an alumni query, Mrs. Maude E. Barnes (Maude Hawkins of the class of 1900) revealed that she had been on the committee to select a design and had submitted the drawing that was used. Mrs. Barnes wrote that:

> It was my idea of the man looking across the lake to the other shore, the rising sun indicating possibilities of service—also hope—being rising. Distance between indicating time for preparation and developments. I know the man who made the etching [for the seal] added sun, rays or made sun rays longer. I know when I made it I hoped it would carry inspiration.[40]

The College has experimented with logos but the Seal has remained constant. The logos that appeared on the College podiums, stationery, and various artifacts in the Halverson years depicted two trees beside a rising sun. More recently several variations of the Victory Arch have appeared on logos and on the College Medallion designed by artist Dennis Dykema in honor of the dedication of Siebens Forum. The new logo designed in 1991 was altered four years later to incorporate the name university instead of college. However, by the mid-1990s the logo no longer seemed totally representative of the new directions in which Buena Vista was moving. In 1998, when Tim Seydel was Director of University Communications, the starburst logo was designed by Sayles Graphic Design. But this logo, although it included the NAC concept, the progressive starburst, the Victory Arch, and the "Education for Service" motto, was soon deemed less than satisfactory. Jennifer Felton, the new public relations director and graphic design professor, pointed out several missing features. President Fred Moore, in the fall of 2001, formed a new Integrated Marketing Team of faculty and staff from various departments to plan a new logo that would better promote the University's image. It was decided that "a logo should be simple in its message; it needs to jump out and grab you, and our existing logo had too much going on inside to do that." The new logo depicted the victory arch and featured the slogan "BOLD VISION, BRIGHT FUTURES." The athletic department chose a "more aggressive looking representation of the Beaver mascot which depicts a beaver protecting its den." The current arch logo and athletic logo were developed and approved in 2002.[41]

During the significant administration of E. E. Reed (1900–06) the tradition of Senior Tree Day was established. The idea originated with Miss Alice Tozer, professor of Latin 1902–06. At 9 A.M. on Monday morning, June 4, 1906, all four classes in the liberal arts college gathered for the ceremony. The seniors were dressed in their conventional black gowns and mortar boards, the juniors wore Roman togas "of a deep red color and heavy rubber boots," the sophomores were dressed in white with gilt headbands, while the freshmen wore green caps and gowns.[42] The object of the gathering was the dedication of a tree surrounded by a seat which was to be "restricted henceforth to the exclusive use of the seniors." There were speeches delivered by respective members of the four classes and a grand procession from the chapel to the campus. An oration was given by Miss Ethel Miller of the senior class, and the "seat, the tree, and the spade with which the tree had been planted were committed to the care of the coming senior class."[43] While the popular Miss Tozer would soon leave Buena Vista College, the custom she innovated would long remain a revered tradition. However, the custom became one of the casualties of the 1960s, and the planting of the Tree of Life in October 1969 as part of Vietnam Moratorium Day services marked the last official tree-planting ceremony on the campus.

Another custom, which originated about the same time and also died an apparently easy death in the late 1960s, was the smok-

ing of the Pipe of Peace. The origins of this custom remain unknown. It is possible that it stemmed from "a beautiful carved pipe
of peace" from the Pipestone quarries given to the College by A. A.
Horton in the mid-1890s.[44] The 1919 *Rudder* refers to both the Tree
Day ceremony and the Pipe of Peace as having originated in 1906.
However, the first *Tack* reference to the Pipe of Peace is in May
1910. The purpose of the ceremony was to bury the hatchet between the warring juniors and seniors. It was a secret ritual at
which the two classes smoked the peace pipe "in the good old
Indian way." In the early years the ceremony was held on Monday
of Commencement week. It was "enveloped in mystery" and no
one talked about it, but at least it ended the rough, though good-
natured strife between juniors and seniors.[45] Of course by the 1960s
such class rivalries had long fizzled out, and the tradition itself became an anachronism.

Other once-flourishing Buena Vista traditions that by the 1970s
had fallen victim to changing patterns of sophistication were the
Senior Swing Out and Farewell Chapel. At first these events were
separate but ultimately merged. The Senior Swing Out originated
on February 24, 1909, and denoted the first occasion at which the
seniors appeared in public in their caps and gowns. At the Farewell
Chapel the seniors said goodbye to College years, and each class
gave a response to the challenges left by the approaching graduates.
Could the class of 1991 imagine the Farewell Chapel of 1909?

> Four black-robed solemn people marched into the chapel and took pos-
> session of the platform. The men did not remove their tasseled boards,
> but balanced them carefully during the speeches that followed. Each
> member of the class took part, the president presiding. Miss Eshbaugh
> recalled to their minds all the picnics, pranks and parties of the past
> years. After this, the most musical members rendered two beautiful
> solos. And then Mr. May, the college booster, stirred up fresh enthusi-
> asm for Buena Vista. As the students passed out of the chapel a card
> printed in gold and white, with a calla lily, the class flower, upon it was
> handed to each.[46]

In those years the students were more likely to have caps and
gowns than the faculty. Even after World War I the trustees re-

scinded a faculty resolution that the professors wear caps and gowns at Commencement time and that the "Board of Trustees be asked to pay for the renting of these." Not until 1925 is there evidence that academic apparel was worn at Commencement by the faculty.[47] Faculty, of course, paid for their own gowns and eventually trustees who participated in the ceremonies were asked to wear academic apparel. However, in those early years major faculty concerns were delays of salary payments and status frustrations. On one occasion the professors were asked "not to give orders to the janitor."[48]

Around 1913 an unusual tradition known as Hobo Day was initiated. It was a day when the student body, dressed in odd assortments of clothing, skipped classes and begged handouts from the citizens of the community. This proved disturbing during World War II when faculty felt students should not be begging from townspeople. Eventually it matured into more of a Campus Day, during which students helped to clean the buildings and grounds and the day's activities ended with a late afternoon picnic at Chautauqua Park and a Hobo Ball in the evening.[49] By the mid-1950s, Hobo Day was losing its hold.

Veterans streaming into college after World War II, the increasing realization that education was vital to national growth, and Buena Vista's own evolving sophistication and maturity brought a new seriousness and purpose to the campus. Perhaps it was significant that the postwar generation sought to emphasize the Fine Arts Week that became a permanent feature after 1951. Dramatic productions, concert performances, and art exhibitions were central features of Fine Arts Week. Beautification Day promoted by Faculty Dames featured planting flowers and shrubbery around the campus during the 1970s and early 1980s. The increasing acreage and new construction made professional landscaping a necessity by the 1980s. Ultimately, Beautification Day became Buenafication Day and consisted of participation by students, faculty, and administration. On Buenafication Day 2005 classes were dismissed, and a campus-wide rally was held at 9:30 in the football stadium. Some fifty teams were organized to clean up local parks, schools, public buildings, hospitals, assisted living facilities, and other areas in the community as well as on the Buena Vista campus. A picnic lunch was held at noon followed by various games and a malt shop dinner. However, *Storm Lake Pilot-Tribune* editor, Dana Larson, while praising the event, lamented that it was "just a day, not an attitude." Larson felt that Buena Vista students while knowing the route to the bars, Wal-Mart, McDonalds, and the theaters, knew little about the city, its citizens, or the churches. The parking lots, Larson asserted, were empty on weekends, and campus events such as Fiesta Latina attracted only a few students.[50] Still, Hobo Day had been transformed and revitalized and enriched both University and community.

The Yule Log Service was originated by Dean of Women Phoebe LaFoy in December 1942. It was the second wartime Christmas at Buena Vista and its purpose was to remind all on campus of "the spirit of Christmas and the hope of the future." The service, originally held in the president's home, was moved into newly completed Swope Hall in 1950. Talks on the tradition of Christmas were part of the candle-lit ceremonies.[51] The Fisher and Halverson years also featured an outside tree-lighting ceremony at the beginning of the Christmas season, followed by caroling.[52]

No tradition is more revered on college campuses than that of Homecoming, which has a meaning far beyond that of the football game. Homecoming was instituted at Buena Vista in 1911 and became a regular feature of the fall season during the 1920s. Graduates returned, reunions were held, there were parades, bonfires, parties, College cheers, skits in Old Main and Schaller Chapel, visiting dignitaries, the autumn nip in the air, the turning leaves, the nostalgia of days forever lost, and the expectation and joy in greeting old and new friends and faculty. The homecoming queens were always beautiful—Mary Ann Dawson (1959), Kay Sullivan Bush (1960), Karen Bluedorn (1965), Teddi Whacker (1966), Rhonda Greenfield (1979), and Luana Root (1980). Returning alumni could watch the two dozen area bands marching down main street followed by carefully constructed sometimes gaudy floats, antique cars, and aspiring political candidates occasionally jostling for position in the parade. And for twenty-five years the football game was preceded by Robert Pfaltzgraff's rendition of the national anthem echoing across the stadium and the lakeshore beyond.

However, by the twenty-first century the day of the marching band had ceased to exist among many smaller colleges. At Buena Vista the colorful musical organization, once led by the immortal Bill Green, was terminated in 1998 following an existence of seventy-five years. Buena Vista was the last Iowa Conference school to maintain a marching band. Furthermore, the Homecoming Parade was now a shriveled reminder of its once glorious past. No longer did area high schools proudly display their colors and march through the downtown area, no longer did college groups construct floats, no longer was the parade held on crisp Saturday mornings. There was a procession, but it was shorter, held on Friday afternoon and was far more mundane. Local citizens still gathered along the streets to watch the cars and dignitaries pass by, but the event lacked the luster of earlier years—another sign that the times were changing.

It is obvious that many early Buena Vista traditions have passed out of existence even though the Tree Day ceremony, the smoking of the Pipe of Peace, Senior Swing Out, the Farewell Chapel, and Hobo Day had once seemed revered and permanent. Other traditions survived only briefly. Among these were a Sing Out started in 1913 and continued for a few years and the Color Ceremony that was established by the class of 1912. The Color Ceremony amounted to a "formal presentation of the freshmen colors by the seniors," followed by a banquet.[53] The freshmen were also saddled with a name (such as the Bolsheviki) that they bore during their four years at the College. The Color Ceremony was still going strong in 1923, but apparently fell victim to the Depression years. A maturing student body may have found such antics childish.

One controversial tradition that developed and survived for a few years in the late 1970s and early 1980s was the Hog Jam. The Hog Jam was moved from the park adjacent to the campus (where late night noise irritated residents) to the industrial park area and finally to the Student Center where it was no less raucous. The Hog Jam of May 1984 cost $7 for admission and featured entertainment, snacks, and all the beer and pop one could consume.[54] However, in 1987 President Briscoe and Forum Director Hal Closson terminated this ode to Bacchus. Among the major factors in sending the Hog Jam into oblivion were the prohibitive rates of liability insurance and state legislation that raised the legal drinking age to twenty-one.[55]

One tradition that seemed a permanent fixture on many campuses even after World War II, but remains only a legend today, was the wearing of the freshman beanie. It was part of a rather rigorous freshman orientation seen in retrospect as more of an effort to terrorize the incoming novices rather than assist them in adjusting to a new and strange environment. Seniors of all sizes, with a glint in their eyes and equipped with stout wooden paddles capable of delivering sharp stings and bruises, grazed across the campus from opening day until Homecoming like early Neanderthals in search of prey. In case the varsity did not win the homecoming football game (happening for which freshmen were hardly responsible), it became necessary to wear the odd-looking, freakish caps until Thanksgiving. There were serious challenges to forcing the beanies on freshmen during the 1960s, and interest in the tradition died during the 1970s. Victory in a celebrated tug-of-war against the hated upperclassmen freed the freshmen from their beanies. Freshmen, who now paid $5,000 and up for the privilege of an education, were too sophisticated to enjoy such harassment. The emphasis of colleges turned to orientation rather than disorientation for incoming students. Certainly no college administration wanted to tolerate a form of hazing that might discourage present and prospective students in an era of intense rivalry for the available pool of high school graduates.[56]

Unfortunately, new traditions have not always replaced the old. Nevertheless, several new traditions have assumed what appears to be a permanent place in the new Buena Vista. A great deal of symbolism and history have come to be associated with the colorful baccalaureate services, much of it the inspiration of professor of religion and philosophy and Calvin scholar, Dr. Charles Partee (1969–78). The reconstruction and relocation of the Arch at the southwestern corner of the original campus has become a major symbol at each Commencement as faculty and students march under and through its stone curvature. The march through the Arch no doubt was more significant for seniors at commencement than it had been when they were freshmen making the trek for the first time. But even the first march through the Arch in 1978 was significant. The faculty leading the freshmen procession split at the steps of Schaller Chapel and started to applaud as the freshmen made their ascent into the building. It became part of the tradition.[57] Chuck Offenburger found it one of the most meaningful experiences he had encountered on any college campus. The memory of the Arch and its historic significance would grow with the passage of time. Many students would refer to the experience in the years following their graduation.

The Founders Day Memorial Service inaugurated by Keith Briscoe in 1978 became a beautiful tradition paying homage to recently deceased members of the Buena Vista community. By 2005 deceased honorees had come to include such Buena Vista legends as Wendell Halverson, Bill Wesselink, Jack Fisher, Vivian McCorkle, Kermit Buntrock, George Reynolds, Luman Sampson, Albert Hirsch, Ted and Gladys Kuehl, Charles Zalesky, Ivan Harlan, Everett and Paul Shafer, Duane Haack, Robert Pfaltzgraff, Ingeborg Stolee, Marilyn Wikstrom, Jay and Jean Beekmann, Jim and Flo Hershberger, John Naughton, Harriet Henry, Laura Inglis, Edgar Mack, A. G. Thomas, James Christiansen, and Jackie Hansen, along with others who devoted their lives to the growth and prosperity of Buena Vista University. Sadly, the line lengthens with each passing year. The Founders Day Memorial Service inaugurated by Keith Briscoe in 1978 has become a beautiful tradition that pays homage to recently deceased members of the Buena Vista community.

There is the Student Recognition banquet each spring, which honors and presents awards to students for academic excellence and leadership and might be regarded as the offspring of the Senior Swing Out. At this time the Rollins fellowships, the outstanding man and woman, the Wesselink, Steif, Zalesky, and Cumberland award winners are announced. It is a significant event and for the moment reinforces the belief that the purpose of Buena Vista College has been and remains "Education for Service." The annual muscular dystrophy dance marathon established itself as an important tradition of service during the 1970s as Buena Vista students raised thousands of dollars to assist those stricken by the disease.[58] A very appealing tradition has been Trick or Treat Night introduced as part of Halloween festivities. Youngsters from kindergarten through the fourth grade knock on dormitory doors asking for candy. In order to assure their protection they register in the Forum and are met by Resident Hall members and by Buena Vista foot-ballers.[59] One newer tradition is the annual Christmas Madrigal Feast first established in 1999. The Renaissance-style dinner featured seven courses, two hours of singing, playing, and comedy. The 2005 Queen Ryann Ruedeman and King McKenzie Rieling presided over the Royal Court.[60]

Each year since 1987, during the Christmas season, Buena Vista faculty and staff members volunteer to serve meals to the student body. There is a short program, the lighting of the Christmas tree by the young children of faculty and staff, holiday selections performed by the Vista Chamber Singers, and a rousing Sing-Along climax to the evening festivities.[61]

Still those symbols and traditions that arouse emotion, promote unity, and create unbreakable bonds remain undeveloped at Buena Vista College. There were more traditions during the difficult years, and old-timers always felt a strong sense of loyalty to the struggling College. However, twenty-first century students tend to be more detached and seem to prefer traditions, such as those described, that are serious and certain to have a lasting impact. There appears to be, in any case, less rah-rah than in earlier days, perhaps partly explained by the cost of education, the increasing seriousness of the endeavor, a greater awareness of the pressure-laden world around them, and the fact that an overwhelming majority have part-time jobs and must carefully budget their time.

Though the College enrollment was small, no program seemed too ambitious for the pre-World War I student body to undertake. The climate of bankruptcy that constantly challenged the trustees and administration failed to dampen the enthusiasm of the young men and women attending Buena Vista. C. M. Drury recalled that when he enrolled as a student in the college section in 1914 total attendance at the College was probably under 100, with half taking the college work and the others in the academy or commercial departments.

> We had an abiding loyalty to the College. The whole student body turned out for all events whether such were athletic, music, debating or social. We had no fraternities or sororities—these were considered somewhat snobbish—nor were dances allowed. Very few of the students smoked and never in the buildings.[62]

The enthusiasm of the student body was manifest in the whole-hearted support given to the oratorical contests. Already during the 1890s Buena Vista's traditional interest in forensics was developing. An oratorical contest during the winter of 1895 was called the "greatest event of the college year." The contests became an annual event and Buena Vista became a member of the Oratorical Association of the Colleges of Northwest Iowa.[63] In a spirited contest held May 15, 1896, at Sac City, Buena Vista emerged the victor. The rivalry between Buena Vistans and the institute that then existed at Denison was intense. The *Pilot-Tribune* reported that Buena Vista had the best speaker in Willis Edson, whose oration on President Lincoln carried away first honors. Bad weather kept some Storm Lakers at home, but still the College out shouted their rivals by "singing and giving the College Yell."[64]

> Ricka chicka boom,
> Ricka chicka boom,
> Ricka chicka, ricka chicka,
> Boom, boom, boom,
> Hoopla ha, hoopla he,
> Hoopla, hoopla, BVC[65]

The *Pilot-Tribune* noted that the return trip was made "without accidents or mishaps by way of Newell, and the citizens of that place were serenaded in royal style by the College songs and yells of all colors."[66]

The enthusiasm for forensics equaled or surpassed interest in athletic contests. When Buena Vista's debaters won from Central and Ellsworth colleges it was headline material for the *Tack*. And one of the high points of the academic year 1917–18 was when

Miss Dewey Deal, coached by Willis Edson, won the state oratorical contest at Morningside on March 1.[67] Dewey Deal later became
a faculty member at Buena Vista College, and prize-winning author
Marjorie Holmes remembered her as a professor who encouraged
her to embark upon a writing career. Deal told Holmes, "You can
write beautiful things for people who crave beautiful things."[68]

One of the landmarks in the development of Buena Vista's
forensic tradition came in 1924 when the College was granted a
chapter of Pi Kappa Delta, national honorary forensics fraternity.[69]
In April 1926 L. Dorothy Greene of Rolfe won third place in the
first national oratory contest held at Estes Park, Colorado. Also representing Buena Vista was Maxine Ross who had won the state
contest. There were 350 delegates from every state in the union. L.
Dorothy Greene Lester would eventually become a distinguished
author, theologian, the first woman president of the Presbyterian
National Town and Country Fellowship of the United Presbyterian
Church, and Arkansas Woman of the Year. She was a recipient of
the Buena Vista College Alumni Association's Distinguished
Service Award in 1970.[70]

Marjorie Holmes, who did outstanding work in forensics while
a student at Buena Vista College, was elected president of the Iowa
Collegiate Women's Forensics League in the spring of 1929.[71]
Holmes left Buena Vista College to complete her undergraduate
studies at Cornell College in Mount Vernon. Her ties with her native Storm Lake remained strong, however, and as her literary
career blossomed into national prominence as a feature writer for
the *Washington Star* and the author of the best-selling books *I've
Got to Talk to Somebody, God; Two From Galilee;* and *God and
Vitamins,* her interest in Buena Vista was rekindled. Watching the
steady progress of the College in the 1960s, she could readily see
there was little resemblance to the institution somewhat conde-
scendingly described in one of her earlier works, *World by the Tail.*
Marjorie Holmes became a frequent and much honored visitor at
Buena Vista, whose progress she recognized through the establishment of the Marjorie Holmes Endowed Scholarship Fund. The nationally known author of twenty-one books maintained a strong interest in Buena Vista until her death at age 91 in 2002. Her literary

ingredients of diet, vitamins, exercise, and prayer proved a successful formula. Many of her papers and journals are now located in the
special collections area of the Buena Vista University Library.[72]

The real peak of forensic achievement came with the arrival of
Professor Gladys Kuehl in 1947. The late years of the Depression
and the declining enrollment during World War II had shredded the
program. Gladys discovered that she was the only member of the
speech department, and speech was required of all students for
graduation. She not only ran the speech department but had the responsibility of directing all dramatic productions. Furthermore,
1947 was the year that World War II veterans took advantage of one
of America's great examples of social legislation—the GI bill.
Brilliant, persistent, and personable, Professor Kuehl molded a
forensics squad consisting of ex-GIs, and incoming high school
graduates into one of the most formidable debate units in the
Midwest. Funds were limited, and students helped subsidize expenses "through judging at high school speaking contests and book
sales and rummage sales."[73]

Since there was no such thing as a College vehicle, either
Gladys or the students furnished the car, students paid for their own
meals, and they lodged together in the dormitory of the host school.
When the College finally supplied a station wagon, it "was held together with chewing gum and paper clips, and there were break-
downs, and snow storms and desert winds." Sometimes they traveled all night to save on expenses, arriving tired but ready to debate
the following day. They struggled through car trouble, through limited and carefully rationed funds. They packed picnic lunches. They
learned a resourcefulness that stood by them throughout life. It was
an era of not-to-be-matched camaraderie extending into the middle
1960s.[74]

There was, of course, a fair share of incidents along the way.
Working together produced amorous relationships. On one trip in
desolate Montana a "frisky" couple in the back seat (not unusual)
spilled hot coffee over Gladys's lap, burning through her ski pants
and sending her to the hospital. The strict moral code of the era
kept one outstanding forensics member from being recognized in
Who's Who in American Colleges when she was seen drinking "too

much" at the Cobblestone Inn.[75] But nothing could stop the accomplishments of the Buena Vista forensics team; excellent and superior ratings were accorded at each meet. Among the great teams were the 1951 squad led by Dix Lohman and Bill Richards[76] and the 1962 squad headed by Lynn Phelps and Dave Lampe. This squad won the Sweepstakes Trophy, the top prize awarded by the Iowa State Forensics Association, at the 1962 state forensics tournament in Ames.[77] The 1958 team achieved a forensics rarity by sweeping all debate rounds among twenty-three competing schools in the discussion and debate conference at the University of South Dakota.[78] The 1965 team—Bill Wolff, Peder Halverson, Maxine Warnke (Lampe), Elsie Heikens, and Alice Madsen—returned with high honors from the Pi Kappa Delta national convention at Pacific Grove University in Tacoma, Washington. Also among the great forensic competitors for collegiate honors during the Kuehl era were Clair Abbott, Norbert Sauter, Jean Waisner, Helen Gaherty, Ken Beatty, Ken Green, Maureen McKenna, Doyle Hanson, Jean Moe, Carol Hammer, Carolyn Claussen, Norman Van Klompenberg, Bob O'Rourke, Ruth Eichstaedt (Lampe), Luella Wohlers Wolff, Ed Bodaken, Joe Meusey, Vicki Morton, Jim McDermid, Marilyn Lewis, Carol Coburn, Phil Redenbaugh, and Rosemary Shaw Sackett. Joe Meusey, Jean Moe, Carol Hammer, David Lampe, and Vicki Morton were chosen in state competition to represent the State of Iowa at interstate oratory contests.[79] Sackett, now a distinguished jurist, recalled that having Gladys Kuehl as her speech instructor was one of her most fortunate college experiences. It was Dr. Kuehl who encouraged the rather shy college student to try speech and debate.[80] In addition to her successful state and national programs, Professor Kuehl instituted a campus forensics contest for high school students, which by 1961 had 300 participants. Winners received scholarships to Buena Vista College. The Kuehl years brought prestige to the College and participants. Some of the most successful graduates in the College's first century were the products of Professor Kuehl's heroic battle to make a little go a long way. Dave Lampe, Ed Bodaken, Bill Wolff, and Luella Wohlers were among those who entered graduate programs, earned Ph.D.s, and embarked upon academic careers. Joe Meusey and

Rosemary Shaw Sackett won distinction in the legal profession. All found their contact with Professor Kuehl an important ingredient in their success. Unfortunately, the great tradition Dr. Kuehl had established in speech weakened after her departure. Student interest in forensics declined during the late 1960s and 1970s. It was not until 1979 that Dr. Sandra Madsen and her valiant debaters temporarily revived the earlier days of forensics glory. Susan Hutchins, Rai Peterson, Dan Lintin, and Brian Mathers led the squad that Dr. Madsen said "earned more trophies this year and had more people participating than ever before."[81] Sue Hutchins Cameron, after working as an editor and copywriter at Drake University, would return to Buena Vista as Director of Public Relations.

A commercial (business) department had existed at Buena Vista since its founding in 1891. Some forty-eight students were enrolled in the business, shorthand, and typing courses during the year 1892–93. Students might follow the commercial program from two months to two years, and the coursework did not lead to the B.A. or B.S. degree until shortly before America's entry into World War I. Because commercial courses attracted a large number of students they were highly valued. College catalogs emphasized the value of a commercial department located within a liberal arts college compared with that offered by a purely business college. The College boasted that "our students go into the best positions open to anyone." Furthermore, commercial students were exempt from entrance examinations and Bible classes (although the value of the latter was stressed).[82] By 1917 a full-fledged program in business administration had been introduced, and students were able to major in commerce and obtain a bachelor's degree in business administration. In 1920 William A. Abernathy appears to have been the recipient of the first B.A. in business administration. Abernathy became the principal of the commercial department at Morris, Illinois high school. Donald Ambler and George P. Diehl were awarded the B.S. in business administration in 1921. Ambler continued on to graduate school and became president of the Dryden Press.[83] During the North Central accreditation process in the late 1940s the business department became part of the Division of Education and Physical Education. It was moved into the Social

Science Division during the late 1960s and finally became a separate school following the Siebens gift in the early 1980s.

The 1980s would, partly as the result of the Siebens gift, witness the enormous growth of the School of Business. There was even some apprehension that as desirable as this growth was it might submerge the liberal arts tradition of the College. Consequently, business faculty sought to limit the number of business majors to 300 and to encourage their students to delve into the liberal arts curriculum. Actually, the business program was a major force on campus even before the Siebens gift. The arrival of a Cuban refugee and former professor of accounting at the University of Havana, Dr. Felix Cruz, ably supported by professors Paul Russell, Norman Bonnema, and Everett Shafer gave Buena Vista a small but outstanding business program during the 1960s. Cruz, who had had many American contacts while in Cuba, had written accounting texts. He left his homeland when he could no longer tolerate Fidel Castro, and directed the accounting program at Buena Vista from 1961 until his retirement in 1969. Cruz was popular with his students and was named "favorite professor" by the class of 1967. The honor signified the contribution that Dr. Cruz had made to "college careers in and out of the classroom."[84]

Joining Cruz in the mid-1960s was a seasoned businessman and former treasurer of Motorola, Everett Shafer, who also brought needed business expertise. Shafer taught on two different occasions on the main campus before moving to Omaha to serve the Council Bluffs branch campus in 1983. Shafer also had stints as treasurer of Admiral and president of A-M International Leasing Corporation. Shafer possessed an engineering degree from Iowa State, an M.A. from the University of Chicago, and a J.D. from the University of Iowa. His ability to merge his academic know-how with his practical experience in the business world greatly benefited his students. Shafer was still actively promoting Buena Vista University when he died suddenly in Omaha in April 1998. His wife Kathryn, a gifted music teacher at several colleges including Buena Vista, had died a few weeks earlier. Another stalwart was Norman Bonnema who came to Buena Vista as a young assistant professor in 1964 and during the late 1970s was lured into administration as the director

of the College's Lakes and Prairies Center in Spencer. Veteran professors Wayne Higley, Margaret Redenbaugh, Stan Ullerich,
Houston Poulson, and Henry Hardt were instrumental in maintaining the excellent reputation of the School of Business as the
University moved into the twenty-first century. Wayne Higley, an
outstanding professor of accounting, won the Wythe Award in 1995.

An eager twenty-five-year-old economics professor, Paul
Russell, came to Buena Vista College in 1967 fresh from the
University of Missouri graduate school. He ultimately received his
Ph.D. from the University of Northern Colorado. Russell was a
popular lecturer in economics, chaired the School of Social Science
(of which business was then a part), chaired the Faculty Senate, and
was the major force in obtaining the Dows grant for the College.
The Dows grant was a people-oriented program that essentially endowed the small business program, the development of computers,
the Florida interim program, and European interim trips for business students. The grant emanated from a series of trust funds established by Iowa Electric president Sutherland Dows, the grandfather of Pete Dows who was a 1973 graduate of Buena Vista
College. The cumulative total realized from the grant places it
among the foremost benefactors of the College, after the Siebens
gift. In 1972 Russell was already recognized as Storm Lake's outstanding young educator. He organized business interims and trips
for students abroad, and in 1988 enjoyed a semester sabbatical as
lecturer at Templeton College, Oxford, England. Russell also organized the Deans Fellows, which recognized and provided grants for
outstanding students coming into Buena Vista preparing for careers
in business. He also became Dean of the Harold Walter Siebens
School of Business. Russell influenced a generation of business students at Buena Vista. One of them, Lowell Jacobsen (B.A. 1979)
completed advanced degrees at the American Graduate School of
International Management and at Edinburgh University, coauthored
The Small Entrepreneurial Firm published by Aberdeen University
Press, and in 1990 was professor of economics at William Jewell
College in Missouri. Russell's lack of reverence for administrative
fiat frequently pricked tender institutional sensitivities, but his main
purpose and considerable achievement was to move both the busi-

ness program and the College forward. These achievements were recognized when Russell was honored at the 1990 faculty recognition dinner as the fourth winner of the Wythe Award.[85]

Russell retired from Buena Vista in 2001 and moved to Kansas City where, for several years, he worked with Baker University.

Social fraternities and sororities at Buena Vista College have always been on a local rather than a national level. The first sorority was Phi Alpha Pi organized in November 1906.[86] The Delta Phi Beta sorority was founded in November 1920 and celebrated its fiftieth anniversary in 1970.[87] Delta Phi Rho (founded in 1925), Gamma Sigma Phi, and Kappa Tau Delta (1963) were social fraternities.[88] The student revolution of the 1960s made sororities and fraternities appear antidemocratic. Phi Alpha Pi held out the longest but became inactive in 1974, lamenting that they could "no longer fight the trend on this campus, which is also a nationwide trend, of women and men who feel that social sororities and fraternities are no longer a necessary requirement of fulfilling college life."[89] At Buena Vista they were replaced by houses (organized on the basis of dorm floors or sections) in the 1970s and expanded into cottages in the 1980s when the College purchased and utilized houses on streets adjacent to the campus. In both instances former trustees, administrators, faculty, and house mothers were honored—thus there was Reynolds house, LaFoy house, (in honor of Jake and Phoebe LaFoy), Beekmann house, McCord house, Follon house (in honor of former dean of women Sue Follon), and cottages bearing the names of Blayney, Boyd, Hays, Fracker, Marshall, Reed, and Olson.[90] The original idea for house names came from Sue Follon in 1971. The purpose was to create a new sense of community and identity within the residence halls.[91] Many of the houses in Swope Hall carried a Greek theme and carried names like Echo, Olympia, Athena, and Discordia. The Morlan house was named in honor of Etha Morlan, the Swope director from 1970 to 1978. The cottages were opened in the fall of 1987 and were headed by a student resident advisor.[92] However, by 1987 new interest in fraternities and sororities was developing, fostered by alumni director Greg Evans, and Gamma Sigma Pi was restored to active status with twenty-two men as members.[93]

Buena Vista College, by the mid-1960s, boasted a number of campus organizations that served almost every social, vocational, or political interest imaginable. The Young Republicans and Young Democrats battled for student loyalties. The revived 1960 Young Democrats club sponsored homecoming queen Kay Bush. In the heated campaign of 1968, senior Dean Kerhulas from Chicago rallied nearly 15 percent of the students in support of third party candidate George Wallace in a mock election. Richard Nixon received the support of 60 percent and Hubert Humphrey 24 percent.[94] The Circle K club, founded at Buena Vista on May 5, 1950, largely through the efforts of Dean William Wesselink, served business administration majors who sought to reach out to help others. The Buena Vista Circle K became part of the international organization in March 1956. The club became coeducational in 1973, and by 1986 there were only four men among the twenty-one members.[95] The SISEA (Student Iowa State Education Association) assisted the growing number of education majors. There were also the Student Christian Fellowship, Music Educator's National Conference (MENC), the Letterman's Club, Women's Physical Education (PEMM), Celtic Cross, Beaver Players, and the new Beaverettes. The Order of the Keys was founded in October 1969. The organization emphasized both scholarship and friendship.[96] The most prestigious organization was the campus academic honorary society. The Buena Vista Honor Society was organized in 1936 by Professor Luman Sampson. A four-year cumulative grade point average of 3.3 on a 4-point scale was necessary for membership. At the end of the spring semester, an honor society tea was held and new members received into the society.

However, there were many changes during the 1970s and 1980s. There was more political lethargy and the political clubs were less active than in the days of the New Frontier and Great Society. Republicans on campus outnumbered Democrats by about two to one throughout the period. Increasingly, political candidates appeared at the College. By the 1980s there were homecoming kings as well as queens. Circle K survived but it was more subdued than the new club for business majors—Students in Free Enterprise (SIFE) brought to campus by Professor Raj Shirole in 1988. A new national academic honors society, the Epsilon chapter of Alpha Chi, was installed in January 1971, replacing the Buena Vista College Honor Society founded and encouraged by Dr. Luman Sampson.[97] The old honor society had approved the change in May 1969 and the Faculty Senate had added its blessing in April 1970. Dr. Leonard Martz, chairperson of the Division of Language and Literature, was elected faculty sponsor.[98] In addition, a new honors program was developed in the 1980s with high GPAs and a research requirement for membership.

Throughout the years Buena Vista College had able cultural ambassadors. John Gooch, Stan Longman, Travis Lockhart, and Michael Whitlach produced masterly dramas. Travis Lockhart (1968–76) and his Buena Vista drama crew performed twenty-one plays in eight years. Among the memorable productions were *A Man for All Seasons, Look Homeward Angel, Death of a Salesman, The Diary of Anne Frank, The Cherry Orchard,* and *Night of the Iguana.* At least three of Lockhart's students, James Hartman (1969–73), Laura Whitmer (1969–73), and Alan Semok (1970–73) continued on to professional careers in theater, films, and television.[99] Lockhart, in 1977, was succeeded by Michael Whitlach, a Bowling Green Ph.D., who would direct the theater program for the next three decades. Whitlach would spend a term as associate dean of the faculty, fill in briefly as acting dean of the faculty, would be twice elected chair of the faculty senate and in 2003 replaced Dr. Mary Gill as the dean of the School of Communications and Arts.[100] In 2004 Governor Vilsack appointed Whitlach to the Iowa Commission on the Status of Women.[101] *Who's Afraid* of *Virginia Woolf, Amadeus, My Fair Lady,* and *Fiddler on the Roof* were among Whitlach's most memorable performances. A scholar as well as a director, Dr. Whitlach's research was published in scholarly journals; "Eugene O'Neill and Class Consciousness in 'The Hairy Ape'" appearing in the East German magazine *Zeitschrift fur Anglistik und Amerikanistik.* He also contributes reviews to drama and literary journals. One of the most important Whitlach publications was his review of "The Cambridge History of American Theater" in *Theater Research International.*[102] Buena Vista students Benjamin Mordecai, Rosey Davis, Ingrid Halverson, Alan

Semok, Laura Whitmer, Kitty Hardgrove, Diana Wesselink, Gayle Mahn, James Larson, Ginger Joslin, Jim Hartman, Brian Mathers, Chuck Spencer, and Mary Cusak were among the great stage performers in the era following the 1963 opening of Schaller Chapel, with its spacious arrangements for theatrical productions. Mordecai became the director of the Yale University Repertory Theatre.[103] Lockhart described native Storm Laker Jim Hartman as "the most talented and promising of the students I taught at BVC and one of the best students I have ever known anywhere in theatre."[104] Backstage design artists such as Gordon Linge and Art Beaulieu helped overcome limited technical capabilities. Linge (1972) continued on to an interesting career as the designer of Storm Lake's Santa's Castle and as the project director of Puppeteers of America, Inc. Beaulieu, who worked at a Storm Lake radio station following his graduation in 1969, continued to assist Lockhart as a "highly knowledgeable lighting designer and technician."[105] Meanwhile, throughout the 1990s and into the first decade of the twenty-first century, Dr. Whitlatch continued to direct quality plays for Buena Vista University. The theatre program was expanded and improved with the acquisition of Dr. David Walker who was a brilliant technical director. Walker's addition and technical excellence enabled a successful expansion of serious productions. Furthermore, the addition of Assistant Professor Dr. Bethany Larson made possible a three-show season. Dr. Larson was not only married to David Walker, but was the granddaughter of George Reynolds and shared with Carla Offenburger the responsibility for the ACES programs. Bethany ran the Cultural ACES while Carla handled the Speakers and other parts of the program until she left the University in 2004. The addition of Walker and Larson meant that theater was no longer a one-person program and that new and additional shows were possible.[106]

One production of great depth, directed by Dr. Whitlatch, was the drama *The Laramie Project,* in November 2004. This drama portrayed life in the town of Laramie following the brutal murder of a young homosexual. The drama explored the "depth to which humanity can sink and the heights of compassion of which we are capable."[107] Whitlatch acknowledged that producing the drama was "emotionally exhausting for all." The significance of the production was heightened by the visit of Judy Shepard to the campus three weeks before production.[108] Both the Shepard visit and the production quickened the consciences of those who took time to witness the performances.

During the spring of 2005 Whitlatch and his cast of actors produced the acclaimed musical *Grease*. On April 28 four teams of cast fanned out across the city to perform fun music from the play, including "We go together." This was the cast's contribution to Buenafication Day.[109]

Other productions that proved popular were *Camino Real*, *American Clock*, and *Copenhagen*. *Copenhagen* was the first production performed in the new Science Center in February 2005. The well-known drama revolved around the tense World War II friendship of German physicist Werner Heisenberg and his Danish counterpart Niels Bohr concerning the development of atomic weapons. Ed Lanning's last musical *La Ma Mancha* received wide acclaim. A production, *Emma's Child,* by Dr. Larson was also a hit. The fall of 2005 saw Whitlatch undertaking the Greek anti-war comedy *Lysistrata* by Aristophanes.[110]

One of Buena Vista's real success stories was that of Ben Mordecai, a 1967 graduate, who had participated in a number of college dramas directed by professors John Gooch and Stan Longman. He completed graduate work at Indiana and started the Indiana Repertory Theatre and then went on to Yale where he served as the director of the Yale Repertory Theatre. By 2003 Mordecai had become "one of Broadway's busiest and most successful producers." He had eighteen productions nominated for Tony Awards and four productions that won Pulitzer Prizes.[111] Buena Vista theatre major and technician Kendra Ramthum worked ten exciting weeks as an intern for Mordecai's company.[112] Whitlatch also laid much of the groundwork for the relationship with Mordecai who unfortunately died suddenly in May 2005 just before he was to be Buena Vista's honored commencement speaker.[113] Mordecai was honored posthumously with an honorary doctorate and the John Fisher Award.

Whitlatch, like Lockhart before him, had some outstanding acting talent in such performers as Ben Jenkins, Brett Winters, Bradley Workman, Amy Calhoun, Brittany Schmitt, Naomi Ziller, and oth-

ers. Whitlatch students have acted in Chicago, Phoenix, Minneapolis, and New York. Others have done graduate work at major universities including Iowa, Ohio, Georgia, and Nebraska. Some are
teaching at the college level, some have gone through law school.[114]
    The Buena Vista choir was directed by Robert Pfaltzgraff for
twenty-five years. He was replaced by a new master and veteran
choir director from Yankton College, Stan Rishoi, who directed the
choir until his retirement in 1999. Under the direction of Pfaltzgraff
and Rishoi, the a cappella choir continued its tradition of excellence. The choir was founded in 1929 with the explicit purpose of
presenting the great heritage of religious music with artistry and
simplicity. The directors also sought to train choral leaders and foster fine music in the churches.[115] The achievement of the founders
of the choir have been demonstrated by the capacity crowds that annually fill the 900-seat Schaller Memorial Chapel.
    The Buena Vista College band founded in 1924 was directed
by Will Burke Green from 1950 until his retirement in 1975. Green,
an amiable and talented maestro, had many successors including
the popular Reggie Schive, a skilled jazz artist whose alleged failure in recruiting students cost him tenure, much to the consterna-
tion of music students. Beginning in the fall of 1987, the band was
directed by a vigorous young conductor, Gary Fugman, who rapidly
built a reputation for excellence. Fugman, however, left Buena
Vista, entered seminary, and became a minister. Another very competent member of the music department was colorful Ed Lanning
who retired in 2001 after thirteen years on the faculty. Lanning
served a term as chair of the School of Communications and Arts.
He also directed the Buena Vista Jazz Band. Lanning was a wonderful colleague and a popular professor described by faculty and
students as "intelligent and funny."[116] Meanwhile, although the era
of the marching band was drawing to an end, the concert band still
performed at Christmas and in the spring. By 2000, Buena Vista's
Jazz chorus directed by Paula Keeler performed an annual program
in Siebens Forum. Professor Keeler also directed the University
choir and has built a reputation as a strong, new leader in the music
department.[117] The band served the College in a variety of ways—
as a marching band during the football season, as a pep band at the

basketball games, and as a concert band.[118] Like the choir, the band performed for a general audience at Christmas and in the spring.

Students who attended Buena Vista College appreciated the campus setting that featured the great natural beauty of Storm Lake. Of course, during the 1890s the barren campus needed development. South of the campus the land down to the lake was vacant "swampy land where we used to stake out our cows for pasture."[119] But the natural beauty of the area was lost on no one, and from the beginning it moved sensitive students to pen their love of the campus and the lake:

> The moon was shining high up in the heavens and there was scarcely a breath of wind as I walked along the lake one evening last week. . . .
>
> The wind is blowing hard and the waves roll up on the shore dashing against the stones with a resounding splash. Farther out on the lake the waves seem to be racing. They roll after each other and fall from the crest making a beautiful white spray which glistens in the sunlight. This gives the appearance of a large bluish gray sheet covered with queer white figures, constantly changing in shape and position.
>
> And now I stand on the campus facing the lake where it bends to the north. I gaze at the beautiful effect of the sunset on a calm lake. Near the horizon the sky is a deep golden color and gradually fades to a pale yellow. Above this is a beautiful stretch of red shading into a delicate rose color which is lost in the blue of the rest of the sky.
>
> Three colors are reflected in the lake exactly as they are in the sky, except that the motion of the water gives life to the picture and a greater beauty to the tinting.[120]

The prospect of attending college, even a small college like Buena Vista, could be a frightening experience for young people from rural western Iowa. The College catalog, eager to attract the best students, made city and College seem inviting. Rural students coming by train felt Storm Lake was a city that offered adventure as well as education. Members of the YMCA and YWCA generally met the train and helped the new students become oriented to their new environment. One young lady arriving in the fall of 1909 recalled: "She arrived at the hotel and [was] left in the middle of the street—after being gazed upon by many curious eyes and hearing whispers until her ears burn, she is escorted into the president's office and enrolled as a student at Buena Vista College." The accommodations at Ladies' Hall were not quite as elegant as she had been led to expect. (Such complaints about dormitory life were still being voiced in the late 1980s.) She found two windows that were "void of screens or curtains" with the wardrobe, dresser, and other furniture certainly "guiltless of any germs, as they were too plain for the concealment of a single bacteria."[121]

However, dormitory life during the pre-World War I era had its mischievous turns. The large boarding house, Gentlemen's Hall, in the mid-1890s was not always the scene of studious tranquility. The February 1895 issue of the *Tack* reported:

> On the night of Feb. 8th the orator of the dormitory took it into his head to practice in the hall during the midnight hours, interspersing his gestures and emphasizing his remarks with the remains of a bed slat. The occupants endured this as long as possible, until suddenly four ghostly figures were seen stealing noiselessly toward the unsuspecting night hawk. In a moment the voice, and the orator himself was being drowned beneath a double torrent of cold and boiling water.[122]

Ladies' Hall was also the scene of good sport. On cold nights the young models of deportment kept warm by indulging in pillow fights. Also it was noted that "a couple of boys and two girls seem to have a monopoly of the parlor." On one occasion a sneak thief entered the cottage and escaped with $30. The culprit had been about for several days and "carried plumber's tools to hide his design."[123]

Pranks at Ladies' Hall continued well into the twentieth century. The hall was an attraction for the young gentlemen at the College. Nor was it just the parlor that was appealing. When C. M. Drury was a student, the hall matron discovered that an intruder was coming through the dining room window and raiding the icebox. The matron discovered which window was being used and

> placed a tub of water inside the window early in the evening and then sat down by the electric light switch to wait. After a time, the culprit returned, carefully raised the window, balanced himself on the window sill and dropped down into the tub of water.
>
> She then switched on the light and there stood the surprised and embarrassed senior.[124]

The Hall could accommodate around forty young ladies. It contained twenty-one rooms, parlor, dining room, and kitchen.[125] The rules were brief but rigid and apparently enforced. The 1911 handbook listed the following regulations:

    I.   Anything that disturbs others during quiet hours, as loud talking, reading aloud, studying aloud, or singing must be avoided.

    II.   Quiet hours are: Before breakfast every morning; after 10 every night; 2 to 5 Monday, Tuesday, Wednesday, Thursday; 3 to 5 Sunday; 7:30 to 10 Sunday, Monday, Tuesday, Wednesday and Thursday.

    III.   The bell rings at the beginning of quiet hours.

    IV.   Pianos are not to be used during quiet hours or for lesson practice at any time.

    V.   The bathroom is to be vacated by 10:30 P.M.

    VI.   Persons needing to walk through the halls after 10:30 P.M. should move quietly.

    VII.   All lights in the rooms must be turned out at 10:30 P.M., and whenever the resident leaves her room even if only for a few minutes.

    VIII.   The doors are locked at 10 P.M.. If for any reason a resident desires to be out after 10 P.M., or to be gone overnight, she is to notify the matron.

    IX.   Students may not have guests overnight without previous consent of the matron.[126]

The two dormitories, Gentlemen's Hall and Ladies' Hall or Cottage had been built in the late 1890s. Around 1903 the original women's dormitory became the Mather Music Conservatory, as Flora S. Mather of Cleveland, Ohio, provided the funds to buy one of the two buildings that had been constructed by a Storm Lake syndicate. The young women were then moved into the men's dormitory, which became Ladies' Hall, and the men sought private lodging. Unfortunately, Ladies' Hall was destroyed by fire in 1915 and it was not until the construction of Swope Hall in 1950 that the College erected a satisfactory women's dormitory. This meant that Buena Vista College lacked the qualities of a residential college. Students who were not local or within commuting distance were forced to rent approved rooms from nearby residents. Undesirable as this situation was, and it continued until well after World War II, it neither prevented nor dampened the development of a strong College spirit.

College pranks (distinguished from vandalism) remained part of the College scene during every decade. In January 1964 nineteen-year-old Richard Betten crawled into an automatic dryer and his companions, Richard Troup and Joseph Niedziejka, "gave him over to the new era of automation by inserting the required coin to start things spinning." Justice of the Peace R. E. Manly fined the three "revolutionaries" $10 each.[127] More serious was the spring 1964 party at Casino Beach where a large group of students were apprehended and fined for illegal consumption of beer. A number, including a former homecoming queen, were placed on probation and several dismissed in an administrative action that seemed unduly harsh not only to students but to some members of the faculty.[128]

Federal grants and loans during the 1950s and 1960s resulted in the construction of additional dormitories, and although Buena Vista continued to have a large number of commuting students it became much more of a residential college. Changing patterns of student life and values in those decades brought some new and serious problems. These ranged from adequate parking space for on-campus and commuting students, alcoholic beverages in the student center and the dormitories, vandalism, and even arson. In January 1976, $70,000–80,000 worth of damage was incurred and several lives endangered in a fire that was later discovered to have been arson. The culprit, who signed his name PYRO, was ultimately apprehended.[129] While Buena Vista dormitories were functional, they were in need of consistent overhaul in order to maintain the living accommodations expected by the affluent generation.

During the 1920s and 1930s some of the old taboos began to crumble and the social life of the College became more flexible. Enrollment continued to increase until by 1933 there were 260 students, more than double the attendance just prior to World War I. By the 1920s the preparatory features of the College had disappeared, and all Buena Vista students were collegians. Drinking and smoking were still frowned upon. Room regulations for women were strictly and carefully defined. The 1930 *Beaver* handbook cautioned young women that "picnics, automobile trips of couples should be discouraged."[130] But the real breakthrough came in the gradually changing attitude toward social dancing. Historically the College officials had adamantly opposed social dancing. Merrill Drury records the puritanical standards that dominated his collegiate days (1914–18), not only was dancing forbidden but "young lovers could not show public affection such as putting arms around each other." Dean Wilcox often rebuked the demonstrative Drury.[131] In 1918 President Stanton Olinger presented a series of recommendations to the faculty concerning the status of dancing on campus which stipulated that:

(1) No dance shall be given under the auspices of the college nor in any building of the college.
(2) Students who wish to dance may do so by written consent of their parents or guardians. If a student is of age and paying his own way, he is on his own responsibility. If parent or guardian is paying his way, the written consent is required.
(3) Violation of 1 or 2 makes the student subject to discipline— the maximum penalty being expulsion.[132]

Some members of the faculty apparently felt that President Olinger's position was too liberal. They requested that the "words referring to age" be stricken from the recommendation and later asserted that "no dance whatever shall at any time be held under the auspices of the College or in any College building." However, the era of the flapper and the Charleston and the enthusiasm of young people for emerging trends inevitably softened faculty resistance, and in the fall of 1926 a committee was appointed to study the "advisability of holding authorized college dances."[133] By 1930 dances had seemingly become acceptable, although College parties appear to have been carefully supervised. They were nonetheless held in the Cobblestone Inn, with students and faculty dancing to the music of Rudy Vallee "through the medium of the Orchestrope." The dance continued until Professor F. F. Smith arrived to throw "a monkey wrench into the works of the jazz machine"[134] by calling a midnight curfew. Of course there were always ways of circumventing the rules. Russell Anderson, a student during the 1920s, recalled how his buddy Rowland drained off alcohol from professor F. F. Smith's basement lab "and mixed it with strawberry pop for schnapps."[135]

It would be a short step to the Gaslight Singers and the New Christy Minstrels and an even shorter but noisier step to Maynard Ferguson and the high voltage concerts of the 1970s and 1980s. Of course, with the influx of World War II veterans, official control of student social life had to be relaxed. The College continued, however, to stress a strong moral tone, and the taboos on alcohol continued well into the 1960s. But American life was changing rapidly and Buena Vista College, always ecumenical rather than sectarian, could not avoid those changes.

The construction of the new dormitories of the 1950s and 1960s, which (except for Swope) were built with government loans, provided not only new conveniences and a more collegiate setting but new problems as well. During the 1960s traditional, somewhat Victorian, regulations were challenged. Already by 1968 first year women, historically imprisoned on weekdays at 8 P.M., were free until 10 P.M. with one o'clock curfew permitted on one week night. The following year women, properly escorted, were able to visit the men's dorms during weekends, a policy brought about by popular dean of students, Dave Palmer. Soon women's hours were completely abolished. Considerable resistance to the new plan became evident on the Faculty Senate with some senators trying to rescind the policy. By the 1980s visitors of the opposite sex could remain until midnight on weeknights and 2 A.M. during weekends. The new policy disturbed some but was regarded as too stringent by others. Opponents claimed the College was trying to dictate morals in an age when being in loco parentis was passé. Coed dorms were also on the agenda, with those in support arguing that this type of living accommodation did not result in excessive sexual experimentation or animalistic behavior but increased maturity and the reduction of vandalism. Dorms became partly coed in the late 1970s, with men and women on alternating floors in White Hall but not in alternating rooms, nor sharing the cottages. However, other dorms remained single sex and a student request for twenty-four hour visitation was rejected by the Faculty Senate in 1985.[136] By 2000 several residences including recently completed Grand and Liberty halls were coeducational. Pierce Hall housed men and women on different floors. Briscoe Honor, McCorkle, and Constitution halls accommodated upper-class students and are coeducational. White Hall was now solely for men, and Swope housed approximately 200 women.[137] Buena Vista students still had a choice when selecting dormitory-style living. By the twenty-first century a vast majority of America's colleges and universities had coed residence halls.

There was a growing feeling that no party could succeed "without booze." Eventually alcohol was tolerated on campus, and beer was permitted in the rooms and at campus parties. September 8, 1982, was a momentous day for many students because it marked the first time that beer and wine could be purchased on the Buena Vista College campus. This marked a complete retreat from the Halverson years, for as late as 1972 no alcohol was permitted on campus. Indeed, during the late 1960s a student could still be dismissed (and sometimes was) "for having a drink even off campus."[138] But a 1972 poll revealed that 84.4 percent of Buena Vista students wanted the privilege of possession and consumption of alcohol on campus.[139] The poll was a factor in softening the Board as the College reasoned that social drinking had become so accepted by American society that it wanted to promote "responsible drinking" in a proper atmosphere, to move parties out of the dorms, and reduce alcohol-related dorm damage.[140] A new alcohol policy permitted only five in a room at one time—a dictum strongly resisted by students who preferred a maximum limit of ten. The lowering of the drinking age to nineteen had produced an increased demand for a more open policy among students. The raising of the drinking age in 1987 would create new tensions. Perhaps it can be said that no policy, from prohibition to permissiveness, has been successful.

During the 1990s Buena Vista developed the unenviable reputation as a drinking university. One study claimed that 90 percent of students drank and that 63 percent had practiced binge drinking. Eight Buena Vista students, several of them on the *Tack* staff, questioned the poll and conducted their own study in what the *Storm Lake Pilot-Tribune* punned as "a sobering new book."[141] The new study, undoubtedly far more accurate, discovered 85 percent of those surveyed insisted that they limited their consumption of alcohol and had no intention of reaching the level of intoxication. They insisted that they did not allow drinking to interfere with learning. The results of the survey were publicized in a small volume, *Behind the Arch, The Truth About Drinking At Buena Vista*, seriously challenged the methodology and results of the original survey.[142] Courtney Weller, one of the authors, hoped "to dispel some rumors that we're all a bunch of drunks." Advising the project was Associate Professor of English, James McFadden, in whose Advanced Writing class the volume was produced.[143]

One new effort to mitigate the effect of youthful drinking in downtown bars was the use of a bus to transport students to and from the downtown area. This method first used at Buena Vista in 1998 was politely called "Rides" although a more popular term was the "drunk bus." The bus had an army of critics as it cranked along during late night hours with riders' renditions of such catchy and noisy tunes as "Your Mamma ain't got no socks" or "Sweet Caroline." The exhilarating impact of too much alcohol penetrating the cerebellum resulted in sporadic fights and on at least one occasion the bus suffered a broken window. No doubt Loyal Y. Hays who once freed the old Collegiate Institute from the temptations of Fort Dodge saloons was stirring in his grave. These excesses, although the behavior of a minority of riders, made it more difficult to attract and retain competent drivers. Some local citizens complained both about the noise and the cost feeling that it raised the price of an education. Actually, the employment of "Rides" was not unique to Buena Vista, but used on many campuses, and no doubt has been important in saving lives, avoiding injuries, and indeed arrests. As one member of the administration remarked, the University was not "trying to make it a dry campus, we're trying to make it a safe campus."[144] Students rode the bus without charge, not all riders intended to drink, and the bus stopped at other establishments, not just the bars. Funding for "Rides" sometimes became a problem because of rising transportation costs. The cost in 2004 was, for the University, at least $20,000.[145] The cost again exceeded the budget in 2005 and was made up by contributions from several bars and from funds in the administrative budgets including student services.[146] Buena Vista's alcohol policy mirrors state law in that it does not condone underage, high risk, or binge drinking. For those of legal age the resident hall rooms are treated as a private residence. Students who wish to be free of alcohol and tobacco may choose to reside in substance free Liberty Hall.[147] Substance abuse remains a problem virtually every campus in America has to confront. No doubt many of these exuberant youths will become the parents of tomorrow and, with equal effect, caution their offspring not to engage in similar or new yet unheard of behavior. Meanwhile, a modicum of guidance and protection appears necessary. Colleges and universities cannot imprison young people who have made their first break with home.

Most students spent the bulk of their time in activities outside the bars. Noteworthy, were the Buena Vista students who tutored IBP workers in order to assist them in their language skills. Buena Vista students and faculty also traveled to St. Peter, Minnesota, to help with the clean up following the April 1998 tornado that had plowed a path of devastation throughout the area. When Katrina ravaged the Gulf region in August 2005, the Buena Vista Campus Community's ON TASK force collected supplies to benefit 5,000 victims.[148]

Virginia Henrickson, a Social Work major from the small town of Cylinder, Iowa, was one of five winners of the Elie Wiesel prize in 1996. Her essay, "Silence" dealt with the tragedy of child sexual abuse. The other winners of the $500 prize were from Hunter, Barnard, Maine, and Harvard.[149] Obviously, hundreds of Buena Vista students were swimming elsewhere than in the Sea of Alcohol.

Since most students owned and brought their cars to campus, new parking lots were constructed after the Siebens gift in 1980. There was even a parking lot for faculty, but the choice spots in front of Dixon-Eilers remained reserved for administrators and visitors.

During the remainder of the Briscoe Era and the Moore administrations additional parking areas were added . This, of course, was a necessity since the student body had increased by nearly 400 since the 1980s, and students continuously let their frustrations over the lack of parking space be known. New construction contributed to the frustration. There were 1200 spots but several hundred more were needed. Staff, faculty, and University vehicles occupied 117 of the available spaces. The area immediately in front of Dixon-Eilers was now landscaped and no longer served as a parking area.

Vandalism, including several episodes involving arson, became a mounting problem and one that had serious budget implications. During the 1990s and on into the twenty-first century, vandalism, especially damage to student cars, became a frequent occurrence. This was not always the work of Buena Vista students. Furthermore there were incidents of sexual harassment including several assaults. Parking areas were especially vulnerable to wanton damage to vehicles and even assaults. Lot E, which was the western most lot and furthest from any dormitory, was somewhat inappropriately called "rape lot," and was regarded by some as a virtual no man's land. Consequently, there were increased calls for safety, which did not go unheeded by the administration.

A May 1980 graduation survey conducted by *Tack* writer (later public relations director) Susan Hutchins revealed that while students might concur that Buena Vista College was a friendly place, some even wished they could repeat their four years at the College, but a number noted the campus atmosphere was dull, social life lacking, and the administration stifling.[150] This was a problem that the Buena Vista College community focused upon and endeavored to alter during the 1980s. Unfortunately, the perception continued on into the Moore Administration.

Dr. Bernadine Sikorski, a New York native with a Ph.D. from St. Louis University, proved a popular dean of students during part of this era. Dean Sikorski developed and promoted an educational experiment known as the second curriculum, which fostered expertise and experience in nonacademic areas. The second curriculum stressed the importance of student involvement and leadership in all areas of campus life. Students participating in the program assumed much of the responsibility in the renovation of Pierce and White halls. Dr. Sikorski enjoyed working with students, and her pleasant demeanor in the face of serious problems enabled her to retain the confidence of the entire College community. She left Buena Vista after her marriage in December 1981, but was soon appointed a trustee and continued to serve in that post in 2005.[151]

By the middle 1980s the new, more modern campus was plainly visible. The Forum provided dining facilities far more luxurious than Lage; the Grand Ballroom could be utilized for dances and public events; there was a new student-leadership area and computer center; the snack bar and centennial room remained steeped in tradition; Lage was remodeled into a mass communications center with state-of-the-art technology; there were improvements in energy management and in dormitory conditions. BVTV matured into Innovation Video. KBVC was said to be the only college radio station in the United States with AM stereo. There were 123 mass communications majors when Lage Mass Communications Center was dedicated on October 15–16, 1986.[152]

Tuition costs remained modest at Buena Vista until well after World War II. In 1913–14 a year's tuition in the collegiate department was only $40.[153] During the Depression, President Henry Olson publicized that a good liberal arts education could be obtained at Buena Vista for $285 a year—a sum that included living expenses as well as tuition. Meals could be obtained in the campus dining hall for $4.50 a week. Students, since there were no dormitories on campus, could room and board in the community for $10–15 a week. It was, however, a substantial sum for families hit hard by the Depression, and students knew they would have to work.[154] Those who attended Buena Vista during the Depression years recalled good times and much merrymaking in spite of lack of money and rather limited wardrobes. There were many jam sessions, and it was an era when students did not mind walking. Only two or three students had cars and "it was quite an event if you had gasoline and a car that would run." The pushing and overloading of the partly serviceable cars was one form of entertainment.[155] Apartments were created on the upper floors of Old Main to help financially stressed faculty members. Louise Zerschling recalls how one summer, men students took up "arms in a war against pigeons infesting Old Main's nooks and crannies." After the struggle "we had an all college roast squab feast, served with a flourish in her Old Main apartment by French teacher Miss Lockwood."[156] Wartime inflation, the GI bill, and mounting costs saw tuition, and room and board rise to around $800 by 1954—a seeming pittance when compared to total costs of more than $26,000 faced by entering freshmen in the fall of 2004. However, federal and state grants were not yet available to the students of 1913, were still rare in 1954, and businesses, alumni, and wealthy friends were much less generous in providing scholarships. All that had dramatically changed by the 1990s so that few students paid the total bill for their education. In 2005 approximately 98 percent of Buena Vista students benefited from aid packages that provided both scholarships and federal and state grants and loans. The aid, on the average amounted to $20,000 per student.[157] Loans, of course, still meant considerable indebtedness upon graduation. However, the default rate on loans was less than 3 percent. Furthermore, more than 95 percent of Buena Vista graduates had jobs or had entered graduate school within six months following graduation.

Candidates for the ministry and children of ministers could attend for one-half the normal tuition. During the era 1891–1918 especially a large number of Buena Vista students entered the ministry. C. M. Drury, who had no intention of becoming a clergyman when he enrolled at Buena Vista in the fall of 1914, recalled that "a high religious idealism permeated the student body." Drury was one of eight graduates in the class of 1918. Five became Presbyterian ministers and the sixth a missionary. This class survived to celebrate its fiftieth anniversary on the Buena Vista campus in 1968. At that time they encountered a much larger class of 106 graduates.[158] Drury went on to receive the Ph.D. from the University of Edinburgh, served as missionary in China, a Navy chaplain during World War II, a faculty member at San Anselmo Theological Seminary, a highly respected scholar on the American West, and the official historian of the Chaplain Corps. In 1968 Drury was the recipient of the first Distinguished Service Award presented by the Alumni Association.[159] The other members of the class of 1918 who entered the ministry were J. S. Brown, Edmund Marousek, Harvey Hood, Russell Ensign, and Florence Mitchell. It was a distinguished class.

Drury was one of many Buena Vista students who found it necessary to work part time. Young Drury's board cost $4 a week and he rented a room for $5 a month. He remembered that he had a job beating carpets for twenty-five cents an hour and on one occasion worked for seven and one-half hours in order to earn the money to buy a season ticket to the lecture course. During the summer of 1915 he hauled gravel, which had to be "shoveled by hand onto the wagon and then taken about half a mile where it was dumped in the middle of the road. No effort was made to rake out the larger stones or even to level it." For this work Drury earned fifty cents a load and up to $3 a day. Nor was it easy to travel the fifteen miles between Storm Lake and Drury's home in Early during the winter months. When Drury traveled home via train during the Christmas holidays, he had to go first to Sac City then walk with luggage for two miles in order to take a freight train to Early. He rode in the caboose and recalled that it took over five hours to make the trip. It was also an era when cars and roads were unreliable. Among the hazards to automobiles were the many nails on country roads. Cars lacked demountable rims, and the tires had to be pried loose and the inner tube patched. After the tire was "pried back on" the inner tube was pumped up with a hand pump.[160]

Buena Vista College, small and struggling as it was, left a lasting impression upon Drury. He found Dr. Parkhill, dean of the College and professor of Latin and Greek, an inspiring teacher. And Drury recalled that it was Walter Benthin, professor of Bible and sociology, who in 1915 first presented him with the challenge of the ministry.[161] Furthermore, because of the limited student body, everyone could participate in the extracurricular activities.

Campus, community, and summer work has always been necessary for Buena Vista College students. By the 1980s, abetted by federal work-study grants, students labored for the minimum wage of $3.35 an hour. The elite corps of academic assistants (outstanding majors assigned to an individual professor) received $4 per hour. In Drury's era there were few jobs for students on a campus of under ten acres where a single academic building housed all departments, administrative offices, chapel, laboratories, and library. The increasing size of the campus, a growing enrollment, the new building programs, and the bureaucratic mentality of the modern era—local and government—meant increasing job opportunities at the College.

Increasing college costs and rising standards of living forced most students to seek not only campus but outside employment. Extracurricular activities became more necessary and more demanding. (What employer wanted a total bookworm?) The ubiquitous Dan Ott became a role model for the emerging student of the 1960s and 1970s. An activist in the positive sense, Ott was elected president of the Student Council in May 1966. He was described as "hyperactive" because of his many activities, which included the Lettermen's club and the Gamma Sigma Phi fraternity. He was vice president of the Phi Alpha Theta history fraternity, chairperson of the Student Religious Activities Committee, a member of the football squad, and worked a forty-hour week at a local gas station and dry cleaning establishment.[162] With all that, Ott managed to retain a B-plus average. Following graduation he obtained an M.A. in history at Southern Illinois University, returned to Buena Vista as director of admissions, and later achieved success as director of planning at the University of Florida.

Another student leader during the 1970s was Stephen D. Peterson. Peterson was an excellent student, a history major, a member of the choir, and a participant in the Joint Conference Committee (students, faculty, and administration). He was also a victim of Hodgkin's disease, which claimed his life shortly before graduation in 1970. Although he struggled across campus supported by iron walking aids, suffered repeated hospitalization and fierce challenges to his waning strength, he managed to become an integral part of the College scene—all this in an era, unlike today, when Buena Vista had no easy access facilities for the handicapped. His degree was granted posthumously and he was honored by an "in memoriam" dedication in the 1971 *Log*.

There are many examples of student creativity and initiative. One day while taking a shower, *Tack* editor Quent Wittrock, realizing that the College had no yearbook and that he had many pictures revealing campus life, decided to write a book. His small volume about Buena Vista dorm life in the 1970s entitled *The Long and the Short of It* was printed at a newspaper office where he had summer employment, cost $350, and sold 100 copies. Selling at $2 a copy the book was not a moneymaker, some of the revelations were not entirely pleasing to the administration, and there were complaints from students that the book was too expensive. Wittrock responded, "I would wallpaper my room with it before I would lower the cost." But John Karras gave it publicity in his column in the *Des Moines Register* and the book retained its value as a social document.[163]

A favorite among students during the early 1980s, although more an inspiration than a leader, was the canine mongrel the intrepid Tripod (proper name Casey). Actually, Tripod or Casey was a much-traveled Irish setter whose owners moved him from Alaska to Colorado to Iowa. An unfortunate victim of cancer, Tripod's left foreleg was amputated to save his life (thus the name). When his owner left Storm Lake for a metropolitan area, historian Jeff Perrill, whose liberal leanings made him sympathetic toward the homeless, adopted Tripod. Tripod wiled away the hours sleeping in Dr. Perrill's office, sometimes attending the Russian history class, and occasionally assisting in proctoring exams. Definitely a senior citizen by 1981 (equivalent human years, 78), Tripod was generally passive except at those rare cultural events he disliked.[164]

Social activism among Buena Vista students during the Vietnam War era may have appeared tame when measured by national standards. Nevertheless, the student generation that emerged during the 1960s insisted not only on greater social freedom but an increasing role in the governance of the institution. Student calls for change went far beyond expanded parking, assessments for dorm damage, all night visitation rights, and beer in the dorms. They also demanded the exciting, concerned, entertaining brand of education pictured in college publicity, which they sometimes found lacking upon arrival. One young 1960s collegian wrote the *Tack*, "Most of the courses are anything but challenging, many teachers are just plain dull, and much of the curriculum seems designed for high school juniors." This critic not only placed the blame on those students who were concerned "only about the job after graduation" but with faculty who "are not using their intelligence to challenge the student."[165] Jay Campbell who edited the *Tack* in 1966, continued the cry for higher standards insisting that "standards must be of the highest degree and expulsion rules must be understood by all and frequently enforced."[166] Many would echo the sentiments of one distinguished graduate who recalled:

> Most of all, my time at Buena Vista made me think (in many ways, for the first time in my life). Whether it was figuring out why (name deleted) should not be dismissed from school for drinking a beer, what Walt Whitman said . . . , or what was wrong with Roosevelt's first-year economic policies, I had to think. And, life hasn't been the same since.[167]

Actually, all thinking segments of the College community sought higher standards. Buena Vista's academic success during the period 1960–85 can be measured by the outstanding life and career performances of its graduates as seen from the vantage point of the early twenty-first century.

Buena Vista attracted its share of charismatic professors whose magnetism soon pulled large numbers of students into their academic and social orbits. Duane Merry, a handsome and colorful professor of sociology, who completed his graduate work at New York University and as part of his studies had spent six months studying the way of life of Bedouin tribes in Jordan's central desert, excited Buena Vista students during the 1960s. Merry's office in the northwest wing of Dixon-Eilers was directly across from the women's dormitory. So many women students stood at their windows staring at the Roman-featured, dark-haired Merry that he felt it necessary to put up curtains (which he did with considerable flair). A popular lecturer throughout northwest Iowa, Merry in 1964 decided to seek the sixth district Republican nomination for Congress. "If the people of northwest Iowa believe in me as much as I believe in them, I'm sure I will be elected," he announced. However, Merry lost his bid for the GOP nomination, became engrossed in some personal trials, and soon left Iowa for California.[168] He had been seen as heir apparent to Dr. Luman Sampson as chairperson of the Division of Social Science. Instead the post passed to the pedestrian but more stable William H. Cumberland. Another sociologist, Dr. Ron McClay, arrived in the mid-1970s to present his radical albeit soft brand of sociology. McClay's pointed challenges to accepted orthodoxy prompted a following among small town students still unaware of how much antiestablishment feeling boiled within them. Unfortunately, McClay's fondness for heterodoxy moved beyond the realm of iconoclastic behavior that college authorities were willing to tolerate and he, too, departed for California.

The students' chosen professor of the 1980s was Dave Diamond (a pseudonym as it turned out). Diamond's tall, slim figure, his long strides, and dark sunglasses provided an imposing silhouette on campus. Like Merry, Diamond attracted a large student, especially female student, following. Diamond, like Merry, was born and raised in North Dakota. He had been a disc jockey in California, a program director at Los Angeles radio station KFI, and an author of dramas, poetry (including *Storm Lake Suite* published by his own vanity press—Barking Dog), and westerns. The *Slade* series, under the pen name of Link Pennington, was vivid, robust, fast-moving, and introduced a coating of rather explicit sex into the traditionally clean-cut literature of the American West (read the books). Between 1982 and 1988 Diamond was a major force in building Buena Vista's strong mass communications program. He was also a key figure in Buena Vista's decision to purchase the Ida Grove radio station KIDA-FM, which he was expected to manage.[169] Many students were outraged when Diamond was denied tenure for what appeared to be rather obscure reasons. Diamond made it known in interviews conducted by the College paper, the *Tack*, and the local press that his feelings had been ruffled. The vocal Diamond could not understand how he could have been selected as Teacher of the Year by the Student Senate, featured in College brochures, and still denied tenure—all in the same week. Diamond must have felt a little like his fictional hero, Slade, as he reviewed his predicament charging that the seven-person tenure committee "hid behind rocks" as the candidate (Diamond) rode "into the canyon unarmed. They can shoot at you, wound you, but you can't defend yourself."[170] Students organized a "Save Dave" campaign, all to no avail as President Briscoe upheld the recommendation of the Promotion and Tenure Committee. Diamond withdrew only as far as Sioux City, where Morningside College hired him to teach and promote their budding mass communications program.

It was Dr. Laura Inglis, who was, perhaps, the University's most charismatic and sometimes controversial professor during the decade of the 1990s until her tragic death of pancreatic cancer in August 2001. Inglis was determined in her pursuit of social justice. She opposed AHLS and ACES speakers whom she felt did not meet acceptable standards. She fought for gender justice in the area of faculty salaries. She was an opponent of the first Gulf War and urged for understanding of the world's ethnic, cultural, and religious differences. She was not an orthodox Christian, but a seeker who personally assimilated what she discovered as the deepest meanings in a variety of faiths. She seemed, in her final struggle, not to fear death, but to find in it another challenge of mystery and experience. Typical were her remarks in March 2001; when faced with her terminal illness; she insisted that she was "having a wonderful time seeing how reality fits the material that has been written about it."[171] Her life had been a continuous quest for personal meaning and global social justice.

Those students who were seeking stability and solid professional advice along with academic depth and considerable personal charisma found a champion in Dr. John Madsen, Associate Professor of Business and Corporate Communications. Madsen worked in several areas during a career that ran from his first steps across campus in the fall of 1973 until his retirement on August 31, 1999. Madsen had received his doctorate from the University of Kansas and had taught at the Haskell Indian Community College. He performed a variety of tasks at Buena Vista including organizing the mass communications along with the corporate communications program, saving the *Tack* from extinction in the early 1970s, working closely with President Briscoe on the Siebens Grant, and being the parent of Buena Vista's Pacific Rim overseas program. Madsen also taught a number of courses in the Business Department. Four of his students won the Cumberland Award for Research and a dozen were winners of the Rollins Award.[172] Madsen was a forceful, dynamic, sometimes blunt, always energetic teacher who knew how to inspire confidence in his students. He had uncommonly good judgment and possessed a way of getting people to listen to him, from the CEO on down. His retirement in 1999 left a difficult gap to fill. One always knew where one stood with John Madsen on an issue. Madsen remained occupied following retirement by teaching at various colleges, including St. Ambrose, in the Quad Cities area. He also served as a member of the editorial board for the book *Encyclopedia of Public Relations,* Robert L. Heath, Editor, Volumes 1 and 2, Sage Publications, Thousand Oaks, California.

Students also had their favorites among the custodial staff. Among the three most interesting was "the man in white," Carl Peterson, who tended the New Building (later Dixon-Eilers) from its completion in 1958 until his retirement in the 1960s. Peterson wore a white uniform as his trademark and conversed freely with faculty and students on a variety of topics. George Krohn, a venerable St. Louis Cardinals baseball fan who often accompanied Jay Beekmann and the Beaver baseball team on trips, came to Buena Vista in 1969 and for a time was superintendent of buildings and grounds. Krohn retired in 1980, but within a month returned on a part-time basis and served Buena Vista in a variety of ways, including that of mailman, until his permanent retirement in May 1987.[173] Jim Barber, the custodian-student of the beginning of the second century, compulsively cleaned the floors of Dixon-Eilers. The insight and influence of these men on student life and learning rivaled those of the professors.

The early classes provided the College with a gift upon graduation. This must have originated with the class of 1905, who desired to leave "on campus some little reminder of their companionship and work together." They secured a stone and placed it on campus where it might do its part in "holding the memories of those days." The class of 1908 presented the College with a large bust of General Grant; the class of 1909 replaced trees that had died; the class of 1910 established a fund of $600 from which interest was to go to the winner of the state oratorical contest. The class of 1913 "erected a gateway for the N.E. corner of the College campus." The two columns of mason work were 4 feet square and 10 feet high. A stone inscription plate bearing the date of the class graduation was cut into the portals, which still stand undisturbed.[174] The class of 1913 could denote some sadness, too. That year Mrs. J. W. Countermine, the former Anna M. Godley, died in Des Moines of cancer at the age of forty-three. She had been the first female faculty member at Buena Vista, women's principal and instructor in English, 1891–95. One of her pupils had been Willis Edson, who remembered her with affection throughout the years. Death also claimed C. W. von Coelln, a stellar member of the faculty, 1892–96. The New London, Iowa paper recorded that von Coelln was a "man of pronounced ability."[175]

Lecture series were popular before World War I. Sometimes lecturers were obtained through the Redpath Lyceum Bureau of Chicago.[176] Among the lecturers to appear was Champ Clark of Missouri, the Speaker of the House of Representatives. It was the Progressive Era and the students had a keen interest in politics. In a straw poll conducted in 1921, the student body supported Woodrow Wilson, with one student (perhaps for shock appeal) voting for socialist Eugene V. Debs.

Of course, prominent speakers and groups continued coming to the Buena Vista campus including Bennett Cerf, nationally acclaimed publisher, author, and lecturer, Erwin Canham of the *Christian Science Monitor,* scientist James Van Allen, the Vienna Boys' Choir, Lorin Hollander, Gerald Ford, Jimmy Carter, and Carlos Montoya. During the 1960s the Danforth Foundation provided funding for many of the campus speakers. The development of the Academic and Cultural Events Series (ACES) program already under way in 1988 promised an exposure to cultural programs unprecedented not only in the College's first century but on few small college campuses anywhere.

It was Briscoe's wish to bring the "world's ideas and culture to Northwest Iowa." Hal Closson was the first coordinator until his retirement in 1994. Carla Offenburger and Bethany Larson added to the success of the program as they found ways to revitalize the important series at a time when it seemed to be on a downward spiral. The ACES program was destined to be part of the academic curriculum at Buena Vista. Students were required to attend eight events including two concerts and six lectures out of a total yearly offering of seven concerts and fifty lectures.[177] Most of the programs were of high quality with class artists and speakers. However, the fact that they were involuntary and did not always appeal to student interests aroused considerable criticism. Some students frustrated both the artists and serious members of the audience by talking among themselves or through other forms of rudeness during the performance. By October 1994 a few students were urging that ACES be abolished, a clamor that still occasionally echoed into the twenty-first century. It was noted that one speaker spoke 90 minutes on "Iowa's Ice Age" receiving, because of the length of his narration, an "ice cold" reaction.[178] However, a majority of students recognized the value of the programs. Already by 1995 Ed Albee, Tom Brokaw (telecast), Henry Cisneros, Shirley Chisholm, Richard Leakey, Lech Walesa (telecast), Robert Waller, the Boys Choir of Harlem, Chinese National Orchestra, violinist Izthak Perlman, and the Vienna Choir had been featured. Programs were timely as they zeroed in on the issues of the day. In September 2005 ACES in an effort to put a human face on the Muslim faith sponsored a program, "Islam in America." Dr. Hatem el-Hag Ali, a physician at Mayo Health Systems, and Mr. Said Khalid, a software engineer at IBM, shared the experience of practicing their faith following 9/11.[179] One could hardly quarrel with that lineup and a majority of students acknowledged the benefits. Even substantially larger institutions could not match the number or quality of the ACES programs. As expected, Buena Vista students preferred creative performances to heavier lectures. When one considers exchange programs, the blending of cultures, the new and ever-changing technology, developing cultural opportunities including travel abroad, no generation of Buena Vista students enjoyed the opportunities of those who enrolled after 1980. The expectations of the millennial students of the twenty-first century would be even higher.

Students were sometimes overawed by the artists they encountered and occasionally wondered when and how to respond. Initial resistance to a compulsory program evaporated when students recognized the quality of the ACES series. Nor were Buena Vista students unique in expecting more than their predecessors.

Buena Vista College also secured a number of national honorary academic fraternities. The first was Pi Kappa Delta (speech) organized on the campus in 1924. A year later the drama department secured a chapter of Alpha Psi Omega. The original English club founded in 1936 became national with the acquisition of a Sigma Tau Delta chapter in 1938. Professor Maryanna Hamer, 1931–47, and Professor J. Luke Creel, 1938–46, were responsible for the steady progress made by the Division of Languages and Literature. Professor Creel, the author of an increasing flow of poems, left Buena Vista for Gustavus Adolphus in 1946. There he wrote a book on the folklore of an African tribe. Carl Adkins, Leonard Martz, Ingeborg Stolee, Darrell Peck, and Manoocher Aryanpur would continue work begun by Hamer and Creel. Eventually, the annual lecture sponsored by the School of Communication and Arts (formerly Language and Literature) would be named in honor of Professor Stolee who taught at Buena Vista from 1961 until her retirement in 1977. Stolee, the daughter of missionary parents, was born at Fort Dauphin on the island of Madagascar. Her undergraduate and graduate days were spent at St. Olaf and the University of Minnesota. Stolee lived and traveled in Asia, was an editor at the Augsburg publishing house, and served on the St. Olaf faculty before coming to Buena Vista.[180]

During the 1960s overseas travel and exchange programs became part of the Buena Vista educational program. Mary Ellen Hughes of Boone and Stephen Schaffer of Balaton, Minnesota, became the first Buena Vista students to participate in the junior year abroad in the fall of 1964. Hughes, a French major, attended the International Christian University in Tokyo, and Schaffer, a math and science major, selected Germany for his study abroad. Mary Ellen Hughes, outstanding not only as a student but as a person, died prematurely in England where she had married and resided. Schaffer attended the Free University of Berlin, worked on a farm for room and board, and improved his German.[181]

In 1959 the School of Science secured a chapter of the coveted Lambda Sigma Tau fraternity. The music department was represented by Alpha Mu Omega and Phi Mu Alpha. In 1966 history obtained the Pi Kappa Delta chapter of Phi Alpha Theta. During the 1970s social work organized and received national accreditation due to the efforts of Professor A. G. Thomas, who had taught both sociology and social work since his arrival on campus in 1964. The most recent fraternity is Alpha Mu Gamma, the national collegiate foreign language honor society brought to campus in 1987 by Dr. Floyd Pace, professor of Spanish.[182] While student support for academic fraternities proved disappointing, an increasing number of Buena Vista graduates continued on to professional schools. The escalating numbers of business graduates meant more Buena Vista grads would be seeking the MBA, but large numbers also sought law and medical careers. The competence displayed by Buena Vista College graduates was a major factor in the College's achievement of regional and national prestige.

Buena Vista students continued to benefit from the development of the second curriculum originated by Dr. Bernadine Sikorski. The second curriculum was designed to develop leadership and decision-making skills, foster latent creativity, improve planning and organizational abilities, and strengthen forecasting and communication talents. Testing, counseling, and the development of a structured framework to discover and promote student talents were part of the procedure. Students whose talents were in the area of communication skills would be channeled into work as disc jockeys for the radio station, or as reporters and editors for the campus newspaper. This was part of the historic goal of "Education for Service" and it suited well the new era where entrepreneurship, leadership, and decision making were emphasized. The second curriculum was not meant to subvert the more intellectual first curriculum, but it was a recognition that book skills were not the only road to success and service.[183]

Although a Presbyterian church–related college, the religious tone at Buena Vista was from the beginning more ecumenical than sectarian. Nevertheless, chapel remained compulsory until well into the 1960s. As late as the middle 1920s faculty were forced to sit in front on the platform in full view of the student body where their absence was easily noted. The *Tack* emphasized that "the faculty did not enjoy this exhibition and neither did the students."[184]

Few Buena Vista graduates after World War II chose the ministry as a career. However, the religious emphasis remained strong until the College pursued a more independent course during the Briscoe administration. President Fisher, a committed Christian layperson, strongly approved of a strong liberal arts program "in a distinctively Christian setting." Spiritual Emphasis Week was an annual event, which provided "a week of concentrated emphasis on Christian values."[185] Fisher's successor, Wendell Halverson, sought to continue the tradition. However, the turbulent 1960s saw a persistent rebellion against involuntary chapel. Still during the early 1960s, College authorities were literally counting heads as they checked attendance—failure to comply could lead to petty fines ($2 for each excessive cut) and considerable resentment. Buena Vista experimented in finding ways of making compulsory attendance more viable; this included better speakers (not just area ministers), a reduction of services, and the formation of a new program, part religious and part secular, known as DISCO (Discovery). Finally by the fall of 1970 the College abandoned forced piety.[186] The introduction of voluntary chapel left both freedom of choice and chapel intact, but attendance atrophied to a handful of students, faculty, and staff. Under the leadership of College chaplain "Parse" DeJong, trustee member, retired pastor, and a revered and respected counselor of students, chapel programs and attendance enjoyed a revival in the late 1980s. However, the new freedom of choice and the availability of secular activities determined that only a fraction of the 900 seats in Schaller Chapel would be filled.

Still, religious life permeated the College. The historic connection with the Presbyterian Church was not severed—only altered. As President Briscoe remarked, "The Synod does not own the College nor dictate to the College what it has to do."[187] Board members were now routinely approved by the Synod, and representatives from the Synod came around less frequently to review the progress of the school. The demise of the old intimacy had been gradual but real as the Church, unable to provide more than a token of the funding, could no longer exercise power in the new era of American education. A joint statement on the status of the continuing but changing relationship was drawn up by the College and the new Synod of Lakes and Prairies in 1984 and approved by the Synod in June 1986. The new covenant reaffirmed "the desire of Buena Vista College and the Synod of Lakes and Prairies to maintain a close inter-relationship while at the same time affirming the need of each institution to retain its autonomy."[188] Thus the relationship, although still valued, was more flexible and less intimate than at any time in the College's history. Nevertheless, the traditional religious aura and moral commitment was much in evidence at the conventional baccalaureate services and in the symbols of the institution. Prayer was still invoked at major College functions. The department of religion, although now in the School of Social Sciences, retained much of its earlier influence; Robert Tollefson's large course, Experiences in Religion, introduced in 1971 and the Staley lecture series, also a product of the 1970s, indicated that at least some threads of church-relatedness remained.

Professor of Religion and Philosophy, Dr. Robert J. Tollefson, who arrived in 1960 and served under three presidents and as many deans, was for three decades the campus leader in promoting spiritual awareness. A navy veteran in World War II, an electrical engineering major at Michigan Technological University, a theology graduate from Princeton, a Ph.D. from the University of Iowa School of Religion, a former mathematics instructor, and a pastor for three years, Tollefson's religious, social, and political underpinnings became increasingly liberal. A social activist and a community leader, Tollefson developed a deep concern for the social and environmental problems of the global village. These concerns were voiced in classes, as president of the Storm Lakes Art Council, as president of Kiwanis, as moderator of the Synod of Lakes and Prairies, in sermons, and in prayers that were sometimes upsetting to traditionalists.[189] But even opponents had to admire his scholarship and the fact that he had an uncanny ability to prick the tranquility of hitherto undisturbed souls. Furthermore, some of Tollefson's students like Herbert Swanson, who taught, ministered, and wrote in Thailand, and Richard Fiete, who upon graduation served in Africa, carried the spirit of their mentor abroad. Another former student, the Reverend Duane Queen, became pastor of Lakeside Presbyterian Church in 1979. Tollefson's relationship with his colleagues was controversial. Some, perhaps unfairly, charged that he was the "prime minister," during the era when John Williams was vice president for academic affairs. Actually, Tollefson was moving steadily left during this period. He became an exponent of liberation theology, which committed him to social action on global as well as local concerns. Tollefson could on occasion appear judgmental and autocratic, attributes that sometimes cloaked his great compassion, humanism, and concern for social justice. His tireless and expert work in the classroom and on committees, his constant call for excellence, his broad commitment to the development of the whole person, his ability to awaken in students a sense of feeling for the environment and the global village, and his stellar service to the Storm Lake community marked him as one of the great teachers in the history of Buena Vista College.

Students moving through the decade of the 1980s were less interested in traditions, less interested in the burning questions of social justice, social reform, or the opportunity for social service that had concerned many of their predecessors. Some faculty found them materialistic, void of enthusiasm, career-oriented to the extent that they cared little for the humanizing virtues of the liberal arts. They also faced temptations and problems no other generation of students had encountered. These challenges included nuclear technology that made instant global destruction a possibility, and the dire consequences of casual sexual encounters, ranging from herpes to the dreaded AIDS. Drugs, including some of the more lethal ones, were a small but ever-present nemesis after the 1960s. However, alcohol remained the drug most commonly consumed and no doubt contributed to the increasing occurrences of violent behavior and vandalism common to all college campuses. Changing patterns of acceptable behavior plagued a series of vice presidents of student services from Jim Petty to Gary Musgrave to Ivan Harlan. Harlan took the post in 1987, having come from Knox College originally to serve as vice president for institutional advancement. But Harlan had served Knox in a variety of posts and would do the same at Buena Vista. As Forum director Hal Closson noted, "Ivan can handle the toughest situation with the utmost calmness." He seemed to have a manner that channeled the volatile urges of his wards in a more positive direction.[190]

At the same time this generation of Buena Vista students would have laughed at the panty raiders of the 1950s, ridiculed the thought of tolerating a beanie for two months, and scorned racism. They were also increasingly concerned about cuts at the national level for student assistance and the mounting costs of a college education that might force them to transfer from private to public colleges or drop out of college. Buena Vista still recruited students who would better have been left alone, but there were also the dedicated and the brilliant, some of whom in 2010 will be among the movers of a fast-developing technological global society. Several faculty believed that they could discern with the arrival of the 1990s a new humanism stirring within the student body, and with it new possibilities for the liberal arts.

The burning of Old Main by no means destroyed the bones of the structure. Indeed, the stone archway remained erect and so rich in memories that Bill Wesselink painstakingly disassembled it piece by piece, numbered each stone, and reassembled the structure southeast of the new building (Dixon-Eilers). Students from the classes of 1954–60, assisted by the administration, headed the reconstruction project. The ground-breaking ceremonies took place in November 1959 with Student Council President Robert O'Rourke turning the first shovelful.[191] After its completion academic processions would pass through the arch, which became a symbol linking the past and present. President Wendell Q. Halverson noted:

> That Stone Arch is also a symbol of the future of the College. It is a symbol of the determination of the Trustees and the faculty to build a private independent institution of Christian Higher Education which will more effectively serve the complex needs of the youth of today and tomorrow.[192]

With this in mind President Halverson, Vice President Gordon Hermanson, and other College officials organized the Order of the Arch. This was an expensive but worthwhile society for friends and alumni of the College to join. Life membership signified a contribution of $5,000 or more within a three-year period. A contribution of $1,000 within a three-year period enabled the donor to become an active member of the Order. Already by 1965 there were 132 active members. The early members received a certificate plus a small marble plaque with the arch medallion and the donor's name inscribed. By 1996 the Order of the Arch designated four categories of donors. These consisted of (1) the Keystone Society ($1,000), (2) Dean's Circle ($2,500), (3) President's Circle ($5,000), and (4) the Trustee's Circle ($10,000 up).[193] The Arch would become one of the major symbols of Buena Vista College, imprinted on the logos of the institution, with the visible edifice rebuilt and standing tall in the southwest corner of the Forum, where twice each year students and faculty perform the binding rites symbolized by the march through the Arch. Is it too much to hope that the rich heritage that those rites symbolize will forever touch the lives of those who joined hands for a moment of eternity?

10

An Athletic Tradition

All thy loyal sons and daughters
Do thy name revere.

—BUENA VISTA ALMA MATER

Athletics have played an increasingly important although not dominant role at Buena Vista College. The athletic program at Buena Vista has passed through at least four phases: (1) 1891–1912, loose eligibility rules, commercial and preparatory students and some professionals participating; (2) 1913–23, Buena Vista was a member of the unstable and now extinct Hawkeye Conference; (3) 1923–70, Buena Vista became one of the charter members of the newly formed Iowa Conference; and (4) the post-1970 era of rapidly expanding athletic emphasis, women's competitive sports, the development of a nationally recognized wrestling program, and the inclusion of the so-called minor sports. During the first two phases football was the major college sport. Although baseball was played during the 1890s, it failed to gain full status in small colleges until after World War II. Basketball started at Buena Vista around 1917, but it was not until the 1920s that the College began to play what might be considered a full schedule. Since 1970 women's softball and men's wrestling, along with football, have given Buena Vista national recognition in intercollegiate athletics at the Division III level.

Football records from the 1890s are rather scarce; however, by

1893 Buena Vista had organized a team. J. Weber Linn, son of
Buena Vista's second president, James M. Linn, claimed that he
was the organizer (as well as the worst player) of the team.[1]
Another instigator seems to have been the Irish-born student, J. P.
Mullen. Mullen had a copy of Walter Camp's rule book and suggested that a team be organized. The squad made their own uni-
forms and marked out a field on the campus. Game and participation rules were rather loose in the 1890s. Writing in what he
believed to be a more modern era, W. C. Edson remarked on the
early phase of the gridiron sport:

> Looking back a dozen years we see teams composed of men of enor-
> mous weight and stature and with about as much speed as a loaded
> freight train on an up-grade. The ball was put in play at the center of
> the field by the center touching the ball with his foot and passing to the
> quarter back, while the eleven men were formed in the old fashioned
> turtle-back wedge.[2]

It was a rough, rugged sport with the opposition team charging
from their own ten-yard line in order to break up the barrage that
was churning down the field. Some moved over the top, some underneath, while others "grabbed arms, legs, hair, or any frayed
edges that could be reached until the whole was finally dismem-
bered and the man with the ball was downed."[3]

The 1893 Buena Vista team opened their gridiron history by
challenging a Cherokee independent squad, "composed largely of
employees of the Illinois Central Round House." The Cherokee
team appeared in Storm Lake on schedule, but the Buena Vista center did not put in his appearance. Furthermore, it was a stormy,
snowy day. Without a center to lead the "center rush," it appeared
that Buena Vista would be buried in the two inches of snow that
had accumulated during the night. While the Beavers were preparing to take the field, a Storm Lake businessman (Mr. Skiff) came to
the dressing room with a husky young man whom he introduced as
"Mr. Root." Root, who weighed 225 lb, was willing to play center
if the Buena Vista squad would "show him how." Root seemed to
learn quickly, and Buena Vista moved through center to score the
lone touchdown of the game and a 6–0 victory. The next morning

AN ATHLETIC TRADITION

1891–1991

1

1 Sports contests were held in the space in front of Old Main until Bradford Field was completed in the mid-1920s. Swope and Smith halls now occupy the area.

2　　　　　　　　　　　　　　　　　**3**

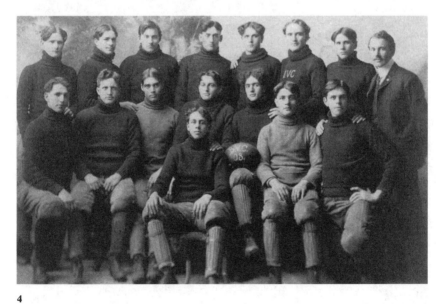

4

2 Players on the 1902–3 football team. (*From left*) Irving Wright, John Beard, Charles Flint, Charley Burgeson.　　**3** Willis Edson, an outstanding athlete who went on to play for the unbeaten University of Iowa in 1899 and 1900.　　**4** The 1904 football team.

5   6   7

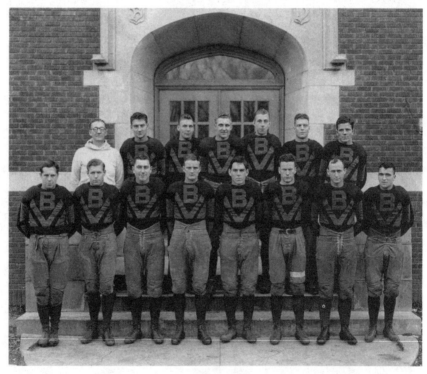

5 Mighty "Beef" Karges, star guard during the Kelly era.   **6** Leslie Rollins, outstanding player of the 1920s.   **7** J. D. "Jim" Kelly took over College coaching from 1922 to 1926. His rugged techniques brought results, and Buena Vista had four brilliant seasons in football and track.   **8** The 1934 football team with coach Frank Casey. (Photo by Mickle Studio, Storm Lake)

9

10

9 The old gymnasium, Victory Hall, built in 1920. It was renovated in 1962 and renamed Edson Hall in recognition of W. C. Edson, lifelong friend of the College and member of the Iowa Hall of Fame. 10 Jay Beekmann, nominated best basketball player in the Iowa Conference in 1962. Beekmann returned to Buena Vista in 1956 as baseball coach.

11

12

13

11 Cheerleaders, 1949.   **12** Bill Tryon, outstanding football player in the 1950s.   **13** Charlie Mulligan, quarterback, an all-time Buena Vista football great.

14

15

14 Bob Otto, one of the Iowa "Ironmen," coached the Beavers during the early 1950s. His 1952 team won the Iowa Conference championship. **15** The victorious 1959 football team, slogan, "every man a most valuable player." Their record 8-1-0 was the best since 1925. Quarterback Lanny Grigsby is no. 16.

16

17

16 Jerry Ibach is congratulated by President Fisher, 1957. Ibach, 1954–1958, was an athletic star who scored 1,036 points in three years of basketball competition, an all-conference first team football selection, and top pitcher for the 1957 baseball team. **17** Coach Merritt Ewalt, athletic director Jay Beekmann, and all-conference college star Jim Ahrens examine trophies of the triumphant 1961–62 basketball season. Ahrens's no. 14 was retired.

18 The 1962 basketball team, coached by Merritt Ewalt, won the Iowa Conference championship. Star performers were Jim Ahrens (15), Larry Dick (53), and Glenn Theulen (35).

19

20

19 Coach Jay Beekmann and all-American Dave Wolfe, leading hitter of the 1965 baseball team.
20 Jim Hershberger directs his quarterback. Hershberger, an outstanding coach of the 1970s and 1980s, became athletic director in 1990.

21 The 1974 Iowa Conference championship baseball squad.

22

23

22 Harriet Henry (*right*), architect of the women's athletic program at the College, coaches volley-ball.   **23** Wrestling coach Al Baxter (*left with tie*) arrived in 1978 to establish the Beavers as a national power. The 1986 Beaver wrestlers were Iowa Conference champions and third in the nation (NCAA Division III).

24   Jeannie Demers, 1983–1987, drives for the basket. Demers was an all-time Buena Vista scoring great, an all-conference, and all-American player.

25

26

25 Charles Slagle stands with his 1982 women's golf team. (Photo by Buntrock-Salie, Storm Lake) **26** John Naughton (*left*) and Al Baxter following regional and national championship performances in women's basketball and wrestling, 1990.

27

27 Aerial view of the football stadium and campus, about 1982.

28

28   President Briscoe with J. Leslie Rollins at the naming of the new stadium, 1987.

two of the triumphant Buena Vistans went to Mr. Skiff's store to thank him for Root's timely assistance. It was then that Skiff informed them that the mysterious center's "name isn't Root and he has played four years at Princeton."[4]

Another member of that first team, J. Weber Linn, later a professor at the University of Chicago, recalled that he was "the worst player on the first football team of Buena Vista College." A player named Steele and Willis Edson were the best players, Linn wrote many years later. He also recalled a game played in a snowstorm when Steele, who had to ride in from the farm, was late. Apparently he was badly needed, for Linn remembered, "Never shall I forget the sight of him on his horse looming up through the driving flakes as he reached the edge of the field after we had been longing for him for a fifteen minute eternity. He looked bigger than Jonah's Whale."[5]

In those days the big, open field in front of Old Main was used as the playing area. Linn recalled another contest with Cherokee on the latter's field, which Buena Vista also won. The field had been covered with tall weeds and on Saturday morning the Cherokeeans had burned them down. The game was played in two inches of black ashes.[6] In the 1890s Willis Edson played for the Storm Lake town team and for Buena Vista College. Seemingly, town and college players performed on both squads. While Edson was an outstanding prep and college player, his great days on the gridiron were when he was a back with the unbeaten Iowa University teams of 1899 and 1900. The Iowa coach during those years was the famous Dr. A. A. Knipe. One of Edson's great games was a 58–0 victory over Illinois in 1899. During a long career, dating from 1894 to a final victory over the Iowa alumni in 1905, Edson played thirty games at halfback. In those games his team was never defeated and they outscored the opposition something like 802–33.[7] In 1959 Edson was elected to the Iowa Hall of Fame.

During the 1890s, the number of contests was limited and scheduled games often canceled. The opposition might include town or high school teams as well as college squads. The 1898 Buena Vista team was undefeated and un-scored upon in three contests. The victories were over Storm Lake High School 11–0, the Fonda town team 32–0, and Morningside College 6–0. This was

sufficient for Buena Vista to claim the championship of northwest
Iowa. The 1899 eleven were blasted by the University of South
Dakota 26–5, but trounced the high school 28–5 and Denison
Normal 28–0. Buena Vista compiled a 4–1 record in 1900 losing to
Des Moines University 40–0 but later defeating the same team 5–0.
Other victories were over South Dakota 11–0, Alta 28–0, and in the
most points ever scored by a Buena Vista team, the Sac City
Institute was annihilated by a score of 100–0. The *Pilot-Tribune* as-
serted that the 1900 footballers were "worthy successors to the ag-
gregations of a few years ago which included such stock as Harlan,
Edson, Rae and Harker and which swept everything before it."[8]

The 1901 team appears to have played only one game, which
it lost to Dakota Wesleyan University 6–0.[9] The attainments of the
1902 and 1903 teams also appear to have been mediocre. However,
in 1904 the College compiled a 5–2–1 record. Drake and South
Dakota won 18–0 games, but Buena Vista defeated Morningside
5–0, Western Union 21–0, Sac City 39–0, Western Union 52–0, and
State Normal (UNI) 56–6. There was also an early season scoreless
tie with Morningside. The 1907 team compiled a 4–1–1 record
against much weaker opponents.

One of the most formidable Buena Vista players during the
1902–04 era was John W. Beard. Beard played during the two years
that Willis Edson coached the team and made a lasting impression
upon his mentor as well as upon everyone else. Beard had come to
Buena Vista from the stockyard district of Sioux City. College
trustee George Cummings helped finance his education. In 1902
Beard was one of the thirteen men who reported for football practice. Edson recalled that he was a solid 185 lb and could "have
made any team." When Beard's fury broke loose Edson would
"have the boys throw him down on the ground and hold him there
until he was able to control himself." The 1902 squad played a
tough Alta team that consisted of "some old footballers, farmers
and blacksmiths." The official called Buena Vista for being offside
and rather caustically informed Beard, "I'll put you out of the game
if you do that again, you SOB." Beard struck out like a bolt from
Zeus and in a flash "the official was lying on the ground with blood
all over his face." Edson had been out of town and on his return

found a complaint filed with the justice of the peace that Beard was guilty of assault and battery. Edson filed a counter-complaint that the official was guilty of using obscene language and ultimately both cases were dismissed. Records show that Buena Vista split two games with Alta that year, losing the first 6–0 but winning the second 16–0, even though outweighed 30 lb to the man.[10]

The temperamental Beard entered the ministry. He migrated to the tough lumber camps of the far northwest and on occasion had to quell the rugged lumberjacks with his fists before gaining an audience. In World War I he enlisted as chaplain in the Wild West Division and emerged a hero, receiving the Croix de Guerre and the Silver Star. After World War II, in which he also served as chaplain, he completed a 3,000-mile trek through the wilds of Canada. He died in 1951 at the age of sixty-eight.[11]

Football at Buena Vista knew some lean years between 1910 and 1915. In 1908 College officials had the good sense not to field a team and in 1909 they must have wished they had not when Morningside mauled Buena Vista 114–4. The *Tack* refused to mention the score for several years, though it did refer to the game as a "holocaust" and noted that the "heat and dust of the field were almost unbearable."[12] During the next five seasons the Beavers won only six of twenty-eight games. One of the defeats was a 31–3 loss to Morningside at Buena Vista's first Homecoming on October 11, 1913. On a beautiful Indian summer day, the Beavers folded in the second period after battling to a 3–3 tie at half time.[13] But Homecoming was a success and launched Buena Vista on a tradition that became permanent after 1923.

In 1915 former Purdue star Edward Ball became head coach. Ball immediately changed Buena Vista's football fortunes into a decade of gridiron brilliance. Between 1915 and 1925 Buena Vista won forty-five, lost twenty-one, and tied five. The 1918 team was unbeaten in a season limited to three games because of the war, and the 1922 team was undefeated but tied once in six games. Coach Ball's well-balanced 1915 team lost only to Dubuque and Wayne and tied Ellsworth while winning four of seven contests. The tragic death of the young coach in December 1915, when he and a companion fell through the ice in Storm Lake, cut short a promising career.

There was, however, one dismal season in this golden era. The 1916 Beaver squad, led by the bruising fullback John W. Fulton, had won five games and lost three. By the fall of 1917 war enlistments had taken their toll and only eighteen men reported for practice. An equally war-torn Ellsworth team was subdued by the Beavers 14–6 in the opening game. A more rugged Yankton eleven blasted the Beavers 41–6, the Wayne game was canceled, and then the mighty Dubuque Germans appeared on the schedule. Dubuque not only had a weight advantage of 20–30 lb per man, but it also had the great Sol Butler who was reputed to be "the fastest man in the Midwest."[14] Cancellation would mean a $50 forfeit that the College could not afford to pay. So the Beavers undertook the long journey to Dubuque.

The weather, which had been warm, now turned cold, leaving the grassless field full of clods of mud and ice. Dubuque had the speedy Butler primed to play and a great advantage in weight. C. M. Drury, who played center in that game, vividly recalled:

> They held us for downs and got the ball and made a touchdown. We couldn't catch Sol Butler. On the average they got a touchdown every four minutes. I remember the crowd yelling, "We want a hundred." They got it and then the cry was, "We want another hundred."[15]

When the game finally ended Dubuque had amassed a 125–0 margin. Drury, who was knocked unconscious during the last five minutes of play, regretted that he had "not been knocked out the first five minutes."

During home games, Drury recalled that the College was still playing on the green before Old Main. There was nothing to keep the spectators out of the playing area, and in one game an "end suddenly emerged from the crowd and made a successful catch."[16]

In the fall of 1922 young J. D. ("Jim") Kelly arrived from Fonda to take over the coaching duties. Kelly had graduated from Fonda High School (where he once scored 75 points in a high school basketball game) and had attended South Dakota and Iowa State universities. His coaching career actually started on a volunteer basis with youngsters at the Brownsville, Texas high school while he was a young army engineer during World War I. He had married a Newell girl, Donna Redfield, and had returned to Fonda High School as the coach. While Kelly's ways were sometimes rugged, they were successful. College officials were proud enough of Kelly's triumphs to refer to them in the 1924–25 College catalog. He even housed some of his star athletes in the "upstairs dormitory" of his own home.[17]

There were many Kelly victories, especially in football and track. The 1922 gridiron eleven were undefeated, and the 1925 team lost only one of nine games. Kelly's four-year football record of twenty-two wins, five losses, and three ties remains the best winning percentage among Buena Vista coaches. The Kelly schedules were the toughest that the College had yet played. Notable victories were a 3–0 win over State Teachers in 1922; 6–0 (1923) and 22–6 (1924) victories over Morningside; a 6–0 (1925) win over Coe; and a 14–0 (1925) victory over South Dakota State. The Beavers also defeated strong Des Moines University 29–7 in 1924 and clubbed Ellsworth 89–0 in 1923. Kelly football teams won six of seven games against foes in the new Iowa Conference during the seasons 1923–24 and 1924–25. The lone conference setback meted out to Buena Vista during Kelly's reign was a 10–0 defeat at the hands of Western Union (later Westmar College, now Teikyo Westmar University) in 1923. Kelly-coached teams during these years outscored their opponents 446–122. Buena Vista stars in this era were Emmett Barron at end, Theodore Karges and Edward Hagedorn at center, and Forrest Gaffin and J. Leslie Rollins in the backfield. Jim Kelly's four brilliant football seasons remained unrivaled until eclipsed by Jim Hershberger in the 1970s. Kelly produced the only undefeated team to play a full schedule in the history of the school. His mark of eight victories in one season (1925) was not equaled until Dean Laun's 1959 eleven won eight of nine games and not surpassed until the 1986 team won nine contests while losing two. (Hershberger's teams also won eight games in 1973, 1975, and 1976.) When Kelly left Buena Vista in 1926, he moved on to De Paul University in Chicago; in 1937 he was invited to become the track coach at the University of Minnesota. In 1933–34 his football, baseball, and basketball teams were undefeated. No one could replace the colorful Kelly, and the local paper greeted his successors with the headline, "De Paul hires three to replace Kelly." At Minnesota, Kelly built a track program from scratch, revolutionized the discus throw by "developing an intricate pattern of footwork that enabled the thrower to build up much more momentum in the ring," won the NCAA track title in 1948, and coached the U.S. team at the first Pan-American games in 1951. In 1956 he coached the U.S. Olympic track team to victory (15 gold medals) at Melbourne, Australia, and in that same year was honored as the Knute Rockne Coach of the Year. He was also honored as a member of the Iowa Hall of Fame and chaired the U.S. Olympic Committee.[18]

By the time Kelly arrived, Buena Vista athletic teams were called the "Beavers." The football team was officially christened the Beavers on November 9, 1921, when George Wanner was in his last season as coach of a team that won three of eight games. There had been some dispute concerning the origins of the name with the *Storm Lake Register* crediting the *Des Moines Register* with having concocted the name. But "Beavers" was conceived by a Buena Vista student, Karl Nicholas, while sitting in the College library (then in Old Main) in the Spring of 1921. Nicholas was tired of sports headlines that referred to the athletic teams as BV or Bvers, and he combined those two names with BEVO a popular soda pop of that era. The name caught on and was officially adopted as the team prepared to travel to South Dakota. Beavers, a *Tack* writer noted, seemed appropriate because "If there is one characteristic our teams have had above others, it is that of being workers. We've had to work for what we've gained, for we have always played bigger schools than ourselves, and we've never been ashamed of the results."[19] On that day amidst the frosts of fall the Beaver student body "pepped out and down to the station to see the men off on their trip to South Dakota." Karl Nicholas eventually became postmaster at Storm Lake, a strong Presbyterian who, until his death, reminded William H. Cumberland each Sunday they met in Lakeside Church that *The History of Buena Vista College* had not credited him with the unique and genuine contribution that was really his. (There is no doubt concerning the validity of Nicholas's claim—I simply used the wrong source.)

Buena Vista failed to win a football game in the year following

Kelly's departure and won only one basketball game, but things would change with the arrival of Frank Casey in the fall of 1927. Although Casey's greatest coaching days came later at Simpson, he was able to raise the Beavers from the conference cellar. The 1929 football team lost only one and tied two of eight contests, and the 1934 club compiled a 7–1 record. Weak teams during the 1931–33 seasons lowered Casey's overall mark to 29–35 in what at that time was a record eight-year tenure for a Buena Vista coach. Casey coached all sports and when he left in 1935 the *Pilot-Tribune* accurately remarked that, "always taking a handful of inexperienced lads, he registered upset after upset."[20] Casey's 1927 eleven tied Upper Iowa 12-12, lost to champion Iowa Teachers by 6–0 and second place Luther 12–6. The 1929 team upset second place Luther 14–7 and gave Columbia (Loras) their only defeat of the season 14–0.

Coach Albert Dallagher's three-year stint 1935–37 produced fifteen victories in twenty-four games with the high mark a 7–2–0 record in 1936. That squad missed the conference championship by one point and three inches when Central edged the Beavers 7–6 early in the season. Penn, Upper Iowa, Western Union, and Dubuque were all victims as Buena Vista compiled a 4–1 conference mark. Prentist Jones, senior quarterback from Cherokee, directed the team and was elected honorary captain at the end of the season. Scott Keister was the leading ground gainer and was an all-conference selection at halfback.

In 1952 Buena Vista finished a mediocre 5–5 season. But with the conference split into northern and southern divisions, Buena Vista won the northern division 2–1 and emerged as champions when they edged Iowa Wesleyan 13–7 in the play-off game. End Don Kamprath, guards Steve Nemeth and Jim Lindlief, and backs Bill Tryon and Charles Rosburg made all-conference. The Buena Vista victory over Iowa Wesleyan was the only setback the Tigers suffered during the season.[21] Bob Otto, one of the members of the famous 1939 University of Iowa "Ironmen" football team that featured Nile Kinnick and Mike Enich, was the Buena Vista coach. In 1948 Buena Vista finished eighth in the Iowa Conference with a 1–3–0 record but won the championship of the Dakota-Iowa Conference of which they were also a member.

Dean Laun's 1959 eleven, which compiled an 8–1 record, was one of the most exciting teams in Buena Vista football history. Lanny Grigsby was quarterback and end Wes Hunziker and center Roger Jaacks were all-conference selections. Jaacks was regarded as one of the great centers in Iowa Conference history. Buena Vista lost only to champion Wartburg 19–6 at Waverly. The 7–6 Ice Bowl victory at Luther was the first time Buena Vista had beaten the Norsemen since 1952. This was Laun's last season at Buena Vista. The former Iowa State star had amassed a respectable 24–18 record in five seasons.

One of Buena Vista's finest football players and all-time great athletes during the 1950s was Jerry Ibach. A native of Bayard, Iowa, Ibach (the "Bayard Bomber") proved to be Buena Vista's best all-round athlete since J. Leslie Rollins. Ibach was an all-conference back in 1956 and 1957.[22] In 1956 he led Iowa Conference scorers with eleven touchdowns and sixty-six points. He amassed, during his four seasons, 2,839 yards running and passing. He scored twenty-six times and passed for ten touchdowns. Ibach did much of the punting and was regarded as one of the best small-college punters in the nation. During those years Buena Vista played a number of close games; seven of the Beaver defeats were by the margin of one touchdown or less. Unfortunately, Ibach never had the privilege of playing on a winning football team. He was a pitcher on the 1957 Buena Vista team that finished fourth in the nation and in 1958 became the first Beaver basketball player to score one thousand points. Ibach was the only Buena Vista athlete to win the President's Award (for outstanding senior athlete) in two sports. He lettered eleven times, won little all-American recognition in football, was co-captain and most valuable player in football, co-captain and second all-conference in basketball, and was an undefeated pitcher on the nationally ranked 1957 baseball team. Ibach's records would soon fall, but no Buena Vista athlete was more versatile or so captivated Buena Vista fans. As one fan pro-claimed when Jim Ahrens surpassed Ibach's career scoring record in basketball, "There'll never be another Ibach" (nor would there be another Ahrens). Upon graduation Ibach's number twelve jersey was permanently retired, and the Ibach award for athletes winning at least nine letters was established.[23] Only four other Buena Vista athletes have won the award—Lanny Grigsby (1960) who won ten letters, Arnold Zediker (1965), Gary Lane (1966), and Rick Wulkow (1967) with nine letters.

A native of Cedar Rapids, John Naughton, came to play baseball for Kenny Blackman and developed into a star athlete at Buena Vista College during the years 1947–50. Naughton's football talents surpassed his diamond skills as he became the starting quarterback. He was also a second team 1950 all-conference selection in basketball. The Korean War was under way almost as soon as Naughton received his diploma, and he quickly exchanged athletic gear for an army uniform and footballs for flame throwers. Naughton followed military service with coaching stints at Marathon, St. Edmond's High School in Fort Dodge, and Fort Dodge Community College.[24] He was appointed head football coach at Buena Vista in 1962.

Naughton's football tenure was not glorious but his 1965 team was a high-scoring outfit featuring the passing of Rick Wulkow and the running of speedy John ("Pete") Peterson, one of the great backs in the Iowa Conference. The six victories of the 1965 and 1966 teams were the best since 1959 and not surpassed until Hershberger's 7–2 mark in 1971. Naughton's greatest success as a coach would not come in football but, surprising to himself perhaps more than to others, in women's basketball where he would produce three championship teams; two in the Io-Kota and one in the Iowa Conference. His caustic Irish wit and homespun view of life provided breathers for those drenched from the perspiration of contemporary pressures.

Jim Hershberger replaced Naughton as head football coach in 1970. Hershberger's first year was spent in rebuilding a team that had lost twenty of twenty-six games the previous three years. The reconstructed squad won only one of eight games in 1970, then Hershberger-coached teams caught fire compiling a 21–5 record the next three years and tying for the Iowa Conference championship in 1972 by upsetting nationally ranked William Penn 26–24. Buena Vista won the title outright in 1973 going unbeaten in conference play. Hershberger's last championship was the 1978 three-way tie with Central, Dubuque, and Luther. Between 1971 and 1989 Buena

Vista would have only two losing seasons (1982 and 1985), win or tie for three conference championships, finish second on ten occasions, and make three postseason appearances. A new football stadium was readied in midseason 1980, and Hershberger's forces celebrated with a 45–15 homecoming victory over Simpson.[25] After the 1989 season Hershberger's overall record was 121–61 and his Iowa Conference record 95–48–1. Hershberger's long and successful career made him the premier, Jim Kelly not excepted, Buena Vista football coach. The pressure of coaching exacts a toll even among small college mentors, and Hershberger suffered a near-fatal heart attack during a game at Dubuque in 1982. His recovery brought more Buena Vista victories, and in the summer of 1989 Hershberger was appointed College athletic director. He relinquished his coaching duties in February 1990 to Kevin Twait who played quarterback for the Beavers in the early 1980s.

One of Hershberger's greatest victories was the 26–24 victory over William Penn that gave the Beavers a tie for the Iowa Conference title (their first since 1952) in 1972. Buena Vista led by quarterback Charlie Mulligan and running back Dave Dolan (605 yards in five league games) rallied from a 17–13 deficit. Mulligan, described by Hershberger as a "car with only three good tires," played gamely on a bad leg. Nevertheless, the all-conference quarterback hobbled eight yards into the end zone for the go-ahead touchdown.[26] It was one of many games in which the oft-injured Mulligan would perform such heroics. The following season, Mulligan came off the bench in the final minutes to spearhead a 13-point rally and a 33–21 victory over Simpson. The undefeated conference season included the first Buena Vista win over Central in fourteen years and a 17–7 conquest of Penn in the game that decided the conference championship.[27] During the 1970–73 seasons Mulligan amassed a record total of 3,918 yards. Through 1989 Hershberger managed to build a victory edge over every conference opponent but Central, whom he was able to defeat on only three occasions and who led Buena Vista in their overall series 33–10. When Hershberger became coach in 1970, Buena Vista led only William Penn among the current Iowa Conference schools in lifetime series. By 1989 the Beavers trailed only Central, Luther, and

Loras. Furthermore, Hershberger had improved Buena Vista's won-lost record to 194–184 (from 98–142 in 1970) since joining the conference in 1923. In 1975 the Beavers defeated St. Mary's 24–21 in the Boothill Bowl at Dodge City, Kansas, and in 1976 won the NCAA Division quarterfinal game 20–14 against Carroll College, after which they were mauled by powerful St. Johns (Minn) 61–0.[28]

The Hershberger era saw Buena Vista teams often ranked among the top twenty in Division III competition and able for the first time in history to compete on equal and sometimes decisive terms with perennial powers like Central, Luther, Wartburg, and Dubuque. Who would have believed prior to 1970 that Buena Vista would one day (1976) defeat Luther 50–0? From midseason 1975 to midseason 1976 the Buena Vista football team was undefeated in thirteen games. The Beavers won their first nine games in 1986 before dropping the title game to Central 23–14. By 1989 Hershberger had obviously won distinction as the premier football coach in Buena Vista College history and, along with Doc Dorman of Upper Iowa, Moco Mercer of Dubuque, and Edsel Schweizer of Luther, as one of the greatest coaches in the football annals of the Iowa Conference. His peers in the Iowa Conference voted him Iowa Conference coach of the year on five occasions. Hershberger continued as Buena Vista Athletic Director until his retirement, hastened somewhat by health problems, in 1994. He had been coach or athletic director at Buena Vista for twenty-four years. His interest in football never lagged and even though plagued by declining health, he served as an assistant coach in the Aztec Bowl at Saltillo, Mexico, in 2001. Hershberger's death on January 25, 2002, at age 67 was a sad moment for the Buena Vista community.[29] Darrel Schumacher who played for Hershberger noted three great attributes of his coach—"a positive attitude, fairness and honesty."[30]

The post Hershberger era witnessed a downturn in Buena Vista football fortunes. His twenty-six year old successor, Kevin Twait, left after six difficult seasons during which Buena Vista had a 12–44 record. Joe Hadacheck followed Twait and improved Buena Vista's football fortunes with a 22–18 four-year mark including two 7–3 seasons. Steve Osterberger replaced Hadacheck and in five years built a 27–23 mark including one 7–3 and two 6–4 seasons.

During his college days, Osterberger had played quarterback at
Drake and passed for an astounding 7,021 yards in four seasons.
Osterberger's 2004 team posted a 5–3 conference record good
enough for third place. This team gained steam as the season progressed, starting out 1–3 and winning five consecutive games before losing a nonconference final to Bethel 34–24. Osterberger was
named the 2004 Iowa Conference football coach of the year. He
was the first Buena Vista football coach so honored since Jim
Hershberger had won the award in 1986.[31] Osterberger also had a
special destiny in 2005. He would be Buena Vista's gridiron mentor during the school's one-hundredth year of fielding an intercollegiate football team.

The longest rivalry in Beaver history has been with Teikyo
Westmar University. These contests date back to 1903 when Buena
Vista defeated the Le Mars school 17–0. All told, Buena Vista has
won thirty-nine, Teikyo Westmar eighteen, and two of the games
have ended in ties. The 1919 Beavers won a 97–0 slaughter. However, a fine Eagle eleven was able to nip the 1923 Kelly-coached
Beavers 10–0 and in 1987 ended a seventeen-year drought with a
24–10 upset.

There were many Buena Vista football stars, dating from the
exploits of Willis Edson and Charles Beard during the first decade
of Beaver football. John Fulton, "Beef" Karges (all Hawkeye
Conference center in 1923), and J. Leslie Rollins starred during the
Kelly era. The great Jerry Ibach thrilled spectators across the region
as he gained all-conference honors and all-American honorable
mention as a multiple-threat back during the 1950s. But it was the
Hershberger years that produced a myriad of stars. Among standouts
of the Hershberger era are Charlie Mulligan and Rollie Wiebers who
were most valuable players (MVPs) and all-conference quarterbacks
on the championship teams of the 1970s. Wiebers set a seemingly
unapproachable total career yardage mark of 6,148 yards. Wiebers
accounted for sixty-nine touchdowns (49 passing, 20 rushing) during his collegiate career.[32] Buena Vista was 22–6–1 during
Wiebers's three-year stint as first-string quarterback. His longest
run was 97 yards in a 28–21 loss to Central and his longest pass a
90-yarder to Dan Richardson in a game against Luther. Linemen

Joe Kotval (1973), who played briefly with the Dallas Cowboys, and Keith Kerkoff (1976) were all-conference and little all-American selections on those great Hershberger era teams.

Dan and Jim Higley were Division III all-Americans in the 1980s. Dan Higley became the greatest rusher in Buena Vista football history, totaling 3,207 yards during the 1982–85 seasons.[33] However, Scott Bailey soon surpassed Higley's single season mark of 1,070 yards by rushing for 1,429 yards in 1989. Bailey broke Higley's record in a 29–16 victory over William Penn when he rushed for 102 yards. However, he saved his miracle performance for the season's finale when he scored six unbelievable touchdowns and rushed for a school record of 350 yards in a 59–26 rout of Dubuque. One touchdown came on a 76-yard scamper and another on a 31-yard romp through the Dubuque line. Bailey was named co-Iowa Conference Player of the Week and was mentioned on ESPN's "Saturday Heroes."[34] The November 20, 1989 issue of *Sports Illustrated* named Bailey as the small college "Player of the Week." Bailey also achieved all-conference honors. The six touchdowns established a Division III NCAA record. Bailey's sixteen touchdowns, ninety-six points, and forty carries in a single game also established new Buena Vista records. The junior back's banner year left him only 540 yards short of Higley's career record. This he broke during the 1991 season finishing with a record 3,780 yards rushing. Hershberger brought Roger Egland with him as an unpaid volunteer in 1970. Egland, a licensed physical therapist, became an important member of the athletic staff. He was appointed Athletic Director upon Hershberger's retirement in 1994. Egland held this post until he retired in 1999. It was at this point Jan Travis became the first woman in Buena Vista's history to serve as Athletic Director.[35] A number of gridiron stars emerged during the post-1991 era. Ben Smith, Troy Nielsen, Carlos Martinez, and Michael Irvin were first team all-Americans. Martinez proved himself a professional caliber field goal kicker. Martinez once kicked five field goals in a single game, and his 251 career points are the second best in Buena Vista history. He was the NCAA field goal kicking champion in 2000. By 2004 Martinez was playing Arena football with the Dallas Desperados. Ben Smith beat Bailey's single season rushing record with a career mark of 1,583 yards in 1999. Smith's 16 touchdowns that season also established a Buena Vista school record. Smith also ran for 305 yards against Dubuque in 1999. Buena Vista's outstanding pass receiver was Joshua Espinosa (1999–2002) who set a school mark of 190 yards against Simpson in 2002. His 60 catches that season were the best in school history. Espinosa's career yardage of 1,848 was second only to the record 2,200 yards set by Barry Jacobsen (1983–86). Quarterback Eric Wiebers threw for a record breaking 431 yards against Dubuque in 2002. His four touchdown passes in that game tied a Buena Vista record for a single game. Michael Irvin was an all-conference and all-American linebacker who finished his career in 2004.[36]

Buena Vista College has been a member of three athletic conferences. The first conference the Beavers joined was the old Hawkeye Conference formed in 1913. This was an attempt among some of the smaller Iowa conference schools to play by more formal and stable rules:

(1) Athletes must be bona fide students, doing full work in any regular department of the College.
(2) Regulations debar the professional athlete and faculty from participating in any athletics of the College.
(3) He must be doing passing work in his studies.
(4) Regulations limit playing period to four years in college.
(5) He may play with any teams representing educational institutions.
(6) A certified list, approved by faculty, of the eligible men who are to take part in contests, must be submitted to each institution before the contest and to the secretary of the association.[37]

Early members of the Hawkeye Conference were State Teachers, Ellsworth, Parsons, Penn, Charles City, Upper Iowa, St. Joseph's, St. Ambrose, and Buena Vista. The Hawkeye Conference was not very effective, and its membership lacked stability. Besides Ellsworth, Buena Vista played few of the teams in the conference.

By 1921 membership in the Hawkeye Conference consisted of Buena Vista, Upper Iowa, Columbia College (Loras), State Teachers, Western Union, Luther, and Lenox. By 1923 the ineffective Hawkeye Conference ceased to function as most of the schools hastened to join the newly formed Iowa Conference. Buena Vista became one of the charter members of the new conference that permitted the participation of freshmen. At the time of its formation the Iowa Conference operated under eligibility rules determined by the Iowa State Board of Education instead of the not-yet-all-powerful North Central Association. Later, conference schools would abide by National Association of Intercollegiate Athletics (NAIA) and finally (in the 1980s) by NCAA rules. During the 1920s commercial students were eligible to participate in intercollegiate athletics as long as they were enrolled in twelve hours of college-level classes. Bookkeeping and typing classes, however, did not qualify.[38]

While membership in the Iowa Conference has vacillated, Buena Vista has remained within the league since its formation. However, between 1946 and 1949 Buena Vista was a none-too-happy member of the Dakota-Iowa Conference, thus belonging to two athletic conferences at the same time. The membership of the now defunct league consisted of Westmar, Huron, Yankton, Sioux Falls, and Dakota Wesleyan in addition to Buena Vista. Buena Vista won the 1948 Dakota-Iowa football championship. Eventually, when Buena Vista was forced to choose between remaining in the Iowa Conference or participating in the Dakota-Iowa Conference, Beaver officials quickly chose the former. By 2004 with the withdrawal of Upper Iowa University the conference consisted of Buena Vista, Central, Coe, Cornell (both Coe and Cornell joining in 1997), Dubuque, Loras, Simpson, and Wartburg. For many years none of Buena Vista's many basketball coaches could emulate Jim Hershberger's successful football program. Merritt Ewalt produced several outstanding teams in the 1960s including the fabulous 1961–62 Iowa Conference champions. Bernie Weiss's 1975–76 team also won the conference crown. However, Buena Vista's overall conference record of 352–591 (through 1996) placed it dead last in overall conference standings. The more modern record of 1979–93 was a miserable 62–163, with every conference season in that period a losing one except 1985 (7–7) and no winning season since Bernie Weiss's 1977–78 squad's 14–12 mark. Former University of Iowa all-conference star and basketball mentor at North Dakota University, Dave Gunther was lured to Buena Vista as basketball coach in 1992. Gunther began to turn things around with 9–7 conference seasons in 1993–94 and 1994–95. He also brought home the first winning season in more than a decade when his 1994–95 team finished 13–12.[39] But Gunther felt his future did not lie with Buena Vista and left, much to the disappointment of players and fans, for an apparent better opportunity at Bemidji, Minnesota. Ed Timm replaced Gunther, and Buena Vista returned to its losing ways with an 8–17 overall and 4–12 conference record. The great Buena Vista star during this period was center Jason Evers whose 1,678 career points (1992–96) places him third among all time Buena Vista scorers. Evers made the first team all-conference squad in 1994, 1995, and 1996.[40] Timm left for Cornell College after a single season, and the future of Buena Vista basketball again looked bleak. Then thin, tall, balding, thirty-two-year-old Brian Van Haaften was appointed head coach. He was an Iowa native and a graduate and basketball star at neighboring Northwestern College. He also coached at St. Mary's high school in Storm Lake winning a baseball championship. Van Haaften (often called VH) was not new on the scene for he had served as an assistant coach during Gunther's final season, and retained that position the year that Timm coached the Beavers. The new coach would prove a miracle man as Buena Vista basketball fortunes changed rapidly and in an unbelievable manner.[41]

None of Buena Vista's many basketball coaches had been able to emulate Jim Hershberger's successful football program. Overall success on the court had been limited, although Merritt Ewalt in the 1960s and Bernie Weiss in the 1970s each produced a conference champion. Buena Vista's overall conference record of 317–530 (through 1990) placed the Beavers dead last in the conference standings.

Buena Vista first fielded a basketball team in 1917 that posted victories over the high school 28–23 and Western Union 39–26.

Losses were to Trinity 66–11 and 49–21 and to Western Union 25–22. There was no team in 1918. The sport was revived in 191 with the results from 1919–22 showing nine wins and twenty-four losses against all opposition. Then Jim Kelly arrived and the 1922 team won six and lost five with two of the defeats being administered by the University of South Dakota. With the completion of Victory Hall, the College could play in its own gymnasium.

Coach Kelly had problems in scheduling Iowa Conference cage opponents in 1924–25 and 1925–26, but his basketball teams won fifteen and lost only three against conference opposition during those years. Kelly's 1926 quintet played enough games to give Buena Vista one of the three conference championships in its history. Buena Vista's 7–2 conference record was nine percentage points ahead of the 10–3 mark posted by Iowa Teachers. Three of the seven Beaver victories, however, were at the expense of weak Ellsworth College (1–10). The two defeats were administered by Central, 37–16 and 22–20. The most satisfying Buena Vista triumph was undoubtedly the 27–26 victory over Des Moines University in the game that sealed the conference championship. Although Des Moines finished with a 2–4 conference mark, the Tigers had a good team that shortly before had upset a highly rated Creighton five. In 1925 the Beavers finished second in the conference with a 6–1 record, losing only to the Des Moines team 24–21.

The championship team of 1926 was led by Captain Marmaduke Christie with Christie and James Leslie Rollins as forwards, Edward Hagedorn at center, and Stanton Beatty and Eddie Saggau as guards. Other members of the team were Glenn Coulson, William Johnson, Charles Morrill, Oscar Erickson, Beryl Wall, Howard Tjossem, and Elmer Moe. Winning the conference championship inspired the campus. The sports editor of the 1927 *Rudder* proudly proclaimed, "Winning the Iowa Conference is a signal feat. The teams in this league rank with any of the Mid-West, North Central or other conferences."[42]

None of the 1926 champions made the all-conference team. However, the Beaver's leading scorer, "Whitey" Rollins, was selected for the all-state honor roll. Rollins was also the star halfback on the 1925 football eleven and was on the second all-conference and third all-state teams.[43] He was also a member of the Student Council and president of the B Club and Delta Phi Rho fraternity.

By 1928 he was, almost as though guided by destiny, at Northwestern University as assistant dean of men.[44] Encouraged by football coach Jim Kelly, the still green Rollins allegedly started out for Northwestern not quite certain of his destination or purpose. Furthermore, because of an unpaid chapel fine he had not received his Buena Vista diploma—the most famous example of misplaced administrative zeal in the College's history—which, after the fine was good-naturedly paid, was finally granted shortly before Rollins's death.

Fortunately, the fact of having graduated and not the possession of the diploma was the vital element in the young man's career. For Rollins achieved distinction as one of the deans of the Harvard Business School, where he remained for twenty-four years (1942–66). He would become a prominent national figure in the field of education as a research fellow for special programs at Ohio University and a management and consultant specialist for eight colleges in the Ohio region. Throughout his life Rollins retained a lifelong interest in the fortunes of his alma mater. Rollins would be honored many times by Buena Vista College—including the Distinguished Service Award, an honorary doctorate, and in 1987 the naming of the newly remodeled football stadium in his honor. He preceded the days of sports scandals on college campuses and was the finest example of the scholar-athlete.

After Jim Kelly's departure, the road to athletic excellence dipped again. Buena Vista basketball teams from 1927 to 1932 won only fifteen and lost forty-eight games in the Iowa Conference. Frank Casey's 1933 team reversed the trend by finishing fifth with a 6–3 record. The star of that team was Ernie Salveson, whose ninety-one points in nine games netted him fifth place in the conference scoring race. Beaver losses were to the league's top teams: Luther (7–3) 41–22, Simpson (6–4) 37–30, and conference champion St. Ambrose (12–1) 26–19. The 1935 Casey-coached squad finished third in the conference with a 5–3 mark. Harold Sweet and the Keister twins were the stars of that outfit. Actually, the Beavers did not miss the conference championship by many points. They were defeated by Luther 21–20 and by champion St. Ambrose 26–22. The only other loss was to Western Union 38–31 in the final game of the conference season. The 1937 team, led by Ralph Layman's 136 points in ten games, won six and lost five for seventh place in a league that had grown to thirteen teams.

Between 1937 and 1952 the Beavers were able to break even in conference play only once, in 1941. The Beavers were led by their great center, Jay Beekmann, an all-conference selection in 1941 and 1942. Not only was Beekmann's 14.5 average the best in the conference in 1941, but he was the first Buena Vista basketball star to make the all-conference team. In March 1942 Beekmann had the distinction of being picked as the best player in the Iowa Conference. In a poll of coaches, officials, and sports writers, Beekmann was deemed the "best scoring, defensive, ball-handling center."[45] Beekmann scored 495 points during those two seasons; 321 of them in twenty-two Iowa Conference games. Still the Beavers were able to win only nine games while losing thirteen. However, Buena Vista's 44–42 victory over St. Ambrose in February 1941 was the most stunning Beaver triumph in a decade. The last time Buena Vista had beaten a first division team in the Iowa Conference had been in 1931 when they nipped third place Luther 31–28. The *Tack* reported "five iron men, namely: Hanshaw, Lashier, Beekmann, Mason and Bye, stayed the whole game against a classy, powerful St. Ambrose team."[46] Beekmann's nineteen points led the way. With most of the 1941 squad returning, there were great expectations for the 1942 team. However, Buena Vista lost two games to powerful Dubuque (14–3) 29–28 and 42–40. Indeed twelve more points in the right place would have given the Beavers a conference record of 8–4 instead of 4–8.

The tide seemed about to turn in 1952 when Coach John Krause's team compiled a 17–7 mark, winning seven and losing three in conference play. Only Wartburg finished ahead of Buena Vista in the conference's northern division. And the Beavers handed Wartburg their only defeat 58–48 at Storm Lake early in the season. Buena Vista also defeated the southern division champion, Parsons

(11–1) 62–59. Center Don Kamprath was the leading scorer with 257 points. Guard Sherwin Sankey was an all-conference choice, becoming the third Buena Vista cager in history to make the all-conference team. Glenn Theulen had been a 1949 selection as one of the two best dribblers in the conference. During these years, Theulen's great natural talents were dwarfed by a carefree life-style as he went through college "like a billiard ball bouncing off cushions."[47] Theulen left school, served two stints in military service, married, and returned to Buena Vista College at age thirty-six as a reserve on the 1961–62 championship team. While he could no longer play like the Theulen of old, he was both a legend and a steadying influence—one who knew what not to do as well as what to do. Afterwards, Theulen became a teacher and coach at Panora-Linden in Iowa and at Leadville, Colorado, where in 1965 he was selected Colorado prep coach of the year. He later received an M.A. at the University of Indiana while assisting Branch McCracken (just before Bobby Knight) and then moved on into university ranks as head mentor at Keene State in New Hampshire where he turned the basketball program around, producing several teams of championship caliber.[48]

After 1952 the Beavers began to slip again, finishing last in the conference with a 2–14 mark in 1957. Merritt Ewalt temporarily revived Beaver basketball after 1958. The banner year was 1961–62 when Buena Vista won twenty-five and lost three and compiled a championship Iowa Conference mark of 15–1. There was no doubt that Buena Vista's 1962 cagers were the best in the conference. The lone conference setback was an early season 71–58 loss to Parsons. Buena Vista later avenged this with a 76–66 win at Storm Lake and an 86–75 victory at Ames that sent the Beavers into the NAIA play-offs at Kansas City. There the Beavers were beaten 95–73 by Flagstaff Teachers of Arizona. The 1961–62 team, unsurpassed in the school's history, was led by all-American center Jim Ahrens with a supporting cast that included Larry Dick, Dwight Subbert, Sherman Wolleson, Ervin Dotson, Rich Hansen, and Glenn Theulen.

The records compiled by the 1962 team were impressive; three times the team scored more than a hundred points. The Iowa Conference champions were led by 6 ft 6 in. center Jim Ahrens who set or tied thirteen individual records. Ahrens set a single game mark of fifty-one points and scored 701 points in twenty-eight games for a twenty-five-point average per game. He led conference scorers with 409 points and completed his four years of varsity play with a then conference record of 1,975 points. He also grabbed 682 re-bounds during the 1961–62 season. Ahrens was all-Iowa Confer-ence, NAIA second team all-American, and Associated Press third team all-American. Thirty years later Ahrens's unbelievable season and spectacular career still mark him as the king among cage stars in Buena Vista history and one of the all-time greats of the Iowa Conference. No wonder Buena Vista retired his number fourteen jersey. Ahrens was an excellent student who was president of the Student Iowa State Education Association, president of the Letter-man's Club, and selected by faculty for inclusion in *Who's Who in Students in American Colleges and Universities.*[49] He went on to pursue a distinguished career as teacher-coach and served a term as alumni representative on the Buena Vista College Board of Trustees.

Larry Dick and Dick Point were two other great basketball stars who performed during the early 1960s. Coach Ewalt's 1963–64 team won eighteen and lost seven and also represented the Iowa Conference in postseason play at Kansas City. The Beavers had finished second in the conference, but in the play-offs were able to nose Central 91–88 and champion Upper Iowa 89–85 to win the desired berth at Kansas City. This time Pacific Lutheran spilled the Beavers in the first round of the NAIA tournament 109–94 when Larry Dick got into foul trouble early in the game. Dick fin-ished his three-year career at Buena Vista with 1,628 points. He was the Iowa Conference scoring champion in 1963 and 1964 and twice, in 1962 and 1963, was an all-conference selection. For some reason Dick was overlooked when 1964 selections were made. Guard Dick Point was an all-conference choice in 1963 and 1964. Point, a junior college transfer, tallied 930 points for the Beavers during his two years of competition. Among the thrillers of that season was a 108–107 victory over Wartburg and a controversial last second 75–73 home win against a strong Central team. The Central coach, Marinus Kregel, claiming the scorer had let the clock run down, uttered a few abusive remarks in the direction of spectators Jay Beekmann and Wendell Halverson and claimed Central had been "robbed." He later retracted his accusations but it made interesting press copy for several days.[50] Ewalt's three squads between 1961 and 1964 were the best ever. They amassed a 57–22 overall record, a 37–13 conference mark, won one conference title, won two conference tournaments, and twice made it to the NAIA tournament. In Jim Ahrens, Larry Dick, and Dick Point, Ewalt had coached three of the great players in Buena Vista College and conference history. Ewalt's three brilliant years surpassed those of the untouchable Kelly. Unfortunately the last nine years of Ewalt's coaching career were unhappy ones. The conference record in that period was only 26–100, and when Ewalt resigned as head coach after the 1973 season his lifetime mark had dipped to 159–228.[51] The 1969 squad failed to win a conference game. Ewalt was a personable individual and excellent recruiter whose coaching abilities were demonstrated during the first half of his coaching tenure. He expected the best from his players and his rather disciplined concept of training did not always fit in with the changing moods of the 1960s athletes. On the sidelines Ewalt occasionally added to the color of the game by kicking the seats. Once when a player hesitated on what Ewalt believed was an open shot, his voice reverberated across the gym; "shoot you dummy, shoot!" (In spite of reduced hearing this author heard it loud and clear at the northeast end of Siebens Fieldhouse.) His later record should not diminish the standout years and the overall contribution Ewalt made to Buena Vista athletics.

Ewalt was replaced by thirty-five-year-old Bernie Weiss who had been freshmen coach at Valpariso University in Indiana. There were great expectations that seemed realized as Weiss moved the Beavers from a 2–12 (6–14) mark in 1973 to an 11–3 (18–9) record and a conference championship in 1976. During this era Weiss coached two all-conference stars, Phil Maynard and Dan O'Hern. Both joined the select 1,000-point club and rank among the top players in Buena Vista basketball history. O'Hern scored over 1,500 points and made the all-conference team on two occasions. O'Hern was the 1979 Iowa Conference scoring champion with a 27.2

average—the highest in Buena Vista College history. Weiss also took his team on a European tour in December 1978. After 1976 Buena Vista basketball fortunes again declined and a frustrated Weiss resigned in midseason 1980, a year when the Beavers won only three of twenty-six games. Weiss's successors, Joey Grau and Jeff Spielman, have been unable to alter a pattern of losing seasons that started in 1979. There was one three-year stretch in which Buena Vista, forced to forfeit several games because of using an ineligible player, went 7–68. There were, during those years, some outstanding players, such as Barry Anderson, Brad Rohwer, and Mark Grintjes. However, recruiting during a long series of losing seasons proved difficult, and overall squad depth was lacking. Gunther and Timm were able to produce better results, but it remained for Van Haaften to eclipse virtually every record in Buena Vista's book of records. The Northwestern College graduate knew how to recruit, how to mold his team into a cohesive unit, how to inspire confidence, how even to come up with some "magical" plays that turned defeats into victories. His goal was to understand not only the game, but the players. Deeply religious but without ostentation he knew how to motivate his team. Under Van Haaften Buena Vista was expected to play like Buena Vista in order to win tight games. During the previous three decades they had had to play like someone else in order to win. Van Haaften's teams began to feel they were the best and acted accordingly. Few expected Buena Vista to win the conference championship during the 1996–97 season. But win they did with a 12–4 conference mark and a respectable 18–8 record for the year. That was followed with 19–6 (17–3 conference) and 15–11 (13–7 conference) seasons. The era of Buena Vista basketball domination of the Iowa Conference had begun. Between 1996 and 2006 Van Haaften's record was an amazing 215 wins and only 66 losses. His conference mark was 148–34. In nine seasons his Buena Vista teams won five Iowa Conference championships and finished second twice. There were no losing seasons. The 1999–2000 Beavers bettered the mark of the 1961–62 squad by winning twenty-seven of twenty-nine games. They set another school record with twenty-three consecutive victories. The 2004–05 team amassed twenty-seven wins and only four losses.

Their 14–2 conference mark left them a game behind Wartburg in
IIAC standings, but they won their way to the NCAA by giving the
Knights a 79–68 thumping in the finals of the conference tournament. Buena Vista's Eric Wiebers, Randy Bissen, and Michael
Cameron made first team all-conference, and Jordan Campbell was
selected for second team honors.[52] Buena Vista won twenty or more
games per season six consecutive times since 1999. They swept
through the Iowa Conference tournaments five times, were runners-
up once, and reached the Sweet Sixteen in Division Three on two
occasions. The seniors of 2004–05 had a 100–19 overall mark and
a 61–9 conference record. No other Buena Vista basketball mentor,
including the great Jim Kelly, had come close to equaling Van
Haaften's coaching performance. In less than a decade the Beaver
coach's success has made him a school and regional legend. Van
Haaften knew how to recruit players who would meld together as a
team. VH told his players to (1) have fun, (2) go to class, (3) graduate on time, (4) play hard, and (5) commit to each other. This formula, Van Haaften expected, would produce a team chemistry that
would be difficult for opponents to overcome.[53] Many of his recruits
came from Western Iowa schools and were familiar with one another from high school days. Van Haaften was able to merge them
into an almost unbeatable unit of determination, confidence, and
teamwork. During his first year at the helm in 1996–97, senior forward Brad Douglas discovered that VH "does not yell and holler."
There was more emphasis on having fun.[54] Still, the once seemingly
impossible goal of winning a National Championship remains. This
lofty ambition was thwarted in 2005 by Puget Sound in the Sweet
Sixteen in an 85–82 thriller that was decided in the final 6.4 seconds. Eric Wiebers hit five 3-pointers and finished with a total of
24 points in the game.[55] There were many outstanding players on
the Van Haaften teams. Adam Jones (1998–2002) was one of the
best. Strongly recruited from Jefferson High School, and probably
capable of playing Division I ball, the 6 ft 5 in. Jones became one
of the most talented performers in the history of Buena Vista.
Jones's 1,831 career points were second only to the 1,975 points
scored by Jim Ahrens 1958–62. Jones was an all-conference selection from his freshman through his senior years, was twice selected

as the conference's most valuable player, and in 2002 became the first Beaver basketball player to achieve coveted all-American status. He was also the recipient of the Jostens Trophy recognizing "the top student-athlete in Division Three men's basketball."[56] Eric Wiebers demonstrated outstanding team leadership and scoring during the 2003, 2004, and 2005 seasons. He was chosen on the all-conference teams in 2003, 2004, and 2005 and was selected conference MVP in 2003–04. Other outstanding players on Van Haaften teams were Nick Dentlinger, Landon Roth, Brett Smith, Nolan Stribe, Robby Beyer, Jeremy Holmes, Scott Weber, Chris Peterson and Casey Pelzer. Landon Roth, a star of the record setting 1999–2000 team was a two-time all-conference selection, a Dean's Fellow in the School of Business, an academic all-American, received an NCAA postgraduate scholarship, and entered the University of Iowa School of Law.[57] Roth was the sixth Buena Vista athlete to be honored with an NCAA postgraduate scholarship. Others were Steve Trost, 1976 (football); Mike Habben, 1987 (football); Monte Merz, 1990 (wrestling); Cary Murphy, 1994 (football); and Nicole Kotrba, 1995 (softball).

Baseball became a major sport in the Iowa Conference after World War II. Only about one-half of the conference members played the game during the 1930s, and official records do not appear prior to 1947. Buena Vista fielded a team throughout its history, but there was no official compilation of statistics until league play began in earnest in 1947. Many of the early games were played against high school or junior college opponents.

Following World War II Buena Vista became the dominant baseball school in the Iowa Conference, and although the Beavers have not won a conference title since 1981, their fourteen won or shared titles are still more than achieved by any other school. The Beaver championships were 1949–51, 1953–55, 1957, 1959, 1965, 1970, 1974, 1976, 1980, and 1981. Ken Blackman coached the 1949–51 champions and John Krause the 1953–55 title holders. Catcher Jim Fanning was one of the stars of the early 1950s and led the 1950 team with a .430 batting average. Fanning reached the majors, serving brief stints with the Chicago Cubs and Montreal Expos and eventually becoming a manager and baseball executive.[58] Jay

Beekmann, baseball coach 1956–86, won more than half of those titles and guided his team to 488 career victories—a mark that is unlikely to be equaled. The 1951, 1957, 1965, and 1972 teams were undefeated in conference play. Unfortunately, too many rain days prevented the 1972 team (6–0) from qualifying for the conference title. Jay Beekmann's 1974–81 teams won four Iowa Conference titles winning sixty-nine games and losing only twenty-one conference games during this period.

On only five occasions were Beekmann-coached teams denied first division in the Iowa Conference. Beekmann's 1957 champions won nine games without defeat in the Iowa Conference. Jerry Ibach and Wayne Paige were Buena Vista's top pitchers, yielding only thirteen runs in nine conference games. Freshman second baseman Lanny Grigsby led the team in hitting with a .412 average. Shut-outs were hurled against Westmar, Wartburg, and Upper Iowa. Ken Evans, Lanny Grigsby, Don Baker, and Jim Nielsen were the leading hitters. Buena Vista finished fourth in the first NAIA tournament that year at Alpine, Texas, and received the sportsmanship trophy. The Beavers reeled off fifteen consecutive victories before losing in the national tourney. The 1957 team mark of 17–3 remains the unrivaled best percentage, but the 1965 team became the first to achieve a twenty-game season. The 1974, 1976, and 1981 teams all won twenty-four games. The 1965 team compiled a 9–0 conference mark and finished second in the regional NAIA play-offs. David Wolfe was the club's leading hitter, batting .430. The star second baseman was lost for post-tournament play when he broke his wrist. The 1965 champions, paced by the hard-hitting Wolfe and the brilliant pitching of Drummond and Naughton, still rank among the best in the school's history. Wolfe was a first team all-American in 1966 and enjoyed a brief stint in professional baseball after graduation.

Beekmann maintained his mastery of the game throughout his coaching career. His 1974, 1976, and 1981 teams all won twenty-four games. The 1980 team dominated the Iowa Conference with a 13–1 mark and was 25–16 in all games. Because time and again they demonstrated the capacity to rally in the late innings, Beekmann remarked, "they never quit . . . they're just one unit."[59] Coach Beekmann was especially fond of the 1981 team that won a surprise victory in the 1981 regional NCAA tournament over heavily favored Stanislaus State, California. Six Beavers were all-conference that year. Barry Larson hit .435, Floyd Athay .429, Dwight Widen .413, and Byron Peyton .396. Pitcher Dale Knight was undefeated during three seasons of conference play.[60]

Beekmann's retirement in 1986 marked the end of an era at Buena Vista College. This quiet, dignified man who won so many games knew how to be gracious in defeat as in victory. He loved the game and he believed athletics developed character, leadership, and personal values. Ethical considerations were as strong with Beekmann at the end of his career as they had been at the beginning. He deplored the contemporary materialism, the infusion of drugs and gambling into sports, and the emphasis upon winning at all costs. He never stopped playing the game the way it was intended to be played, he never elevated it above the basic purpose of college—obtaining an education. He won as much respect off the field as on, and he never boasted about his many honors, such as coach of the year and membership in the Iowa Hall of Fame. It pleased him that the very players he had to discipline or confront returned ten or fifteen years later to tell him "You were right." It also pleased him that two of his players Dan Monzon (Minnesota Twins) and Larry Bittner (Senators and Cubs) made it into the majors. Bittner, who played a number of years with the Senators, Cubs, and Texas Rangers, led the 1966–68 teams hitting .439 for the season, amassing a 15–2 pitching record, and batting a torrid .567 in the 1967 regional championships. He was a 1968 NAIA all-American.[61] The long-standing Buena Vista baseball tradition of excellence seemed to collapse after Jay Beekmann. Lanny Grigsby, Jay Miller, John Ward, and Larry Anderson all struggled to produce winning teams. There were no more winning seasons until 2002, and only two winning seasons (1989, 2002) in conference play. Buena Vista's conference record 1994–2000, a horrendous 24–93, reminded one of the futile play of the old St. Louis Browns. It wasn't until Steve Eddie was hired as coach in 2000 that Buena Vista's baseball fortunes began to improve. Eddie had been a member of the University of Iowa baseball team 1990–93 and played professionally in the minor leagues for the next nine years. Eddie's

2002 team sprinted to a 24–14 season and finished second in the Iowa Conference with a 15–6 mark. Such an improvement following fifteen years of frustration won Eddie the Iowa Conference Coach of the Year Award. Eddie's teams remained competitive finishing fourth in the conference with an 8–8 record in 2005.

There were, in spite of the overall record, some sparkling performers. Infielder Nick Beard was the star of the second place 2002 team hitting .422, scoring 48 runs, collecting 57 hits, 17 doubles, 12 home runs and batting in 58 runs. Beard was selected as the most valuable player in the Iowa Conference for 2002. Beard's .473 batting average the previous year was the highest in the history of Buena Vista baseball.[62]

By the late 1970s the Iowa Conference had mandated that conference members field teams in all sports. This meant that conference competition would be upgraded in the hitherto neglected sports of wrestling, track, cross-country, tennis, swimming, and golf as well as in the long-dominant spectator sports of football, basketball, and baseball. Similar teams would be fielded in women's sports as the Iowa Conference sought to implement the national goal of equality in athletic programs for both sexes. It was not easy for colleges the size of Buena Vista to recruit formidable teams in all areas, but success would be achieved in wrestling and in women's basketball and softball.

Iowa Conference wrestling developed slowly during the two decades following World War II. There were no conference tournaments from 1955 through 1959; Buena Vista only began to field teams in wrestling during the 1960s. Virgil Pithan, John Naughton, and Merritt Ewalt took turns at building a wrestling program with limited success. Virgil Pithan's 1969–70 team went 11–13 in dual meets and won four of nine conference matches. Naughton produced one conference champion in Joe Curry at 150 lb during the 1974–75 season. However, Beaver wrestling fortunes underwent a dramatic renaissance in the 1980s.

Al Baxter, 6 ft and 205 lb, came to Buena Vista from Lisbon High School in 1978 and quickly established the Beavers as a national power in wrestling. His boast that "It's no secret, I hope to make Buena Vista a power in wrestling at both the conference and

national level,"[63] was met with skepticism only by those who did
not know him well. Baxter had starred on the mats at Morning Sun
High School (25–0 and a 1965 state champion) and at Morningside
College where he graduated in 1968. His dual record at Lisbon
High School was 76–15–1 and his teams won twenty-three of the
thirty tournaments they entered. That program had been built from
nothing. The big man also took over a defunct wrestling program at
Buena Vista and had to raid the dorms for wrestlers during a miserable 2–13 first season of competition. He enjoyed working with
young people, he liked to win, he believed in hard work, he was
confident that he could build a winning spirit. Baxter also knew
how to recruit and amazed the Iowa Conference by moving his
team from last to first and by winning the conference tournament
his second year as coach. He was selected coach of the year. That
was only the beginning, for in an eleven-year period (1980–90)
Baxter coached Buena Vista to the conference wrestling championship eight times. Three times the Beavers came in second. On
five occasions (including 1990) Baxter was selected Iowa
Conference coach of the year. More students attended the wrestling
matches than the basketball games. Buena Vista wrestlers qualified
for the nationals, and through 1989 thirty Beaver wrestlers gained
all-American status as year after year Buena Vista ranked among
the top twenty Division III teams. The College enjoyed a lofty third
place finish in 1986, placed fourth in 1990, finished seventh in
1988, and ninth in 1989. Brad Brosdahl in 1988 became the first
Buena Vista wrestler to reach the final round in the NCAA Division
III tourney.[64] Dave Jordan, wrestling at 118 lb and with thirty-two
consecutive wins, became Buena Vista's first national champion in
1989. Jordan's feat was all the more remarkable because he wrestled in the championship round at John Carroll University in
Cleveland with a broken hand and a torn cartilage in his knee and
still managed to win. Along with Jordan and Brosdahl, Rick
Dawson, Curt Cawley, Paul Van Oosbree, John Brown, and Don
Dresser were among the great Buena Vista wrestlers in the Baxter
era. No competition was too formidable as Baxter's squads challenged Division II schools and were able to post victories over
Drake, Oregon State, Mankato State, San Jose State, Air Force,

University of California-Davis, and San Francisco State University. In spite of preseason competition against larger schools, Baxter's dual record through 1990 stood at 145–49–2. The 1990 squad out-pointed favored Simpson in the conference meet 137.75–109 to give Baxter one of his most satisfying triumphs. When the Beavers came in fourth in the national tournament, Baxter was honored as NCAA Division III coach of the year. Baxter's magnificent career was hardly over in 1990 although he made wrestling so popular at Buena Vista that other Iowa Conference schools became interested in upgrading their programs and soon provided intense competition. The 1994–95 and 1998–99 wrestlers finished fourth in the nation-als, while his 1993–94 and 2001–02 teams placed fifth. Baxter's Buena Vista wrestlers went 45–5–1 in dual meets from 1997–99. His career mark in twenty-six seasons, unlikely to be equaled, was 376–119–5. His wrestlers were in the top three of the Iowa Conference in eighteen of those twenty-six years. His teams ranked in the top ten in the nation on twelve occasions. During his long ca-reer at Buena Vista Baxter coached 37 academic scholarship all-Americans, 71 all-Americans, and 6 national champions. Five of the national champions came in the post-1990 period. They were Brian Stewart in 1994 at 150 lb, Jay Huff in 1995 in the heavy-weight class, Ryan Schweitzberger in 1998 at 150, Andy Krueger in 1999 at 165, and Jamie Taxted in 2002 at 125[65]. Schweitzberger had a career record of 87–27 and Krueger 110–22. Brian Stewart was a State Champion from Lisbon whom Baxter described as hav-ing "unbelievable body control." Baxter recalled that if Stewart got into "a scramble on the mat he would always come out on top." He had a career record of 136–38 and was 45–4 as a senior. He was also a three-time conference champion. Jay Huff was a Sheldon na-tive of whom Baxter said "was one of the quickest and most explo-sive wrestlers that I ever coached." Although only 5 ft 8 in. Huff de-feated four opponents who weighed more than 260 lb and towered over him at 6 ft 2 in. to 6 ft 8 in. in height in order to win the National Championship as a junior. He was 36–1 that year and had a career record of 109–22. In spite of a shoulder injury his senior year, Huff still won the conference heavyweight title and placed fifth in the Nationals.[66] Besides being honored as National Coach of the Year in 1990, Baxter was inducted into the National Wrestlers Coaches Hall of Fame in 1999 and the National Wrestling Hall of Fame (Iowa Chapter) in 2000. Baxter succeeded in making wrestling a major sport not only at Buena Vista but in the Iowa Conference. Former Cornell College wrestling coach, Steve Devries, summed up how most people felt about Baxter when he said, "His greatness as a coach is his loyalty to his athletes. He's totally committed to his student-athletes, and that's what a coach is. He's a joy to compete with—you love the guy for his integrity and great sense of humor. I consider him to be my best friend in coaching, and I spent two decades at Cornell College trying to beat him!"[67] Baxter had an enormous impact on all those who knew and worked with him. His humor, graciousness, and sportsmanship infected colleagues, students, and competitors. He is as President Moore remarked, "a Buena Vista legend."

There was no college-level athletic program for Buena Vista women until the 1970s. While the College organized a women's basketball team early in the century the contests were largely intramural or with neighboring high schools. The 1912–13 team split eight games in a home and home series against Sioux Rapids, Fonda, Pomeroy, and Manson high schools.[68] Even this limited activity seems to have terminated following World War I. Harriet Henry, professor of physical education since 1965, was the real founder of the women's intercollegiate athletic program at Buena Vista College. During the critical era of development in women's sports in the early 1970s, Henry became the first women's coach in basketball, softball, track, and volleyball. Women's basketball, softball, and volleyball had small schedules in 1971. Women's sports at Buena Vista began on a competitive basis during the 1972–73 season with membership in the Io-Kota conference. Henry's 1973–74 softball team entered the state tournament with an 8–0 record and finished 9–2 overall. In that year her basketball team shared the Io-Kota championship and had a season's record of 13–7. She fielded a women's track team that competed in the Drake Invitational, the Westmar, and Northwestern relays in 1972–73. Henry turned basketball over to John Naughton in 1976 and softball to Marge Willadsen in 1981. However, her role as the real founder and major architect of the women's athletic program would not be forgotten, nor would her overall contributions to Buena Vista as a professor of physical education and valued colleague. Henry suffered a massive heart attack in December 1993 and never fully recovered. She died in February 1995. Henry's career at Buena Vista had spanned thirty years, she had made the most of opportunities offered by Title IX and influenced hundreds of Buena Vista women athletes.[69] When Siebens Fieldhouse was built in 1969, women were not even considered "except for physical education classes." By the time of Henry's death women were participating in at least eight competitive sports.[70] An appreciative Buena Vista University established a Harriet Henry Dedicated Athlete Award in her honor. Nicole Kotrba who played four years of basketball and softball was the first recipient in May 1995.[71]

In 1982 the Iowa Conference formed an intercollegiate association for women's athletics. Until then Buena Vista women had competed in the Io-Kota conference. A more open society, a new emphasis upon equality, federal support through Title IX, and a positive reaction from the public all helped facilitate vigorous programs in women's athletics during the 1980s. The number of women participating nationally in college sports programs jumped from 300,000 in 1972 to 2.25 million in 2000.[72] Buena Vista College was no exception, as John Naughton's teams in basketball and Marge Willadsen's softball players won regional and national acclaim. Great women athletes like Jeannie and Joleen Demers, Chanel Finzen, Libby Kestel, Lu Ann Thurn, Lori Lane, "Sam" Meyer, Julie Quirin, Missy Neblung, Jenny Delzell, Kim Beckman, Jill Haden, and Lori Gries proved that women's sports were intense, competitive, crowd-pleasing, and exciting.

Marge Willadsen took over the softball coaching duties in 1981 and after a rather mediocre 12–19 first season quickly moved her Buena Vista teams into national contention. Willadsen's teams won the 1983 and 1984 conference titles as well as the Io-Kota championship in 1982 and 1983. The 1982 team reached the national finals, in 1983 they were runners-up, and in 1984 defeated the defending Trenton State champions 2–0 and 3–1 behind the pitching of Chanel Finzen, who yielded one run in thirty-six in-

nings at the national tourney. Trenton State was a top-ranked opponent with a 44–1 record and a pitching staff that boasted twenty-
nine shutouts against opposition. Willadsen's 1984 NCAA championship was the first won by a Buena Vista team in any sport. It was
an accomplishment that was recognized both by the College and by
her peers who selected her as coach of the year. Coach Willadsen
was also presented with the Presidential Citation, the highest honor
the University can bestow. Jeannie Demers at third base and Libby
Kestel at catcher were all-Americans, but it was the arm of Chanel
Finzen that carried the Buena Vista team to the title. Lori Stirn,
who hit .382, and Jill Walquist made the all-regional team. The
1985 team suffered a major tragedy in April when pitcher and left
fielder Nita Skou was killed in an auto accident.

Competition was rugged in the tough Iowa Conference and
in spite of strong teams (10–2 in 1985, 9–5 in 1986, and 11–5 in
1989), Buena Vista did not repeat as conference champs again in
the 1980s. However, the plucky 1989 team, a fourth place finisher
in the conference (although only one game behind champion
Simpson), made its way to the NCAA finals where it finished third.
Buena Vista was granted distinct honors when selected as the site
for the NCAA Division III national softball championship series
in 1987 and 1990.[73] Willadsen's career still had a long way to go in
1990. Her teams proceeded to win conference championships in
1992, 1994, 1995, and 1996. The 1992 team was national runner-
up, and the 1994 team finished fifth. She was selected National
Coach of the Year in 1984 and 1996. She was Regional Coach of
the Year in 1992, 1993, 1994, and 1996 and Conference Coach of
the Year in 1983, 1984, 1992, and 1995. Willadsen's 1995 team
went 25–11 and lost in the NCAA tournament to the eventual national champions, Chapman University 2–1. The 1996 Iowa
Conference champions had a league record of 13–3 and an overall
mark of 27–13. It was Buena Vista's sixth Iowa Conference championship with Coach Willadsen at the helm. Willadsen-coached
teams produced 19 all-Americans and 31 academic all-Americans.
Her twenty-six-year career mark at Buena Vista stood at 539–377–2
in 2005. No other Buena Vista coach had reached the 500-victory
plateau. Her conference mark was 228–134. Her 1983–85 teams

won 33 of 36 games and her 1992–96 teams won 62 and lost 10 in
Iowa Conference play. Buena Vista stars in those years were
Heather White, who won 14 consecutive games in 1995, and
Megan Coe, who hit .591 in 1993 and who set an Iowa conference
record with a .419 average that same year. During her career White
struck out 551 batters in 635 2/3 innings, pitched 31 shutouts and
had an ERA of 0.99.[74] Buena Vista all-Americans during the 1990s
were pitchers Heather White and Amy Haeder along with first baseman Andi Royster. Willadsen also authored a chapter, "Coaching
with Integrity," in *The Softball Coaching Bible,* published by
Human Kinetics.[75] She was one of twenty-eight nationally prominent coaches who were asked to participate. In 2005 Willadsen was
named a Sports Ethic Fellow, one of twelve honorees honored for
"promoting ideals of ethics and fair play in sports and society."[76] A
century is likely to pass before any future Buena Vista softball
coach exceeds Willadsen's achievements. She is the only Buena
Vista coach in any sport to achieve 500 career victories. Willadsen
by 2005 was Buena Vista's Associate Athletic Director and Senior
Women's Administrator in addition to being head softball coach.

The most exciting woman athlete of the century was Jeannie
Demers, an all-American at the Division III level in two sports (softball and basketball), whose heroics on the basketball court won her
national acclaim. Demers did not exactly arrive on campus as an unknown for she was an all-stater in softball and basketball at Albert
City-Truesdale High School, averaging 49.3 points per game. Once
she scored 78 points against Pocahontas. Relatively small (5 ft 5 in.)
but fast, a good passer and ball handler, an accurate shooter with a
devastating running jump shot, and a great heart that often defied
defeat, Demers's 3,171 four-year point total was, at that time, the
most scored by any female athlete at any level. Even as a freshman,
she breezed to the Iowa Conference scoring title with a 24.2 average. As a senior in February 1987, she broke the four-year record of
3,115 set by former Drake star Lori Bauman.[77] Demers was a four-
point student in the classroom, an academic as well as athletic all-
American. Her four years of competition were played after the
rugged Iowa Conference schools forged a full-fledged schedule, and
Buena Vista faced powerful teams from William Penn, Simpson, and

Central. Demers led her squad to an 11–3 co-championship in 1985 and a second place finish in 1986 under the tutelage of coach John Naughton. During her career, Demers broke twenty school records, was the first player to be named player of the month in consecutive months by the Women's Sports Federation, was selected small college player of the year by *Fast Break Magazine* (1984–85), was the 1985 MVP in the Iowa Conference, named to Kodak's Division III Women's all-American basketball team, featured in *Sports Illustrated*, and was athlete of the week on *Wide World of Sports*.[78] She was also selected as one of *Good Housekeeping's* Class of 1987's 100 Women of Promise. When Demers's career ended, the College provided an unprecedented honor—a Jeannie Demers day on the Buena Vista campus.[79] The honors were worn with dignity. More sophisticated, she was still the same person who innocently asked during the first road trip, "Where's the scallops?" Following graduation, she married Mark Henningsen and was employed as a teacher-coach at Storm Lake High School.

In 1985 and 1986 Naughton's teams won twenty-eight of twenty-nine games at home. He had enjoyed success during the days of the Io-Kota Conference, winning or tying for two titles (1974, 1980) and in 1980 had a record-shattering 25–2 season. That team was headed by sophomore Lori Lane, who scored 449 points, and Lori Gries, who became the first woman in Buena Vista College history to score 1,000 points. Lori Lane and Jenny Delzell joined that select group in 1981.

Naughton's 1989–90 Lady Beavers amassed a 21–5 regular season mark and finished second in the Iowa Conference. Kim Beckman made first team all-conference, Jill Haden was a second team selection, and John Naughton was coach of the year. Beckman was also named a First Team Kodak All-American. This outstanding record won them a berth in the NCAA Division III national basketball tournament. At the end of the 1989–90 season Naughton's career mark stood at 244–120. Two more victories were added when the Lady Beavers defeated Washington University of St. Louis 78–71 and Iowa Conference champion Wartburg 78–63 to capture the NCAA Division III regionals at St. Louis. Tournament MVP Kim Beckman scored sixty-seven points in the two games. Carol

Wiebers and Patti Kuhl joined her on the all-tournament team. The previously unranked Lady Beavers prepared for the Division III finals as one of the top eight teams in America. (The Lady Beavers were edged in overtime 85–79 in the first round of the national tournament by eventual champion Hope College.) Two more years of coaching boosted Naughton's career victories to 258 before he retired at the end of the 1991–92 season. This remarkable coaching achievement belonged to the same John Naughton who had at first balked when asked to coach women's basketball. Janet Berry (then Janet Allgood) was hired in 1992 to replace Naughton as the Buena Vista women's head basketball and volleyball coach. Berry was an assistant professor of exercise science who, amazingly, had never played high school or college basketball.[80] She was also asked to coach volleyball, which she did through 1995. Her first Buena Vista basketball team started out slowly, winning only 20 of 50 contests and going 14–16 in the conference during her first two seasons. There then came the Buena Vista women's basketball explosion with three consecutive conference championships in 1995, 1996, and 1997. The 1998 team was a close second with a 15–5 conference mark. The 2001–02 season was a miserable year with a 5–13 conference and 7–19 overall mark. Berry's teams were soon back on track winning 71 and losing 14 overall and going 44–6 in the conference 2002–05. The 2004–05 team was undefeated in conference play and had a 25–3 overall mark. Berry's all time record stood at 231–136 at the end of 2006 and her conference record was 160–82. She won her two-hundredth career victory on January 14, 2005, as the Buena Vista women crucified Dubuque 89–54. In that game the Beavers fell behind 10–0 and trailed 24–13 midway into the first half. During the next twenty minutes Buena Vista went on a 49–6 rampage to notch their thirty-eighth victory in forty-two contests. Berry's teams have won five conference championships and reached the Sweet Sixteen on two occasions. Berry has been honored as Iowa Conference Coach of the Year five times during her thirteen-year tenure at Buena Vista. She is rapidly becoming one of the all time great Buena Vista and Division III coaches. Although no one could come close to reaching the records of the great Jeannie Demers, the Berry years produced a number of stars. Amy Meggers proved to be one of the most talented players in the history of Buena Vista women's basketball. Her 1,632 career points placed her third among all-time Buena Vista scorers. Her 819 rebounds were second to Jennifer Erickson's 854. Erickson starred on the 1995 and 1996 championship teams. Meggers was both an all-conference and all-American selection. She was selected the MVP in the Iowa Conference in 2003 and 2004. By the 1980s Buena Vista women were participating eagerly in nearly all sports. Harriet Henry's 1982 volleyball team finished third in the Io-Kota conference and for the first time reached the state tournament. Debra Leslie became the first Buena Vista woman to make the all-conference squad in volleyball. Melissa Landsness was all-conference in 1984 and Shelly Barr followed in 1985. The 1987 volleyball squad posted a 10–6 mark and Brigid Gute made the second all-conference team. Buena Vista's Harriet Henry was honored as coach of the year. Volleyball enjoyed only average success throughout the following decade, but the 2004 team was 6–6 in the conference and 14–16 overall. A new head coach, Lindsey Johnson, was hired in May 2005 replacing Amy Sanders who had gradually improved the volleyball record at Buena Vista. Jo Denny and Sandra Folden were fierce competitors in tennis in 1981 and 1982. The 1982 women's tennis team was Io-Kota champion. Overall there have been few upper division finishes in women's tennis and the 2004–05 team finished next to last in the conference winning only one of six matches and going 1–8 for the season. Charles Slagle's women golfers managed to finish second in the Io-Kota conference in 1981. However, upon entering the Iowa Conference in 1982 Buena Vista's women's golf team failed to make the first division throughout the remainder of the decade. The years after 1990, however, would be a different story. Beginning with Amy Grigsby in 1989 some fifteen Buena Vista women golfers would be all-conference selections. Carin Skold in 1996, Debbie Zorn in 1999–2001, and Jen Einck in 2003 were the MVPs in the Iowa Conference. Skold was a 1997 all-American and Zorn followed suit in 1999. In 2004, Jennifer Stork was named to the National Golf Association's all-Region team. Buena Vista won conference titles in 1995, 2000, 2001, and 2003. Large institutions, like Oral Roberts University, who had never heard of a Buena Vista, learned the location once they competed on the green. Darlene Still won coach of the year honors in 2000 and Tom Bohnenkamp in 2001 and 2003. Tom Bohnenkamp is the athletic director at Aurelia High School and has coached golf for more than thirty years.

Buena Vista women were less successful in other sports, although Harriet Henry's 1982 volleyball team finished third in the Io-Kota conference and for the first time reached the state tournament. Debra Leslie became the first Buena Vista woman to make the all-conference squad in volleyball. The 1987 volleyball squad posted a 10–6 mark, and Brigid Gute made the second all-conference team. Buena Vista's Harriet Henry was honored as coach of the year. Jo Denny and Sandra Folden were fierce competitors in tennis in 1981 and 1982. The 1982 women's tennis team was the Io-Kota champion. Charles Slagle's women golfers finished second in the conference in 1981. However, since entering Iowa Conference competition in 1982–83 neither tennis nor golf managed to finish in the first division. Women's track also seemed to sputter until the 1988–89 season when Buena Vista led by Barb Buckwalter, Kim Beckman, Julie Evers, and Jonda Black amassed an unprecedented 106 points for a solid third-place finish in the conference meet.[81] The 1989–90 team also finished third while scoring 117 points. Barb Buckwalter in 1989 and Paula Truesdell in 1990 were named MVPs at the Iowa Conference meet.

A number of individual stars emerged in women's track and field after 1991. Teresa Breyfogle won the conference high jump in 1995, 1996, and 1997, and was first in the nationals in 1996. Dawn Puttman-Vinyard won the conference indoor high jump in 1998 and the long jump at the nationals. Jessica Jensen was a champion in the NCAA Division Three 400-meter hurdles in 2002. Melanie Uhl was one of the greatest women's track stars during this era winning the 1996, 1997, and 1998 conference long jump and the 1997 and 1998 100-meter race. She also finished first in the 1998 long jump at the nationals and in that same year finished second in the 100-meter and fifth in the 200-meter races. Uhl, who did not enter competition until her sophomore year and who never dreamed of stardom, won nearly twenty events and set four indoor track records. The Buena Vista relay team of Amy Nieland, Rachel Carstens, Erin

Steinkamp, and Jessica Jensen were victorious in the 1,600-meter relay in 2003. Still, there were no conference championships and Buena Vista women were eighth among nine conference participants in the 2005 IIAC meet.

The best track days were during the Kelly era in the early 1920s. The 1925 Buena Vista catalog boasted that the track men had set the half-mile record at Drake and Dakota in 1923, 1924, and 1925 and had also won the mile and two-mile events at the Dakota relays in 1925.[82] The Beavers also won the half-mile relay in their first Iowa Conference track meet at Des Moines University in 1923 and repeated the feat in 1926 with the record time of 1.31.7.[83] The 1926 half-mile relay team of Rollins, Stevenson, Marshall, and Ellerbroek was a great one. Other great Buena Vista runners during the 1923–26 era were Barron, the 120-yard high-hurdle and 220-yard low-hurdle champion in 1923; Bouck, the 220-yard low-hurdle champion in 1924; Marshall, who ran the 100-yard dash in 10.3 seconds in 1926; and Peterson, the 1926 high-jump champion. The Beaver mile-relay team, Rollins, DeLong, Greene, and Ellerbroek, won that event in 1925 at the conference meet at Des Moines. In spite of great individual performances, Buena Vista lacked depth, and Kelly's best conference effort was in 1926 when Buena Vista was nosed out by Simpson in the conference meet. Wendell Edson, a distinguished Storm Lake attorney and nephew of Willis Edson, was on that team. The Beavers would finish second at Cedar Falls in 1930 and third at Indianola in 1946 but would never win a conference title. The 1930 team was led by Duke Thayer, who won both hurdle events, and by Clark Boggess, who set records in the 100- and 220-yard dashes. Vernon Huseman, Paul Bye, and Sanford Reed were largely responsible for the third-place finish in 1946. The 440-yard relay team set a conference mark of 42.4 minutes in 1968 and Randy Lewis tied the conference pole vault record at 15'6" in 1987. Generally mired in the bottom half of the league, Buena Vista's fourth- and fifth-place finishes in 1988 and 1989 under coach Keith Schmidt marked a hopeful upward surge in track fortunes. The 1990 team also finished fifth at the Iowa Conference meet, with Ken Fox winning the high jump for the third consecutive year. Fox finished third in the high jump at the NCAA outdoor tournament. Previously he had become Buena Vista's first NCAA track champion with a $6'11\frac{1}{2}''$ high jump in the indoor track and field contest held at Northampton, Mass. Schmidt also coached the women's track team to third-place finishes at the 1989 and 1990 conference meets. Buena Vista men's track and field did not flourish after 1991. Robby Beyer won the conference discus throw at the 2002 outdoor meet and also set a school record of 155–9. Henry Johnson won the 1996 400-meter race and Adam Gordon the 400-meter hurdles in 1999. Jason Grubb captured the 3,000-meter steeplechase in 1992. Josh Rasmussen, Jeff Christians, Scott Hermann, and Henry Johnson won the 400-meter conference relay in 1996. Johnson, Christians, Chad Hisler, and Brian Schmulbeck raced to victory in the 1,600-meter relay. In 1996 Don Wolf won the high jump and Mike Wilson the javelin. But no Buena Vista track and field men have been all-Americans since 1989.

Merritt Ewalt's golfers brought home the first Buena Vista title in that sport in 1958. John Naughton's Beavers won back-to-back titles in 1979 and 1980 and over a five-year period did not lose a single dual meet. Naughton coached some outstanding golfers with Jeff Opheim and Tom Geelan being the mainstays of the championship teams and Bill Naughton winning a conference MVP plus all-American honorable mention in 1985. Naughton won recognition as conference coach of the year in 1979, 1980, and 1985. Buena Vista golfers were nearly always one of the top three or four teams in the league. Unfortunately, those halcyon days ended in the 1990s and men's golfing records remained, for the most part, mired in the second division. The 2004–05 golfers were seventh in the Iowa Conference. Neither men's nor women's tennis has been able to win a conference title. The 1985 and 1986 men's teams finished a creditable third in league play under the tutelage of Professor Carl Adkins. Adkins, a scholarly English professor, not unlike Vernon L. Parrington, directed Buena Vista's tennis teams through seventeen turbulent seasons before his retirement in 1997. During his three best seasons he amassed the enviable dual record of 28–12. Adkins-coached teams never failed to win at lest one dual meet. His teams might have done even better had they not been pressured to achieve academic excellence. The Buena Vista Men's tennis teams consistently had the highest GPA of any school athletic squads and there were at least six academic all-Americans. Overall not even Gator Aide could overcome the emphasis on brainpower and the scholarly Adkins' seventeen-year winning percentage stands at .386. Adkins also had the distinction of being the first women's tennis coach in school history. Not long after the passage of Title IX in 1972, a very good women's tennis player sought to make the men's team then coached by Bernie Weiss. Weiss would have none of it even though the woman was obviously superior to some of the men players. The young lady promptly related her woes to Dean of the Faculty Fred Brown who quickly phoned Adkins with the surprising greeting, "How's our new women's tennis coach?" Adkins managed to schedule three contests finishing with a 1–1–1 record.[84] Mike Inman, an All Big Ten tennis star at the University of Iowa in 1984, was named head coach in 2005. Inman would be the first Buena Vista fulltime coach in tennis. However, in 2005 his men's team was blanked in eighteen matches and finished last in the Iowa Conference. The women were eighth in the conference and had an overall record of 1–8. Inman had a long climb ahead in order to reach the top. Future prospects for outstanding teams apparently did not look promising and Inman resigned in July 2005.[85] Cross country and soccer suffered even more difficult times. The 2004 team was twenty-second among twenty-two entrees in the NCAA Regionals and sixth in the Iowa Conference. The Men's Cross Country team, however, had a second place finish in 1999. The women's soccer team has won 12 matches while losing 116 since beginning competition in 1997. The most notable achievement of the women's soccer team came in October 2001 when they ended a thirty-five-game losing streak with a 2–1 thrashing of Mt. Mercy College.[86] Jodi Coleman did, however, make the second all-conference team in 2004. Mark Kosterman became coach in 2002 and has a 7–47 record. The men's soccer team finished third in 2003 and fifth in 2004. The 2003 team finished with a 10–7–2 overall record and the 2004 squad managed an 8–8–4 mark. Nick Fox was a first team all-conference selection in 2003, and in 2004 Chris Bayer won that honor.[87] The late 1980s saw Amy Hoeft and Lana and Todd Cosgrove, a brother–sister combination from Vinton,

Iowa, achieve conference and national recognition in swimming. While Buena Vista swimming teams won no championships, they remained reasonably competitive into the twenty-first century. Unfortunately, the men's and women's swimming program was terminated in 2004 in order to reallocate funds to other "required" conference sports. This created considerable anguish among swimming advocates who were quick to point out that in the last three years twenty-two school records had been broken, nine of them in 2004.[88] In the composite standings of the Iowa Conference, which includes all sports, Buena Vista has consistently ranked fourth or fifth, trailing the perennial champions Central, Luther, and Wartburg. However, Buena Vista has become a Division III power in wrestling, football, baseball, and women's softball.

In 1969 Buena Vista College initiated a sports Hall of Fame. The requirements were graduation from Buena Vista at least five years prior to selection and an outstanding contribution to College athletics. The first six selected were Jim Ahrens (1962), Jay Beekmann (1942), Forrest N. Gaffin (1925), Jerry Ibach (1958), J. Leslie Rollins (1926), and Bernie Saggau (1949). Saggau, a native of Denison, Iowa, would become the executive secretary of the Iowa High School Boys' Athletic Association.[89] Saggau was enticed to enroll at Buena Vista on a $95 scholarship that covered full tuition and a two-hour-a-day custodial task of sweeping floors. Meanwhile he managed to play three years of football and track, a year of basketball, and meet and marry Buena Vista co-ed Lois Kretzinger. Both began their career as teachers, with Lois obtaining a position at Lytton and Bernie in the Cherokee District. Saggau continued his education obtaining a master's in school administration. He also became a principal and businessman and in 1963 began his work with the Iowa High School Athletic Association. In 1967 he was appointed executive director and held that post until his retirement in 2005, when another Buena Vista graduate, Rick Wulkow, was elevated into that position. Saggau also was president of the National Federation of State High School Associations, Chair of the National Basketball Rules Committee, a member of the Football Rules Committee, and a member of the U.S. Olympic House of Delegates Committee. He was the recipient of the Award of Merit of the

National High School Athletic Directors Association, and the National High School Coaches Distinguished Award. In 1996 Saggau was selected by *Referee Magazine* as one of the top twenty in the last twenty years to do the most to improve officiating.[90] Both Saggaus retained their interest in and loyalty to Buena Vista, and in 1997 Bernie became a member of the Board of Trustees. He was also the 2002 Buena Vista Commencement speaker.[91] The original six were joined during the following decades by many other distinguished graduates and former outstanding stars of Buena Vista. One of those Hall of Famers was William Tyron (1954), one of five Tyron brothers who attended Buena Vista College during the 1950s and 1960s and who would soon be ranked among western Iowa's outstanding coaches and teachers.[92]

By 2004 there were eighty-nine members in the Buena Vista Athletic Hall of Fame. No members were selected between 1977 and 1987 and none during the years 1994 and 1995. It was not until 1996 that the first women athletes were included in the Hall of Fame. The first three to receive that honor were Chanel Fizen and Libby Kestal, the almost invincible pitching-catching team of the 1984 national softball champions and Lois Koster Peterson, a star on John Naughton's 1978 and 1979 basketball teams. Jeannie Demers and Julie Quirin were added the following year. By 2004 those selected stood at seventy-four men and fifteen women. The lack of balance is due partly to the fact that women's athletics did not gain parity until Title IX became law during the 1970s, the ten-year gap when no new members were added, and the unexplained reasons why the selection committee did not deem it necessary to honor women athletes with Hall of Fame status until the middle 1990s. One requirement for inclusion is that the nominee has to have been out of school for ten years, which meant Buena Vista's greatest women athletes were waiting quietly on the sidelines until eligible.[93] Since 1996 fifteen of the thirty-four honorees have been women athletes. Since the advent of Title IX, women have amassed sixteen Iowa and four Io-Kota conference titles and the only national championship in the history of the University.[94]

Athletics at Buena Vista College remain at the Division III level where huge stadiums, under-the-table alumni contributions, special privileges, and favoritism do not exist. Athletes enrolled in the regular curriculum and pursued the same general objectives as nonatheletes. The tension and stress, although not absent, were far less than at the Division I level. A few, like Larry Bittner, worked their way to the top in professional sports. More would become teachers, coaches, businessmen, and lawyers.

Originally, the conference decision in 1978 to abandon the NAIA for the NCAA was not entirely pleasing to Buena Vista, which was bound by the majority decision of the Iowa Conference. The additional restrictions placed upon scholarship aid for athletes by the NCAA made recruitment increasingly difficult for schools like Buena Vista where education continues to be the major concern of both coaches and professors. Indeed, some Buena Vista coaches in the past like Henry Hardt, Charles Slagle, and Carl Adkins came from academic disciplines. It was Slagle's 1984 women's golf team that defeated Notre Dame by two strokes.[95]

The caliber of coaching, the techniques and intensity of training programs, and the strength and endurance of athletes improved at Buena Vista (as it did nationally) after the 1960s. Since the 1966–67 diamond jubilee, Buena Vista men have claimed three football championships, eight conference wrestling championships, six Iowa Conference basketball crowns (plus five consecutive conference tournament titles), five conference baseball titles, and two league titles in golf. Buena Vista women won one Io-Kota, followed by six Iowa conference titles in softball, and enjoyed one national title along with second, third, and fifth place finishes, claimed two Io-Kota and six Iowa Conference titles in basketball, and four conference championships in golf. The Buena Vista women also won the Io-Kota tennis title in 1982. This totals forty-four conference crowns (including Io-Kota championships) in eight different sports since 1966. Buena Vista won only fifteen conference titles (nine in baseball) between 1923 and 1966. Two of these were Io-Kota football titles in 1947 and 1948. Jay Beekmann, Jim Hershberger, John Naughton, Al Baxter, and Marge Willadsen have joined Jim Kelly as legendary coaches in Buena Vista sports history. Janet Berry and Brian Van Haaften are still in the early part of their careers, but they are already knocking on the door of coaching immortality.

11

THE FISHER INTERLUDE

Nobody in their right mind would come up here.
— PRESIDENT JOHN FISHER

W hile William Wesselink wrestled with the problems vacated
by the retiring Olson, the trustees conducted a search for a
new chief executive. Their choice was John Albert Fisher, whom
the *Pilot-Tribune* referred to as an "energetic young educator."[1]
The head of the Iowa Synod had asked Fisher if he would mind
having "his hat put in the ring" as a candidate for the vacancy at
Buena Vista. The Fishers had traveled to Storm Lake in March
1954 for an interview. They found the town "gorgeous" but in
evaluating the prospects of the College they counseled one another
that it "was a poor little place," and that "nobody in their right
mind would come up here." Nevertheless, Jack and Ruth Ann
Fisher mused that they knew what a minister went through when he
had a call and that they could not say no if asked to assume the
presidency of Buena Vista College. The letter, not unexpected, asking them to do so arrived in May.[2] The Fishers arrived on the
Buena Vista campus in July 1954.

The new president had considerable experience in the academic world. Only forty-four years of age, he had been registrar,
administrative dean, and chairperson of the Division of Philosophy, Psychology, Education, and Religion at Coe College. Fisher

was a graduate of Nebraska State Teachers College, had received the M.A. from the University of Michigan, and an honorary LL.D. degree from Parsons College. The civic-minded Fisher had been active in a variety of community and state activities: chairperson of the finance committee of the Iowa Study Committee on Higher Education, 1955; a member of the Iowa Citizenship Clearing House, 1954; vice president of the Cedar Rapids YMCA, 1952–1954; a member of the area council of the Boy Scouts of America and member of the executive board 1950–1956. While at Buena Vista, Fisher would be the only layman to serve as moderator of the Synod of Iowa Presbyterian Church, U.S.A. A close associate praised Fisher as an administrator who understood the processes of educational management, knew how and when to compromise, and possessed a contemporary view of the role education should play in a changing America.[3]

The new president was a well-built, dark-complexioned, friendly man. He enjoyed travel, liked to talk, liked meeting new people. He smoked huge cigars which emitted rather odorous black smoke. One suspects that Fisher used the cigars during interviews to test the stamina of prospective faculty members. Jack Fisher slept late and worked late, which made some administrators and trustees wonder where he was during the ordinary hours of the morning. He resided with his wife, Ruth Ann, and seventeen-year-old son, Robert, in the stately but aging Miller-Stuart house on College Street, where they provided much of the labor and paid out-of-pocket for painting, wallpaper, new linoleum, and other expenses. Mrs. Fisher was a graduate of Coe College and former executive secretary of the Cedar Rapids and Marion Council of Churches.[4] She had married Jack Fisher in August 1939. A gracious hostess and veteran of numerous dinners in an era of few funds and little assistance, Ruth Ann helped her husband build solid relationships with community and church. She was also a strong supporter of the Faculty Dames in an era when that organization provided an outlet for many faculty and staff women and she served at numerous brunches and teas. There persisted during the Fisher years a feeling of close community, inspired (as Ruth Ann reminisced years later) by the fact that no one had much and "everybody was willing to share what they had with somebody else."[5]

The Fisher regime, 1954–1960, met many challenges and had much to its credit. While Olson had saved the College, it was Fisher's task to move it forward. Recent years had seen a decline in church support with the Christian Board of Education of the Presbyterian Church having given Buena Vista College only probationary approval. An unavoidable surge of new indebtedness and a questioning of the quality of education at the College had prompted the Synod to insist on change. Dormitories still had to be built and the library was becoming a thorn in the flesh. There was fear that inadequate library and laboratory facilities might jeopardize North Central accreditation.[6] Furthermore, Old Main was in desperate need of renovation. Due to the end of the influx of GIs from the Korean War, enrollment was about 25 percent under the high point of 539 students that had been reached in 1949–50. Like Olson, Fisher followed the Buena Vista tradition of speaking ebulliently concerning future prospects of the College. Soon after assuming his duties in 1954, the new president reminded community and College that Buena Vista "has a great history . . . your College has a challenging future spread over years ahead."[7] Nor was the Fisher administration idle. Early in 1955 bidding opened for the construction of a new $300,000 men's dormitory. With the able assistance of long-time trustee, Z. Z. White, a loan for the desired amount was approved by the Federal Housing and Home Finance Agency.[8] It was the first of four new dormitories to be constructed over a decade, which would alter the appearance as well as the character of the institution. For more than sixty years the majority of Buena Vista students had been forced to find lodging off-campus and commute to classes. Now the College community would be brought closer together by on-campus residency. One of the dormitories would bear the name of Zeno White, a trustee of the College since 1928. White would remain a trustee until his death in 1980 — a period of fifty-two years service not likely to be equaled. Another would be named in honor of Dr. H. A. Pierce, a Board member since 1940.

Although not a clergyman, and perhaps partly for this reason,

Fisher carefully stressed the Christian character of the College.
Fisher indicated in his inaugural address that the purpose of the
founders had been to educate "the youth of this area in a climate
that would be thoroughly Christian." It was an era when faculty
members were expected to demonstrate "personal Christian character" and prayer at faculty meetings was accepted without question.
Not only were all Board members approved by the Synod, but a
majority of the trustees were expected to be Presbyterian.[9] The
Board of Visitors of the Presbyterian Church, U.S.A., which still
exercised control over the Church's denominational colleges, sent
its chairperson, Dr. Charles Friley, out in November 1954 to examine the status of the College and the progress made in the period
since Olson's departure.

Later in 1955 another step forward was taken when Buena
Vista College received a grant of $114,600 from the Ford Founda-
tion. The purpose of the grant was to assist in boosting the traditionally low faculty salaries. While the grant was appreciated and
helpful, President Fisher soberly reminded his faculty that an endowment of $100,000 at 5 percent produces $5,000 per year. "At
this rate," Fisher cautioned, "it would take between one-and-a-half
and two million dollars in endowment funds to produce the
amount your College must raise each year to carry out its program."[10] Nevertheless, the College seemed to be more stable than
at any point in its history. Fisher viewed the first year of his administration as a successful one. He pointed out that the goals
during the academic year 1954–55 had been (1) an enlarged program of Christian activities, (2) financial aid to worthy students,
(3) the maintenance of an outstanding faculty, and (4) the improvement of facilities and equipment.[11] Fisher felt that Buena Vista
College was moving forward along all four lines.

Faculty salaries had risen more than 10 percent during Fisher's
first year as president. Such an increase hardly placed Buena Vista
among the American Association of University Professors's top-
rated institutions, but it did enable the College to become more
competitive with colleges of similar size and purpose. Dedicated
faculty members like the Kuehls, George Reynolds, the venerable
Albert Hirsch, Miss Dagmar Peterson, and the untiring Luman

Sampson continued to serve the College throughout their lives. Younger faculty members, among them Ronald Smith in biology, James B. Christiansen in chemistry, and the Reverend Lester Williams in Bible and philosophy were recruited during the early years of the Fisher administration. The youthful Smith had already published a booklet entitled *The Natural History of the Prairie Dog* and his outstanding ability as a teacher made him a worthy successor to F. F. "Bugs" Smith. Among undergraduates whom he influenced was Richard Lampe, class of 1968, who would years later occupy the same professorial chair.

Ron Smith was a dynamic young professor who quickly assumed a leadership role among the faculty. Compromise was a somewhat difficult art for Smith to master and he was quick to attack administrative policies he found disagreeable. Unable to accept either the policies or the governing style of Dean John Williams, Smith soon left Buena Vista. Because he was a brilliant scholar and teacher, he left a model of excellence for his successors in the science department to emulate. Smith's colleague, Professor James Christiansen had contributed to scholarly journals in his field and for more than a decade had been in charge of a research section with General Mills in Detroit.[12] Christiansen's experience and research interests gave the chemistry department a much-needed scholarly boost and he remained at Buena Vista until his retirement in 1976. His wife, Irene, became a dominant force among the Faculty Dames (as they were known in the 1950s and 1960s). Their son, James B. Christiansen, graduated summa cum laude from Buena Vista in 1962 and quickly launched into a successful academic career of his own as researcher, author, and professor at Drake University. Two other professors who would make long-time commitments to the College, coach Jay Beekmann (see Chapter Ten), and professor of music Fran Heusinkveld, were given faculty appointments in 1955. Heusinkveld remained on the faculty and served as the College organist until her retirement in 1988. It was in 1958 that Fisher and Dean of the Faculty William Wesselink hired a young, inexperienced, history professor with a fresh Ph.D. from the University of Iowa. He could smell the newness of the yet unnamed "New Building," already in use although still receiving its final touches, he could sense the friendly concern for students and staff, and he could feel the optimism of those with whom he spoke. The professor was William H. Cumberland, and he would stay for thirty-three years.

One of the most important appointments made by the Fisher administration was that of Dr. Lester Williams as professor of Bible and philosophy and dean of students. Williams completed his undergraduate work at Ursinus, his M.A. at the University of Pittsburgh, and held a M.Div. from Yale University. He also studied at the University of Pennsylvania, at the American School of Oriental Research, and at Hebrew University in Jerusalem. Even an urbane aristocratic veneer could not cover an ever-present twinkle and love of jest. Williams, liberal albeit independent in thought, was a student of the religions of the world, hated sham and intolerance, thought world government necessary for world peace, and was a perpetual student as well as teacher. The Williamses had lived in India where Lester assumed the position of vice president and professor of English literature and Bible at the Baring Union Christian College in Batala and Punjab.[13] Indeed his travels took him around the world, fine-tuning his scholarly instincts. One such itinerary found the Williamses on a thousand-mile photographic safari across East Africa through the bush country of Kenya. Williams's talents were utilized in many areas as he operated in the dual role of faculty-administrator. Not only did he acquire an outstanding reputation as a faculty member and as dean of students, but he served as foreign student advisor, financial aid officer, and director of the convocation program. He assisted Halverson as executive assistant to the president 1968–1972, returned to the classroom in a new field — sociology — in 1972–73, and was appointed interim president of the College 1973–74. He had also been moderator of the Synod of Iowa of the United Presbyterian Church.[14] In the summer of 1965 he traveled to the Middle East in order to participate in an archaeological survey — one of his four archaeological expeditions to the region. The 1965 expedition involved the excavation of Tell Arad, one of the largest Canaanite sites in Palestine, in which walls and artifacts dating to 3,000 B.C. were uncovered.[15]

Williams, who had watched the burning of Old Main in 1956 and witnessed the rise of the new Buena Vista, retired from the College in 1974 at the beginning of the Briscoe era. Through it all and into retirement Williams maintained his faith in the liberal arts, hoping to witness a renaissance in a world where too much emphasis upon computers and technology produced a dangerous depersonalization.[16]

There were others, too, who devoted much of their lives to Buena Vista College. The Reverend Henry Eggink, for many years the chairperson of Bible and philosophy, and Dorothy Skewis, professor of art, also arrived during the Fisher administration to give long and competent service. Professor Eggink made a lasting impression on students with his sincerity and masterly presentation of course material. Dorothy Skewis, a talented painter, started the art department on its road to prominence. Professor W. B. Green continued to improve the music department, and in 1956 under his guidance the College band undertook the first tour in its history. Green, a native Texan, was a Buena Vista College graduate, a member of Karl King's band in Fort Dodge, and a former Storm Lake high school band director. He was a picturesque personality, adored by students and colleagues. Green's marching band provided colorful half-time entertainment at football and basketball games. He composed a number of marches including "La Roquina" (the Red Head). Tragedy hit the Green household in 1961 when their ten-year-old daughter, Patti, died suddenly of complications following the flu. In 1977 following his retirement, the College music department dedicated the spring festival to the maestro who passed away a few months later after suffering a fatal heart attack while directing a rehearsal of the Karl King band at Fort Dodge.[17] He was an important cultural source and one of the builders of Buena Vista College.

Likewise, Professor T. P. Kuehl's sudden death in 1961 left a gap in the education department. Professor Donald V. Cox, a 1949 Buena Vista graduate and a faculty member since 1956, moved efficiently into that vacancy until lured to Des Moines by the Department of Public Instruction (now Department of Education) where he became associate superintendent of instruction. Dr. Cox continued to maintain a strong interest in Buena Vista College that included serving a term on the Board of Trustees.

During the Fisher administration, enrollment edged slowly toward the five hundred mark. Fisher envisioned the kind of growth among students and faculty that would enhance the quality of the College. "We believe," he said toward the end of his presidency, "that the growth of Buena Vista has been a healthy one — not so rapid that quality could not be maintained and improvement made, yet rapid enough to keep us developing spiritually, intellectually and in the support of those interested in the kind of education we believe in."[18]

The June 1956 graduation ceremonies were celebrated by the return of Donald Ambler who delivered the Commencement address to the graduates. He spoke on "The College in a Changing World." Ambler, now chairperson of the Board of Dryden Press, New York, was a 1921 graduate of the College. His father, the Reverend T. A. Ambler, had been pastor of the Lakeside Church in 1914. Young Ambler had been editor of the *Tack* and the College yearbook, athlete, debater, and business administration major. Upon graduation he coached, taught, and later attended the University of Iowa where he received his M.A. degree in English. For a while he was an instructor at the University of Minnesota, then moved east and became a field representative for the Macmillan Company. In 1939 Ambler, along with four others, became one of the founders of the Dryden Press. His address recalled the long struggle for survival faced by the College and the difficulty of "bridging the gap between the college and the community."[19]

By nature a garrulous, friendly person, Fisher liked to talk with his faculty. The new president, partly from his own apprenticeship as a faculty member, was oriented toward the faculty and faculty concerns. During the years 1954–1956 he was getting the feel of the College and preparing what he believed to be a sound, steady program of growth. Already the look of the future was beginning to show. The College paper in the fall of 1956 proudly announced that "many changes have taken place on the Buena Vista campus during the summer, the greatest of course being the

completion of the new men's dorm." Furthermore, the student union had been moved to more spacious quarters in the basement of
the new dormitory, later White Hall, and considerable repair and
painting work had been completed in Old Main.[20]

And then came one of the pivotal points in Buena Vista history. At 10:15 P.M. on September 27, 1956, someone discovered
smoke billowing out of the beloved but decaying Old Main. Just
before retiring for the evening, Superintendent of Building and
Grounds, Buck Allison, received a phone call that Old Main was
burning. As he looked out, he could see the fire "really flarin',
lighting up the sky." By 10:25 P.M. Fire Chief Harold Stanton and
the fire departments of Storm Lake, Alta, and Newell were rushing
to combat what was rapidly becoming an inferno. It was too late.
Already, the blaze could be seen in Spencer forty miles away.[21] The
symbol and rallying point of the survival struggle of sixty-four
years burned in fierce, hot agony. The exact cause of the fire would
remain unknown although there was speculation that a smoldering
cigarette might have been left on the roof by a workman. Apparently there was no electrical short or outage because the lights
remained on during the early stages of the fire.[22]

The College and community were horrified as they watched
the College's oldest and most revered symbol engulfed in fire and
smoke. To many of them Old Main was Buena Vista College. President Fisher, Dean Wesselink and Public Relations Director Don
Kelly had been attending a meeting of Iowa private colleges at
Lake Okoboji when Ruth Ann Fisher called informing the president that Old Main was burning.[23] Jack Fisher turned to his colleagues and asked, "What would you do if your Old Main was
burning?" Several with old buildings of their own responded, "Let
us know how you did it?"[24] But it was serious business and as
Fisher and his staff sped home for a 3 A.M. rendezvous with the
College community, the future of the institution was in doubt.
Ruth Ann Fisher, like Lester and Edith Williams, had been attending a PTA meeting at the high school. They could hear the sirens
and seeing the red glow in the sky knew the fire was at the College.[25]

Gladys Kuehl was attending a function of Phi Alpha Pi sorority at the Cobblestone Inn. There was a call informing the group of the "disaster in progress" and the party quickly broke up as those in attendance rushed back to the campus. Ted and Gladys Kuehl had their offices in the basement of Old Main. Dr. Kuehl recalled vividly that

> the third floor was occupied by the music department in the west wing, and the speech and drama department in the east wing, while the chapel and the classrooms were on the second floor. Consequently, pianos, musical instruments, chapel seats and stage properties came hurtling down from above, making efforts to remove anything from the building a very dangerous procedure.[26]

Among the items falling from the third floor as the building burned were the Kuehl's old davenport and chairs, bought when they were first married. The set had been donated to the Buena Vista Players for their meeting room and for use in drama productions.[27] Grace Russell, whose father had built Old Main, and Phoebe LaFoy (former dean of women) watched in anguish and horror from the east side of the building. Eight times they heard the mournful twang of pianos, including the baby grand from the chapel, falling into the inferno.[28]

All that had been the College was in Old Main—it had been the spirit of Buena Vista. Members of faculty, administration, student body, and community sought desperately to salvage the vital historic documents. Even as the building became untenable, the students, "without regard to themselves . . . saved all of the school records and virtually all of the stock of books in the bookstore. Filing cabinets, safes, heavy cabinets of addressograph plates—all were carried to safety." Furniture, instruments, and machines too heavy to carry through the flames were thrown out of the windows. Brigades were formed to cart away records and books from the burning building. One freshman mindful of his beanie, put down his books and "buttoned as a senior came along." No danger could halt the heroic work of salvage. Indeed, it was not until the roof of Old Main began to collapse that the students, "ordered out and away from the structure by police," gave up the struggle. Ruth Ann Fisher believed that had the men students not been concentrated in the recently completed dormitory, where they could quickly organize salvaging efforts, many invaluable student and administrative records would have been lost. A legend persists that the following day the students were unable to lift the heavy files they had carted out of the burning building. The fire started on the top of the building and worked its way down, which meant it moved more slowly than if it had started in the basement or main floor. Les Williams had a sickening feeling as he watched his office burn along with a lifetime collection of several hundred books.[29]

The blaze continued to rage for more than three hours before it could be brought under control. Unfortunately, the fire fighting equipment was not adequate to reach the blazing roof.[30] Finally, with the flames ebbing and sick reality replacing the early numb shock, President Fisher and his staff "joined in a circle on the canvas-covered and equipment-cluttered gym floor to bow their heads in prayer." They were, as the *Storm Lake Register* commented, "a student body and faculty united by one thought . . . loyalty to Buena Vista College."[31] One more time adversity would rally the spartan forces of Buena Vista.

It was John Fisher's finest hour. He could have surrendered to the despair he must have felt and temporarily suspended classes and even operations. Rather, he announced that classes would continue as usual and at 1:15 A.M. he began his plans for Buena Vista's future. As he looked at the charred skeleton of Old Main, he could see the Christian flag "which hung on the west wall of the Little Theatre," still unscathed by the conflagration. Fisher would never forget that moment. He would speak of it often as a new Buena Vista began to rise phoenixlike from the ashes of the old. Nor would he forget Buck Allison, who at considerable risk crawled through the ruins to retrieve both the Christian flag and a badly charred United States flag. A moment later, what was left of the top floor of Old Main crumbled.[32] The flag would become a memento of the past and a symbol for the future. Now, more than three decades after the great fire of Buena Vista, the Christian flag is displayed at baccalaureate and other major College functions and the charred United States flag remains encased in glass in the Centennial room of Siebens Forum.

Professor Luman Sampson was grateful that his honor scroll had made it through the fire without harm. The honor society, started in 1936, had become another revered tradition of the College. And yet, as Sampson knew, the loss from the fire was too great to be replaced. "Not only was there the material loss of the building," he said, "with its classrooms, offices, studios, pianos and a considerable amount of equipment, but also the loss of this landmark of memories for all those who had entered the building in the years it had stood as the symbol of Buena Vista College."[33]

At least the College had been spared the loss of life or serious injury, nor had the fire spread to the homes across the street. In the days that followed, the bonds that united Buena Vistans would be strengthened. Old Main had many mourners, and faculty and former students poured out many eloquent words on her behalf. The mandate for a new building program would challenge the growing intellectual climate that President Fisher had hoped to foster. Sensibly, he reminded the College and community:

> We regret the passing of a building that for many years has housed a considerable portion of the activities of the College. A college, however, is much more than a building and so the students, faculty and staff have not seen fit to interrupt the normal routines necessary to fulfill the purposes of the College. We believe in the future of Buena Vista.[34]

Nor did Fisher permit the tragedy to disrupt classes or the ordinary functioning of the College for a single minute. Storm Lake churches offered their buildings as temporary havens for classes. Jack Fisher's home became his office and planning center for a new Buena Vista. Events were held as scheduled. The Kuehls found office space in the men's dormitory. A small cottage near the football field housed forensics and advanced speech classes. Classes moved into the new building as it was being completed — even before the walls were finished when "there were only canvas partitions for division of space for classroom."[35] In those days, one could feel (if not define) the "soul" of Buena Vista College!

Whereas Old Main had cost $25,000 to construct, the value of the building in relation to its insurance coverage was $111,500 at the time of its destruction.[36] The total cost of replacement would be over $400,000, of which $100,000 was promised by the Church and $33,000 from the Board of Education.[37] Indeed, in destruction Old Main may have performed its most valuable service. For it steeled Buena Vistans to make the greatest effort they had yet made on behalf of the College and to fulfill the purpose envisioned by the founding fathers. Former trustee Willis Edson walked painfully to the campus to view the ruins. He noticed that "not a single brick or stone in those walls was out of place. What kind of men built those walls so long ago?" Edson mused. Later, that same brick and stone would be used in building the Victory Arch. New and magnificent buildings would dot the campus of a rising Buena Vista College. But the "spirit of Old Main" would not be forgotten.

A new main building and a new chapel dominated the last part of President Fisher's six-year term at Buena Vista. Lumberman and trustee Paul Dixon drew the plan for the new building, but Jack Fisher, assisted by Bill Wesselink, designed the interior office and classroom space. Dean Bill Wesselink remembered that "many long hours were spent at Jack's kitchen table drawing up the floor plans." Although they were not architects little of their work had to be altered.[38] Construction on the new administration building started early in 1957 and was completed by the time classes opened in the fall of 1958. The half-million dollar structure with its spacious, functional rooms seemed like a paradise to those who had wrestled with the creaking stairs and falling plaster of Old Main. About the only similarity was that the new building still "commands a panoramic view of the campus and lake as its predecessor once did."[39] The new Georgian colonial structure was ultimately named Dixon-Eilers Hall in honor of trustee president Paul Dixon of Sac City, and trustee Tom D. Eilers, president of the World Insurance Company of Omaha, Nebraska. Both men would continue to be among the leaders in the drive to move Buena Vista forward.

In the fall of 1958, the prominent banker George J. Schaller presented the College with a challenge gift of $125,000 for the construction of the new chapel.[40] George Schaller, once a student of P. B. S. Peters in the commercial department, had acquired a fortune in banking and real estate. He could now see the phoenix-like resurrection of the College, its importance to the Storm Lake community, its future within the stable complex of Iowa's private colleges and sought to aid in its development.

In the nineteenth century the Schaller family had been wagon makers in Alsace-Lorraine. In 1866 the father, Fred Schaller, had emigrated to the United States. Only eighteen years old, he endeavored to continue his trade at Buffalo, New York. The following year, 1867, he moved to western Iowa with $100 in savings. Fred Schaller took advantage of rising land values in a rapidly growing state, became a successful farmer and in 1902, after some urging by his son George, purchased the banking business of Thomas and Bradford. The Schaller enterprise was a private bank until 1911, when it was reorganized as the Citizens National Bank.[41] At this point George Schaller was on his way to national prominence. By 1927 he was the president of the Iowa State Bankers Association and in 1928 became a director of the Federal Reserve Bank of Chicago. In 1934 he was elected governor (president) of the Federal Reserve Bank and served in that capacity until 1941.[42] During his nine decades George Schaller contributed to many philanthropic enterprises. The Citizens Bank remained in the hands of the Schaller family (son Harry and grandson George), and the Schaller's support of Buena Vista College continued far beyond the naming gift of the Schaller Memorial Chapel.

On May 12, 1963, Schaller Memorial Chapel was formally dedicated. It was a stately and graceful structure with its

> Georgian colonial design, its flush columns, the expansive steps, its imposing doors, its beautiful and functional interior, standing as a distinguished architectural landmark, a spiritual as well as cultural focal point on the Buena Vista College campus.[43]

Another veteran Buena Vistan who watched the growth of the College with pride was W. C. Jarnagin, editor of the *Storm Lake Pilot-Tribune* since 1922. Distinguished careers in journalism would embrace three generations of Jarnagins. William C. Jarnagin's career began in 1901 when he started work as a proofreader on the old *Des Moines Daily Capitol*. Eventually, he became the paper's managing editor and on February 1, 1922 purchased the *Storm Lake Pilot-Tribune*. Nearly half a century in Storm Lake produced many honors for the Jarnagins and the *Pilot-Tribune*, which they built into one of the best weeklies in the Midwest. Of equal significance was the twenty years that William Claude Jarnagin served on the College Board of Trustees and the outstanding public relations he conducted on behalf of the College.

Throughout his long life Jarnagin maintained his undiluted enthusiasm for the Storm Lake community. The editor's spirit of boosterism manifested itself in community service, for Jarnagin was a president of the Chamber of Commerce, a founder of the local barbershoppers, a solid promoter of the Storm Lake community chest, and the heart and soul behind the Mr. Goodfellow's Christmas fund for poor families. The annual Goodfellow's fund saw to it that many children of needy families were supplied with warm mittens, caps, jackets, and boots.[44] His son, Philip C. Jarnagin, followed in his father's footsteps producing the same quality paper and serving as a trustee until his retirement in the early 1970s. The *Storm Lake Pilot-Tribune* kept the College before the public and its columns provide a rich and accurate source of historical information.

There was, of course, much more to the Fisher regime than unexpected concern with bricks and mortar. The embryo of modern technology was hatched during the Fisher years when a rather flamboyant professor of business administration, former Boston attorney and Boston University professor Bill Parks, introduced IBM data-processing machines in 1959. Parks had also been a statistician with a large insurance company and a branch chief accountant with General Motors.[45] Never modest about such innovations, the *Tack* boasted "Buena Vista is believed to be the first college in the United States in such a program of instruction."[46] Installed under the IBM Educational Contribution program, each machine included a card punch to record data on cards, a sorter to arrange facts, and an accounting machine to print results. Parks was to teach the courses in the new program but he soon was swinging out with the soon-to-be graduates at the Senior Swing Out and the machines (no one else could operate them) were left to gather dust.[47] However, while the expectations of this early version of computer technology were not then realized, President Fisher insisted that the College pioneer new methods of study and tieing the collegiate program to business and industrial applications as Buena Vista added "modern machines to the teaching process."[48] Charles Slagle was one young undergraduate who tinkered with the new technology. Years later Slagle would introduce the first computer course at Buena Vista College.

Many College executives felt in the post–World War II era that six years was a lengthy tenure at one institution. Perhaps because of this, and possibly because he saw increasing resistance to his own educational vision, John Fisher, by the time Schaller Memorial Chapel was dedicated in May 1963, had departed for Jamestown College, North Dakota. By now however, it could be said that while an untried, incoming president inherited the frustrations inherent in such a post, he also inherited a continuing design that contained more substance than fantasy. Jack Fisher's six-year tenure, 1954–1960, had seen Buena Vista march into a new position of respectability. The area press began to acknowledge that Buena Vista College "isn't the little one-horse college as some of us may have thought, but it's a fully accredited school that can take its place among the colleges of the state and the nation."[49] Jack Fisher had put the Ford grant to good use, church pledges of $169,000 over a five-year period surpassed all such previous support, and the net equity of the institution increased from $521,000 to $1,432,240.[50] The size and quality of the faculty had been increased, student enrollment had grown, the liberal arts heritage had been maintained, and Fisher had led the College community as it hacked a path through adversity. Of course adversity was nothing new for Buena Vista College, but under Fisher's inspired and determined leadership, the fire had hardened the steel. Fisher's heart would remain at Buena Vista. After his premature death at age sixty-four in 1974, Ruth Ann would return to Storm Lake to live. The big man with the cigars had left his mark. There would be no turning back.

12

HOLDING THE LINE WITH HALVERSON

I am going to enjoy thoroughly being president of Buena Vista College.
—PRESIDENT WENDELL HALVERSON

F isher's resignation meant the College would have to search for a new president — one who could continue the institution's march into the modern era. The mantle fell upon Dr. Wendell Q. Halverson, a strong-boned, handsome Scandinavian, serving as an executive in the presbytery of New York and a graduate of the University of Iowa and Union Theological Seminary with postgraduate studies at Oberlin graduate school of theology, the University of Chicago, Chicago Lutheran Seminary, and the University of Oslo. He had served the Presbyterian church as pastor at Clyde, Ohio, and La Grange, Illinois, and as a philosophy professor at Heidelberg College in Ohio. He had met his wife Marian while they were students at Iowa. As first lady of the College, Marian Halverson demonstrated a strong civic and social conscience, an honesty and integrity that was refreshing and frank although not always in harmony with conservative local politics. Accompanying the Halversons were their three children, Peder, Ingrid, and Timothy.

The Q. stood for Quelprud — and it was the Viking-sounding middle name that was the deciding factor in Halverson's appointment, said crusty trustee Tom Eilers.[1] Actually, Halverson was aware that Buena Vista was seeking a new president and he had

315

been toying with the thought of leaving congested New York City for such a post, should it present itself in his native Midwest. The Halversons recalled wonderful days with students and colleagues at Heidelberg College that certainly whetted their interest in returning to the campus scene. Presbyterian church executives had approached Dr. Halverson concerning the prospects of his accepting a college presidency in a national meeting at St. Paul. Later a call came from Buena Vista trustee Tom Eilers inviting the Halversons to come to Storm Lake for an interview, and Halverson accepted the challenge. Halverson, who was born in Austin, Minnesota, and had lived as a youth in Eagle Grove and Webster City, Iowa, was impressed by the professionalism of Board, administration, and staff. He sensed, however, the need to change the parochial atmosphere and broaden the horizons of the College. He immediately surmised that the student body (which came mostly from a hundred-mile radius) needed to be exposed to a wider diversification of people. This, plus a major construction program, coupled with endeavors at enlarging and improving the quality of the faculty would be the major challenges of the Halverson era.

Halverson described himself as a "Christian realist," a liberal theologian in the Niebuhrian sense. He was a man with a strong social conscience and an ecumenical global and spiritual view, an intellectual with powerful oratorical gifts. His faculty respected him as an intellectual, but sometimes found him distant and occasionally too prone to theorizing rather than responding to the call for practical action. Halverson's liberal theology, however, did not extend to life-styles and he was committed to the sacredness of the family unit and belligerently opposed to a lenient alcohol policy on campus—a view that caused some conflict with students and faculty in the generation of the 1960s which espoused radical changes in traditional life-styles. His regime would undoubtedly mark the end of clergyman-presidents and the zenith, although not through lack of dedication on Halverson's part, of the historic closeness of the church relationship. Halverson brought with him not only a Niebuhrian social and theological piety, but a solid commitment to the liberal arts. The traditional humanities, bolstered by the historic Judeo-Christian commitment, provided the solid core of

Halverson's approach to education. However, he appreciated the challenges of a pluralistic society and readily accepted what he saw as the three main Buena Vista traditions — the classical, the normal or teaching, and the commercial. Those business leaders he respected most, he said in a 1988 interview, felt the importance of the liberal arts. Halverson assumed basic humanities requirements, including those in philosophy, religion, and physics, were essential for the culturally literate graduate. He firmly believed in the necessity of exposure to other cultures and endeavored to bring representative faculty and students on campus — among his appointments were Manoocher Aryanpur (English) from Iran, Felix Cruz (accounting) a Cuban refugee, Soon Kang (history) who had fled from North Korea, A. G. Thomas (sociology and social work) a native of India, and Iftikiar Bhatti (biology) from Pakistan. A scattering of students from Africa, Europe, and Asia would dot the campus. And during the 1960s Buena Vista witnessed what some felt was certainly a radical departure from tradition: the influx of hundreds of students from the East — especially New York and New Jersey.

Halverson's approach to higher education should have been clear to those six hundred Buena Vistans who gathered in Edson Hall on Pearl Harbor Day in 1961 to listen to the new president speak on "Challenge and Response." He hoped the days when others perceived Buena Vista as a mediocre institution were over, and told the audience he envisioned a three million dollar building campaign that would bring about the construction of the chapel already planned by Jack Fisher, add new dormitories, a library, and a student union. He optimistically forecast a student body of eight hundred by 1965–66. "The crisis of our day," Halverson informed his audience, "is to help students not to get but to become children of the highest; to see life and see it whole." This, of course, had been the vision of Loyal Hays, of E. E. Reed, of James Patterson Linn, of Evert Jones. Was the vision and faith of the founding fathers destined to become a reality?[2] Plans for the next decade were outlined in a twenty-four-page brochure entitled *Design for Learning* and presented to the audience by trustee Kermit Buntrock, chairperson of the Development Committee.[3]

The big event of the academic year 1961–62 was Dr. Halverson's inauguration as the College's fifteenth president. It was fitting that the three-day event should take place during the first week in October. Nearly seventy years before, the dedication services surrounding the building of Old Main and the beginning of the College had been conducted in the splendor of early autumn. The colored leaves of Storm Lake's elm-lined streets formed a majestic archway around the city. On October 7, as the red-orange and yellow leaves were falling from maples and elms, a large crowd gathered to see the long procession in full academic apparel march to the Victory Arch at the edge of the main campus grounds. There dignitaries from across the nation watched the installation of Wendell Q. Halverson as the new president of Buena Vista College. The Rev. Dr. Arthur McKay, president of McCormick Theological Seminary, and Dr. Frederick H. Sparks, head of the Council for Financial Aid to Education, were featured speakers. It was a three-day ceremony complete with receptions, the annual college-community banquet, seminars, and ground-breaking ceremonies for the new dormitories and Schaller Chapel. Assisted by his son Harry, George J. Schaller broke ground for the building named in his honor. "Buena Vista and I grew up at the same time," Schaller remarked, "the only difference is I have grown older, while Buena Vista has grown bigger and better. . . . We owe our pioneers a debt of gratitude for the heritage they left us here."[4] Letters were read from former presidents Arthur Boyd and Henry Olson. For those who thirty years before had listened to the drums beating the death knell of the College, it was the beginning of a new era.[5] Halverson revealed that he understood the essence of the liberal arts when he told those gathered that "Ignorance of the past foredooms us to prejudice in the future. Students are in demand who know how to think, write and speak, and who have an understanding of history, of people and the world around them." The church-related college, he argued, "is uniquely called to fight the battle [for a liberal education] on behalf of all of higher education. I am going to enjoy thoroughly," he said, "being president of Buena Vista College."[6]

The twelve-year Halverson presidency had its share of excitement and turbulence, paralleling the youth rebellion of the 1960s,

the Vietnam War, the Civil Rights Movement, political assassina-
tions, the programs of the Great Society, and foreign policy somer-
saults that saw the United States and the Soviets move from nuclear confrontation over Cuba to détente and cooperative space
exploration, from frigid hostility toward China to Nixon's careful
preparation for extending recognition. The state and federal governments provided increasing grants to higher education and with
them increasing regulation. How private were the private colleges?
And should a religiously affiliated institution be the recipient of
such grants? The Halverson years, 1961–1973, posed a challenge
to traditional academic and political conservatism. Halverson, less
appreciated than the facts warrant, paved the way for the modernization of Buena Vista College. His broad perspective, his commitment to the liberal arts tradition, his theological and social realism
uprooted provincial views that impeded progress. He was willing to
build buildings with federal assistance, he was willing to seek out
minority students, he sought a more diversified body of trustees,
faculty, and students, he enlarged the cultural programs, and he
maintained a tight fiscal ship under the direction of Charles Zalesky, his able and occasionally cantankerous business manager.
Student ACT scores and class standing edged upward, and an annual student academic awards banquet was instituted where intellectual achievement was given long overdue recognition.[7] The Iowa
Epsilon chapter of the Alpha Chi National Honor Society was
approved by the Faculty Senate in April 1970, with Professor
Leonard Martz serving as sponsor.[8] At the same time, faculty salaries were steadily increased and new fringe benefits were introduced, including expanded medical coverage, life insurance, and a
much-improved pension plan under the auspices of TIAA-CREF.[9]

One of the immediate tasks undertaken by Halverson was to
obtain funding and complete the buildings envisioned in the *Design
for Learning* plan. The gift and planning of Schaller Chapel right-
fully belonged to Jack Fisher although it was completed by Halverson. However, it was the Halverson administration that added
most of the dormitories, the long-sought college library, Lage Center, Siebens Fieldhouse, the Science Building (now named after
Estelle Siebens), and the new Smith Hall remodeled at a cost of

$376,000 making it into an up-to-date educational center.[10] The Halverson administration successfully raised over $8.5 million of which $5.6 million came from government grants and nearly $2.9 million from private funding. Slightly under $400,000 came from alumni, nearly $250,000 from trustees, and over $60,000 from faculty. Contributions from church bodies totaled $648,000, a sum that was disappointing to Halverson and which indicated that weakening of church-college ties was inevitable. What many have found remarkable is the consistently enthusiastic response of the 9,000 residents of Storm Lake to the annual College campaigns. Between 1961 and 1973, more than $753,000 was provided by local residents. Aware of the significance of this generosity and its importance for private education, Halverson paid tribute to the community in his farewell statement asserting that "We can have no volunteer society if we have no volunteers."[11] Halverson acknowledged the dorms lacked the amenities he would have liked to have included, but he did what he could considering budget constraints. This included adding two new wings to Swope Hall, thereby increasing room capacity to 202; adding a 126-student addition to White, thus creating room space for 492 students; and completing Pierce Hall in time for the 1962 academic year.

Mr. and Mrs. (Merle Garton 1930) Leonard C. Philips of Wheaton, Illinois, were among the foremost supporters of Buena Vista College during the Halverson years. The Philipses provided a $17,450 challenge gift (if the alumni could raise an additional $35,000)[12] and presented the College with bell chimes for the steeple tower. The twelve bells were cast in the Netherlands and weighed from 140 to 1,000 lbs. They were dedicated to members of the Philips family and to former Buena Vista College deans Harriet Banghart, Walter O. Benthin, and J. F. Saylor who had meant so much to Merle Philips during her college days at Buena Vista. The dedication of the bells was part of the June 2, 1963, Commencement and the Rev. Gilbert T. Bremicker, pastor of the American Protestant Church in The Hague, Netherlands, was the speaker.[13] The bells are electronically controlled and use a timer system, with a bell company providing biannual inspection. The bells were used to play special music at Commencement and at Christmas. However, after two decades of use, the parts began to wear, were expensive to replace, and difficult to find.[14] The Philips's interest in natural science led them to provide a unique butterfly collection consisting of 4,350 specimens donated in 1970 and 543 more presented in 1973.[15] In recognition of their generosity to the College, the Alumni Association presented the Philipses with a plaque at the 1963 Homecoming festivities.

Dean and Mary Persing, who became one of the College's most beloved couples, arrived on the Buena Vista College campus in the spring of 1964. Dean Persing served as assistant business manager and as manager of the Buena Vista College bookstore for many years. He succeeded in making the bookstore into an academic palace stocked with the best paperbacks the scholarly world had to offer. Unfortunately, the venture was not profitable and did not survive Dean's retirement. Mary Persing worked for the College as reference and circulation librarian until her retirement in 1977. The Persings had been brought to the campus by Wendell Halverson, who had been their pastor when he served a parish in Clyde, Ohio, and had benefited from their close friendship and wise counsel. They provided the same service at Buena Vista not only for Halverson but for faculty and students. Mary Persing's courageous death in face of incurable cancer in June 1989 saddened an entire community. In the struggle against disease she revealed with true nobility that in death, as in life, we can find inspiration.

When Halverson became president, the College's most pressing need was for a new library—a need that had existed since the original collection was housed in a room in Old Main, where it remained until 1928. At that time the collection was moved into Smith Hall and in 1947, after World War II into a makeshift ex-army barracks.[16] There the fewer than 40,000 volumes that now constituted the College collection remained in 1961 for students and faculty to squeeze between the shelves (of a not completely open system) and to study at the ageing tables, if an empty space could be found.

A library committee was appointed in 1962 to survey libraries in the region. Dean Bill Wesselink, business manager Charles Zalesky, trustees Luther Powell and Gib Geisinger, librarian Lucille Vickers, and faculty representative William Cumberland constituted the committee. A trip to Minneapolis in $-15°F$ temperatures in mid-January found the group on the way to visit St. Catherine's College with scheduled stops at Gustavus Adolphus and Carleton along the way. After a quick stop for coffee, the team piled into the station wagon with Zalesky at the wheel—only to discover after a few miles that Wesselink had been left behind. An embarrassed but unruffled dean was retrieved, and the group proceeded through blowing snow and a windchill that must have approached $-50°$ before Zalesky discovered the gas tank was nearly empty—a discovery alarmingly verified a few minutes later. Fortunately, a Minnesota highway patrolman was making his rounds and after a bitter delay the group was able to proceed. Such efforts produced results, however. The library was planned, Donald Rod, librarian at University of Northern Iowa, was hired as consultant, and a small but viable structure was built for the modest cost of $330,000. Designed for future expansion either south or west, the building maintained the tradition of the Georgian colonial architectural style on campus. As Halverson noted, "one would have been blind" not to have seen the need for a library.[17] The naming gift came from Loyal Ballou, president of the Security Trust and Savings Bank and a long-time friend of the College. The structure was sound, and though small, it certainly seemed beautiful to senior faculty members who felt euphoric about a dream that had taken nearly three-quarters of a century to come true. In a few years the collection, carefully guided by librarian Lucille Vickers, would pass the 60,000 mark with both federal and private grants utilized in building the number of volumes. The library marked the eighth new building to be constructed at Buena Vista College since 1957.[18]

Other building projects included remodeling Smith, the construction of the science building, the Campus Center, and finally the field house. All of these projects were completed between 1964 and 1971 and absorbed much of Halverson's energy. It was at this time that the College made its initial contact with oil magnate Harold Walter Siebens. Director for Development Robert Siefer

learned from banker Harry Schaller that Siebens had been in
Storm Lake attending funeral services for a relative and had indicated his desire to do something for Storm Lake. Siefer's correspondence with Siebens illustrated the opportunities for naming
gifts for either the new science center or the recently constructed
physical education building and requested data on Siebens's father
who had attended Buena Vista as a commercial student during
1899–1900.[19] Siebens, the master of brevity, informed Siefer that "I
expect to have some surplus funds available during 1972 and will
give your proposal serious consideration. You may expect to hear
from me by July 1." While the funds did not materialize as Siebens
anticipated and the original correspondence with Siefer was lost,
Siebens responded to a new inquiry in September that "I have
definitely planned to do something for Buena Vista College and
you will be hearing from me."[20] In May 1972 Siebens wrote:

> If I should subscribe a $100,000 naming gift for the main Physi-
> cal Education Building as a memorial to my father, Walter C.
> Siebens, could I expect the same recognition given George J.
> Schaller, that is a photograph, plaque and the words "Siebens
> Memorial Physical Education Building," engraved over the front
> entrance?[21]

Siebens suggested that since the mail was slow to the Bahamas
(where he resided) the College might call collect. Little time was
wasted in affirming the stipulations, and Siebens was invited to a
hastily prepared banquet in his honor and to the May 21 Commencement ceremonies where the gift was announced.[22] The new
physical education building was named in honor of Siebens's
parents, whose photographs were exhibited in the foyers. This field
house was one of the largest of such structures in western Iowa and
included a swimming pool, faculty offices, and weight-lifting and
training rooms. It would become the scene of college and high
school basketball games as well as Commencement and cultural
activities. Its tartan floor (replaced with a new wood floor in the
late 1980s) would be one of the first in the region. Siebens appeared to have enjoyed his initial contact with Buena Vista College.[23] In reaching Siebens, Bob Siefer, perhaps the catalyst in this

early relationship, and Halverson provided the opening for a more intimate association in the future.

The Halverson years also brought increased faculty participation in governance and a general acceptance by the Board and administration of traditional American Association of University Professors (AAUP) guidelines on academic freedom and tenure. Young Turks on the faculty aggressively pushed for the creation of a Faculty Senate to replace the unwieldy college community concept embodied in the much-criticized 1962 faculty constitution that had given lower-level administrators and staff (including the College nurse) an equal voice on curriculum matters. The new structure still provided for four general faculty meetings per year, but the real deliberative body was the Faculty Senate, consisting of six senators, chair, chair-elect, and faculty secretary along with top-level administrators. Within three years, student representation was written into the new constitution.[24] The first elected chair of the Senate was William Cumberland, and the new system took effect during the academic year 1966–67. There would be alterations in eligibility for the Senate and in the number of participating administrators as the bureaucracy and complexity of a modern college increased.

The Senate structure still survived in 1990, often coming under fire by newer faculty who had not witnessed the old structure and who could now take the existence of academic freedom for granted. Halverson did not resist but encouraged the change even though it was not high on his list of priorities. He had been surprised that the existing structure had not encouraged more faculty participation and he was pleased at the way in which the changes had been brought about. While the Senate sometimes moved too slowly and took time to "grow into," Halverson felt it made an overall positive contribution to the development of the College. The change was undertaken with much enthusiasm although some of the Young Turks occasionally fought among themselves concerning the nature and extent of the revolution. In the early years faculty eagerly sought the leadership roles the Senate offered, but time eroded the desire to participate. The feeling that an expanding institutional bureaucracy increased the administration's hold on decision making contributed to the reluctance of many faculty to run for vacant seats on the Senate.

Controversy over questions of tenure were rare but not unknown during the Halverson years. However, few faculty questioned the solid entrenchment of academic freedom, and free expression of ideas flourished uncensored in every classroom. Wendell Halverson understood and supported the importance of academic freedom stating that "our colleges could be criticized for not helping students understand as fully as they should, the truth about academic freedom, especially in regard to its high value, the high cost of establishing it, the terrible alternatives to it, and the high responsibility it places on everyone, citizen and scholar alike."[25] In fact an early Senate effort to gain institutional approval of 1940 AAUP guidelines was successful in the spring of 1968. Professor Ron Smith set the tone for a new academic emphasis when he insisted that "curricula matters, especially strengthening curricula, should be the first business undertaken by the Academic Standards and Policies Committee."[26] Of the twenty-five faculty members who served on the first Senate and its committees, only four (Tollefson, Cumberland, A. G. Thomas, and Bonnema) remained with the College as it moved into the 1990s — retirement, death, and new opportunities depleting the ranks of the original Young Turks. Carl Adkins, as a newly hired young faculty member in 1966, noted that AAUP membership and the Faculty Senate and its committees seemed inseparable. He quickly grasped the significance of the changes occurring and joined the "rebellion." Adkins (Ph.D., Kansas State), a talented teacher and authority on the poet Richard Wilbur, would remain at Buena Vista and eventually serve a term as associate dean of the faculty. He was also instrumental in founding and providing for the continuation of the Stolee lecture.

New state and federal interest in higher education during the Kennedy and Johnson administrations led to new cooperative efforts among "developing" institutions. Halverson guided Buena Vista College into becoming a charter member of the Colleges of Mid-America (CMA) consortium at its creation on August 5, 1968. The CMA was an association of ten colleges in western Iowa and southeastern South Dakota (Buena Vista, Briar Cliff, Dakota Wesleyan, Dordt, Huron, Mount Marty, Northwestern, Sioux Falls, Westmar, and Yankton). The purpose was to maximize efforts through the use of available resources and to streamline the efforts to obtain Title III money. There were consortium meetings that featured speakers, issues, research, and progress in the various disciplines, new ideas for the improvement of education, assistance for faculty travel, establishment of student leadership programs, and funds for library acquisitions. Eventually, fund money became increasingly scarce, several schools (Yankton and Huron) failed to survive the academic crisis of the 1970s, and by 1980 Buena Vista, although it continued to participate, felt it had achieved a status far beyond that of a developing institution.[27] However, in its heyday, the CMA provided a positive stimulus for institutions seeking to enlarge their horizons.

Nor was the Board of Trustees inflexible to change. Halverson increased the membership of the Board to twenty-one members, expanded its geographical distribution, and worked to enhance its understanding of educational issues. There was a blending of local veterans on the Board with new appointees from urban centers, including Charles Scanlon of the Federal Reserve Board (appointed June 1972) and John Bartizal, a Chicago businessman who had been president of Amocodyne corporation. Bartizal served as chairperson during the turbulent middle 1960s until forced to step down for reasons of health in 1969, although he remained on the Board until 1971.[28] Bartizal worked to build a strong spirit of cooperation between Board, faculty, and students. He inaugurated a special committee that consisted of trustees, students, and faculty to discuss issues and concerns of the College. Bartizal's sensitive probes helped institute often small but critical changes. The Board, though not with unanimous enthusiasm, followed the Faculty Senate's recommendation and accepted the 1940 AAUP principles on tenure and promotion. The Board was less receptive to the recommendation that one or two members of the faculty be placed on the Board.[29]

When Halverson arrived as president in 1961, the student body did not yet number 500, but by the 1968–69 academic year total enrollment reached 1,017 (some figures show 506 and 817). It would decline for a few years after 1969, but the pattern of overall growth and stability was programmed. For the first time Buena Vista College could boast a diverse student body with 100 of 259 freshmen coming from New York and Chicago areas. Twenty-one states, eight foreign countries, and twenty-six different religious groups were represented in the student body.[30] Student ACT scores reached new highs in 1968: 21.93 for men and 20.52 for women.[31] New buildings had been constructed, state and federal governments provided grants and aid, students remained on campus, and the number of faculty increased along with expanding academic offerings.

Recruitment and maintenance of high-quality faculty was now a must if Buena Vista was to adhere to the rigorous standards set by North Central. Therefore, Halverson concluded that Dean Wesselink's role as dean of the faculty and dean of students (he had earlier been registrar as well), a position he had held since 1947, needed to be divided into two positions — vice president for academic affairs and vice president for student affairs. Wesselink had been an outstanding dean of faculty and perhaps favored that position, but Halverson felt his real strength was as dean of students where his considerable counseling abilities and his unique insight into the problems of young men and women could be fully utilized. It took some persuasion and resulted in not a little bitterness, but Wesselink was to provide a decade of brilliant service, developing a rapport, respect, and even affection among college students during the anxious and frustrating decade 1966–1975. While Wesselink believed he could have handled either and perhaps both posts, he graciously accepted the challenge and established the model for future vice presidents for student affairs. His death in 1989 was mourned by many past and present Buena Vista students whose lives had been touched and molded by his strong, yet kind and gentle friendship.

The search for a new dean of faculty yielded John Pennington Williams, a University of Michigan Ph.D. in education who had been dean of the University of Akron night college. Williams, a devoted but conservative Quaker, would suffer through what was perhaps the stormiest tenure of any dean of the faculty in the history of the College. He was a man of considerable ability and organizational skills, but a number of faculty found him tactless and inquisitive in areas of life they felt were private. Halverson believed the faculty found Williams's piety irritating, and certainly his conservative theological and moral stance seemed beyond that which the faculty could endure. He tried to censure what he considered suggestive dramatic productions; some felt he would have liked to bed-check faculty and students to make certain alcohol was not present. He opened every meeting, no matter how trivial, with prayer and had the unique ability of making people think he was insulting them when he was actually dispensing praise. The faculty believed that he had favorites, that he was rigid and unbending, and that he entered offices secretly in order to exchange furniture thus ensuring a kind of household equality. Although he was tenacious in defense of his ideas and irritating in his dedication to trivia, he did not hold grudges — waging his battles openly and generally accepting the results. He had an uncanny knack of hiring the best candidates for vacancies and was instrumental in hiring James Rocheleau (later president at Upper Iowa), Gunnar Wikstrom (who would chair the social sciences and move on to become dean at Idaho State College), Gerald Poff (winner of the first Wythe Award), Paul Russell (instrumental in building the new business program), Leonard Martz (dean of the Fort Dodge Center), Al Lewis (who chaired the academic program in physical education), Dennis Dykema (professor of art), and Floyd Pace (chair of the School of Education and professor of Spanish and French) among others who would make significant and long-range contributions to the College and who would often be sought by rival institutions. He also appointed as College registrar colorful Paul Shafer, a local businessman who had taught part-time at Buena Vista since arriving in Storm Lake in 1946, thus assuring the efficient operation of that office. Shafer retired as registrar in 1984 but continued to assist the College as a consultant and as a math instructor at both the centers and on the local campus. Dr. Al Lewis, renowned as a teacher who emphasized the "education in physical education," was forced because of illness into premature retirement in 1988.

Furthermore, there were those innovative and unusual features in the approach to education fostered by John Williams that sometimes occasioned friction. The changes he sought in educational focus sometimes irritated those wedded to a more traditional approach. Williams took "Education for Service" seriously and encouraged the career approach to education. Thus practical areas, such as business education, teacher training, the beginnings of an international program sparked by the classroom in Mexico, and an expanded evening program to facilitate the needs of the nontraditional student were important segments of his vision for the future.[32] The classroom in Mexico was held in the Institute Allende, San Miguel Allende in Guanajuato some two hundred miles northwest of Mexico City. Floyd Pace and Felix Cruz were among Buena Vista professors who assisted in developing and overseeing the program. In 1969–70 Williams flew to Venezuela to arrange for three skilled academicians from that nation to come to Buena Vista for a year of teaching and research.[33] The three worked as administrative interns in a program sponsored by the Agency for International Development. Dean Williams noted with pride that eight Buena Vista professors had lived much of their lives abroad and that four others had studied a year or more in foreign countries. He prophetically insisted that "teaching an awareness and appreciation of non-western cultures is one of the priority frontiers of higher education."[34]

Williams worked with Drake University in order to bring the Drake graduate program in education (the first such expansion for Drake) to the Buena Vista campus and promoted the first management conference for business at the College.[35] Working closely with the president, Williams pushed for summer grants for faculty travel and research and assistance for those desiring to complete their doctoral studies. For the first time the College actively offered inducements in the forms of loans, leaves of absence, and bonuses for those completing doctoral studies. There was active encouragement for young professors like Jim Rocheleau, Paul Russell, and Gunnar Wikstrom who completed doctoral work while teaching at Buena Vista. Halverson thought highly of Williams's dedication and felt that academically he had aggressive and even radical ideas that he was forced to limit because of the difficulty he had in building rapport with the faculty. Halverson found the controversial dean professional in all his relationships and one who made a good contribution to the institution. His religious piety inspired a strong social consciousness. John Williams and his wife worked hard in community affairs, which included participating in the foster parent program. His seven years at Buena Vista left a stronger faculty and a stronger academic program than he had found in 1966. He prepared diligently for North Central reviews and met criticisms that the curriculum was stagnant by instituting the 4-1-4 plan that continues today, by encouraging assistance for faculty research, leaves, and graduate study.[36]

Williams also served a term as president of the Iowa Association of College Deans, chairperson of the dean's group of the CMA consortium, host administrator of the international administrative internship program of the American Association of Colleges for Teacher Education (NCATE), and worked successfully in the North Central Association review of Buena Vista College and in securing the highly coveted NCATE accreditation—thus making Buena Vista teaching graduates more marketable across the state and nation.[37] However, his deteriorating relationship with faculty helped force his resignation and departure for Friends University in Kansas. An objective appraisal of the Halverson years must recognize the forward impetus provided by Dean John Williams. By the spring of 1973 both Williams and Halverson recognized the time had come for a change—a change that would bring in not only an academically talented ivy leaguer but a charismatic personality who would be able to rebuild administrative-faculty relationships.

The 1966–67 academic year saw the College celebrate its seventy-fifth anniversary selecting the (perhaps not most appropriate) theme "From Goodness to Greatness." The kickoff dinner for the anniversary celebration was held at the Hotel Bradford on July 8, 1966, with local businessman, Deutsch Kraut festival music director and anniversary committee chair, John Dvergsten, presiding. Seventy-five distinguished Iowans were honored at a convocation on September 17, 1966, including Marjorie Holmes, E. Howard Hill, Ralph Neppel, Paul Engle, Dr. Ronald Dierwechter, and speaker Clark Mollenhof, a Pulitzer Prize–winning journalist (1958), who reminisced about famous Iowans he had met during his twenty-four year stint as a reporter.[38] Donna Reed and John Wayne were among those invited, but unable to attend.

Governor Harold Hughes received his first honorary degree (LL.D.) when he spoke at the January Commencement (the College's first midseason graduation), and American history scholar and president of Drake University, Paul Sharp, was the featured guest at the Spring Commencement.[39] Many former students including nationally renowned author Marjorie Holmes (honored by a tea at the college bookstore) were around during Commencement week.

Expenditures for the anniversary year were modest but appropriate—trustee Tom Eilers supported self-financing. Clarence Richardson headed the campaign drive. Guest artists and distinguished speakers including Bennet Cerf (publisher, editor, columnist, and panelist on television show "What's My Line?") and theologian and author Dr. George Buttrick were featured at various times during the seventy-fifth anniversary year. William Cumberland wrote *The History of Buena Vista College: Education for Service*—thus compiling the first complete account of the institution's existence.

The seventy-fifth anniversary year saw Buena Vista undertake a $1,925,000 fund drive, which was bolstered by a $100,000 greater teacher beneficence from Mrs. Ethel Heater of Fort Dodge and her son, Robert, from Joplin, Missouri.[40] The Heater grant was only the second gift of more than $100,000 from an individual since the founding of the College. The Heater grant came at a critical time, and the Heater family later provided an additional $30,000. Their overall contributions to the College exceeded $180,000. Local businessman H. E. Stalcup headed the seventy-fifth anniversary fund drive, which included a $38,500 donation from the Lehnus family as well as the Heater gift. Nearly $250,000 was raised in the fiscal year up to May 31, 1966—representing a real surge for the 1960s.[41]

Numerous guest artists were brought to the campus, the Hirsch library collection was started in honor of the admirable professor of German, and the College received a new pipe organ—

a gift from highly respected local physician, Dr. Russell R. Hansen.
The organ was custom designed and built for the chapel by the
Reuter Organ Co. of Lawrence, Kansas. Dr. Hansen loved organ
music and his hopes that the organ would be "a source of renewal
to all who hear it," was fully realized through the years.[42] Hansen's
daughter Charlotte, an accomplished organist, would perform pe-
riodic recitals before appreciative audiences.

The euphoria surrounding the anniversary year did not stifle
student protests. Students in November 1966 launched a major
protest when the College shortened the academic year by a week
but scheduled classes for the Friday following Thanksgiving. Students collected six hundred signatures, and seventy walked out of
mandatory chapel and at 7 P.M. on November 22, staged a torch-
light parade and marched en masse into Schaller Chapel. Police
and the state highway patrol were somewhat needlessly placed at
strategic places around campus. President Halverson called out the
Faculty Senate to face what might have developed into a tense
situation (violence on other campuses had sometimes grown out of
protests).[43] Eventually, the students won their case and lost neither
the shortened academic year (which actually brought Buena Vista's
academic calendar more in line with other institutions) nor the
Friday following Thanksgiving. This, of course, was the era of the
Vietnam War, of the youth cultural revolution, an age when all
dared speak although there was not always substance in what was
said. Nevertheless, there was an explosive energy, a zeal and passion, and a concern for bettering the human condition—a raw,
unripened thrust for social justice which by the 1980s seemed under
siege from a neolethargy ground fine by materialism and the machine technology.

The Halverson administration met the challenge of the Vietnam years and the cultural revolution with dignity. There was dis-
content and violence in America that often masked the concrete
achievements of a nation that seemed at times not only involved in
war abroad but at war with itself. Even college campuses became
battlegrounds and sanctuaries of escape and protest. There was a
quickening of social concern, conscience, and protest at Buena
Vista College, but it was couched in moderate terms and rarely

moved beyond the boundaries of vigorous democratic dissent. Buena Vista students protested the American intrusion into Cambodia not only during a convocation for that purpose in the science building, but also with petitions in front of Storm Lake churches on a May morning in 1970. There they were generally politely (but critically) received, except for an incident in front of one church where a local legislator protesting, "This is the House of God not of Harold Hughes," seized the petition from two students, Steve Heikens and Lonn Kaduce.[44] Publicity generated by the intervention of the Iowa Civil Liberties Union helped persuade the legislator to return the seized document. One orderly demonstration was staged through the halls of the administration building.

More typical was the increased awareness of the global community that burst forth through a new awareness and more stimulating discussions with students on questions of civil rights, the black revolution, the nature of American foreign policy, and the meaning of education. Buena Vista students sought service in the Peace Corps and an increasing number endeavored to find the means to spend a semester abroad. Faculty acceptance of student input into the process of institutional governance resulted in greater social and academic freedom. Among the casualties were the rigid requirements of the 1950s as general education requirements were reduced from fifty to thirty hours. Buena Vista students, like their counterparts across the nation, were free to escape mandatory foreign language requirements and often did. Programs in the humanities and mathematics struggled for students. A department with a long-standing tradition, like history, was reduced from four to two faculty members.[45] Those who had reservations about the long-range impact of the new general education package were, perhaps, proved correct a decade later as the nation came to grips with the ignorance of its young and began a painful reassessment of American education at all levels.

Gerald Ford, then House minority leader, was brought to the campus as Commencement speaker in May 1968. Mr. Ford sensed the spirit of a heartland college's struggle for responsible social action in accordance with its historic Christian quest for social justice. There were 108 young graduates at the May 26 ceremonies held in Schaller Chapel, where the future chief executive was awarded the honorary Doctor of Laws degree by Professor George F. Reynolds. Opposition to the Vietnam War and social tension was perhaps at its height in America as Ford addressed the audience of nine hundred that filled the chapel. Ford called for a rebuilding of American cities through assisting people to become self-reliant, through the restoration of self-esteem and pride. "Terror and coercion are alien to American ideals," he said. "We must not act out of fear, nor should we fear to act." He praised Buena Vista students for their example of self-discipline and restraint.[46] President Halverson reiterated that sentiment before the trustees in May 1970, when he noted that in an era of student strikes and campus disruptions "Buena Vista students expressed their dissent in constructive and legal ways and were most commendable in their behavior."[47]

A fine example of the dedication of Buena Vista students and faculty to enlightened dissent during the years of national turmoil was the planting of the Tree of Life during the Vietnam War Moratorium Day on Wednesday, October 15, 1969. Overcast skies and a gentle drizzle somewhat hampered but did not mar the activities, which were led by Lonn Kaduce, a junior from Klemme, Iowa. At 7:30 A.M. the flag was raised as the national anthem was played, then it was lowered to half-mast to the sound of taps. This was followed by brief remarks from the Rev. Dr. Robert Tollefson. From 9:30 A.M. to 3 P.M. a vigil was held in the chapel with a continuous reading of the names of the Iowa war dead. Folk songs were played and sung, a history of the war read, and several short addresses given. During the noon hour president of the student body, Ned Lenox, supervised the planting of an evergreen Tree of Life at the corner of Swope Hall. Professor William Cumberland spoke briefly, and President Wendell Halverson offered a prayer. Students then canvassed the city with antiwar petitions. At 6:15 P.M. carolers singing protest songs paraded candles in the campus area maintaining a quiet and reverent program as intended. The spirit of protest was rational, reasonable, without rancor, but still deep and meaningful, disdaining violence and intimidation. The Tree of Life still stands and the memories remain.[48]

Halverson's Christian realism enabled him to appreciate the beauties in a pluralistic society, to tolerate and even encourage the dissent that could promote constructive growth. In a presidency that covered more than twelve years, he had been a builder of buildings — a finished chapel, a new library, the field house, science center, dormitories, and a remodeling of Smith and Swope. Budget expenditures had grown from $688,000 to $2,316,000 and the value of the plant now reached $7,191,000.[49] Assisted by Bill Wesselink, Lester Williams, and John Williams, Halverson carefully selected and improved the quality of the faculty, brought stimulating cultural programs, and presided over the beginning of federal and state grants for the institution and for students. He had hewed the stones that made Buena Vista into a quality institution. Halverson had maintained the small college concept and the church relationship upon an ecumenical basis. There were, of course, frustrations that had caused pain to the tall Scandinavian. The Church, pressed by its own financial concerns, found it increasingly difficult to respond to the financial needs of its colleges, thus limiting one hoped-for source of support. Limited resources and a declining enrollment during the latter stages of his administration forced Halverson to make the difficult decision of dismissing people in whom he had believed. The decline in enrollment and uncertain prospects for the future forced him to terminate five faculty and one administrative position.[50] He now began to feel the tiredness of a presidency that had become too long and too burdensome for the continued growth of the College and for the renewal of his own spirit. He was, perhaps consoled that he had resisted temptation and remained true to the traditional church-related, liberal arts purpose of the College.

"There was a sense of something," Halverson believed that permeated the Buena Vista College community.[51] You found it in graduates like Clifford Merrill Drury who in order to attend classes hitchhiked from Early to Sac City then took the train to Storm Lake. Drury later served as a missionary, a navy chaplain, and a respected historian of the American West. Among his major works were *Henry Harmon Spalding: Pioneer of Old Oregon* (1936), *Marcus Whitman, M. D.: Pioneer and Martyr* (1937), and *Chief*

Lawyer of the Nez Perce Indians (1979). He also edited and compiled the six-volume *History of the Chaplain Corps, United States Navy, 1778–1954.* Drury often returned to the campus he loved. He received the College Alumni Association's first Distinguished Service Award in 1968.[52] Drury, was one of many distinguished alumni whose horizons were first broadened by their encounter with the liberal arts at Buena Vista College.

Furthermore, Halverson could point out graduates of distinction whose lives were molded during his own era. There was Glenn Theulen, all-conference basketball guard who floundered in youthful rebellion then returned at age thirty-six to finish his degree and go on to a successful coaching career in Colorado and at Keene State College in New Hampshire. There was Steve Smith, the 1968 valedictorian who would receive recognition from the Iowa Bar Association as the outstanding all-around student in the University of Iowa Law College, become the recipient of the first Buena Vista College Young Alumnus Award, enter the academic world as a professor on the University of Louisville law faculty, followed by an appointment as associate dean at the University's Law School, and in 1988 be appointed dean at the Cleveland State College of Law.[53] Smith's academic contributions included articles in the broad field of mental health and law that appeared in such journals as the *George Washington Law Review, Kentucky Law Journal, International Journal of Law and Psychiatry, New York Law School Review, Wayne Law Review* and the *Journal of Contemporary Health Law and Policy.* In 1986 Smith and Robert G. Meyer, a University of Louisville professor of psychology coauthored, *Law, Behavior, and Mental Health: Policy and Practice,* an important comprehensive volume that focused on the common interests and problems in the professions of law and mental health. There was 1960 honor graduate Rosemary Shaw Sackett who became judge of the Iowa Court of Appeals and the recipient of the College's 1984 Outstanding Service Award. There was Dennis Young, an outstanding 1965 graduate, who became senior vice president and treasurer of Norwest Financial Services, Inc. and a member of the Buena Vista Board of Trustees. There was Dave Lampe, a 1962 English graduate, a University of Nebraska Ph.D., and now professor of English at State University College at Buffalo who by 1989 had written or coauthored three books, *The Fifteenth Century, The Legend of Being Irish,* and *Five Irish Poets.* He was also the author of more than a dozen articles with such interesting medieval titles (Lampe's field of expertise) as *The Cuckoo and the Nightingale, The Truth of a 'Vache',* and *Country Matters and Courtly Eyes.* Lampe's vita also contained more than two dozen papers presented at scholarly conferences. There was also George Christakes who came to Buena Vista from a Greek community in Chicago. He not only received his degree in 1964 but learned to appreciate what he originally regarded as the somewhat dull environment of rural northwest Iowa. Christakes went on to receive his Ph.D. in history from Kansas State University, become a distinguished teacher at the City Colleges of Chicago, and the author of *Albion W. Small* (1978), and coauthor (with George M. Kren) of *Scholars and Personal Computers* (1988). They were part of that "institutional marrow" that combined liberal education with career goals and the Judeo-Christian heritage. Their minds discovered channels yet unexplored and a new sense of freedom in the liberal arts. More than twenty-five years later Lampe would insist "that the liberal arts offer solutions and perspectives for even (or especially) a technological, post-imperialist society."[54] While not everyone respected or grasped the liberating strength of a liberal arts education, many students found an essence or a "soul" at Buena Vista that gave a spirituality to their lives they could continue to nourish. In 1991, thirty years after his arrival at Buena Vista, Wendell Halverson could see the product of those lives that he, his staff, and his faculty had touched.

Now, in September 1973, a call came for Halverson to head the Iowa Association of Private Colleges in Des Moines, where he would serve until his retirement. He felt there were new needs at the College that could be best served through a changing of the guard. He prepared the way by appointing the multitalented and much-respected Lester Williams as assistant to the president so that the College would have an interim executive familiar with the administrative process of the institution.[55] There had been during his nearly thirteen-year tenure, "a thousand little experiences that

make up a life." The retiring president predicted a great future for
the College, a future that he hoped would be "focused on providing
an experience of wholeness combining competence and conscience
for public service." He hoped Buena Vista students would catch
that spirit and "in joy and freedom, they would lay themselves out
for the cause of truth, beauty, and above all justice. Do justly, love
mercy, walk humbly."[56] That was the soul of Buena Vista College
that Wendell Halverson had endeavored to nourish. He had raised
the institution from the abyss of its long struggle for survival and
marked the path into a more certain future. He had remained
steadfast in the faith. He had not sacrificed his principles. He had
contributed mightily to the lives of those whom he had led.

The College also had recently appointed a vigorous dean in
Dr. Fred Brown who had arrived from Gustavus Adolphus where
he had served as an assistant dean. This was one of Halverson's last
but most important appointments, for the destiny of the academic
program and the quality of the faculty would be largely in the new
dean's hands until his departure for the presidency of his alma
mater, Doane College, in 1987. Brown had graduated from Doane
College in Crete, Nebraska, and had a Ph.D. in history from the
University of Pennsylvania. Here was a scholar who had turned
administrator and whose scholarly and humane instincts always
took precedence over the trivia inherent in what was perhaps a
necessary but not entirely desirable educational bureaucracy. Only
thirty-eight years old and in his first few months as leader of the
faculty when Halverson resigned, Brown would have his management skills sorely tested. Along with Lester Williams, he was instrumental in providing for a smooth transition. Brown quickly
established a solid rapport with the faculty and a confidence in the
dean's office that had become somewhat eroded. A search committee was appointed by the Board of Trustees to review and select
Halverson's successor.

The faculty elected Dr. Leonard Martz, professor of English,
to serve as faculty representative on the search committee with his
colleague in the English department, Dr. Darrell Peck, as alternate.
The choice of a new president was critical. Halverson's successor
would carry the College to the completion of its first century of

The New Buena Vista

1960–1990

1

2

1 Ballou Library, completed in 1965 and remodeled in 1989.   **2** Congressman Gerald Ford at Commencement in 1968. (*From left*) Robert Tollefson, religion; Louis Duncan, trustee; Wendell Halverson, president; Gerald Ford, future president; Rev. Robert Dickson, baccalaureate speaker; George Reynolds, history and political science.

3

4   5

3 Schaller Memorial Chapel, completed 1963.   4 George J. Schaller, banker and philanthropist. His
$125,000 gift made Schaller Chapel possible.   5 Parse De Jong, trustee and chaplain, speaks at Found-
ers Day.

6

8

7   **9**

6 Freshmen in traditional beanies search for textbooks in the College bookstore.   **7** Mary Persing, always helpful reference librarian of the 1960s and 1970s.   **8** Professor of English, *Tack* advisor, and Austrian spy, Karl Lichtenecker with President Halverson.   **9** Charles Zalesky, vice president for business affairs, whose budgeting kept the College financially stable during the 1960s and 1970s.

10

11

12

13

10 Professor George Reynolds is awarded an honorary degree on his retirement in 1973. During his thirty-seven years at Buena Vista the historian and lawyer was an excellent teacher, enthusiastic sports fan, emergency basketball coach, and beloved faculty member. (*From left*) Dean of faculty Dr. John Williams, Reynolds, trustee Louis Duncan, President Halverson, president of Alumni Association Ron Michener. **11** William D. Wesselink, vice president for student affairs, advising music and drama student Karlene Bahrenfus in the 1970s. **12** President Wendell Halverson and trustee president Paul Dixon plot the new Buena Vista. **13** Darrell Peck, super teacher, winner of Wythe Award, in class.

14

15

16

14 President Briscoe with Edith and Les Williams at a College banquet in 1985. **15** Two men to whom Buena Vista owes much: Robert Siefer, vice president of development, and Floyd Pace, former dean of the School of Communications and Arts. **16** Marjorie Holmes, prize-winning author who attended Buena Vista 1927–1929, was 1980 recipient of the College Alumni Association's Distinguished Service Award. Holmes attributes her success in part to the encouragement of Professor Dewey Deal.

17

19

18

17 Provost Fred Brown and associate dean Sandra Madsen express the gratitude of the faculty to Vivian and Paul McCorkle for the establishment of the Wythe Award. 18 Professor of biology Dr. Jerry Paff, winner of the first Wythe Award. 19 1989 Wythe Award winner Dr. Rick Lampe, professor of biology.

20   **21**

22

20   1990 Wythe Award winner Dr. Paul Russell, professor of business and economics.   **21**   Dr. Marilyn Wikstrom, professor of education, is nationally known as a poet and a reading program innovator.   **22** Professor Carl Adkins (*left*), originator of the Stolee Lecture, with Professor Emerita Stolee and guest speaker Chuck "Iowa Boy" Offenburger, 1988.

23

24

25

23 President Briscoe and Governor Terry Branstad at Commencement, 1983.   **24** Dr. Joe Traylor, director of the College computer program, professor of physics and computer science, 1985.   **25** Dr. Manoocher Aryanpur, professor of English, 1989.

26

27

26 Dr. James Christiansen and his chemistry class visit the Fort Dodge water plant.   **27** President Briscoe with Asian students.

28 The College choir, directed by Robert Pfaltzgraff in the early 1970s. (Photo by Buntrock-Salie, Storm Lake)

29   **30**

29 Harold Walter Siebens, oil magnate, philanthropist, and benefactor of the College, 1982.   **30**
Breaking ground for construction of the Forum, 1983. (*From left*) President Briscoe; Carmen Briscoe;
Dennis Dykema, professor of art; Sandra Madsen, professor of communications and arts.   **31** The new
campus with (*from front*) the Siebens Forum, Schaller Chapel, Dixon-Eilers classrooms and administrative
building, and (*left*) the new location for the Victory Arch.

31

32

33

32 H. W. Siebens as honorary Doctor of Humane Letters, with his family, May 13, 1979. (*From left*) Rhondda Siebens, granddaughter; Bill Siebens, son; H. W. Siebens; Evann Siebens, granddaughter; Clarice Siebens, daughter-in-law; Carter Siebens, grandson.   **33** Portraits of the parents of H. W. Siebens hang in the foyer of the Siebens Center.

352

34 Sue Follon performed outstanding service as dean of women in the early 1970s. (Photo by Buntrock-Salie, Storm Lake) **35** L. Dorothy Lester (Green), 1926, outstanding Presbyterian woman in America and recipient of the College Alumni Association's Distinguished Service Award in 1970. **36** Dr. Michael Whitlach, associate dean of faculty, associate professor of speech and drama, 1988. **37** Dean of Faculty Dr. James Zabel, 1988. **38** Edgar E. Mack, the third generation of the Mack family to chair the Board of Trustees. His grandfather's leadership was vital in the founding of the College, and he has played a leading role in its growth in the 1980s. **39** Dr. John Madsen, one of the most formidable faculty leaders during the 1980s. He was a builder of the mass communications and business programs. **40** Steve Smith, currently dean of Cleveland State University Law School, as 1968 valedictorian. **41** Stephen D. Peterson waged a heroic battle against Hodgkin's disease. His degree was awarded posthumously in 1970.

42

43

42 Mac Hornecker and Dennis Dykema, the rocks of the art department, have drawn regional and national attention.   **43** *River,* sculpture by Mac Hornecker, 1989. (Farm Bureau Collection; West Des Moines, Iowa)

44

45

44 Archie MacKay pipes in the Commencement procession. **45** Faculty and students march into Siebens Center during Commencement, 1987.

existence and possibly into the twenty-first century. The acceleration of change and the increasing importance of computer-technology would necessitate an innovator who could bring and accept rapid growth, who could be flexible in management style, who respected the liberal arts tradition and career education, and who could find the donors willing to support programs and build the endowment that in 1973 was around two million dollars. Somehow the committee discovered just such a person in Keith Briscoe.

13

Burgeoning with Briscoe

> Let us stand in awe of the distance Buena Vista College
> has come and the challenge of the road ahead.
>
> —PROVOST FRED BROWN

As Fred Brown reminisced, Keith Briscoe was the most curious person he had ever run across. He was a man "who has a knack for the unusual," who was always probing, and "who doesn't always know what he is doing." There was, Brown mused, no relaxing with Briscoe at the helm, no sitting still. Briscoe was endowed with the instincts of a fighter; he possessed a vision of a unique future and the daring to implement that vision. Halverson had set the stage for the energetic and creative Briscoe by moving the Board of Trustees out of the daily routine of managing, thus enabling him to direct the business of the College in the modern terms of a corporate executive.[1] Briscoe and his academic dean (eventually provost), Fred Brown, would form a working relationship that spanned thirteen years and that resulted in the creation of a new Buena Vista.

It was June 1974 when the College announced Briscoe's selection as the sixteenth president of Buena Vista, thus culminating an intensive six-month search. Briscoe had served as vice president of the College of Steubenville, Ohio, since January 1970 and prior to that had held posts as director of student activities and college unions at Baldwin-Wallace, the University of New Hampshire in

Durham, and the University of Wisconsin-Stevens Point. He completed his undergraduate work at the University of Wisconsin-La
Crosse, and his graduate degree was obtained from the University
of New Hampshire with additional study at Case Western Reserve,
the University of Iowa, the University of Texas, Oklahoma State,
and the University of Wisconsin-Madison. The search committee
had been impressed by Briscoe's outstanding administrative record
and his impressive community and church service.[2] He was married
to the former Carmen I. Schwinler (a University of Wisconsin-
Stevens Point graduate) who as first lady would add style, grace,
and elegance to the campus scene. A former home economics
teacher, a world traveler, a volunteer worker for many causes, a
first-class decorator, Carmen Briscoe would make her presence felt
throughout the community. The Briscoes' first date was to the
movies and their eighteenth was their wedding at church. Two days
later young Briscoe began a two-year army stint.[3] The Briscoes had
one daughter, Susan, who in 1974 was in the sixth grade. The
Briscoe presidency, almost frenetic at times, would expand Buena
Vista's interests across region, nation, and globe. Keith and Carmen
Briscoe would operate such an active presidency that evenings
alone at home became a rarity.

The selection committee had seen in Briscoe qualities of leadership and a management style more entrepreneurial than academic.
Those qualities were paramount if the College were to reach out to
substantial donors and build the regional and national reputation it
sought. Academics would be the province of the dean of faculty and
the faculty. The president would see that the means existed to hire
the best teachers available, to fund attendance at professional meetings, and to build a support staff that would recruit a quality student
body. If the College were to move boldly forward, it was time for
risk taking, and Briscoe was willing to take those risks.

Among the new president's sources of inspiration were Woody
Hayes, whom he regarded as a "great human motivator," astronaut
John Glenn, and Barry Goldwater. Briscoe described himself as an
avid reader, admiring particularly biographies of General George
Patton and Winston Churchill. These were, in Briscoe's opinion,
dynamic, highly motivated individuals who were capable of getting

the maximum out of themselves and others. "My field," Briscoe said, "is human motivation."[4]

At the impressive inaugural ceremonies held in October 1975, Briscoe proclaimed his faith in traditional liberal arts education and the free enterprise system. "Only those with solid, broad foundations of knowledge can plot a course for a nation with a shrinking frontier, sprawling, decaying cities, and polluted, abused land," the new president told his audience.[5]

A man with enormous energy, Keith Briscoe would be a different kind of president as he built a different kind of college. Along with Vice President for Academic Affairs Fred Brown, Briscoe was a staunch advocate of global education. He was particularly fascinated by the Pacific Rim theory, which predicted that Asian countries, particularly Japan and China, would become the future centers of economic and political power. This inspired Briscoe to seek academic connections with Asian institutions of higher learning.

The Taiwan exchange program developed through contacts between the Buena Vista president and the Taipei Language Institute through the auspices of the College and University Partnership Program (CUPP). Professor Bob Borgman served as coordinator of the program during its early phase, and in December 1981 Gunnar Wikstrom took the first group of Buena Vista students to Taiwan for a semester of study and teaching the English language at the National Taiwan Institute of Technology. In return, the Taipei Institute sent student-instructors of its own. The first Chinese instructor to arrive on the Buena Vista campus was Linda Hsieh in 1982. Even earlier, in 1979, John Madsen put a summer program together to host Japanese students from Showa Daiichi High School in Tokyo for several weeks. Madsen remained the overall director, but as the program grew he was assisted by Dr. Charles Slagle and Professor Bruce Ellingson. Additional exchange programs developed between Buena Vista and Koka Women's College in Sapporo and Hokusei College in Kyoto, Japan.[6] Hokuse involved an exchange of students; ten Buena Vista students studied there in the spring of 1990. Buena Vista and Koka exchanged faculty during alternate years.

Briscoe's ideological conservatism and dislike of communism

did not stop him from leading a four-week educational tour of the Chinese mainland in the summer of 1979. There he met with leading Chinese educators who were interested in establishing exchange programs. Out of the negotiations, which were part of an exchange agreement with the Chinese People's Association for Friendship with Foreign Countries (Hebei Friendship Association), came the first visit of Buena Vista faculty to mainland China in January 1988. It was a thrilling experience for professors Paul Bowers, Bruce Ellingson, Mac Hornecker, Lanny Grigsby, and Raj Shirole. Noting the great contrasts in China, Hornecker reminded Americans that "the rest of the world doesn't live by our standards." The People's Republic of China now joined Taiwan and Japan as part of the Buena Vista College exchange program. An increasing number of students from Asian countries would come to Buena Vista not only to study but to assist in the growing Asian languages program at the College.[7]

One of Briscoe's first tasks was to examine the changing relationship between Church and College. "What does it mean to be a Christian institution?" Briscoe asked his Board at their October 18, 1974 meeting; a question that Briscoe would partly resolve by weakening Synod influence in the governing apparatus of the College.[8] Of course the traditional Church-College network had begun to disintegrate even earlier, since the Church was unable to provide the enormous monetary funds necessary for modern education. After 1976 the College reported the addition of new trustees to the Synod rather than submitting names for approval. The Synod retained the right to appoint one trustee. The Church, while remaining a strong moral force in the affairs of the College, would henceforth lack the structural power that it had possessed since 1891. There would remain a lasting sense of church-relatedness and strong emphasis on spirituality as contained in the mission statements, but the Church could no longer topple a president nor formulate policy. There was no desire on the part of either the Briscoe administration or the Synod to end the relationship only to reform it to meet contemporary exigencies. These arrangements were codified in a new covenant between College and Church approved by the Synod in June 1986.[9]

The new president sensed that long-range planning needed to be undertaken immediately and he suggested action at the January 1974 meeting of the Board of Trustees. The selection of new trustees was imminent, and Briscoe recommended that two or three educators be brought on the Board. There should be, he said, a contingency fund that could be used at the discretion of the president, a policy on granting honorary degrees, and the College needed to be aware that women's sports would soon be as important as men's on college campuses.[10]

Briscoe inherited an enrollment that had declined from a peak of over 1,000 to 747. Quickly, recruitment was stepped up, and a branch campus was established at Fort Dodge where third- and fourth-year students could attend six eight-week terms and eventually earn a Buena Vista degree. The branch campus formula proved so successful that nine such campuses were in operation by 1987, with Provost Fred Brown as instrumental as Briscoe in their origination and in directing their activities. It was a novel experiment that made Buena Vista's presence felt across the state from Council Bluffs to Ottumwa and from Clarinda to Mason City. Each Center had a director responsible to the academic vice president or provost at the main campus. By October 1987 total enrollment at the main and branch campuses had reached 2,686 students.[11] Dr. Leonard Martz and Dr. James Lockard both served as directors of continuing education and were instrumental in establishing the early guidelines for the successful operation of the Centers. Dr. James Rocheleau was the first director at the Council Bluffs Center and, after he was invited to assume the presidency at Upper Iowa, was ably followed by Dr. Helen Wanken. Norman Bonnema, former professor of business administration, provided long-term continuity and steady counsel for the small but vital Center at Spencer.

The new president's first on-campus remark was, "The school is ten times better than it thinks it is."[12] He promised that he would work from the institution's strengths not its weaknesses, and early in 1975 Briscoe formed the Committee on the Future (COF—often pronounced "Cough") to do just that. This committee, which drew the early blueprints of the Briscoe administration, was staffed by key administrators and faculty, including Fred Brown, Bob Borgman, William Cumberland, Leonard Martz, and Robert Tollefson. The purpose of the committee was to crystallize Buena Vista's long-term goals for the next decade. The committee did come up with some heavily worded statements concerning the institution's purpose. It was also aware of the vital necessity of creative change. Furthermore, it reaffirmed institutional commitment to the Judeo-Christian heritage and the principles of academic freedom, and paid attention to the search for community and harmony of life. An intensive self-study of strengths, weaknesses, and characteristics of the College was undertaken. Two critical characteristics in 1975 were the low endowment and low gift income. But there were other concerns besides the lack of adequate financial resources, namely, the largely residential nature of the institution, its homogeneity, and the lack of cultural opportunities.

The COF committee concerned itself with many areas of institutional planning, including the organizational, political, societal, academic, and budgetary aspects of management. The committee predicted growing diversity, an increasing age mix, and a growing trend of changing careers—asserting that there would be an increasing emphasis on techniques and processes of learning rather than on subject matter. Thus in what would become an understatement, the committee noted that "demands for measurable objectives and competency-based education, may produce conflict with discipline-based curriculum."[13] The committee included an elaborate statement of beliefs, mission, and function. This statement placed a strong emphasis on the College's historic commitment to Church, society, and faith and reaffirmed its belief in academic excellence and academic freedom. The key assumption was a responsibility to teach "the meaning of academic freedom processes; facilitate the open search, and protect the individual's right to be a critic in society." Furthermore, the statement of mission noted that the College "will guard against diminishing other individuals and groups, intellectually, socially, culturally or physically through rumor, harassment, or innuendo, will provide for the free expression of ideas, will create the atmosphere for responsibility to truth by all persons in the college community, will provide a responsible community built on respect and consideration for other individuals and groups within which there will be a freedom of expression for all ideas."

Thus the "spirit" or "soul" of the Briscoe administration during its early years attempted to codify the commitment of the College to the liberal arts and Judeo-Christian heritage. It was within this atmosphere, led by the liberal and humane vice president for academic affairs, Fred Brown, that the College supported affirmative action through the appointment of women and minorities, adopted a policy on sexual harassment, and sought to foster dissenting opinions through more vigorous cultural programs. The COF committee knew the world of academia was changing and that technology, federal and state programs, social changes in manners and morals, a persistent and gnawing inflation, intensifying competition for students and funds, and the increasing gap between private and public education would pose challenges for the future. But in 1975 the College indicated it would remain loyal to its historic liberal arts and, at least nominal, church commitment.[14] Briscoe would feel that the work of the COF committee marked a turning point in the College's history. It performed the spadework that would enable future donors, among them Harold Siebens, to feel that they were investing in a college that had the potential for progress and possibility for greatness.[15]

Paul and Vivian McCorkle, two trustees from Sac County, had a long and intimate interest in Buena Vista College and were well aware of the difference good teachers could make in the life of students. Paul was a lumber executive and Vivian, a 1959 Buena Vista graduate, an elementary teacher for many years. The McCorkles, while supportive of general scholarship money that was provided for students at all levels, sought to redress the balance by providing a generous stipend for the "great teachers" at Buena Vista College. "We wanted to do something for faculty," said Paul McCorkle, "so that Buena Vista can become an even better teaching institution."[16] The McCorkle development fund was first announced in December 1982, with the first award granted in 1987. The stipend, one of the largest in the nation's history for such purposes, was originally $18,000 but eventually rose to $30,000. It is awarded annually to a great teacher on the Buena Vista University faculty. The recipient fulfills the terms of the grant with a project of his or her own design—travel, study, research—there are no boundaries placed upon the use of the money, except it must be used (not banked) for educational, creative, or inspirational purposes. The award was named after lawyer George Wythe, signer of the Declaration of Independence and tutor of Thomas Jefferson, John Marshall, and Henry Clay. Wythe, while largely self-educated, had schooled himself in the classics, was intellectually indebted to John Locke (as was Jefferson), and inspired his students with his liberal political and social ideas that became part of the ideology of the American Revolution. Jefferson had marked Wythe as a man whom "he would trust with anything he had in the world."[17]

This was the spirit the McCorkles wanted to emphasize at Buena Vista and they worked carefully and closely with President Briscoe, Provost Brown, and a faculty committee to hammer out stipulations that would be flexible enough to do justice to the spirit of George Wythe and to realize the expectations of the McCorkles and the College faculty. It was not to be an "old boy" award, nor for research and publication. It was an award for teaching excellence that might release the creative impulses, the free and unfettered spirit of the "Age of Enlightenment." Felix de Weldon, who had molded the Siebens sculpture, was now called upon to create a bust of George Wythe with room for each winner's name to be chiseled into the stone. In the process many Buena Vistans, including some of the winners, would reap a warm acquaintance with George Wythe.[18] For the McCorkles, it was only one of many benevolences (among them the new president's mansion on Shoreway road and the Pinecrest Apartments), but it was the one that would survive the decade and perhaps the century. An appreciative faculty presented them with an engraved silver tray in 1987.[19] It was a well-deserved recognition. Paul and Vivian McCorkle had spent much of their lives savoring, loving, and promoting Buena Vista. Paul was a 1932 graduate of Iowa State University. It was about that time he met 18-year-old Vivian Olson at her sisters' café in Sac City. Their initial conversation was over an apple pie. From that encounter a long romance ensued ending only with Vivian's death in 2002. Eventually, Paul became a successful entrepreneur in Sac City, and Vivian a

Buena Vista graduate and esteemed teacher at Lytton for twenty-three years. Together the McCorkles traveled the world experiencing the broadening wonders of nature and different cultures. They graciously shared their growing business and financial success with Buena Vista not only as philanthropists but in service on the Board of Trustees. Paul became a trustee in 1978, and Vivian served from 1982–2002. There were few Buena Vista enterprises since the 1970s in which Paul and Vivian did not play an important role. A grateful Buena Vista honored the McCorkles with the University's highest honor, the Citation of Excellence and renamed the Heritage Residence Hall McCorkle Hall in their honor. Buena Vista student Andy Offenburger assisted the McCorkles in their bio narrative *Over the Hill Twice.*[20]

The first Wythe Award went to Gerald Poff, a popular professor of biology and a member of the College faculty since 1969. The first award was announced at the faculty banquet in September 1987; subsequent awards would be recognized at the spring recognition dinner. Poff's undergraduate work had been completed at McPherson College in Kansas and his Ph.D. at Colorado State University. Poff had served with distinction on virtually every faculty committee, including a stint as chairperson of the Faculty Senate. Provost Fred Brown noted that Poff was a teacher-scholar of "rare capacity" whose teaching exhibited the "traits of a great professor."[21] Dr. Joan Nilles recalled that as a student Poff had made her look "with a scrutinizing eye at my stand on the issues of medical ethics." Poff activated the award with a scientific expedition that would carry him across the Pacific into remote areas of Australasia in search of the elusive tuatara.

Briscoe and Brown inherited the nucleus of a strong faculty from the Halverson-Williams years. Among the most distinguished members were Paul Russell in economics, one of the leaders in the Florida interim program and the catalyst in obtaining Dows Foundation money, who assumed administrative and teaching responsibilities; Gunnar Wikstrom, a sage political scientist, trusted senior professor, campus and community leader, scholar, and author; Gerald Poff, distinguished general science and biology teacher; Floyd Pace, the venerable and versatile professor of Romance languages, who also taught effectively in the education department and tackled with verve any assignment the College might designate; Leonard Martz, an outstanding administrator as well as teacher, who as director of continuing education would be instrumental in making the Fort Dodge and Spencer centers successful; and Darrell Peck, the first faculty member hired by Halverson who would teach until temporarily immobilized by a serious heart condition in 1989.

It was Peck who in the mind of many faculty members during the era 1960–90 personified the spirit of Fracker, Sampson, Hirsch, and Reynolds. While Peck achieved verbal acclaim as a regional scholar of Mark Twain, his essential prestige came from his work as a teacher of American literature and writing and as a counselor of students. Interested in sports, Peck especially helped young athletes as well as others who had difficulty in mastering basic skills. He wore the invisible badge of a great teacher—one able to uplift those who lacked skill, one who could brighten the lives of the marginally educated, moving them from an intellectual purgatory into an appreciation of literature and art. Peck completed his academic work at Hastings, Drake, and the University of Nebraska and taught for several years at Estherville Community College before arriving on the Buena Vista campus in the fall of 1961. He would achieve virtually every honor the College and community had to offer— Outstanding Educator Award, Outstanding Young Educator, faculty marshal, chair of the Faculty Senate, chair and dean of the School of Communications and Art, faculty athletic representative to the Iowa Conference, president of the Iowa Conference, alternate on the committee to select the president, and the second winner of the Wythe Award.

It was an emotional night for Dr. Peck when he received the coveted Wythe Award at the College Recognition Dinner in May 1988. At the time, Peck was still recovering from quintuple bypass surgery on a damaged heart. He managed to give a compelling speech as he told the Buena Vista community that he felt highly honored and "deeply humble." He expressed appreciation to past mentors and friends such as the Kuehls, George Reynolds, and Jay Beekmann who had contributed much to his success. Nevertheless,

Peck soon felt it necessary to resign his professorship.[22] He had been a key figure in both the Halverson and Briscoe administrations.

Another colorful holdover from the Halverson years was Charles Slagle, a graduate of Buena Vista College and the University of South Dakota. Dr. Slagle, who returned to the Buena Vista campus in 1969 as an assistant professor of chemistry, was one of the early Buena Vista pioneers of computer technology and offered the first course in the College computer program (1972). Slagle was described by Provost Fred Brown as a Renaissance scholar because of his versatile interests, the ease with which he could cross the barriers in academic disciplines, and his mastery of several foreign languages—put to good use when he guided College interim tours abroad. Because of his interest in and work on the presidency of John F. Kennedy, President Briscoe selected Slagle as the coordinator of the College's commemoration of the twenty-fifth anniversary of Kennedy's assassination, which featured the presentation of a bronze bust of President Kennedy sculpted by Felix de Weldon. Slagle was also the founder and coach of the Buena Vista College's women's golf team and one of the organizers of the European interim.[23]

The Briscoe-Brown team quickly hired new faculty members who would not only support the distinguished faculty already in place but play a role in the forward thrust of the College. Among them were two couples—John and Sandra Madsen in speech and Jeanne Tinsley and Ken Schweller in psychology. These young professors brought intellectual curiosity, teaching excellence, and administrative competence to the College. Drs. Sandra Madsen and Jeanne Tinsley would become school deans; Madsen would also serve a term as associate dean of the College. She took a leave of absence during the years 1991–93 in order to obtain a law degree from the University of Iowa. Dr. Madsen, upon her return to Storm Lake, decided to enter the local political scene. She was elected Mayor of Storm Lake in November 1993, and reelected in 1996. She was the first woman elected to that post in the history of the city. During her terms in office the city passed a local option sales tax (1995) and a Telecommunications Utility bonding meas-

ure in 1998. The council also put through a burning ban and hired
Alan Windsor as the new and very successful city administrator.
Her terms in office also saw a substantial increase in Storm Lake's
minority population leading to increased pressures on the school
district, the hospital, and the police department. The School District
instituted a Diversity Day "involving community leaders and minority members in explaining elements of their cultures." Storm
Lake students were involved in statewide conferences with communities that faced similar problems due to the rapid growth of the
city's minority population. The year 1997 also saw Dr. Madsen
honored as Storm Lake's Woman of the Year.[24] She retired from
both Buena Vista and as mayor in 1999. Her contribution as mayor
and her ability to deal effectively with minority representatives, police department, the School District and long-time citizens helped
Storm Lake ride through a difficult period. Still, Dr. Madsen felt
that there remained room for improvement in town/gown relations.[25]

John Madsen, Briscoe noted, was really the father of the new
mass communications program and center and was also an important cog in the business program being developed in the Harold
Walter Siebens School of Business. An energetic, sometimes blunt,
and always forceful individual, Madsen (Ph.D. Kansas) possessed
strong journalistic and communications skills well-honed as a
newspaperman in Wisconsin. In 1986 John Madsen was named one
of the nation's faculty leaders in *Change* magazine—one of only
eight faculty members from Iowa colleges to make the list. Twice
he was honored as outstanding faculty member by Buena Vista students.[26] Madsen was a strong supporter of the post-1980 trends at
Buena Vista as his essay in *Buena Vista Today* on the entrepreneurial teacher indicated. "We should demand that our teachers become
entrepreneurial in outlook," he wrote. Teachers, Madsen argued,
must be allowed the freedom to take risks. Failure was acceptable
in the pursuit of lofty goals. Buena Vista must seek "excellence not
safe mediocrity."[27] His versatility made him a valuable resource for
the College where he directed the public relations office for several
years, originating the *Vistagram* (now *Vista Vue*),[28] and with his
wife, Sandra, launched the College's exchange program with Japan,
thus actively endorsing Briscoe's Pacific Rim theory. Asian lan-

guages and Asian students would soon be heard and seen on an increasingly cosmopolitan campus. And the Madsens would divide their time between the Buena Vista campus and sister campuses in Japan.

Ken Schweller, a brilliant Wesleyan University and University of Illinois graduate, moved from psychology into computer science in 1986. Schweller was a Vietnam veteran who had walked point and patrolled along the Ho Chi Minh trail,[29] a quiet but reflective man, an excellent scholar in behavioral psychology. His love of computers and his interest in robots led to his transfer from one field into another. His colleague and wife, Dr. Jeanne Tinsley, continued her research interests in psychology, publishing and presenting scholarly papers at academic conferences. Both served on numerous faculty committees, with Schweller heading the search committee for a new academic dean in 1987 and Tinsley chairing the original Wythe committee. Tinsley also assumed the post as dean of the School of Social Sciences, Philosophy, and Religion in 1987.

Professor Joe Traylor, an expert in the field of physics, was lured away from Iowa State University in 1976. Traylor, a University of Tennessee Ph.D. in solid-state physics, was the author of *The Physics of Stereo/Quad Sound* (1976) and a significant article "The Lattice Dynamics of Rutile (T_iO_2)," which appeared in the *Physical Review* (1970). Traylor quickly established himself as a leader on campus as he proceeded to direct the design and installation of the academic and administrative computer systems at the College. In fact, Traylor played a major role in designing the new computer science curriculum.[30] He improved his knowledge of computers during a 1987 sabbatical at Worcester Polytechnic Institute, served a term as chairperson of the Faculty Senate in 1980, was involved in the establishment of the Science Lecture Series for Laymen (1977), and chaired the 1977–78 campus energy committee that sought means of conserving fuel during the energy crisis of the late 1970s. Traylor also served as the Director of Technological Services until 1997 when he resigned in order to devote full time to being professor of physics and computer science.[31] Traylor's well-known oratorical abilities were further utilized when in 2005 he was selected to be Buena Vista's Commencement speaker. President

Moore referred to Traylor as an "inspirational teacher" and a "masterful orator."[32] Traylor was the 1998 winner of the Wythe Award. A devout person, Traylor was active in the religious life of the College and the community.

Dr. Richard Lampe, a 1966 Buena Vista College graduate armed with a University of Minnesota Ph.D. in the natural sciences, returned to the campus in 1975. For the next fifteen years Dr. Lampe would work his way up through the ranks to the deanship of the School of Natural Sciences, achieving an international reputation as a scholar of the natural habitat of the badger, publishing his findings in significant scholarly journals, and attending both national and international conferences. Lampe's lonely vigils along winding county roads in a strange-looking pickup truck made isolated homeowners, unaware of his interest in the North American badger, wonder if he were not engaged in livestock mutilations or surveying the area for a break-in. Grants for Lampe's work were made by the College, by the Iowa Academy of Sciences, and by the American Museum of Natural History.[33]

In a strong show of emotion for the institution that had nourished him as a student and revered him as a maturing teacher-scholar, Lampe accepted the third Wythe Award at the 1989 recognition dinner. Dr. Lampe, wrote Fred Brown from Doane College, "is Buena Vista's most renowned scholar/teacher. He is known nationally and internationally for his work on the North American badger and on other small creatures of the Midwest."[34] Lampe's scholarly efforts included articles in the *Prairie Naturalist* and the *Journal of Wildlife Management*. In 1982 Lampe was one of thirty-two authors recognized by the Iowa Natural Heritage Foundation for his contribution to Iowa's natural heritage. He had also starred in the Iowa public television series, *Land between Two Rivers*, which featured the natural heritage of Iowa.[35] Lampe soon moved into administrative work becoming first associate dean of the College and in 1991 he succeeded Dr. James Zabel as Dean of the Faculty. He was given the title Executive Vice President in 1994 and remained in that post until resuming his professorship on the faculty in 1997. Dr. Lampe had the task of dealing with the increasing growth of the Centers and the completion of the new

Information Technology Center. Lampe was the recipient of the John Fisher Outstanding Service Award and the winner of the coveted Wythe Award in 1989. Lampe used the funds from the Award to traverse Africa and pave the way for students to travel to southern Africa for biological studies. The Lampe family had a long tradition at Buena Vista. An uncle was a 1909 graduate, Lampe's mother completed her degree in 1929, and his brother David received his B.A. in 1962.[36]

In an increasingly strong science department, Lampe's work was bolstered by veteran Dr. Robert Borgman, who served more than a decade as administrative head of the school and as assistant to the president, where he impressed Briscoe as the best concise writer on the faculty. Charles Slagle (chemistry, a Buena Vista graduate), Gerald Poff (biology, first winner of the Wythe Award), Lanny Grigsby (mathematics), Ben Donath (mathematics), Nasser Dastrange (physics), and Jonathan Hutchins (chemistry, another University of Minnesota Ph.D. and a native of England) formed the complement of senior professors in a school that many thought was the best in the College. Along with Lampe, this brilliant and veteran corps of scientists gave the School of Science an eminent reputation, attracted outstanding scholarship students from throughout the Midwest, and saw an increasing number of graduates accepted at the major medical colleges.

The list of outstanding young scholars brought to the campus or given encouragement during their formative years by the Briscoe-Brown team is a long one. Professors Hornecker and Dykema brought prestige to the art department. Hornecker's work in sculpture would win regional recognition, appearing on college campuses, in city squares, and at museums. Hornecker had roamed up and down Highway 71 much of his life. The artist liked the rural settings that his work reflected and staunchly defended his work against the criticism of the uninformed, insisting that "You've got to be a surly old devil and fight back."[37]

To Hornecker, his environmental sculpture was "bigger than life." He wanted to awaken a public that he found more "concerned about nostalgic ideas than about new ideas." While Hornecker expected open criticism and controversy concerning his art, he was upset when his critics resorted to vandalism, once commenting in irritation, "You see more vandalism here [on the campus] than you see in the slums." Most of Hornecker's art embodied futuristic designs, and while his work was occasionally greeted with hostility from the local public, it was highly regarded by professionals in the field. Furthermore, as Hornecker noted, "environmental psychologists have proven that original, contemporary art is mentally stimulating to people in a work atmosphere."[38] A new honor came to Hornecker early in 1990 when his architectural design ranked among the three finalists to honor the victims of United Airlines flight 232 in Sioux City.

Dennis Dykema proved a challenging teacher and a sensitive painter whose work was displayed in numerous art exhibitions. Dykema's exhibitions appeared not only regionally but in the summer of 1989 the artist was invited to bring his art to Poland for the first international show by a Buena Vista artist. Dykema paints "what he sees in his mind not with his eyes," letting viewers draw their own conclusions.[39]

Dykema was also one of many faculty who helped plan the layout and landscape around the newly created Siebens Forum. Both Hornecker and Dykema stress the integrity of their work. As the colorful Hornecker remarked, "If you do art just for the money, you become an art whore."[40] It was only fitting that professors Dykema and Hornecker would retire together in 2001 and that they would share the honor of giving the commencement address—the first faculty members so honored. While Hornecker soon departed for his native Oklahoma, Dykema established a studio in Storm Lake. Both were presented with honorary degrees. Dykema was also the 2001–02 recipient of the Distinguished Service Award by the Art Educators of Iowa Association.[41] Dykema also joined the growing number of Wythe Award winners in 1999.

Another newcomer was Professor Jeffrey Perrill who brought renewed verve to the study of history. A University of Missouri Ph.D., Perrill specialized in the history of India, where he had studied, researched, and published several articles. A unique and creative teacher-scholar, Perrill acquired a solid following among the student body. The School of Social Sciences also enjoyed the brief tenure of a sensitive and probing philosopher, Dan Keller (Ph.D., University of the South), who in 1983 wrote a thought-provoking volume much deeper than its title, *Humor as Therapy*.

The School of Education could also boast of its creative faculty. Education professor Marilyn Wikstrom not only established a state-wide reading program but won considerable acclaim as a poet. In June 1988 she was chosen by World of Poetry as a recipient of the Golden Poet Award for her 1988 poem, "Encounter." Her poem, "Fog," was published in *Best New Poets of 1988*.[42] Professor Wikstrom expanded both her work in education and her poetry well into the 1990s. She was honored, in 1991, as the fifth recipient of the Wythe Award. Unfortunately in June 1998, Wikstrom was suddenly stricken and diagnosed with a malignant brain tumor. She died in September of that year. Many members of the faculty came to her assistance as she waged a valiant struggle to retain as much mobility as possible during the devastating illness. Professor Wikstrom, a few years earlier, had spent a semester sabbatical teaching at Sheldon Jackson College in Sitka, Alaska. She became so enamored of the region and its people that she directed her ashes be scattered there. A memorial tree in her honor was planted on the Buena Vista campus. Dana Larsen, editor of the *Storm Lake Pilot-Tribune*, called her "the master educator of educators," noting that "she was strong enough to admit her fear, and maintained her style and dignity to the end."[43] Marilyn was a regionally recognized poet whose life, teaching, and poetry influenced more people than she realized. Marilyn's spouse, Gunnar, was also inspired to write poetry and these moving few verses of tribute from one of his poems help capture the essence of her life and the sorrow of her loss.

> He walks along the beach
> Alone in his thoughts–about things past
> Looking for a special sea shell
> By which to remember her
> Then before him, he spies one
> Brought to the shore by recent tide
> Like the one she gave him
> On their first encounter

He picks up his cherished prize
And as he holds it close
He feels again her presence
Lost in her mortal passing
He remembers happier times
And together their love for the sea
Two lovers walking along the beach
In bare feet on the white sand
Even through the wind and waves
He hears her gift of laughter and soft voice
Now but a remembrance
To be tied to his new found treasure.[44]

Briscoe's emphasis upon leadership, the entrepreneurial spirit, individuality, and creative discipline had produced a campus of academic scholars and leaders. School chairs and deans rotated, thus building a corps of experienced administrators often sought by other colleges. In the spring of 1985 the divisions became schools with a school dean over each. Seven schools merged into five with the fine arts merging into Communications and Arts, and religion and philosophy becoming part of the new School of Social Science, Philosophy and Religion. The latter also included psychology, which was moved out of education into the social sciences.[45] The new academic structure at the College now consisted of the Harold Walter Siebens School of Business; the School of Communication and Arts; the School of Education; the School of Science; and the School of Social Science, Philosophy and Religion.

The competition for merit pay increases at Buena Vista became intense as did the competition for travel grants, sabbaticals, promotion, and tenure. A college determined to achieve distinction was generous in its allotments for projects that might enhance individual excellence and institutional prestige. The new intensity sometimes led to stepping over or on one another rather than stepping to the side, but overall the faculty enjoyed considerable harmony despite the tensions inherent in a rapidly changing academic environment. The exceptional growth and emphasis upon business and mass communications, however, would produce more challenges and tensions.

A serious crisis, a personal illness, a tragedy, brought about the traditional unity in the case of Nasser Dastrange, a newly hired professor of mathematics, who left Iran in 1986 to present papers at mathematical conventions in Czechoslovakia and California. Oregon State University, where Dastrange had obtained his doctorate in 1973, invited him to teach for a semester. His wife Shahin advised him to remain in the United States until the family could be reunited. Buena Vista needed an additional professor in mathematics, and Dr. Dastrange seemed to be the ideal candidate. He quickly established himself as a capable teacher. Students liked his courses; faculty liked Nasser. Unfortunately, Nasser's passport had been lost, imperiling his status as a legal alien and temporarily negating his right to work in America. Before it was over, Nasser was threatened with deportation, was not permitted to continue work, and Buena Vista College, which had employed and harbored him, was fined $74,000 for an alleged 135 paper violations of improper documentation. Through it all the College had endeavored to follow proper procedures while continuing to assist Nasser in what became a family crisis of international proportions. Ultimately a compromise settlement was reached with the immigration authorities that resulted in a drastically reduced penalty.

Meanwhile, Nasser's family suffered innumerable delays as they sought to leave Iran for America. Legal fees, money that had to be sent home, personal living costs, and a law that kept him idle soon depleted Nasser's resources. However, the Buena Vista College faculty and staff combined to raise $3,800 and the Prospect Hill presbytery contributed $500 per month, enabling Nasser to survive the ordeal. Finally, the needed visas and passport were obtained. The family was reunited in Canada and upon their arrival in Storm Lake found a newly furnished college house and a kitchen filled with groceries awaiting them. Nasser returned to teaching mathematics at Buena Vista, and the family began the process of Americanization. While the Dastranges were profuse in their gratitude, President Briscoe simply remarked, "That man owes us nothing. That wasn't something we were doing for him. It was something we were doing for ourselves."[46]

At Buena Vista Nasser joined another Iranian exile, Dr.

Manoocher Aryanpur. Aryanpur, one of several members of a distinguished Iranian family to come to America, had completed his graduate work at the University of Colorado during the 1950s. Married to an American, he taught at Wartburg College 1959–61, Buena Vista 1961–64, and University of Missouri-Kansas City 1964–69, before returning to Iran as vice president of an Iranian college. The victory of the Khomeni forces put the College and the Aryanpurs in jeopardy. Once Aryanpur was threatened in the hallway by student revolutionaries carrying firearms.[47] In the spring of 1979, the Aryanpur family returned to the United States. It was a quick and courageous getaway in which the bulk of family assets had to be left behind. A telephone call to William Cumberland revealed a literature vacancy at Buena Vista. Because of his previous reputation as an outstanding teacher and the international scope of his scholarship, Aryanpur was promptly selected by the administration and English faculty to fill the position. Among Aryanpur's contributions to scholarship were the internationally acclaimed English-Persian and Persian-English dictionaries. Six of the seven volumes of the dictionaries were coauthored with his father, the late Abbas A. Kashani. Other works by Manoocher Aryanpur include *A History of Persian Literature*, publications in several scholarly journals, book reviews, and articles that appeared in the *Kansas City Star* and the *Christian Science Monitor*. The Aryanpurs were the founders of the Tehran College of Translation, which offered majors in six languages. Royalties from the dictionaries were lost when the publisher was imprisoned in Iran. However, the dictionaries remained valuable during the negotiations and settlements leading to the release of the American hostages in Iran. The name Aryanpur to Iranians was the equivalent of Webster to Americans. Author, teacher, world traveler, fluent in several languages, Aryanpur had much—this second time around—to offer Buena Vista College.[48]

The leadership of Keith Briscoe and Fred Brown innovated, renovated, altered academic programs as well as intellectual and social life at Buena Vista College. The star that guided Fred Brown was never to say no to an idea if he felt it had a chance of success. Faculty would speak of Brown's "deep pockets" as he funded faculty programs, faculty travel, and proposals seemingly out of nowhere. High morale, nourished by strong administrative support and growing self-confidence, led the faculty to support new ventures of their own. Furthermore, the new image of Buena Vista College began to attract national attention and support. Of course, the watershed event in the College's history occurred in the spring of 1980 when the $18 million challenge gift of an anonymous donor was announced.

The magnitude of the gift electrified more than the College and community—it inspired academia throughout the nation. There were, it seemed, yet philanthropists who were willing to give their resources to maintain the heritage of America's liberal arts colleges—colleges that had promoted democracy; propagated the Christian faith across the frontier; and supported American values of individualism, free enterprise, capitalism, and family solidarity. Many denominational and private colleges had fought the good fight and disappeared, others struggled and accepted mediocrity, a few found the support that enabled them to realize the vision of their founders. Buena Vista had never lacked vision, it had been steeled by struggle, kindled with high aspirations, but thwarted by the harsh realities imposed by economic factors. The 1980 challenge gift changed all that. Buena Vista's leaders were challenged to find matching funds and design new programs to depart from those limitations that had chained the College to the past. A daring president had secured a mightier benefaction than all the Buena Vista campaigns and campaign managers combined in the history of the College. What might E. E. Reed or Henry Olson have done with one-tenth of that sum? It remained to be seen what Briscoe would do—what might be the expectations and limitations of the gift and the provider?

The anonymous donor was Harold Walter Siebens whose interest in Buena Vista College stemmed from his early life as a resident of Buena Vista County and later experience as a Storm Lake businessman and close friend of Harry Schaller, president of Citizens' National Bank. Siebens's father had been a student in Buena Vista's commercial program, 1898–1900, and this factor, plus a correspondence with Vice President for Development Robert Siefer, had prompted Siebens to give the naming gift for the new field house in 1972 in honor of his parents. As a portent of things to come, both Briscoe and Siebens received honorary degrees at the eighty-eighth Commencement on May 13, 1978. Brown bestowed the honor (L.H.D.) upon the mildly surprised Briscoe, praising the "pride and teamwork the president has instilled in everyone at Buena Vista College." Meanwhile, Briscoe had found in Siebens "the finest spirit of concern for the advancement of higher education." The relationship between College and philanthropist had begun to blossom.[49]

Siebens was a product of modest circumstances. His grandparents were among the early Storm Lake residents. Arriving about 1890, they purchased two quarter sections for a shotgun and $100, leased the land and bought lots in town, and later retired on the income. The swampy, quicksand characteristics of land around Storm Lake were well known. As Siebens's grandfather told him—a quarter of a mile out of town "you were up to your hips in mud."[50] Fortunately, early European settlers (particularly the Dutch) knew how to drain the land by tiling it. Siebens's father had trapped and sold muskrats and worked as manager of Lamson Grain Company before becoming a full-fledged trader dealing in real estate, bikes, automobiles, and so on.

In 1910 when Harold was five, the Siebens family sold out, packed, and embarked on a new merchant venture in St. Louis. The family was well-off enough to send Harold to a military school in St. Louis where he carried a gun and wore a uniform. Young Siebens was more of an activist than a scholar and at the end of his third year in high school the principal wrote Harold's father, "We don't seem to be able to teach Harold much of anything so he will not be accepted back at Principia next year." Siebens attributed much of his problem to a faulty memory—a memory so poor he whimsically remarked that he could not remember his teachers' names. His early academic experiences also convinced him that "Education isn't everything." To succeed, Siebens mused, drive, goals, and interest are essential. Furthermore, while feeling strongly that education was not everything, he did endorse academia—"Just because they threw me out of high school doesn't mean I don't believe in education. If I would have gone through school I think I would have done a better job than I did." Siebens was convinced that money does not determine human happiness. Modern students had become too dependent on alcohol and drugs; they had not been taught the value of a dollar. (Siebens endeavored to make certain that members of his family were instilled with the work ethic.) He believed education could provide short cuts and in the process instill values. Nevertheless, he took pride in having done things the hard way and that he had, after all, exceeded the performance of his classmates who had graduated from Principia.[51]

Fortunately, young Siebens could work in his father's general merchandise and sporting goods business—a business he inherited when his father died in 1939. But during the 1920s Siebens returned to Storm Lake and for six years managed a discount store, The Bargain Basement, which sold everything from soap to nuts.[52] He had built the Siebens American Sporting Goods business into a nationally known enterprise when health problems intervened. These, plus some unfavorable business trends, led Siebens to sell the enterprise in 1948 and embark upon a fishing and hunting expedition into Alaska with two house trains and two house trailers loaded with equipment. There Siebens learned of economic opportunities in oil development.

Siebens was soon in Alberta opening an office and dealing with gas leases. The small original investment of $10,000 in January 1950 peaked in 1979 when he sold the company to Dome Petroleum for $350 million. He was known as a man who "had a nose for oil." He would buy the land, and oil would be discovered. Siebens Oil and Gas had become a family enterprise with Siebens's three children Gloria, Nancy, and Bill from his first marriage, his second wife Estelle, whose son, Stewart, from a previous marriage he adopted, and their daughter, Mary Jane. There were ten grandchildren and five great-grandchildren by the time of his death in January 1989. His marriage to Estelle and family ties crossing generations (his oldest daughter was fifty-seven and youngest thirty in 1986) were major elements in Siebens's life. It made him aware of the differences in generations—"Every generation has a more advanced thinking. . . . It's a little difficult for the generation behind them to understand them."[53] But the generations did appreciate

Harold Siebens. As daughter Gloria remarked, "He has been a source of security to all, knowing that behind us stood a solid caring father." His son, Bill, echoed those remarks, pointing out that his father was the "greatest teacher I have ever known; he has his nose into everything, but not his fingers."[54]

Of course, there was much more to Harold Siebens than his sharp nose for oil or his ability to amass great wealth. As Keith Briscoe said, "Whatever he did, he was on top." Siebens was captain of the skeet team in Missouri; he made his sporting goods company the third largest in the country. He was a world-class hunter and fisherman who found his way into the Guinness Book of Records "for having caught a swordfish in the Pacific Ocean, a rainbow trout in the Rockies, and a Spanish mackerel in the Atlantic—all on the same day."[55] He also provided the wild game for a dinner that Winston Churchill hosted for heads of state during World War II.

Siebens had become a premier philanthropist, providing gifts to Miami Heart Institute, Toronto General Hospital, Mayo Clinic, Principia College. It was Siebens who provided the naming gift for the Canadian Olympic Hall of Fame (dedicated in Canada during the 1988 winter Olympics) and to various outdoor and sporting organizations.[56] While he loved to succeed, success was not all. The entrepreneur and philanthropist insisted that "the soul, the passion, the excitement, the fulfillment was in the doing." His hunting and fishing records brought him as much joy as his business successes. Nor did failure, which for all his creativity and drive he occasionally encountered, daunt him. "Failure," Siebens remarked, "is a wonderful lesson. It should be one of the first lessons people learn, not one of the last."[57] Siebens, certainly a self-made man, attributed his success to persistent dedication to the historic American work ethic. It cemented his belief in conservative political democracy and the free enterprise economic system. Siebens's money would support conservative political candidates in his adopted Canada and, if Reed Irvine representing Accuracy in Media and Mike Walker speaking on behalf of the conservative Fraser think tank in Vancouver were correct, Siebens's presence and money did make a difference. Some academicians present at a memorial service for

Siebens were stunned not so much at the denunciation of Jane
Fonda from these two speakers but by their call from the podium to
"stuff and mount liberals," a sentiment apparently compatible with
Siebens's conception of desirable political orthodoxy.[58] Siebens
made no secret of the facts that he wanted to be remembered as one
"who stood behind statesmen with the right stuff" and that he had
endeavored to "advance civilization through education, medicine,
and a conservative life-style."[59]

Furthermore, there was an impish side to Harold Siebens. He
loved to pull hoaxes and practical jokes. Harry Schaller recalled the
time Siebens was chauffeured into Storm Lake in a huge Cadillac
attired as an oil sheik ready to buy Citizens Bank on the spot. The
Storm Lake Pilot-Tribune carried this adventure on page one. Then
there was the time he entertained hotel guests masked and attired as
Jimmy Carter. The accumulation of his unbelievable fortune had
not shredded his loyalty to old friends, to Storm Lake, or robbed
him of the approachable aspects of his basic nature. He was rich;
he was powerful; he was rigidly and uncompromisingly conservative, but he was neither distant nor arrogant. And he did want his
benevolences used for ends compatible with the Siebens's view,
which included no bonanza for art forms he did not like and a nervous reaction to the "liberal" in liberal arts, which he associated with
leftist academicians. However, according to Keith Briscoe, Siebens
came to see and approve the liberating features of the liberal arts
that provided the freedom, the drive, the curiosity, and inventive-
ness that Siebens had come to prize.[60] From this, one might con-
clude that while Siebens was good for Buena Vista, Buena Vista
was also good for Siebens.

Of course, Keith Briscoe, Fred Brown, Bob Siefer, presidential
assistant Bob Borgman, and others who helped write the proposal
carefully nourished and directed the interest in Buena Vista College
that had become apparent when the oil magnate donated $100,000
as the naming gift of the new College field house.[61] As President
Briscoe recalled, Siebens did not warm up immediately—there was
no instantaneous friendship. Siebens was perhaps somewhat taken
aback when in 1979 an impulsive Briscoe arrived on his doorstep
hoping to impress the entrepreneur and philanthropist with the pos-

sibilities of Buena Vista College. In order to achieve these goals, of course, Buena Vista would need to raise more money than ever before in its history. Siebens listened and then posed a question to the audacious Buena Vista president, "How many alumni and friends of the College do you plan to visit to raise such a large amount of money?" In typical Brisconese, the Buena Vista president replied, "Only you."[62] Somehow, Briscoe's frankness had struck a note as the two men began building a lasting friendship. Early doubts evaporated and Briscoe found in Siebens a true friend, "a man of vision, compassion and deep caring." Why did a man of Sieben's stature choose Buena Vista College as the recipient of one of the largest benevolences to a small college in the nation's history? Certainly, Siebens's remembrance of his youth, his parents' love of the community, the fact that his father had been an early graduate of the commercial program, his long-standing friendships with local citizens like Harry Schaller, the sensitive but persistent cultivation of Briscoe, Brown, and other members of the College community were all important. Siebens never forgot that he had started in Storm Lake ("where I let out my first loud cry to the world"), the place of his roots, where he loved the people, the lake, a place where he found the essential human and spiritual values and that had given him respect "even before I became the poor boy who made it big."[63] Beyond that, Siebens felt his belief in the value of hard work, broad knowledge, and the entrepreneurial spirit all existed in this small Midwestern liberal arts college. Siebens envisioned a strong School of Business that would emphasize "the principles of free enterprise and enhance the entrepreneurial skills of young men and women" within the broad concepts of American freedom.[64] It was his hope that such a program might be built on the long-standing traditions of Buena Vista College. Siebens and Briscoe realized that business leaders needed a broad education if America was to be competitive in a rapidly changing world. In this context, they expected the $18 million gift to affect all areas of the College.

President Briscoe jubilantly announced the gift at an all-faculty meeting on May 18, 1980. The donation required the College to raise $9 million in matching funds by December 31, 1987.[65] This money was to be enlarged by a $27 million capital fund drive

launched in February 1982, making a grand total of $54 million.
The drive to raise the required fund would be known as the
Foundation for the Second Century and was to be completed by
1991.[66] The donor wished to remain anonymous, and there were
supposedly dire consequences should the secret be divulged. While
Siebens was widely suspected as donor, his identity was never dis-
closed by the College or by anyone employed at the College. The
Des Moines Register, after checking through tax records, published
an article in 1984 revealing that Siebens was the donor. This was a
violation of the philanthropist's privacy for which the College bore
no responsibility.

The official unveiling of the donor's identity came at the dedication of the Harold Walter Siebens School of Business in October 1985. This $10 million, largely underground edifice had been
under construction since 1981. The building encompassed two and
one-half acres underground and contained a computer center, a
business resource room where television monitors and computer
terminals kept abreast of the world's commodities and financial
markets, a 385-seat auditorium, Harvard-tiered classrooms, luxurious faculty offices, bookstore, mail service, centennial room, grand
ballroom, kitchen and serving areas, placement offices, and information desk. The south wall of the new building, facing the lake,
consisted of a series of twelve arched windows and doorways,
each eighteen feet high—the arches representing a historical tie
with Old Main. The Victory Arch was relocated to the roof of the
new facility where it would become a symbol of Buena Vista's historical presence.[67]

Care was taken to provide appropriate landscaping and maintain the visual unity of the campus, with professors Lampe, Dykema, Poff, and Sandra Madsen chairing committees and serving as
consultants for the architectural firm of Dober and Associates.[68] It
became the showplace of the College, attracting regional and national attention, and making Buena Vista's business facilities, programs, and faculty the envy of the Midwest.[69] Substantial new gifts
poured into the institution. Among the major donors were George
Anderson, a California oil man who provided the naming gift (in
honor of his wife Thelma) for the Anderson Auditorium, and an en-

dowed scholarship fund from the estate of John, Ida, and Frederick Vast. Both of these gifts were over the half-million-dollar category. Mike Whitlatch, Professor of Theatre, used his expertise to assist in the construction of Anderson Auditorium. Much has been made of Siebens' dislike of modern art and his refusal to permit art exhibitions or displays from being housed in his Forum. It is true that Siebens disliked some of the forms of contemporary art and felt the Fine Arts were overemphasized. What he most strenuously objected to, however, were having art classes in his House of Business, moving art exhibitions, and student and faculty displays. He did not oppose art that was part of the permanent collection of the University. Indeed, a special University art committee existed to select appropriate and permanent art for the Forum.[70]

Buena Vista College, aided by the investing skills of the international fund manager and philanthropist, John M. Templeton, by the eve of its second century had acquired an endowment that the visionary Loyal Y. Hays (no pessimist) would have dismissed as fantasy. The year 1980 was the watershed of Buena Vista College. Keith Briscoe and Harold Walter Siebens had combined forces to create what would become within a decade the new Buena Vista. Fred Brown called the Siebens gift a "capstone." While there had been a feeling of confidence at Buena Vista, "it needed a demonstration . . . that this work we have been doing together is truly as fruitful as we thought it really was." Briscoe saw the gift as a new charter for Buena Vista College, enabling it to "make an assault on becoming America's next great college."[71]

Although the Forum opened for business on February 21, 1985, and the cafeteria was already serving by March 4, the gala day for the unveiling of the magnificent "underground pyramid" was October 3, 1985. Presidential assistant Lynn Harlan called it the second most important day (the first being the founding) in the College's history.[72] Dennis Dykema cast a new Buena Vista medallion in which the glaze was made from a nearly pure vein of clay extracted from the earth above one of the tiered seminar rooms. The medallion bore the imprint of the Arch and would be worn by faculty and administration at future graduation and honorary processions. Briscoe provided faculty, staff, and guests with a key chain engraved with the College motif. A bronze bust of Siebens, sculptured by Felix de Weldon, who was known for his busts of Truman, Eisenhower, Kennedy, and Johnson as well as the Iwo Jima monument, was unveiled.[73] Numerous dignitaries, including Governor Terry Branstad, John Marks Templeton (whose wise investment counsel would quickly balloon Siebens's $18 million gift into more than $30 million), and conservative economist George Gilder were honored guests among the large crowd that attended the opening ceremonies.[74] Like many others, Buena Vista students had long known the identity of the donor, but were still anxious to observe the philanthropist's wish for anonymity. Reporters discovered that Buena Vistans found the new facility "awesome," "the students love it." They found it fantastic that Siebens "thinks so much about education." "The school's emphasis in the future will be to build entrepreneurs," Briscoe explained, "people who are innovative and productive in their business careers."[75] There were even suggestions that Buena Vista should change its name to Siebens College—ultimately, perhaps, to Siebens University.[76]

Indeed, wherever one strolled on the Buena Vista campus one could find reminders of the Siebens family: the Estelle Siebens Science Center, the William W. Siebens American Heritage lecture series endowment (to promote the American heritage of freedom), the Stewart D. Siebens Computer Center endowment, the Gloria Siebens Freund Center for Free Enterprise, the Mary Jane Siebens Polubiec scholarship endowment, the Nancy Siebens Binz building endowment. The sustenance of the Siebens family had merged with the soul of Buena Vista College. Edgar Mack, Chairman of the Buena Vista Trustees, also caught the significance of the gift when he remarked, "It gets you away from the struggle with poverty. It gives us an opportunity to do things we could never do."[77] As for Harold Siebens, his dedication to the new Buena Vista he helped to create remained intact until his death in January 1989. The Siebens family also presented the City of Storm Lake a statute of Harold entitled "The Boy Fisherman," depicting the young Siebens holding a string of fish garnered from his efforts on the Lake. He would be cremated and his ashes scattered in his beloved Storm Lake. The legend is that Siebens's close friend, Harry Schaller, drove the boat while spoonfuls of ashes were distributed near the philanthropist's favorite fishing spots located at Tadpole Bridge, Stony Point, and the Inlet. Then the urn and the remaining ashes were deposited, "about 100 yards off the shoreline, straight south from where the statute of the 'Little Fisherman' is now located."[78] The University's greatest benefactor had also given instructions that most of his office furniture and personal historic documents be permanently placed in the care of Buena Vista. A special room known as the Siebens Den was provided, and Lynn Harlan was appointed Curator with the task of arranging documents, photos, clippings, and other memorabilia in some 125 special albums. Harlan, who worked on the project from 1991–97, proceeded to catalog every item on a computer database. The exquisitely furnished den with its great variety of material portrayed Siebens' life as an outdoorsman, businessman, and philanthropist. The Den would not only perpetuate the memory of the University's benefactor, but would provide a rich source for future historians.[79]

With the completion of the Siebens School of Business, it was now possible to renovate Lage Center (the campus dining hall) into a modern center for mass communications, complete with the newest technology. With $500,000 in the latest equipment, the new center could provide facilities for Innovation Video (the College television station), KBVC (the College radio station), the *Tack* editing and production rooms, and faculty offices. The dedication of the New Center for Communication (Lage) was held on October 15, 1986, with Dr. James Grunig of the University of Maryland giving the keynote address. Led by professors Paul Bowers, Bruce Ellingson, and Dave Diamond, the productions of the center soon had not only a campus but a regional impact. The number of mass communication majors had grown from 35 in 1982 to 105 in 1986. Earlier, on May 2, 1985, the College had introduced its new broadband telecommunications system by bringing Ted Turner, chairperson of Turner broadcasting network and president of the Atlanta Braves baseball team, live via teleconference to Anderson Auditorium.[80]

There were other notable achievements during the Briscoe years. One of them was the establishment of the Rollins Fellowship, which was endowed in honor of J. Leslie Rollins, a 1926 graduate, by former students who had benefited from Rollins's counsel at the Harvard Business School where he served as an administrator for twenty-four years. The fellowship provided unique educational experiences for outstanding Buena Vista students in their sophomore or junior years. The first recipient was Lynette Ludemann of Riceville, Iowa, who spent the first semester of the academic year 1977–78 as an intern at Carnegie Hall and attended the Juilliard School of Music. Numerous other internships followed. The 1988 recipient, Kim Hunter, headed east during the spring semester of 1989 to be a research assistant for Joseph Califano (former secretary of HEW) as he prepared a book on Lyndon B. Johnson. The Rollins Fellowship became one of the most coveted academic awards at Buena Vista College.

Rollins's brilliant and unmatched record of twelve letters in three sports was not forgotten. In 1986 his former students donated $250,000 to endow a new stadium, later named the J. Leslie Rollins Stadium in his honor. Vernon Alden, a Harvard MBA and former president of Ohio University, coordinated the project. George Mathews, owner and CEO of Intermet Corporation, led the way with $100,000. Mathews believed that he owed much of his success to Rollins's inspirational counsel while he was a graduate student at Harvard. Other former students of Rollins echoed those sentiments. Harry Hensel (chairperson of the Board of Bulova) remarked, "Nothing could be a more fitting tribute to you than to have your name on a beautiful stadium on a college campus that meant so much to you. . . . Honesty and the spirit of competition are two things you stand for."[81] All this was for a man whose diploma had been withheld in 1926 because he could not afford to pay (or refused to pay) a fine of thirty cents for missing chapel. While Rollins never paid the fine (his son wrote a check for $14.10 in May 1988 to pay the fine plus interest, enabling Rollins to finally receive his diploma) he never lost interest in Buena Vista College. This interest began during the Halverson era and blossomed during Briscoe's presidency. Although his B.A. diploma had been withheld, the College honored Rollins with the Doctor of Humane Letters in 1971 and the Distinguished Service Award in 1983. He was the Grand Marshal of the 1987 Homecoming parade.[82]

One of the most caring features of the Briscoe administration was the creation of Founders Day in September 1978 in honor of those persons who had faithfully served Buena Vista College and who had died the preceding year.[83] At a morning service surviving family members were presented a certificate, a memorial book was signed by visitors, and the names of those who had contributed much to the College's past were placed upon a plaque on the backs of seats in Schaller Chapel. Among the saddest entries were the names of Leonard and Louise Martz who died prematurely in 1985 and 1986. Dr. Leonard Martz had demonstrated a crisp, concise mastery of the English language while professor of English and outstanding administrative talents as chairperson of the Language and Literature Division and, beginning in 1979, as director of continuing education. More than that, he was a close advisor, friendly critic, and confidant of President Briscoe—roles he performed without compromising the trust placed in him by faculty colleagues. Louise Martz had been a part-time instructor in the accounting program. Lorraine Weber, who had brilliantly served both the Halverson and Briscoe administrations as administrative secretary until her death from cancer in 1983, was honored at the 1983 Founders Day ceremony. Weber was one of those organizational geniuses who could produce order out of chaos and make others look organized and effective when they would have floundered without her clear-headed assistance. Her long tenure was marked by the fact that she knew when to talk and when not to talk to those faculty and staff who came into the presidential sanctum seeking more information than they dispensed.

The academic cement that made the College hum with a new confidence and vigor was supplied by Provost Fred Brown. Brown, who had arrived on campus the year before Briscoe, knew the Midwest and the psyche of small liberal arts colleges, having grown up in Nebraska and graduated from Doane College. There he distinguished himself athletically (football and basketball) and academically (graduating cum laude). He never lost his interest in sports and could see no reason why a solid athletic program should be incompatible with intellectual pursuits. Thus, he was supportive of enhancing athletic as well as academic programs without short-

changing either. Furthermore, he had a charisma that many found
irresistible, and that he used effectively in promoting Buena Vista
College. Faculty found that Fred Brown had deep pockets, that his
door was always open, and that he would buffer faculty against the
excessive use of administrative power. Although his desk was so
cluttered that he appeared to lack organization, he had an uncanny
memory for details and the ability to sift the important from the
trivial. Perhaps Brown's greatest asset was that he understood the
problems of students and faculty—indeed he knew the people
around him well, which was one of his secrets of management and
the maintenance of institutional morale. President Wendell
Halverson, who hired Brown shortly before his own departure, correctly prophesied, "He will be creative and resilient in reshaping the
learning programs of the college for the demands of the new day."[84]

Fred Brown disliked "staying by the book," and he felt part of
his job was trying to find ways of saying yes—if not right now then
as soon as possible. To say no (of course he could say no emphat-
ically) might be to stifle creativity, and he wanted a faculty that felt
free to suggest and implement new ideas. He sought to create an atmosphere where "people would do more than expected." Brown arrived at Buena Vista as a young man of thirty-eight and remained
for fourteen critical and vital years. Vigorous and energetic, he always found it "fun to get up and go to work in the morning."
Brown enjoyed his relationship with colleagues who funneled "a
brilliant set of ideas" to him, which he then had the task of making
workable.[85] Briscoe found Brown a source of strength in the first
year of his presidency and the two developed mutual respect and
confidence. Advanced to the rank of vice president and provost,
Brown was the second most powerful individual at the College.
Briscoe had enough trust in Brown's loyalty and insight to permit
him to function as an internal executive, thus enabling Brown to
make important decisions in the academic area. Brown had been instrumental in the creation and management of the campus Centers,
which by the time he left in 1987 were located in nine cities across
the state—Fort Dodge, Spencer, Council Bluffs, Marshalltown,
Denison, Mason City, Ottumwa, Creston, and Clarinda. He was a
consistent motivator for curriculum change, initiated the honors

program, the Basic Skills Center, and the career development program.[86] The honors program, which insisted upon the public presentation of student research or art, inspired Buena Vista's brightest academic students while the Skills Center, ably directed by Mary Slagle, sought to improve weaknesses in verbal and math areas.

Brown firmly believed that Buena Vista was playing a unique role in higher education as it combined liberal education with hard technology. The day had passed, he remarked, when professors could teach with a slate.[87] Small colleges were in a better position to humanize technology than larger institutions, but they must realize that being small and friendly was not enough, they could not ignore the fact of technology. Brown also realized that technology by itself was not the answer for the eternal questions worth asking; human and humane probes of the liberal arts were still necessary in creating the civilized person. When Brown departed in 1987 to accept the presidency of his alma mater, Doane College, the faculty after a prolonged search settled for Dr. James Zabel, a Grinnell and University of Chicago graduate, then dean of the School of the Ozarks. Dr. Zabel was also a historian by training and his credentials indicated that he shared the liberal academic assumptions of his predecessors. Zabel would be largely responsible for developing and implementing the new Academic and Cultural Events Series (ACES)—originally conceived by President Briscoe and modeled on a similar program at Baldwin-Wallace—designed to bring outstanding personalities and creative performers to the Buena Vista campus. In the fall of 1989 he undertook his own search for ways to promote academic excellence, a feeling of community, and a new loyalty for Buena Vista College. These efforts included a massive effort to enhance library holdings, the remodeling of the library interior, and the continued utilization of the newest in technology. By early 1990 Dean Zabel was seeking new ways to promote faculty development.

Nor can one ignore Edgar E. Mack, the third member of a dynamic triumvirate that pushed Buena Vista into regional and national prominence during the 1980s. Mack followed his grandfather, E. E. Mack (founder and second chair of the Board of Trustees), and his father Guy as the latest member of a distinguished and civic-minded local family to help direct the fortunes of

Buena Vista College. Edgar Mack first joined the trustees in 1971 and in May 1979 was elected to be chair of the Board, replacing Dick Eilers of Omaha who had ably guided trustee-College affairs for the previous six years. Edgar Mack graduated from Buena Vista during the Great Depression, obtained his law degree (J.D. from the University of Iowa, and worked as an FBI agent until 1947 when he returned to Storm Lake to join his father's law practice. Mack would pound his gavel in the elaborately furnished Mack, Mack, and Mack room in the new Forum—a setting neither grandfather nor father could have imagined and which the younger Mack might have found incredible as a College student during the Depression-ridden 1930s or even when he joined the Board in 1971.[88] The choice of Mack to direct the Board was a good one because he could blend his understanding of the national psyche with that of the local community. Because Mack was sophisticated and ap-proachable and his loyalty to both city and College was unwaver-ing, he inspired confidence.

Moreover, Mack was flexible and open and knew how to tol-erate controversy without losing harmony of purpose. He would di-rect a strong Board that included internationally renowned business leaders like Harold W. Siebens; John M. Templeton; William Cairnes, who was instrumental in establishing and providing much of the direction of the Florida internship program; Dr. Russell R. Hansen, a respected local physician, who willed the Hansen Medical Arts Building to the College and as a lover of fine music provided the Hansen organ; Kermit Buntrock, a University of Iowa graduate in journalism whose interest in photography brought busi-ness success and national acclaim; Gilbert Geisinger, whose inter-est in the institution dated back to the Olson years; and Dick Eilers, president of World Insurance of Omaha, whose successful six-year reign as chair had seen what Mack called "the most dramatic, aca-demic growth in the college's history." There were, of course, many others. It was perhaps fitting that Briscoe, Brown, and Mack were presented with citations for their endeavors by Senate chairperson Paul Russell representing the faculty, at Founders Day ceremonies in September 1980.[89]

The achievements of the Briscoe administration were monumental. The small endowment of 1974 had surpassed $35 million by 1990. Not even the precipitous stock market losses in October 1987 could stop the escalation of the endowment fund. Losses of $3.8 million were easily weathered through the investment counsel of John Templeton.[90] The overall net worth of the College had increased by 825 percent from $5.8 million to $54 million. The debt remaining on the plant had decreased by 40 percent. The total funds raised during 1974–87 were $27,324,985 compared to $2,655,467 during the years 1960–73. There were nine branch Centers where none had existed. Visitors came to view the Forum, the Lage Mass Communications Center, and the state-of-the-art technology that dominated the campus. Buena Vista became the first small college in Iowa to have a VAX 780 computer with terminals located across the campus.[91] There were new parking lots, meticulous attention paid to landscaping, wellness programs, summer computer and science institutes. The College purchased area housing to provide for a record number of residential students. There were presidential fellowships, a new cultural ACES program, record enrollments, greater campus accessibility for the handicapped, and the gradual upward spiral of student ACT scores. No wonder President Briscoe told the large audience gathered at the faculty recognition dinner May 21, 1988, that the year 1987–88 had witnessed "an academic turning point" in the College's history.[92] The College successfully weathered a National Council for the Accreditation of Teacher Education (NCATE) accreditation review in 1986 and looked forward to preparing for a similar review by the North Central Association of Colleges in 1991. The College was also able to formulate an M.A. program in education in conjunction with Drake University.[93] The size of the faculty had doubled with most professors having completed earned doctorates or terminal degrees in their fields. Only Grinnell among small, liberal arts colleges in the state had a higher salary scale in 1990. The enrollment escalated, surpassing by more than one hundred the desired cut-off figures of 950 decreed in 1981.[94] Students now came from all parts of Iowa, from neighboring states, and from foreign countries. An increasing number of Buena Vista students attended graduate and professional school, and Buena Vista graduates were sought across the nation.

During the 1980s student and faculty travel abroad became commonplace. Six Buena Vista professors even went to Beijing and other parts of China during the student demonstrations of May and June 1989. For a few anxious days in early June the Buena Vista six appeared isolated, their whereabouts unknown except that they were somewhere in the midst of a history-making revolution. They knew the danger and they had wanted to go—as professors of psychology, Dr. Robert Ferguson said concerning the dangers of the revolutionary tremors shaking China, "We're children of the '60s and we've been there ourselves."[95] Risk-taking, it appeared, extended beyond the art of capital investment. The College administration, conscious of the growing importance of China (and ignoring the protest of those who called for sanctions because of the tragedy at Tiananmen Square), initiated an expanded exchange program in the fall of 1989. The new exchange with the Friendship Association of Guangdong Province allowed for a tour by eight Buena Vista representatives beginning in the summer of 1990. Because of the "economic significance" of Guangdong, faculty from the School of Business were given preference among Buena Vista representatives. It was expected that up to twenty Buena Vista faculty would tour China in the summer of 1990. In return Buena Vista would host representatives from Guangdong Province.[96]

Future college historians will see the Briscoe presidency as unique, for unlike his predecessors he acquired the means to realize the long-standing visions of the founders. That in itself was an unprecedented accomplishment and perhaps only an individual with Briscoe's unusual blend of creativity, innovation, salesmanship, and intuitive insight could have so successfully scaled the peaks of academia. Of course, he had support his predecessors lacked—federal and state aid, substantial scholarship money, and a growing class of donors capped by the great donor himself, Harold W. Siebens. At the same time Buena Vista, like other colleges, faced spiraling inflation, declining high school enrollments, and mounting tuition costs. Inflation alone caused College expenses to rise by $240,000 during the fiscal year 1977–78.[97] The Briscoe years would bring radical change and radical progress and construct an institutional edifice that no one dreamed possible the day of his arrival. He had maintained all along that Buena Vista, to achieve the distinction it sought, needed to be different from the state's other colleges.[98]

Sound management and selection of able lieutenants were two keys to Briscoe's success. Among those able lieutenants was Robert Siefer who served nearly two decades as vice president for development and who made the initial contact with Harold Siebens. Quiet, unassuming, and with impeccable integrity, Siefer enjoyed the confidence of the faculty and the community throughout his long tenure. His ceaseless efforts were important in achieving the first million dollar year in gifts from July 1977 to June 1978.[99] The confidence the entire College community placed in Siefer was further demonstrated when he was appointed acting president while Briscoe was on a six-month sabbatical in 1989–90.

Dr. William Wesselink finished his long tenure at the College as vice president of student affairs during the early years of the Briscoe administration. A skilled craftsman, Wesselink constructed and presented to the College what would become the official mace now used in all academic processions. Not long before his death he also fashioned a mace now used by the student marshal.[100]

Meanwhile, Charles Zalesky, Bill Irons, Norman Krueger, and Randy Fehr provided steady if sometimes controversial terms as vice presidents for business affairs. Most of the Zalesky years were served under Wendell Halverson when he established the tradition of balanced budgets and sound fiscal management. These were continued by his successors and from 1959, when Zaleksy took the post of business manager, through 1990 there were only three years when the College ran deficits.[101] Bill Irons was expert in conservation measures during the oil crisis of the late 1970s and early 1980s, assisted by Joe Traylor's energy committee he promoted energy-efficient measures that saved the College thousands of dollars. Irons, a former Westinghouse executive and a professional engineer, was a strong personality who liked to ride alone in the saddle and whose policy differences with Briscoe led to an abrupt departure. But his management was sound, and he appears to have known how to inspire the loyalty of his staff. Briscoe's dealings with Bill Irons and his constant pressure upon administrative personnel brought out what some charged was a ruthless streak in his nature.[102] There were few, besides Fred Brown, who could keep abreast of Briscoe's rapid transitions of thought and action on uncharted seas with no visible direction.

President Briscoe, however, respected the autonomy of the academic area. There he knew what to manage and what to leave to others. For example, he elevated Fred Brown to provost with substantial control over the academic side of the College. Many faculty felt Brown provided not only a desirable but necessary buffer from presidential whims. Others questioned if faculty impact on institutional governance was not a casualty in the process. American Association of University Professors (AAUP) membership dwindled with only W. H. Cumberland still paying his dues by 1990. Cost, confidence, and indifference were all factors in the decline of faculty support of AAUP. Some faculty saw themselves as prospective administrators. There was also the increasing tendency to concentrate on one's field or research and ignore collegial concerns. Others were idealistic in their assessment of the secure status of academic freedom and tenure. Moreover, the McCarthy era had receded from common memory, and not a few complained of the high cost of membership. The concerns of the 1980s were obviously different from those of the 1960s.

Visitors enjoying the campus mall, the finely decorated Forum, the homey courtesy, the fine dining, the efficient personnel, the constant vibration of movement and life could not miss the new dynamism and the feeling that Buena Vista had become a class operation. Of course the College and community were inseparably linked. For years the Storm Lake community had averaged in excess of $75,000 in annual support of the College. By 1984 the College employed 133 people in Storm Lake with salaries totaling $4.1 million. This meant a disposable income of $3.2 million, most of which was spent in the town. Buena Vista spent an additional $3.4 million in the area. The total economic impact of the College on the community was more than $20 million.[103]

As the centennial year approached, Keith Briscoe, the architect of change, readied himself for another decade of action as he molded the new Buena Vista for his successors in the twenty-first

century. The mandate in the final decade of the Briscoe presidency
would involve the renewed challenge of strengthening those humane and spiritual aspects of a liberal education that enable service
to triumph over greed, freedom over tyranny, compassion over sen-
sation. As early as 1982, more than 300 of the College's 952 students were business majors, up from 122 in 1975. Interestingly,
one-third of the business majors were women. The new computer-
science program attracted 43 majors.[104] With the increasing emphasis upon business, mass communications, and technology would
there be enough energy to rejuvenate the humanities, the social sciences, and the arts? If the traditional components of a Buena Vista
education were ostracized or left behind, friction would be inevitable. Somehow, Briscoe needed to harmonize rather than polar-
ize elements of the campus community who differed over the new
commitments of the College. There were those who found in his
style too much slick advertising, and at times he was given to hasty
dicta and a disregard for basic academic privileges, including
tenure. But even his most severe critics recognized his enormous
energy, his capacity for hard work, and his total dedication to the
dream that Buena Vista might enter the twenty-first century as one
of the great small colleges in America.

Even as the president shared with the donor the dream that students be "exposed to the free enterprise system and the concepts
that have made America the great nation that it is," several hundred
Buena Vista students were gathering in Eppley auditorium protesting President Reagan's proposed cuts in higher education.[105] Like it
or not, Buena Vista College remained dependent upon the federal
largess with 80 to 90 percent of the student body receiving federal
and state grants and loans. Furthermore, national and professional
accreditation agencies—North Central, NCATE, the Department of
Public Instruction, the National Social Work Council—would demand regulations and standards unknown in the days of academic
laissez faire; days that were not likely to return. Perhaps the spirit
of uninhibited enterprise remained, however, as across the nation
students moved away from the social justice issues of the 1960s to
the more material concerns of the 1980s. Would they return to basic
humanitarian and social concerns during the last decade of the

twentieth century? The task at Buena Vista College remained to reconcile "Education for Service" with its long-standing liberal arts tradition. Some faculty members argued that excessive reliance on entrepreneurship, unrestricted individualism, weakening of Church-College ties, constriction of humanities programs such as foreign language, philosophy, and history in favor of computer literacy (not undesirable in itself), mass communications, and a four-tier business program threatened the historic goals of the liberal arts. Officially, it was assumed that the liberal arts would remain an integral part of the institution's program, performing not only a service function but providing the humane and moral underpinnings of a rapidly changing civilization that would have to wrestle continuously with the question of values. It was obligatory that the College heed 1986 Commencement speaker Uwe Kitzinger's warning that "engineering has become too important to be left to engineers."[106]

Fortunately, the survival mentality ("You don't build quality schools with that kind of mentality," said Brown) was no longer part of the Buena Vista psyche. The gift had seen to that. Buena Vista's assault on becoming the next great college in America went beyond the classical liberal arts tradition. "If you want a pure, classical liberal arts education you should go to Carleton or Grinnell," said Fred Brown. This did not mean the College had abandoned its liberal arts heritage, but that it now tied it to career education buttressed by state-of-the-art technology. The new soul of the institution centered in its modern business and mass communications programs and in the traditional education major.[107] The Briscoe administration still wanted to stress Christian values. Although the College had become more independent than Church-related, it still maintained a strong sense of vision and mission and still believed strongly in the liberal arts that passed on the nation's cultural heritage. However, the new Buena Vista was not bound by "weighty tradition," but would be "entrepreneurial, flexible and futuristic." Great emphasis would be placed upon developing leadership talent, upon combining and synthesizing liberal and career education.

The sudden surge in fortune brought national attention as Edward Fiske, *New York Times* education writer and author of *Selective Guide to Colleges*, found Buena Vista one of "16 hidden gems" among the nation's colleges.[108] In November 1985 *U.S. News and World Report* classed Buena Vista among the ranks of the nation's best colleges.[109] For the first time in its history Buena Vista found itself at the same party as institutions like Carnegie Mellon, Carleton, Emory, and Trinity. "Let us stand in awe of the distance Buena Vista College has come and the challenge of the road ahead," Fred Brown told the audience gathered for the ground-breaking ceremonies for the Siebens Forum.[110] More than anyone present, Brown realized Buena Vista's struggle, weaknesses, potential, and the long road yet to be traversed. But there was something out there and as Briscoe said, "Our greatness may lie in our spirit, our energy, and in our willingness to go for the dream."[111]

Part of going for that dream could be seen in the construction of a new, modern dormitory undertaken in the fall of 1990 and in a probing discussion of whether the College should transform itself into a university. Expansion, overseas exchanges, and NCATE accreditation demands appear to make such a transition desirable. University status might more adequately describe what Buena Vista is in the process of becoming. The three main components of a restructuring would be (1) Buena Vista College (the historic main campus), (2) Buena Vista Extension College (the nine campus Centers), and (3) Buena Vista International College (the overseas programs).

As the centennial atmosphere ripened and the celebration began, College historian William H. Cumberland wrote that "As a historic community, Buena Vista's collective memory embraces the life-spirit of all those who labored valiantly on behalf of 'Education for Service,' from Loyal Hays and George Fracker, to Keith Briscoe and Richard Lampe, from the Edgar Mack of 1891 to the Edgar Mack of 1991. It was, as always, education with a purpose—that purpose being to reconcile the real and the ethereal, to pass on the revered traditions while meeting the challenges of the new, to put the parts together so life could be viewed as a whole, to find release from the shackles of fear, to seek truth and to understand love, justice, and fellowship. Where is the elusive 'soul' of Buena Vista? It is in all of us—the deceased and the living, the mighty and the small, the scribes and the technocrats, students, teachers, administrators, and trustees. Whether the struggle was for survival or prestige we somehow found the strength to let our more noble motives overcome our frailties. Together we endured, bound closely by events, symbols, and memories that gave meaning to our lives and sustenance to our dreams. At the beginning of the second century we can call back to those who began the first century and say that together we labored not in vain to preserve and enhance Buena Vista College and leave the world a little better place because we did." Certainly a part of Iowa, a part of the Midwest, and even a part of the nation was better because Buena Vista had persevered. What would the future bring?

Keith Briscoe still had four more years remaining as Buena Vista president following the Centennial celebration of 1991. They would be exciting years. During this period the College endowment would grow by millions, new buildings would be planned and built, the size of the student body, the faculty, and the number of trustees would increase, new Centers would be added, and university status achieved with the addition of the Master of Science in Education program.

It was also the period when the first, brief, Gulf War erupted. As might be expected, faculty and student opinion were divided concerning the merits of the U.S.-led invasion to free Kuwait and subdue the forces of Saddam Hussein. Students Linda Sauser and Dave King were among those who strongly supported the war.[112] Former *Tack* editor Debbie Houghtaling took a different position arguing that the "ramifications of U.S. actions will haunt this country forever."[113] Several Buena Vista National Guardsmen and Reservists were called into service. The College promised a refund policy for anyone called into service. The war also forced the curtailment of some trips abroad. Peter Steinfeld and Laura Inglis, both who questioned the war, were upset that "people aren't addressing deeper issues, especially the complex relationship of Islam, Christianity, Judaism and the Palestinians." Professor Steinfeld also maintained that Americans failed to "understand the anger the Third World continues to have for the U.S."[114] Fortunately, the war was short and successful, but within a dozen years the area would once again explode.

By the 1990s the young Turks of the 1960s and 1970s had become older and were retiring or preparing to retire. These included the now elder statesmen and prominent members of the faculty— Aryanpur, Borgman, Cumberland, Heusinkveld, Pace, Pfaltzgraff, A. G. Thomas, Tollefson, and Norman Bonnema—who had moved into administration as a Center Director. In 1994 the Order of Cumberland and Tollefson was established to honor retiring faculty members with long years of distinguished service. Members were Cumberland, Tollefson, Aryanpur, Borgman, Slagle, John and Sandra Madsen, and Marilyn Wikstrom (posthumously) with Adkins and Poff also being honored upon their retirements. The seed for the award came from Paul Russell who among others felt that a different kind of recognition other than presenting each retiring faculty member with an honorary doctorate was in order. Another purpose was to keep retirees feeling that they were still part of the University. The Cumberland-Tollefson club is supposed to be recognized annually at some public gathering, although that has not always happened.[115]

Membership on the Board of Trustees was also undergoing major changes. Long-time member of the Board, Gib Geisinger became a Templeton Life Trustee in 1994 at the age of 84. Geisinger had become a member of the Board in 1948, thus serving through four college presidential administrations, and was an important figure in the many changes that took place at Buena Vista during that long period.[116]

Meanwhile, the trustees were devastated by the sudden death of Board Chairman, Edgar Mack, who died of an aneurysm in March 1992. He was, as Professor John Madsen remarked, "a tremendous spokesman for the college." Vice President of Development, Robert Siefer recalled Mack's "great compassion." There were indeed many who felt that Edgar Mack "made everyone a winner."[117] A few weeks later Buena Vista graduate and trustee member Peter Dows died. Peter Dows along with the Dows Family contributed heavily to Buena Vista.

These losses, however, did not deter the forward march of the College nor did it lessen Briscoe's determination to see Buena Vista recognized as one of the elite regional institutions of higher learning. New faces replaced old. John Mark Templeton, internationally renowned stock analyst became a valuable member of the Board in the 1980s. Edgar Mack was replaced by his son Warren who served as chair during the mid-1990s. Donald Lamberti became a member of the Board in 1993. James Haahr, a 1962 graduate and now the CEO of First Midwest Financial Inc. and First Federal Savings Bank, joined the board in 1997. New, ambitious ideas were constantly fermenting.

Viewing both the internal and external landscape of the soon-to-be university, Professor William Cumberland prior to his retirement in the spring of 1991, and just before the publication of his *History of Buena Vista College,* visualized that the "college history will never be finished." He somewhat innocently forecast should he still be living when the next chapters were written that college representatives would come to the "nursing home, give me a big magnifying glass and ask me to write it again."[118] Those words were closer to the truth than he imagined at the time.

The most significant new project undertaken in the waning days of the Briscoe Administration was the planning of a new, modern, technologically advanced addition to Ballou Library. The new construction was in the planning stages as early as 1991, but funds had to be raised and the actual building was slow getting under way. Finally, ground was broken in May 1994 but the state-of-the-art library would not be completed and opened until the first year of the presidency of Dr. Frederick Moore.[119] The 50,000-square-foot structure would be underground and would be accessible to the nine branch campuses via the utilization of the fiber optic network. This was a new and somewhat dramatic way of transmitting audio, video, and data signals over distances.[120] It was under Briscoe's leadership that Buena Vista, in 1991, took the leadership among Iowa colleges in subscribing to the worldwide computer network.[121] Meanwhile, a new dormitory, Centennial Hall, was added in 1991, Pierce and White halls were renovated in 1992–93, and a revamping of Edson Hall was started in 1990 although destined to be finished under Briscoe's successor.

There was still the dream of achieving university status. Briscoe felt that with the upgrading of faculty, facilities, and endowment, and the addition of the Centers, Buena Vista was ready to move into a "new frontier." The Board of Trustees approved the addition of a Master of Science degree in Education in the fall of 1994 and Buena Vista obtained NCA accreditation to offer the advanced degree, with the first classes scheduled for June 1995.[122] Dr. John Mouw, professor emeritus of Southern Illinois University, was named as the first Dean of the Graduate Program. Mouw had worked twenty-four years with graduate students at Southern Illinois.[123] He was replaced by Dr. Jon Hixon in 1998. It was, then, in the summer of 1995 that Buena Vista College passed into history and Buena Vista University became a reality.[124]

The growth of the Centers, the increasing number of students at the home campus, and the achievement of university status all put a strain on the traditional governing structure of the institution. The faculty senate and administrative structure had served the institution well many years beyond the 1960s, but was now conceived as having become something of an antique. Even the name *faculty senate* seemed something of a misnomer since both administrators and students were included as members. Consequently, the faculty senate approved a proposal that would create a governing structure consisting of three branches:

(1) A university council that would replace the senate and be responsible for all policy decisions. The council would consist of nine members of the Storm Lake campus, the Dean of the Centers, the Dean of the graduate college, and two students.

(2) A Planning and Budget Council that would be responsible for all matters of planning the budget and would consist of the Executive Vice Presidents, the Deans of the five schools, the Dean of the graduate college, and the Dean of the Centers.

(3) The Administrative Cabinet that consisted of the President, Executive Vice President, and Vice Presidents. [125] However, Briscoe's remaining tenure was too short to implement these changes, and major innovations in the governing structure and general education waited for his successor to consider.

It had been expected that President Briscoe would hold office almost to the end of the twentieth century. It was then, something of a bombshell, when Briscoe announced his retirement at a press conference on October 21, 1994. "It's time," Briscoe announced, "for the school to get new leadership and I can't wait to watch it."[126] It was, perhaps, one of the most significant moments in the life of Keith Briscoe. President Briscoe, a complex and sometimes misunderstand man, realized not only what he had done for Buena Vista but the measure of meaning that the University had brought into his life. Here, he said as he jostled with his Buena Vista supporters, he had found joy "in the clear skies, fresh breezes," and also the "thunderstorms, rainbows, droughts, subartic fronts, torrential rains, wild wind storms—and the weather was pretty crazy too."[127] Buena Vista's First Lady, Carmen Briscoe echoed her husband's feelings noting of all the things she enjoyed about the city and the College it was most of all "the people, the people, the people."[128]

Trustee George Schaller praised Briscoe for bringing Buena Vista an administration "based on management principles." Furthermore, Schaller noted that Briscoe had "made it possible for the college to survive and then to grow and expand and to have a future." Lynn Harlan said it best of all when she commented, "I have a real appreciation for his sense of the whole place."[129] Briscoe, now sixty-one years old had served as Buena Vista's president for twenty-one years. He had been seen by some as controversial; he rowed at times with padded oars, but he never feared uncharted seas. There were occasions when disgruntled faculty found him vindictive or capricious. There were some whom he may have unnecessarily hurt. There were occasions when some of his comments would have been better left unsaid. Philosophically, he ranged from extreme individualism to a much higher ground. Actually, Keith Briscoe could show unusual human compassion when he sensed real need among faculty, administrators, or students. Substantial salary increases, improvements in health benefits, travel opportunities, and sabbaticals all belong to the Briscoe Era. He was always a risk taker but if one looks objectively at his twenty-one years (the second longest term for a president in the College's history) his risks paid enormous dividends. He had made Buena Vista a force in the academic world.

Furthermore, President Briscoe recognized that some tension was necessary in an academic community. In a 1988 essay entitled "Interiors of the Presidency," he insisted that "to seek harmony at a college is to stop learning." It was Briscoe's assumption that "from chaos come new order, discussion and progress." He realized that learning is not always harmonious and that a certain amount of tension was not only inevitable but desirable.[130] Briscoe's overall record indicates that he was a strong, although occasionally silent, supporter of academic freedom throughout his two decades of service. He may not have solved all of the problems, he may have left a number of things undone, and some of his personal dealings with faculty may have been erratic, but he bequeathed a solid academy to his successor. No wonder Briscoe received a heartfelt standing ovation on the day he announced his retirement. He had given Buena Vista a future. The Buena Vista Board of Trustees, at their spring meeting decided to bestow rather unique honors on Keith and Carmen Briscoe. President Briscoe would be presented, at the May Commencement, with the University's Citation of Excellence and Carmen would be granted the honorary Doctor of Humane Letters. Dr. Briscoe was also named President Emeritus of Buena Vista University.[131] These were rare honors for rare people.

14

More with Moore

The Buena Vista Trustees, supported by faculty and administrators, chose Fred Moore, a soft-spoken but determined North Carolinian as Keith Briscoe's successor. Moore, only thirty-nine years old, had served North Carolina Wesleyan College from 1990–95, first as special assistant to the president, then as vice president and General Counsel. While at North Carolina Wesleyan Moore had the formidable task of coordinating projects for fund raising, financial analysis, and constituent relations. The new Buena Vista president possessed degrees (B.A., MBA, J.D.) from the prestigious University of North Carolina at Chapel Hill. While interviewing at Buena Vista Moore became impressed by the institutions innovative spirit and bold entrepreneurial approach to education. He stressed his personal values of excellence, faith, and integrity and confidently proclaimed that he was a leader by nature.[1] Moore represented a newer type of small college CEO in Iowa in that his training and experience were in business and law, not academics. Former president Keith Briscoe would be a tough act to follow but the next decade would establish the Moore presidency as the most successful in the school's history.[2]

Entrepreneurship and leadership were magic words at Buena

Vista. This coupled with an impressive resume and confident demeanor were instrumental in Fred Moore's invitation to take the helm as Buena Vista's seventeenth president. Although it wasn't easy for the new president to tear himself away from Tar Heel basketball,[3] Moore took the reins of command in the fall of 1995 as president of what was now Buena Vista University. The new Buena Vista president was accompanied by his attractive and talented wife Susan, whom he met during his junior year at the University of North Carolina and their two children, Allison and Stephen. The Moores were a close, devoted family unit even further cemented because Stephen, an autistic child, had special needs and President and Mrs. Moore were determined to meet those needs. The Reverend Mrs. Moore held a Masters of Divinity degree from Duke University and was an ordained UCC minister.[4] Both Moores were native North Carolinians and had not envisioned spending a part of their lives outside the South.[5] However, they quickly identified with the Midwest and Iowa, which they quickly came to appreciate.

President Moore inherited an executive office much different from that of his predecessors. Keith G. Briscoe, the dynamic personality he replaced, had built a highly successful institution, one with an increasing enrollment; an endowment, which among four-year Iowa colleges had crept into second place among Iowa private colleges trailing only Grinnell; a highly professional faculty; satellite Centers in communities across the State; a modern emphasis upon technology; overseas academic exchanges; and an expanding, attractive home campus. Furthermore, Briscoe had been instrumental in constructing an institution that now possessed a growing self-confidence. The new president's task would be to build on success, to move from stability to prestige, to continue to upgrade programs, students, faculty, and resources. He would need to find a way to make Buena Vista's star shine across the nation. The challenge would be formidable because competition in higher education was now more intense than at any time in the nation's history. The new Buena Vista president would endeavor to create an innovative and original concept and an enticing, sound, and creative academic program. Indeed, Fred Moore occupied his office in early July 1995, just as Independence Day fireworks exploded over Storm Lake as

part of the annual Star Spangled Spectacular.[6] Moore, himself, was
primed and ready to burst into action as he set out to discover a uni-
fying theme and program that would mark his administration and
continue to move Buena Vista into the ranks of America's most distinguished colleges. He quickly sought to incorporate his faculty
into his vision and program. There was even an unprecedented
summer planning session in which the faculty was paid to attend.[7]
The new administration, according to a number of faculty, seemed
to bring in a breath of fresh air. This view remained intact during
the next decade as few found it possible to argue with Moore's success.[8] The University faculty began to feel that Buena Vista was an
even better place to work. Fred Moore looked and acted like a
leader, he was intelligent, articulate, straightforward, and solid in
his convictions. He sought consensus and did not appear vindictive
toward those who disagreed.

The Buena Vista educational program and rallying point would
soon revolve around the New American College theme, which the
incoming president brought with him. The New American College
was an approach to education conceived by Dr. Ernest Boyer, the
highly respected president of the Carnegie Foundation for the
Advancement of Teaching, in the early 1990s.[9] Boyer was the author of several scholarly works including *Scholarship Reconsidered,*
a study that emphasized discovery, and integrating, applying, and
teaching knowledge. His goal was to break down barriers between
academic and real world experience while demonstrating a deep
concern for humanity.[10] His purpose was to challenge and update
the very heart of liberal education and possibly mitigate what he
perceived as an emerging trend toward elitism. Boyer who feared
what he saw as the diminishing of the quality of life insisted that
the academy needed to become more involved in the pressing issues
of our time. Boyer hoped to escape the stereotype of the ivory
tower and channel knowledge to humane ends.[11] He was not attempting to minimize the importance of research, but wished to el-
evate the role of good teaching, to some extent diminished by the
post-World War II emphasis on publication at the college and university level. Teaching and research were not, in Boyer's view, an-
tagonistic. The New American College would connect thought to

action, theory to practice. A number of mid-sized colleges and universities were moving in this direction emphasizing that they were serving the public good. Moore saw the NAC concept as a celebration of the interaction of pre-professional education and the liberal arts, the scholarship of engagement, nontraditional programs for nontraditional students and interdisciplinary programs. The Buena Vista version of the NAC, Moore insisted during his inaugural address, would turn out graduates who could write cogently, read critically, reason quantitatively, communicate orally, work on teams, appreciate diversity, and exhibit a sense of personal ethics.[12]

One of the things that had impressed Moore during his interview was the degree to which Buena Vista was student centered. This was an aspect of education in which he strongly believed. There would be no change in that emphasis. The close relationship among faculty and staff and students, which had existed since the institution's founding in 1891, had been a major reason for Buena Vista's survival and recent success. This academic and personal intimacy, this sense of community would remain the heart of the New American College concept as carried out by Buena Vista University under the Moore Administration.[13] But a strong sense of community does not mean, Moore stressed in his inaugural, the absence of dissent or lack of conflict. Ideas needed to be vigorously challenged in institutions of higher learning where the virtuous endeavor is the pursuit of truth.[14]

Buena Vista had long possessed the unenviable reputation of being a suitcase college, with most students living close enough to their communities to head home almost every weekend. The Moore Administration would seek to garner not only Iowa students, but students from across the nation including those from different ethnic and racial backgrounds. The international program would also be enlarged. The campus, Moore said, would have no borders.[15] He was also determined to develop recreational and cultural activities that would keep most students on campus on weekends rather than only on Homecoming.

By 1997 Buena Vista had revised its mission statement in order to incorporate the conceptual structure of the NAC. The new mission statement clearly affirmed that:

> Buena Vista University is an independent, regionally acclaimed, com-
> prehensive, teaching institution dedicated to education for service.
> Buena Vista University aspires to become the nation's leading New
> American College while retaining its Presbyterian heritage. The
> University prepares students for leadership and service in an informa-
> tional global society. The traditional disciplines provide a framework for
> a curriculum which prepares students for the professions and life long
> learning.[16]

It was argued that the values inherent in the New American
College concept would be instrumental in preparing students for
leadership and service in an information-driven, global society. This
would also give the University a more visible image.[17]

There was of course, some questioning as to what the New
American College concept meant for the traditional liberal arts program and even the college-church relationship. Although Boyers'
scholarship did not succumb to the fog of educational jargon, The
New American College seemed to defy easy and concrete defini-
tions. Did the NAC concepts mean the traditional liberal arts were
being reduced to secondary importance? It was already clear by the
early 1990s that Buena Vista had strayed from being a pure liberal
arts college, if indeed that pure state had ever existed. The internal
debate, it appeared, was largely over. Buena Vista's academic mission would be one that provides career education with a strong liberal arts foundation.[18] The career education components, Teacher
Education and Business, dwarfed other majors. By the early 1990s
the majority of Buena Vista graduates remained education majors although those entering the business and accounting professions remained a not too distant second. It was also the education sector that
would offer a Master's Program. Meanwhile, it was expected that the
liberal arts (English, history, philosophy, foreign languages) would
remain a strong and vibrant part of the curriculum.[19] These assumptions would make it easier to adapt to a new, more evident mission.
There were, however, questions to be considered. To what extent
would the New American College concept actually change Buena
Vista? What changes in the curriculum would the new mission necessitate? How many institutions in the country had already adopted
the New American College concept and how were they faring?

Changes in academia generally proceed cautiously and new programs and ideas take time to build. Existing programs cannot simply be demolished without sometimes incurring disastrous consequences. Faculty involvement and support would be the key in making the new concept work. Nevertheless, it now appeared certain that whatever mission Buena Vista might embark upon, the University had the facilities, the capital, and the personnel to succeed. The Board of Trustees was bringing in new members who were anxious to make Buena Vista an institution of distinction. Furthermore, the Siebens Family was not likely to lose interest in an institution that bore their imprint in so many ways.

Among the newer trustees were Dr. Paula Brownlee, Ed Bock, and Dr. Norman Nielsen. Dr. Brownlee is a nationally known research chemist, educator, and administrator who earned her doctorate in organic chemistry at Oxford University. She became a chemistry professor at Rutgers, then the academic dean at Douglass, the women's college at Rutgers. By 1976 she was the dean of faculty and professor of chemistry at Union College. From there she became the CEO of Hollins College in Virginia where under her leadership the endowment was increased from $14 to 40 million. In 1986 the Council for the Advancement and Support of Higher Education (CASE) designated her as one of the most effective presidents in higher education. Brownlee left Hollins to serve as president of the Association of American Colleges and Universities for eight years. In 2000 she became a welcome addition to the Buena Vista Board of Trustees and quickly became Vice Chairman of that body. Buena Vista was appealing to Brownlee because it was putting its words into action, and really trying to do what it says it will do.[20]

Ed Bock also became a member of the Buena Vista Board of Trustees in 2000. Bock's connection with the University is an amazing story, which covers a time span of more than seventy years. Bock's father was a UCC minister who arrived in Northwest Iowa in 1931. Three years later, during the height of the depression young Ed enrolled at Buena Vista. Twice he was forced to drop out, once because of the lack of funds, a second time because he had contracted tuberculosis. For the next twenty-six months Bock battled the disease instead of struggling with classes at Buena Vista. He recovered and by 1940 had completed two years of college after a six-year struggle with finances and illness. Bock went on to Iowa where he obtained his B.A., served a short time in the Air Force, and by the late 1940s was on his way to becoming a successful accountant and partner with Peat Marwick. Meanwhile, Bock accumulated profitable investments in what he called his three Rs— radio stations, real estate, and restaurants.[21]

The ruddy, curious, conversational Bock who reached eighty-nine years of age in December 2005 possessed the verve and energy of a healthy fifty-year-old. In the last decade the still active entrepreneur has traversed the seas of the Antarctica, rafted on the Colorado River, visited Australia and Europe, besides handling his numerous business interests. He also drives the 250 miles between Cedar Rapids and Storm Lake—occasionally at night. Bock's long association with Buena Vista has spanned every president from Henry Olson to Fred Moore or two-thirds of the school's existence. He has watched the cost of a Buena Vista education mushroom from around $200 in the depression year 1934, when few students had typewriters or other possessions for that matter, to more than $26,000 in 2005 when every student is equipped with a laptop. His accounting expertise was put to good use by the Trustees who quickly made him chair of the auditing committee, but Bock took the greatest pride in his establishment of the Henry Olson Endowed Scholarship Fund in 1992. The fund enables several deserving BVU students per year to study abroad during the January interim.[22]

Dr. Norman Nielsen was a terror on the gridiron, who won the Buena Vista MVP award in football during the 1960 season. He also lettered in baseball and basketball. Furthermore, Nielsen was an excellent student who decided to devote his life to education. His career was destined to be a steady upward spiral. Nielsen taught a year at nearby Alta while waiting for Marian Jaycox, his wife-to-be to graduate from Buena Vista. There followed stints at Webster City, Northeast Hamilton, and several years as superintendent at Belle Plaine. It was 1979 when Nielsen was persuaded to relocate as Vice President of Administration of Kirkwood College in Cedar Rapids. Six years later Nielsen assumed the presidency, which he held until his retirement in 2005. During his career at Kirkwood the institution literally rose from the cornfields.[23] Meanwhile, he obtained an M.A. from Iowa State University in 1969 and a Ph.D. from the University of Iowa in 1986. Nielsen directed a tremendous growth at Kirkwood in buildings, students, and prestige during his twenty-year tenure. Enrollment increased from 4,000 in 1979 to 6,300 in 1985 to more than 12,500 in 2004. In the fall of 2001 Nielsen was honored by the Association of Community College Trustees who presented him with the Association's most prestigious recognition, the Marie Y. Martin CEO of the Year Award.[24] Buena Vista quickly pounced upon Nielsen as he retired from Kirkwood, bringing him on board as the University's newest trustee.

Nine members of the Buena Vista Board of Trustees in 2005 were Buena Vista graduates, who had become successful professionals and entrepreneurs. These include Marc Brinkmeyer (1968), owner and president of the Riley Creek Lumber Company, Laclede, Idaho; Laura Horn (1973), whose upwardly mobile career included a stint as vice-president of systems development at AOL and recently as co-founder of Wondir, Inc.; and Dennis Young (1965) of Des Moines. Young, senior vice-president of Norwest Financial, Inc., has served as a trustee since 1979. He received the Young Alumnus Award in 1975 and the John Fisher Outstanding Service Award in 1993.

Ernest Boyer's work continued to inspire Moore, who by 1999 was pressing for full implementation of the goals of the NAC. To Moore the NAC values signified excellent teaching and advising, learner-centered connectedness, theory and practice, liberal learning, service, innovation, a seamless web of learning—academic to co-curricular, community, and outreach to all learners.[25] The main emphasis of the NAC would hopefully clarify and define the educational goals of Buena Vista University in the twenty-first century. It did not, as noted, signify a radical departure from the past. It was not meant to be a violation of the institution's history and tradition of liberal arts education. After all, the college motto, Education for Service, had always emphasized liberal learning for service to humanity. President Moore felt service to humanity was the soul of the New American College concept. Moore, himself, had been a political science major at the University of North Carolina and at least philosophically recognized the importance of the liberal arts.[26]

The new emphasis was also compatible with the institution's religious values and the College, although essentially independent, insisted that it had no intention of severing its historic Presbyterian roots. The University would employ a full-time chaplain, the religion and philosophy major would continue to be offered, and weekly voluntary chapel was still available. The University's long affiliation with the Presbyterian Church (U.S.A.) was not in question even though the Church now played a subdued role in the daily life of the institution. The Presbyterian Church, of course, no longer possessed either a decision-making role nor had official representation on the Board. Its monetary contribution was now an almost infinitesimal part of the total budget, which grew larger while the Church grew smaller. It was not likely that the University would ever have another clergyman as its CEO. While the Church connection was valued and an ecumenical spiritual life pursued, more secular interests would dominate. Still, it was estimated that 65 percent of the major donors to the institution were Presbyterians.[27]

Buena Vista graduates had throughout the institution's history become teachers, coaches, accountants, physicians, businessmen, scientists, attorneys, ministers, and missionaries. They would continue to do so in increasing numbers. But in an age of rapidly rising educational costs, the NCA concept indicated a dedication to see that the University's graduates were well prepared for the changing American and global market, that they had a solid grasp of emerging and changing technology, understood how to integrate it with liberal learning and that they took their responsibility to the community seriously. Nor did Buena Vista intend to completely turn its back on the humanities, which traditionally provided the cement that held all aspects of learning in place.[28] Still, while there would be no conscious effort to disparage the traditional disciplines, students and faculty in those fields sometimes felt relegated to a secondary role and occasionally made known their dissatisfaction by caustic references to the School of Business. One somewhat dissatisfied student vented his frustration in a letter to the *Tack* writing that students were expected to gaze blindly upon the obvious inequality between departments.[29] Quite obviously, the latest mission statement of the College consciously sidestepped reference to the liberal arts. Instead, the new statement used life-long learning, global society, and leadership as words embracing the institution's liberal arts values in a more accurate manner.[30]

The transformation of the old liberal arts concept could also be seen in the newly adopted General Education requirements. General Education requirements now consisted of four foundation areas—mathematics, written communication, oral communication, and technology skills. It was possible for well-prepared students to test out of mathematics, technology, and the written requirement. The second part of the GE requirements now called Intellectual Explorations enabled students with seemingly minimal effort (frustrating to liberal arts proponents) to graduate should they desire with no more than three hours in history or three hours in literature along with a semester of a foreign language or a class in religion, philosophy, or social work. This would fulfill the humanities requirement with selections made by students on their first real academic safari. Other alignments might exclude history or literature altogether, a hardly pleasing prospect for humanities proponents. Students would be required to complete nine hours from science, nine from social science, and three from fine arts. Future Buena Vista graduates would also be required to register for .5 credits in ACES each semester. Majors ran the gamut from thirty-two to sixty-four hours and the minor was abandoned[31] although concentrations were available. However, such trends in General Education had been in the making for several decades and was part of a national trend in the nation's colleges and universities.

It was increasingly clear that Buena Vista now assumed that survival in modern education meant a full grasp and utilization of the rapidly changing tools of knowledge and learning. The mastery of skills took on new meaning. Libraries still reserved room for books, but computers and access to the world of the Web were a more rapid way and to some a more interesting method of acquiring information. The information-driven global society demanded new approaches to education. Moore sensibly recommended not moving radically or recklessly but carefully and judiciously. The goal of

Buena Vista as it implemented the new concepts was to become a different type of an institution, compared to large universities and traditional colleges. Our focus, said Moore, is more extended, practical, and pragmatic.[32] Buena Vista could serve as a powerful beam of light, sweeping over the restless seas of higher education.[33] It was Moore's feeling, echoing Ernest Boyer, that much of Higher Education was in danger of losing touch with the needs of the world. It was necessary, Moore asserted, to teach not just what we want but what students need to learn.[34] That, of course, would necessitate the acquisition of something more than knowledge; namely wisdom and the ability to apply it. Buena Vista would embrace the kind of pragmatic education that would make employers welcome its graduates in the constantly changing highly technical global society.[35]

At the same time Buena Vista would hopefully retain much of the spirit of the liberal arts, an essential extra for a successful career and a meaningful life. The twenty-first century graduate, if he could work it into an increasingly overcrowded schedule, would still need to have an understanding of history, philosophy, literature, and the arts. The methods of gleaning that understanding had changed somewhat and went far beyond classroom instruction.

Learning was now at a student's fingertips although it still had to reach his mind. It was apparent that the world would be open to Buena Vista students whether sitting on the campus lawn with their laptop, viewing the Holocaust concentration camp at Auschwitz, or interning with a major accounting firm during the interim. The emerging technology could be viewed as a tool that would enhance not retard the more traditional humanities and social sciences. Still the NAC applied better to some disciplines than to others.

Critics found the new program a marketing device, which could sell education as something more than cloudy theorizing. To some genuinely concerned liberal arts advocates the new approach to General Education diluted the life of the mind. Perhaps a course or two in European history might deepen the understanding and feeling when students visited the former concentration camps at Buchenwald or Auschwitz. Some through interest or happy scheduling would find their way into such classes, but large numbers would stumble onto the forces of disastrous human experience with limited background preparation. Hopefully, the liberal arts at Buena Vista would remain a viable force and not wind up on life support.[36] That, however, is a national problem.

The Buena Vista Board of Trustees was receptive to Moore's proposals and already in 1996, contributed $1 million to the New American College Venture Fund. A key component of the Venture Fund was a $465,000 gift of stock by Ken and Ira Kaplan. Ken Kaplan was a member of the Board of Trustees and the founder of the Microwave System Corporation in 1977. He was also the chair of the trustee's Institutional Advancement Committee.[37] The fund would increase money available for the professional development budget by tenfold.

Some members of the Buena Vista community felt that the institution's religious commitment had diminished during recent years. Chapel attendance was down, the very able trustee and part-time chaplain, Parse DeJong, retired in 1994, and there seemed to be less to remind more pious students of the University's Christian roots. One student vented his criticism by reminding the *Tack* in May 1996, while there were numerous pictures of Siebens around the campus, there were no pictures of Jesus or the last supper. Somehow, he could not see how Buena Vista could serve God and Siebens at the same time.[38] These sentiments were an exaggeration, but there were few volunteers at voluntary chapel. Furthermore, the institution had difficulty finding a permanent chaplain, at least one who gave promise of settling in and becoming part of the University. In September 1997, however, Buena Vista employed its first full-time chaplain, Elizabeth Clark. Clark had been a student at Denison University and Princeton, had traveled widely, and had studied the impact of religion on many cultures. Her views were ecumenical and she was very capable, but her stay was short.[39] By 1999 Buena Vista was again looking for a new chaplain.

Fortunately, the University's religious program received, during the summer of 2001, an enormous boost when Henry and Lucile Eggink left an endowment of nearly $1 million to promote student mission enhancement programs, and training or educating students in effective Christian mission service. Projects were also to be created or offered through Campus Ministry and Spiritual Life. Already, by July 2002, endowment funds had been used to support more than two dozen projects.[40] The Reverend Mr. Eggink served Buena Vista as professor of religion and philosophy for twenty-one years between 1954 and his retirement in 1975. He remained sincerely interested in the religious life of the University until his death in 2001.

Buena Vista once again endeavored to find a full-time chaplain who could reinvigorate spiritual life on campus, but all such efforts seemed short-lived. One historic requirement was that the chaplain must be a Presbyterian.[41] Finally, the University discovered the Reverend Mr. Ken Meissner, a pastor who was serving a Presbyterian Church in nearby Alta. He had earlier, in 1999, assisted the Buena Vista program on a part-time basis and had also participated in the clown ministry. Meissner accepted the position and arrived and began his efforts to revitalize the role of the chaplain, chapel programs, and Buena Vista spiritual life in early 2001. The Reverend Mr. Meissner saw his role as being accessible for the special needs, counseling, and support students may want or need while they are connected to the Buena Vista community.[42]

Buena Vista also continued to sponsor the annual Tollefson Lecture, named in honor of professor emeritus Dr. Robert Tollefson and his wife, Barbara. The lectureship was established in 1993 by the four Tollefson children in honor of their father. Dr. Charles Partee of Pittsburgh University and former Buena Vista professor of Religion and Philosophy gave the first Tollefson lecture.

One of the major achievements of the Moore Administration, and certainly an integral part of the New American College concept, was enhancing the continuing technological revolution on campus. Buena Vista was the first private college in Iowa to sign on to and use ICN, the state's fiber optic network.[43] The University remained, in 2005, the largest private user of that facility. This has enabled Buena Vista, Moore maintains, to offer courses and programs in the Centers in an efficient and effective way.[44] The latest in technology was also prominently displayed in the beautiful and functional new Information Technology Center. However, the potential of the developing technology reached new heights in the spring of 2000. President Moore in a dramatic announcement to the University community in February 2000, declared that:

> We are building the first wireless community in the nation. Our plan to install a wireless network system and give each of you your own laptop computer next Fall is regarded by other universities as a significant leap in the field of education. And without a doubt it is an innovation which will make Buena Vista University Graduates stand out to employers.[45]

The first computer to be used in the new wireless technology would be Gateway Solo 2550 Laptop. The Gateway possessed a 13.3-inch screen, Intel Celeron 550 MHz processor, 96 megabytes of RAM, 6 gigabytes hard drive, CD drive, and floppy disc drive. The laptops, of course, would be continuously upgraded. Buena Vista had reached the "cutting edge of technology." It was becoming increasingly evident that survival in the future workplace meant being familiar with the latest technology. It also might mean, as *Storm Lake Times* reporter and Buena Vista graduate Keith Madsen noted, "You can do more work for your employer—at home."[46]

This new, innovative program would be known as eBVyou and would attract national attention. The laptops would be included, perhaps somewhat clandestinely, in the price of tuition. But it would be worth the extra cost. Students were informed that possessing their own laptops meant they would no longer have to wait their turn at a computer in the lab. There "would be no more long files during network downtime."

Furthermore, the new laptops under the program eBVyou could "access all learning resources of the campus internet and world wide web from any place on campus." The small computers could be easily carried on one's shoulder in a backpack. Furthermore more than 1,375 laptops would be replaced every two years as the computers were continuously updated. It was another triumph for the small Northwest Iowa University that had also been the first to place a desktop computer on every faculty member's desk as well as being the first private institution of higher learning in the state to participate in Iowa's fiber optic network.[47] Indeed, Buena Vista, no matter how short-lived the triumph, did become the first totally wireless campus in the nation. Others, of course, would

follow. The challenge would be to maintain the edge. Advertise-
ments quickly sailed through various media outlets.

A Cedar Rapids advertising firm, Stamants Communications
Inc., hit upon using Dr. Seuss characters in publicizing the Buena
Vista triumph in technology. The ads featured Dr. Seuss characters
proclaiming, "Would you, could you by the lake?" These ads appeared on billboards in major communities like Omaha, Cedar
Rapids, Council Bluffs, and Des Moines. "Would you, could you
by the lake," meant that the new wireless technology could be utilized anywhere. As the Director of Communication Services, Ken
Clipperton, noted it meant "not simply anywhere, anytime, but
everywhere all the time."[48]

Nevertheless, the ads were not totally appreciated. While some
Buena Vista students and faculty were supportive of the ads, others
were not amused. The ads appearing on large billboards in shop-
ping malls were, it was argued, too wacky and had too much of an
aura of silliness about them. One ad that attracted attention was
"Would you, could you in the john?" No doubt they could but
would they? Critics did not only find this an unsatisfactory depic-
tion of the academic work ethic, but a challenge to their dignity. It
did not, they argued, capture the "heart and soul of Buena Vista,"
and they endeavored to persuade the University CEO that their view
had merit.[49] Supporters, and there were many, believed the ads not
only alerted prospective students of the existence of the wireless
community, but that Buena Vista had a sense of humor. President
Moore did not feel the ads were demeaning and believed that they
had interested a number of teenagers who were beginning to think
about college. Although the ads were eventually removed, there was
considerable feeling that they had been successful.[50] Buena Vista, of
course, realized that being the first wireless campus in the nation
would be short-lived. Other institutions across the nation were ob-
serving, and some sent representatives to campus. However, Buena
Vista sought to make the most of a brief "window of opportunity."
They had for the moment, Professor and Director of Teaching and
Learning with Technology Paul Bowers observed, a "competitive
edge." Buena Vista students would now receive the "skills needed
for the digital age."[51]

The new approach of merging technology and learning was not only innovative but daring. Buena Vista was well staffed to move into the arena of wireless communication. The new library ably headed by Jim Kennedy already possessed the latest in technology. Professors Paul Bowers and Ken Schweller had established reputations as leading experts in the area of computer science. Bowers, who had served Buena Vista for sixteen years as a Professor of Mass Communications, now became full-time Director of Faculty Development of Distance Learning.[52] Schweller, a professor with a versatile almost renaissance mind, had been on the Buena Vista faculty for more than two decades starting out in the field of psychology, but finding a more compelling interest in computer science.

As early as the mid-1990s the brilliant Schweller had created a virtual academic community in cyberspace known as College Town. This program enabled users all over the world to communicate simultaneously. It was a virtual academic community that was modeled on the real Buena Vista. During the 1996 interim Schweller's class held plays and poetry readings in College Town and were joined by students from other institutions. There were even a few participants from abroad.[53]

By 2001 Schweller with the assistance of his Java Programming class had designed a cyber feedback tool. Students could attract the professor's attention by clicking on a screen with illustrated areas designated as "Swamp of Confusion, Daydreaming, Solid Ground, Boredom City, or Heights of Enlightenment." One student had the habit of clicking in, "I need an aspirin." This type of program appealed not only to "devilish students," but to students accustomed to playing computer games. It also provided a way out for those students who were shy or feared they might be asking a stupid question.[54]

Buena Vista's rapid movement into the latest state-of-the-art technology quickly attracted a number of bright and eager students. These students were anxious to take advantage of the opportunity made available by the expansion and development of the new technology along with the excellent instruction provided by Buena Vista professors. Some students had even been involved in the installation of the wireless infrastructure.[55]

Buena Vista students led by their mentors, physics professor Sean Stone, and Schweller conducted a successful experiment in the construction of a robot, which they named RED PLANET ROVER. The machine was designed to resemble the robot used for exploration on Mars. Funds for the experiment were provided by Harry Stine of Midwest Oilseeds in Adel, Iowa. Among its purposes was to acquaint the showcase wireless technology to middle school students attending a science camp on the Buena Vista campus during the summer months. A digital camera on the robot could take one picture per second, which it beamed back to the laptop. The miniature robot was able to move twelve feet per minute and was as Schweller remarked, "hardly a greyhound." While it could not, as their creators joked, mow the lawn or haul out the trash, it could pick up small objects. It was operated by indirect commands on a laptop computer.[56]

Professors were left with the freedom to decide on how and whether to use the new technology. Buena Vista encouraged but did not mandate the use of the new technology. There continued, however, an energetic effort to mobilize faculty and students in bringing about a "smooth implementation" of the new and changing techniques in higher education. Some faculty members, originally skeptical, quickly became convinced of the possibilities of the new technology. Training programs for faculty, administration, and students were also provided. The Moore Administration did considerable planning with faculty in respect to technology. President Moore wanted to be certain that "faculty were adequately supportive" of the emerging technology.[57]

One convert was Dr. Michael Whitlatch, Professor of Theatre, who had been at Buena Vista for nearly three decades. Whitlatch quickly discovered how the new technology could enhance his classroom lectures and discussion with the use of electronic slides. Course syllabi could be placed online. Broadway review of plays could be followed. As Director of Teaching and Learning, Paul Bowers explained that eBVyou expanded student access to materials, provided more introverted students an alternative way to participate, and improved general communication. One English professor remarked, "teaching writing without using a computer would be like teaching piano without a piano."[58]

Both faculty and students could see that the wireless communication placed the globe at their doorstep. It broadened the arena of research for faculty and students as well as enhancing communication between student and professor. The new technology acquainted students with new methods of research. It was, indeed, a valuable tool, which their University was determined to exploit. Wireless communication changed the scope of learning and no doubt would continue to do so as the twenty-first century progressed.

Still there were problems especially evident to professors in the social sciences and humanities. Students doing research had the tendency to bypass books, periodicals, and documents as they relied primarily upon what they could glean from the Internet. For students trained on computers it was easy to ignore the more traditional but still pertinent tools of research. Furthermore, they often did not know how to evaluate Internet sources nor were they always interested in learning—although faculty endeavored to school them on proper use of sources. To make matters worse, some faculty found that eBVyou contributed to the number of plagiarism cases. It became too easy to find material, "download it, put their name on it, and turn it in."[59]

There also developed a tendency for students to communicate with their professors via e-mail rather than one on one. E-mail communication was more impersonal, and occasionally a student would use it to vent frustration in a manner they would not dare use in a professor's office. Should the laptops be permitted in class? Certainly, the laptops might be an asset in note taking and no doubt more complete than those tools of scholarly antiquity—paper and pen.

Unfortunately, a number of students used their wireless devices to play Internet games, shop, send instant messages and e-mails, or surf the Internet. Irritated professors sometimes took extreme measures and banned the laptops from the classroom. As the use of laptops increased across the nation, professors from other campuses reported similar problems.

These problems would have to be resolved if the efficiency and potential of the laptops was to be fully realized. No matter what the roadblocks, the clock of progress continued to move forward. Education in the twenty-first century would be vastly different than in the twentieth. Challenge in academia, perhaps more so than in most places, is eternal. In 2005 the University announced that it was "leveraging technology to broaden Web-based instructional programs and forge ahead with integrated campus communication."

President Moore along with administrative and faculty leaders no doubt correctly insisted that technology improved learning. Universal access to the latest technology could (1) address different learning styles, (2) provide everyone being on the network with a real campus community "in virtual interactions as well as face-to-face," (3) provide access all the time meaning no waiting for students—and, as Moore mused, "in our society that's important."[60] It was also possible for classes to become virtually paperless.

Buena Vista was also preparing to "launch over the next five years, several fully Web-based programs at the undergraduate and graduate levels." Buena Vista was also exploring "wireless voice convergence," which would "enable individuals using a single instrument to receive calls through the network in areas without cell service." Media Studies faculty were prepared to explore a move to HDTV in TV product facilities. This would enable "students to create, edit, store and broadcast digital media."[61]

There was no way that Buena Vista would be willing to relinquish leadership in the area of wireless communication. The University was, President Moore insisted, "an institution that's on the move all the time. We are constantly reinventing ourselves."[62] The revolution in technology taking place on the Buena Vista campus was one of the great successes of the Moore Administration. The emphasis would be on quality. The technology would "enhance the learning and living environment of students."[63] Paul Bowers, Director of Technology and Learning, also insisted that the emphasis of the new technology was "upon teaching and learning," and that technology was "always a servant, not a master."[64] In August 2005 the Higher Learning Commission of the North Central Association of Colleges and Schools approved Buena Vista's online delivery of degree programs in addition to the University's Master Education degree designation for graduate programs in education. An online program for the Bachelor of Arts in business administration was also available.

It was during the first year of the Moore Administration that the new university Information Technology Center (library) was completed. The new underground facility had been conceived and planned during the waning days of the Briscoe administration. It was a must if Buena Vista was to gain the necessary space and technology required for university status. Groundbreaking ceremonies had been held in May 1994, and a jar of on-the-site dirt was collected "to serve as a token of history." Jim Kennedy, the technologically brilliant head of library facilities, was no doubt tired of being cooped up in the small Ballou Library. Kennedy, excited by the expansive plans, could see rising from the ground "a library of vision, a library of the future."[65] It was this vision that had attracted him to Buena Vista in 1990.

Keith Briscoe, of course, retired in the spring of 1995 and it was left for the Moore Administration to complete the task. For quite some time the proposed state-of-the-art library moved slowly. Its debut was set for January 1996, and by Moore's inaugural in April that year the new Ballou Library was finally ready for business. It was no longer a library with essentially books and periodicals, but an Information Technology Center with a national and global reach. Some 50,000 square feet had been added to the original 20,000 square feet of the existing library. The cost approached $20 million compared to $330,000 for the original structure.[66] By 2004 the Ballou ITC possessed 161,000 volumes and 916 print periodical titles. The library also had a chat-based reference service, "Ask Us Online." There existed desktop computers and wireless access for laptop users along with multiple other services. In addition to in-house periodicals more than 3,000 database journals were available. Library head, Jim Kennedy, cited the advantage of having databases rather than other types of learning materials. He insisted that if "two people check out a book, that book may circulate only twice a semester." The new underground ITC had spacious seating for 400, was beautifully carpeted, had readily available computers, was well staffed, and was one of the academic wonders of the region. There wasn't much it could not access.

In less than a century the Buena Vista library had moved from a meager room in old Smith Hall, to a dingy World War II barracks, to a beautiful but small building constructed in 1965, and finally to a modern and magnificent underground structure. It was an impressive achievement and a long way from the confining army barracks with a closed shelf system that had served as the college library only three decades before.

Building a modern campus would be one of the defining features of not only the Briscoe Era but even more so during the Moore Administration. The new IFTC edifice and the Harold Walter Siebens Forum were both part of a massive underground building complex causing the *New York Times* to exclaim that their reporter had witnessed "an academic wonderland."[67] However, the completion of the Ballou Library was only the beginning.

Edson Hall, left in a state of decay following the building of the Siebens Field House, but once the scene of Jim Kelly basketball triumphs in the early 1920s, was in 1996 and 1997, refurbished into a modern music hall. The major donor for this project was Dr. Frederick Stark, a retired neurologist and psychiatrist from Sioux City.[68] Edson Hall could now boast of state-of-the-art practice rooms, a new separate rehearsal area for choral and instrumental groups, a piano lab with electric keyboards, a piano teaching studio, and a student work area. New practice rooms could also "reproduce acoustics of major concert halls or cathedrals."[69] Although Edson Hall (once Victory Hall) would no longer reverberate with the throaty voices of athletic triumph, the sounds of music would henceforth cast a more permanent spell upon those who ventured inside. Schaller Chapel also underwent a $500,000 cosmetic treatment in 1999 and 2000. The lighting system was upgraded and a new steeple and steeple roof were added. Although 50 seats were removed the chapel could still seat 820 patrons.[70] It remained the site of the afternoon American Heritage Lecture Series.

Since 1991 Buena Vista has built new and remodeled old housing units. Briscoe Honor Hall, completed in 1991, was a co-ed dormitory housing 102 students. Originally named Centennial Hall it was renamed Briscoe Hall in honor of the former president. Other modern dormitory units were Constitution Hall (1995), McCorkle Hall (1996), Grand Hall (1998), and Liberty Hall (2002). Meanwhile, in 1992–93 Pierce-White Hall was renovated by installing new windows, new heating and plumbing, carpeting, and lighting. Buena Vista now had attractive new housing structures conducive for twenty-first century student living.[71]

One of the most significant construction efforts in Buena Vista's lengthening history was completed in 2001. This was the $9.5 million Lamberti Recreation Center named after then president of the Board of Trustees, Donald Lamberti. Don Lamberti had been a Buena Vista Trustee since 1993 and in 1996 became president of the Board. He would serve in that capacity until replaced by Jim Haahr in 2001. During his presidency Lamberti personally recruited nine trustees to the University Board.[72] Lamberti had grown up poor in a "tough neighborhood" on the north side of Des Moines. His father was an Italian immigrant who arrived in the United States at the age of 16 working in the coal mines in the winter and as a gardener during the summer. Eventually, he established a store that became Casey's General Store and which was sold to Don in 1968. Under the direction of Donald Lamberti, Casey's mushroomed into a $1.5 billion annual business with 11,000 employees in nine states. Lamberti became interested in the College following an invitation to give an on-campus speech to business students.

During his visit to Buena Vista, Lamberti managed to stay awake through the labyrinths of a Keith Briscoe speech. After missing a meeting of the Trustees, he discovered that he had been elected president of the Board.[73] Lamberti proved to be an alert and aggressive Board CEO. He was the major donor (more than $3 million)[74] for the new construction, which would consist of more than 50,000 square feet. The Recreation Center contained three multipurpose courts, and a six-lane 200-meter indoor track named in honor of long-time trustee, important donor, and Buena Vista graduate, Dennis Young.[75] Buena Vista had long emphasized healthy diets, sensible exercise, and physical fitness programs. It now had the facilities to make that possible for the entire Buena Vista community. Even President Moore found himself jogging 30–35 miles a week—a feat that enabled him to shed more than 40 pounds, reaching a lean and trim weight level that enabled him to meet the stress involved in a modern university presidency.[76]

Most members of the Buena Vista community were accustomed to thinking of the 1968 Estelle Siebens Science Center as a well-equipped, functional, and modern building. There was certainly no comparison between this attractive 1960s edifice and the acrid-smelling Smith Hall, where the venerable "Bugs" Smith had once taught, conducted his research, and popped skeletons out of closets to the delight of his students. The building named in Smith's honor had served as the College monument to science from 1927–68. The new science building constructed in 1968 had represented a step into the modern era while Smith Hall was remodeled to house the School of Education. Furthermore, the 1968 structure had a good-sized auditorium that served as a gathering place for numerous college events. In the early 1980s the science center was named in honor of Harold Siebens's wife, Estelle. However, by the mid-1990s, the science department and science students realized the Estelle Siebens Center was approaching obsolescence for scientific study and research. In 1995 a new science center had been "identified as a critical need."[77]

A new science edifice would be an expensive undertaking. Necessity dictated that plans and strategy be outlined, fund-raising plotted, the possible attempted. In early 2002 the dreams of the planners took on the aura of reality when a "secret" donor (sometimes referred to as Dr. Anonymous) offered a challenge gift of $13 million. Challenge meant Buena Vista would have to raise an additional $13 million by September 30, 2002, or forfeit the gift.[78] Furthermore, ground would have to be broken within sixty days of completing the fund-raising campaign. The challenge was quickly accepted, and Buena Vista embarked upon the most costly venture of its 100-year history. The new building would encompass more than 70,000 square feet and be located just west of the current Estelle Siebens Science Center. The new two-story building would be "flanked with massive arched windows," thus maintaining the "arch" architecture theme of the campus.[79]

Seven classrooms, eighteen labs, research, and informal study areas plus twenty-four new offices would be added. Construction costs were estimated at $18 million with an $8 million endowment for future operating purposes. The firm BWRB of St. Paul designed the project. The major scientific fields of biology, chemistry, computer science, and physics would now be in one building, "fostering collaboration among these disciplines as well as between students and faculty." Dr. Ken Schweller, dean of the School of Science, proudly asserted that "students need a place to practice being scientists."[80] They would now have such a place—constructed with such a magnificence not yet seen in the history of the emerging university. All could agree that the official opening of the exciting new structure marked a historic day in the life of Buena Vista. As VPAA Karen Halbersleben announced, Buena Vista would now become the "hub of scientific efforts for the entire region."[81]

September 17, 2004, was set as the day of dedication of the new Estelle Siebens Science Center. Many Storm Lakers braved threatening weather to attend the events. Although Estelle Siebens was unable to attend, many of the grandchildren of Harold and Estelle were present for the event, which would mark the official opening of the state-of-the-art building. Archie McKay of Aurelia, a performer at nearly every Buena Vista commencement and numerous special events since the 1970s, arrived dressed in his usual kilts, sash, and glengarry hat and carrying his bagpipes. There were commemorative speeches, colorful streamers, and "explosions of confetti."[82] The same expectation, the same excitement and hope for the future was in the air that existed when the completion of "Old Main" had been celebrated in 1891 or during the opening of the Siebens Forum in 1985. The completion of the magnificent building expected to serve the science needs of the University for the next thirty years was high on the list of monumental events in the University's history. The future had arrived. It had been achieved in large part due to the generosity of the Siebens family. As Art Cullen, editor of the *Storm Lake Times* wrote, "Buena Vista might not even be open were it not for the Siebens family." After all, historic colleges like Westmar and Marycrest had folded. Cullen further mused, "Imagine Storm Lake without Buena Vista and imagine Buena Vista without the Siebens.'"[83]

Dr. Stephen Russell from the Mayo Clinic, a noted cancer researcher, gave a major address in Anderson Auditorium. When President Moore spoke he referred to the new building as "a breathtaking venue for learning." A Buena Vista student remarked, "This building makes you want to go to class."[84] Dr. Jacqueline Johnson, recently appointed Vice President for Academic Affairs, observed that "science is as much about creativity and imagination as it is about fact and knowledge." She hoped that students would experience science as "poetry in motion."[85]

However, the original Estelle Siebens Science Center was not pronounced dead. The 1969 building, which some old timers still thought of as "new," was sound, attractive, and functional. It could serve Buena Vista in some capacity for a long time. The university plan was to renovate the structure for nonscience disciplines and to fulfill office needs for a growing faculty. Social Science, some areas of the Humanities and Education were three disciplines scheduled to benefit.

Nor would President Moore be satisfied with the massive building program that had already taken place during the first decade of his administration. That decade witnessed the completion of the new Information Technology Center, considerable renovation of Schaller Chapel and new residence halls, and the construction of the Lamberti Recreation Center as well as the Science Center. Next on the planning board would be a new Student Center. University leaders and students were already, during 2004, visiting various campuses, plotting architectural designs and possible location. A Student Center would relieve some of the pressure on the Forum and could be used for various activities and social functions.[86]

It was, however, recognized that following the monumental effort put forth in making the Estelle Siebens Science Center a reality, Buena Vista's local and outlying supporters needed a break. The Siebens family had contributed $13 million, but some 450 donors had raised an additional $13 million. As always, the Storm Lake community had responded to a challenge. They would no doubt be willing again, for Buena Vista had become the prize symbol of the city.

On September 11, 2001, the Buena Vista community felt the same jolt as the rest of the nation when three hijacked planes manned by Al-Qaida terrorists smashed into the World Trade Center and the Pentagon. More than 3,000 people, most of them

Americans, met death from the ensuing inferno. The incident permanently warped the calm confidence that followed the downfall of communism and the end of the Cold War. The nation was stunned—American casualties on American soil. The world, it appeared had not, after all, become a better or safer place.

Fred and Susan Moore, like millions of Americans, watched in total disbelief as the horror unfolded on television.[87] They knew the tragedy might impact morale, alter plans, and no doubt change lives. Moore quickly addressed the Buena Vista community insisting, "language does not allow for adequate expression of our reaction to this kind of evil."[88] Senior student, Luke Fast, organized a vigil and special prayer session at the Arch, which several hundred students attended. Five Buena Vista students had internships in Washington not far from the Pentagon. The political atmosphere across the globe was forever changed. But as President Moore insisted, "we are wounded, but we will recover."[89]

An immediate consequence of 9/11 would be the status of overseas programs and travel abroad during the interim. It was painful, but deemed necessary to immediately cancel six proposed trips to Ireland, Australia, Hawaii, Costa Rica, Europe, and England. A concerned Vice President for Academic Affairs, Karen Halbersleben, informed disappointed students and faculty that, "I want our students and faculty to be in a location where we can get them home if the situation worsens and planes are once again grounded."[90]

Nine/eleven ushered in a New Era as the American response included not only increased home security, but an expanding global front in the War against Terror. First the United States crushed the autocratic, fundamentalist Taliban in Afghanistan and then expanded the war into Iraq where Saddam Hussein was alleged to be harboring Weapons of Mass Destruction—an assumption that was questioned by many and later proved to be false. Several Buena Vista students were in the reserves and would be called into service. Many wondered what impact the war would have on their future. It also had an almost immediate impact on at least one faculty member. Professor Houston Polson, Dean of the Harold Walter Siebens School of Business and Professor of Business, was asked to report for military duty in December 2003. Polson, who held the rank of Lieutenant Colonel would be located at Sarajevo in Bosnia where he would serve for six months as Military Advisor to the Commander of Stabilization Forces.[91] Polson would return, but the son of a Buena Vista employee in the food service was to die tragically in Afghanistan in 2004.

The post-9/11 tragedy also had an impact upon financial markets. Buena Vista's endowment, which had reached $124 million, sank to $74 million before recovery brought it back over the $100 million mark. The short-term decline in interest rates also made effective stewardship imperative. Moore, however, felt pleased that Buena Vista was able to steer through the crisis without having to curtail programs for students.[92]

One of the most significant achievements of President Moore was his determined effort to promote diversity on the Buena Vista campus. Buena Vista remained somewhat indifferent to the benefits of campus diversity throughout most of the first century of its existence. As late as 1992, the always aggressive and progressive *Tack* charged that the administration was "oblivious to the vulgar racism that dominates the campus." The *Tack* editorial board recommended the hiring of a minority recruiter and a concerted effort to make minority students want to stay at Buena Vista. Otherwise, the institution would continue to "pump ignorant graduates into the work world."[93] This was strong language, which could not be ignored.

There had, of course, been attempts to acquaint Buena Vista students (still overwhelmingly white and from small towns in western Iowa) to the realities of the wider world. A handful of African-American students had enrolled since the 1960s, and an international program was created to promote faculty and student exchanges with Taiwan, China, and Japan. Asian languages were introduced on campus, and courses in African-American history, African-American literature, and the history of India, China, and Japan were taught. However, the retention rate of racially and ethnically diverse students was unsatisfactory. Such students often felt unwelcome or out of place in the community and isolated on campus. Julia Keehner, Vice President for Student Services, who arrived on campus in 1996, recalled that she would never forget one student who "told me that when he arrived on our campus, he had never felt so black."[94] A Japanese student discovered that, while there were classmates who were friendly, some students would not sit by him in class and others did not speak to him. He felt stared at when downtown and was surprised at the general indifference toward other countries and cultures.[95] These were problems that Buena Vista would take seriously and work hard to address during the early years of the twenty-first century.

Gay students may have felt the most and angriest discrimination. National Coming Out Week in 1995 resulted in numerous expressions of intolerance. These included uncomplimentary, occasionally vulgar chalkings and some vandalism across the campus. Andy Offenburger, a BV student and son of "Iowa Boy," felt that unless this type of intolerance was confronted it would weaken the acceptance of both ethnic and gender differences on campus.[96] A significant number of Buena Vista students, it seemed, were unfamiliar with other cultures and hesitant to bridge the gap.

Still, an effort to lift the albatross of indifference was already visible as early as the fall of 1992 when the largest number of international students in school history enrolled. There were now at least thirty such students, eight of them from Taiwan. Some of the students spoke little English and found American customs interesting but often difficult to comprehend. The only available mass transit in Northwest Iowa was the automobile, the holidays were totally different, and nowhere else in the world did students dare call professors by their first names.[97] Nevertheless, some international students managed to bridge the gap. Megumi Fukami arrived from Japan in 1993 feeling very nervous. During her first year at Buena Vista she recalled that she felt like a "Japan student." By her third year she could finally say, "I am a student at Buena Vista."[98]

However, integrating the campus would prove almost as difficult as integrating the community. Since the 1970s, Storm Lake had reeled from the influx of Vietnamese and Hispanic immigrants who arrived to work at the Iowa Beef meat packing plant, which established roots in 1982. This had an enormous impact upon the Storm Lake school system, and by the early years of the twenty-first century, more than 40 percent of the city's schools consisted of ethnics.

Their cultures were bound to clash with that of the traditional conservative, white, affluent majority. Daniel Boscaljon in a letter to
the *Tack* editorial page remarked, "Iowa has always been an Aryan
heaven, but now it is being threatened."[99] Resulting tensions eventually brought forth critical and unwelcome articles in *U.S. News &
World Report* and the progressive magazine, *The Nation.* The articles noted, perhaps with slight exaggeration, the problems of immigrant workers, their poor housing conditions, low wages, and discrimination. There was some increase in crime and even several
murders. There were, in 1997 more than 600 mostly Vietnamese
and Hispanic workers living in the city. Twenty-five years earlier
there had been 25.[100] It was increasingly evident that the College
and community would need to grow together. Dr. Sandra Madsen,
professor of Speech and Communication and never known for
timidity, was elected mayor and served for several years in the
1990s. Her administration was instrumental in improving ethnic relations in Storm Lake as well as in promoting cooperation between
university and community. She worked closely and successfully
with city leaders and the Chief of Police.

Furthermore, diversity on campus would mean more than recruiting international students. It meant extending equality to
women, to the gay community, to African-Americans, to Asians,
and to Hispanics. President Moore was hardly on campus when a
football recruit left the team because of what he interpreted as a
racial slur. The persistence of racial and gender slurs posted across
the campus was of concern to Buena Vista faculty and administration. This attitude led President Moore to ask, "What is the depth
of our problem? How should we work to solve it?"

At the same time, the Buena Vista president realized problems
could not be solved with an "80 yard bomb." Progress would more
likely be achieved in former Ohio State football coach Woody
Hayes' terminology, "three yards and a cloud of dust." This approach might be slower, Moore acknowledged, but more effective.[101]
In any case, Fred Moore was determined that Buena Vista address
the question of diversity. Already in his inaugural address the new
president stated the necessity for such a program. "A community of
scholars," he told his audience, "invites differing backgrounds, cul-

tures and points of view." Moore also recognized that it was to the benefit of Buena Vista to implement a program that reflected the cultural shift that was transpiring in American society. Moore's early and certainly significant step was the creation of a Diversity Task Force in 1998. The purpose of the Task Force was to "identify and address intercultural issues on campus."[102]

A long recommended and dramatic breakthrough came in 2000 when the University reached out and hired a young African American, Leon Williams, as its first director of intercultural programs. The new director would be involved in recruiting, building new programs, and developing student support organizations. He would have to be able to "connect" with students and faculty. He would be responsible for building something Buena Vista had not yet quite attained for people of color, "a hospitable and welcoming environment."[103]

Williams spent his youth in the "tough inner city" of Youngstown, Ohio. This did not stop him from obtaining a bachelor's degree in management from Ohio Northern and a master's in counseling from the University of Dayton. It also provided him with a background and understanding that would enhance his future career. Still, could he create a successful program at a small traditionally homogenous school in Northwest Iowa? It was possible, friends informed him, that "he did not realize what he was getting into," when he accepted the position as director of multicultural affairs at Buena Vista. Williams, however, liked a challenge and felt confident that he could build a successful program. "I wanted," he said,

> To teach people why we struggle with race relations, and that's because of the history. The history has not provided us with a fair start, so our minds are corrupt, and the less we know about each other keeps us segregated. So the more we teach the more we know about others, and the closer we become. If I can help people understand diversity a little better and challenge people while I'm here, then I've been successful.[104]

The Buena Vista Diversity Program that Williams devised was meant to be inclusive. That meant including not only students of color, but all students. Williams felt diversity programs sometimes failed because the programs did not "allow mainstream white stu-

dents to be involved."[105] Meanwhile, numerous intercultural clubs
came into existence on campus, including Women of Color,
African-American Student Union, Student Organization of Latinos,
Voices of Praise Choir, Asian-American Alliance, Multicultural
Club, International Club, and Time Out (gay, lesbian, bisexual,
transgender, and straight alliance).

Special events were sponsored throughout the year such as
National Latino Heritage Month, Chinese New Year, Kwanza,
Black History Month, Martin Luther King birthday, Asian Awareness Month, Women's Month, Fiesta Latina, and Pride Week. There
would soon be more than fifty cultural education programs at
Buena Vista. It was Williams' goal to bring people of all colors (including white) and lifestyles together. Some students saw a real advantage to the new multicultural emphasis at Buena Vista. Freshman Ben Stevenson arrived with a strong interest in Japanese
culture. His first day on campus led to a meeting with Yuji Ishihara.
The two quickly became good friends and roommates. Stevenson
and Ishihara worked to acquaint each other with the language and
culture of their native countries. Stevenson felt the experience
would assist in putting him "in the business position I want to be in
someday." Like many Asian students, Ishihara discovered the "common style" as his "biggest shock."[106]

Leon Williams also sponsored a Spring Break trip to South
Carolina in order to "connect with people who are direct descen-
dants of slaves." There would also be a trip to Alabama for the purpose of exploring the history of the civil rights movement. Williams
participated in college fairs in Omaha, St. Louis, Kansas City, and
Chicago as well as in Iowa and neighboring states. Buena Vista
now offered four substantial multicultural scholarships, with two of
them reserved for Storm Lake residents. One key program instituted
by Williams—the cultural leadership conference—provided high
school students the opportunity to visit the Buena Vista campus.
Through his efforts the level of diversity on campus moved toward
5 percent.[107]

By the fall of 2003 Williams had recruited 30 more minority
students, boosting the total to 77. One Buena Vista student remarked, "I am amazed and thrilled at how much more diversity

Buena Vista University has this year than in the past few."[108] During the academic year 1999–2000 there had been seven incidents of racism reported to the Office of Student Services.[109] Furthermore, racially motivated incidents were nonexistent during the 2003–04 academic year.[110] Buena Vista was making enormous strides and had managed to avoid some of the ethnic and racial ugliness that had occurred on other campuses.

Leon Williams also demonstrated that he was not only an able organizer and leader, but something of an artist. He developed an original monologue entitled, "The Only Life I know," which he presented to an audience in Anderson Auditorium. The 90-minute performance demonstrated to those in attendance "how African-Americans have survived from past to present." He also sang songs dating from the Harlem Renaissance.[111]

No matter how successful, recruitment of students and expanding programs would not, in the long run, be enough. Williams recognized the necessity of Buena Vista addressing the issue of limited diversity of faculty and staff and the need for developing ethnic and urban studies majors. Prior to Williams the only African-American faculty or staff member to be employed at Buena Vista was Professor Bill Hervey who served briefly as assistant professor of political science in the late 1980s. However, Buena Vista has achieved much through the efforts of Leon Williams. Students of diversity were now making important contributions to the campus. As Professor Whitlatch asserted, "I think Leon has done a terrific job. For the first time in years we've been able to put African Americans in our college shows or as in the case of *The Laramie Project* have them serve as the Stage Manager."[112] At Buena Vista racial, ethnic, and cultural appreciation was winning out over intolerance.

Buena Vista, during the Briscoe and Moore presidencies, increasingly contributed to the cultural life of Western Iowa. A stellar service was rendered by sponsoring the American Heritage Lecture Series founded in 1989 by Harold W. Siebens. Siebens' money provided the endowment to bring national and world leaders to the campus. The series was named in honor of his son, William Siebens. Justice Blackmun, presidents Jimmy Carter and George H. W. Bush, British Prime Minister Margaret Thatcher, newspaper

and television magnate Michael Gartner, Secretary of State Colin
Powell, scientist Carl Sagan, economist John M. Templeton, former
Pakistan president Benzai Bhutto, and journalists Walter Cronkite,
David Gergen, and John Major were among the guests who spoke
at the afternoon session reserved for students and university friends
and an evening banquet attended primarily by large donors and
trustees. Sharp questions welcomed from student panelists and audiences brought seasoned and enlightened answers.

There were occasional criticisms of invited lecturers. This was
particularly true when F. W. de Klerk, the former South African
premier, made his appearance. De Klerk had released Nelson
Mandela from prison and worked with him to end apartheid. De
Klerk and Mandela had shared the 1993 Nobel Prize and came to
Buena Vista in October 1996 as AHLS lecturer.

Professor Laura Inglis, seldom reluctant to provoke a challenge, failed to find in de Klerk the "powerful, courageous, even
noble," world leader deserving of the Nobel Prize. As far as Inglis
was concerned, de Klerk was "one of the bad guys" who "rose to
power supporting racism," and who changed only because of a devastated economy and fear of civil strife.[113]

Professor Inglis may have been largely correct in her assessment of de Klerk. After all he had been among those who tolerated
Mandela's imprisonment for 27 years and seemed to have few
pricks of conscience during that long period. Certainly, Inglis's
protests sparked heated discussion, along with some serious
thought, which was not incompatible with the purpose of the series.

As for de Klerk, he seemed to have genuinely realized that
apartheid had been a monumental evil and that no society could call
itself "civilized" while tolerating racial intolerance. During his lecture he stressed the necessity of reconciliation and the importance
of cultural diversity. Negotiators, he felt, must take risks and think
creatively. He believed that seemingly intractable problems could
be resolved through negotiations. There, must be, he asserted, win-
win outcomes. "We've got to," he said, "create room and space for
a diverse society. You have got to breed a culture of tolerance and
pride."[114]

Nor did sometimes petulant though often brilliant Margaret

Thatcher please all elements on campus when she appeared as AHLS lecturer in 1993. One student remarked that she now understood why the American Revolution had been fought. Others found Thatcher's worldview more pleasing.

Certainly, the AHLS attracted regional and national attention. It brought to Buena Vista a variety of recognized world leaders in politics, journalism, science, and economics. The lecture series remains nonpartisan in its composition. It seeks to enlighten rather than indoctrinate. It became, perhaps, the most significant event of the campus each year. The University now offered lectures and first-hand contact with former presidents, journalists, and scientists. Buena Vista graduates will fondly recall having seen, met, and conversed with Carl Sagan, Jimmy Carter, George H. W. Bush, or Walter Cronkite. As President Moore remarked, "the series demonstrates to the world the dangers of viewing freedom from a limited viewpoint. It attacks the naiveté of us all by serving as a spectacular reminder that the loss of one freedom diminishes all others."[115] David Gergen, editor-at-large of *U.S. News & World Report*, and the 2004 American Heritage guest more than echoed Moore's remarks when he reminded his audience that "what we do as Americans over the next 30 years while we're so powerful, how you lead this country in your generation, is going to shape the world for the next 2,000 years."[116] This rather sober statement made clear the essence of the lecture series, which bore the Siebens name. It came as the critical presidential election of 2004 approached.

Part of the success of the total Buena Vista program and its new status as a university can be traced to the growth of the Centers. The first Center, of course, was the one founded in 1975 at Fort Dodge. By 2005 the number of Centers had grown to an astonishing eleven on seventeen sites. The Center locations stretched from Ottumwa and Creston to Council Bluffs and Le Mars to Mason City and Marshalltown.

There were, of course, concerns about adequate staffing, available library facilities, governance, and control. By 2000 external responsibility for the Centers were concentrated in the hands of a full-time Associate Vice President of External Programs and Marketing or Dean of the Centers. Dr. Janet Stremel occupied that

position. Each Center had an individual director. A Center representative does serve on the Buena Vista Faculty Senate. There was also
supporting staff. Storm Lake faculty maintained only minimal control, but the Senate approved new programs. Faculty members from
the Storm Lake campus, unlike in the early years, only rarely taught
at the Centers. This necessitated a concentrated effort to recruit capable teachers and to acquaint faculty members on the main campus with their counterparts now spread across the state. Many of the
professors have been highly qualified individuals living in the area
of the Centers where they taught. A 2000 study indicated that 25
percent of the Center faculty had terminal degrees in their fields
while 71 percent possessed nonterminal Master's degrees. Sixty-
two percent of Center faculty had been employed as Center faculty
for more than two years and 22 percent for more than ten years.[117]

Also use of the statewide fiber optic system and Internet services provided important technological support. This has facilitated
use of Buena Vista resources plus instruction and advising. Training
sessions helped acquaint Center faculty with the use of available
technology. During the three decades since the first Center began
operation at Fort Dodge, more than 8,000 students have obtained
Buena Vista degrees from the Centers. It is indisputable that the
Centers have established themselves as a vital part of the total
Buena Vista program providing not only expanding opportunities
for education, but spreading knowledge about Buena Vista
University across the state. Furthermore, 82 percent of Center graduates remain in the State of Iowa.[118] Center students tend to be con-
siderably older than those on the home campus in Storm Lake.
They are seeking a Buena Vista degree by completing their final
two years under the Buena Vista satellite program.

Naturally, students found the Centers lacking in student social
life, absent athletic teams, and without special programs. These
adornments were not deemed necessary by nontraditional students
who find the lower cost of education appealing and who are intent
upon obtaining their degrees. Outstanding Center teachers have
been honored. In 2001 Mark S. Cady, Associate Justice of the Iowa
Supreme Court and a member of the Buena Vista Fort Dodge faculty, was selected as the outstanding professor among the seventeen

nominated by the Centers.[119] Many Center graduates eagerly participated in commencement ceremonies on the Storm Lake campus.

The graduate program originally conceived by the Briscoe Era
continued to grow under the Moore Administration. Once it was decided that it was possible for the Master of Science in Education to
be accredited, Buena Vista changed its status from college to university. Two 36-hour tracks leading to the graduate degree were implemented. These were School Administration and Leadership and
Guidance and Counseling. The graduate program met the requirements of the Iowa State Board of Education and licensing board.
Twelve courses per year were offered with eight of the courses
taught by the Storm Lake faculty. The remaining four courses
would be taught by practitioners in the field. By 2001 more than
100 students were working toward the Master of Science degree at
Buena Vista University.[120] Furthermore, the size of the graduate faculty was increased, and all members possessed either the Ph.D. or
the Dr. Ed. The Education Department was led by one of the
University's most effective professors, 1997 Wythe Award winner
Dr. Kline Capps. Another outstanding professor in the School of
Education was Stan Bochtler, also a Wythe winner (2001) and a
twenty-five-year veteran.

As early as 1991 Buena Vista had decided not to seek renewal
of NCATE accreditation, which it had held since the 1970s. The
basic reason was that there existed no NCATE model for assessing
"non-traditional delivery stems for teacher education." NCATE was
not prepared to handle the complex educational structure offered by
the Centers.[121] There were no major consequences resulting from
this decision. The Buena Vista teacher education program was held
in high esteem throughout the state and its graduates in great demand. Buena Vista was graduating more teachers than any other
private college in Iowa. In 2001 education graduates totaled 236 of
the 1,261 degrees granted on the Storm Lake campus. The Centers
reported that 40 percent of 1,500 graduates were in the field of
education.[122]

The obvious success of the Moore Administration was not free
of controversy. Moore inherited from the preceding administrations
festering problems related to faculty salaries, particularly parity be-

tween male and female faculty. The University had difficulty coming up with acceptable policies in the area of sexual harassment and student drinking. Furthermore, what seemed at times an unusual rate of turnover among faculty was troublesome to many Buena Vista students. There were years in which resignations, retirements, and leaves totaled almost 20 percent. Heavy teaching loads and a lack of opportunity for research were reasons given for leaving by departing faculty. Some departments were small, often staffed by only two to four faculty members so the loss of an advisor or major professor could easily interrupt the continuity of instruction.

Nevertheless, Buena Vista moved successfully into the marketplace and was often able to recruit its first choice among new faculty.[123] Furthermore, nearly half of the Buena Vista faculty have been at the institution a decade or longer. Buena Vista faculty can boast of terminal degrees from more than three-dozen institutions of higher learning.

One issue that may have begun to fester in the last years of the Briscoe Era, but particularly plagued the Moore Administration was gender equality in the matter of faculty salaries. Several women faculty had been embittered for years by what appeared to them to be rank discrimination. Furthermore, Briscoe possibly in jest is alleged to have remarked, "I love to hire women because they will work for less."[124] It was one of those remarks that during a tense period (whether he said it or not) was believed by many on the faculty. Then in 1997 John Mouw, acting VPAA, noticed "some variation in salaries." It was suggested that the variations could be based on gender differences. The upshot of this was that six female faculty members, Laura Inglis, Nadine Brewer, Susanne Gubanc, Hollace Drake, Robbie Ludy, and Ann Peterson, sued Buena Vista University in an effort to obtain what they deemed as economic justice. Buena Vista University was charged with violating Iowa Code 216, which prohibited sexual discrimination in the workplace.[125] The case, first filed with the EEOC and Iowa Civil Rights Commission in September 1999, dragged on for more than three years before being dismissed by Sioux City judge, Mark Bennett in December 2002.[126] The reason for the judge's action was that the statute of limitations had run out "so the case was no longer timely." It was also obvious that the majority of women faculty along with their male colleagues were not overly supportive of the suit.[127]

The dismissal hardly satisfied the plaintiffs and their supporters who insisted they had received no justice from the court. Professor Laura Inglis, leader of the group, who died in 2001, argued for fairness and urged the University to make salaries public. Dr. Karen Halbersleben, Dean of the Faculty, maintained the charges were groundless.[128] Meanwhile, the Moore Administration undertook a study of equity in faculty salaries. The Minneapolis accounting firm of McGladrey and Pullen was employed as early as 1998 for the purpose of making a study of the University pay structure. Progress was made and most conceded that the firm helped Buena Vista to establish "reasonable and comparative salaries."[129]

The McGladrey Report found some inconsistencies, but the imbalance, they concluded, was based more on years of service and rank rather than gender. Consequently, adjustments were made in all areas of employment in the University. The adjustments that took place in 1999–2000 amounted to $832,886.[130] One set of criteria for establishing salaries, however, was the market system that caused one prominent faculty member in the social sciences to proclaim, "I'm not thrilled." The Business faculty still felt that their salaries were below the norms.[131] Still, several top faculty salaries in 2004 were slightly more than $85,000 in a profession where great riches are rarely accumulated. No women appeared to be at that level although several may have been close.

Among Iowa's private colleges the mean average for male professors outdistanced the pay for women of equivalent rank by nearly $9,000. The publication *Academe* for July–August 2005 revealed male professors at Buena Vista receiving an average of $77,500 per annum and female professors $67,100. The gap of $10,400 was higher than average, but the $67,100 average for female faculty appeared to be the highest among Iowa Conference schools.[132] However, gender differences evened out at the rank of associate and assistant professor. Buena Vista female faculty at the associate and assistant professor level were only slightly behind male faculty. Obviously a more equitable and fairer salary system was being gradually worked out during the decade of the Moore presidency.

Nevertheless the plaintiffs felt that the University had not adequately addressed their individual cases. Still, the struggle of the six female members of the faculty who brought the discrimination suit was not in vain even though their protest did not succeed in the way they had envisioned. Several of the plaintiffs benefited from the new adjustments. Furthermore an increasing number of women held key posts at the University with most of them having been brought in during the Moore Administration. The last two Vice Presidents for Academic Affairs, the Vice President for Student Services, the Athletic Director, and the chair of the School of Social Sciences, Religion and Philosophy have been women. Several women have served as Associate Dean of the Faculty. Still, only three women faculty members have been among the eighteen winners of the prestigious Wythe Award. During the decade of the 1990s the percentage of female faculty at Buena Vista University increased from 24 to 36 percent. Four of the six women who participated in the suit were still on the Buena Vista faculty in 2005.[133] By 2000 the full-time faculty consisted of 81 members.[134] Gender discrimination has been a national problem at colleges and universities. Some, including Buena Vista, have made progress but the march toward full equality remains an evolutionary process for most American colleges and universities.

One area in which Buena Vista did not overindulge was hiring nontenured adjuncts on the Storm Lake campus. Overall, fewer than 10 percent of the University's academic courses were taught by adjuncts. Adjuncts were generally hired to replace faculty on leave, for specialized course offerings or because they could bring a unique academic offering to the campus.[135]

A number of highly competent administrators left Buena Vista during the mid-1990s and early years of the new century. These included John Klockentager, Vice President for Enrollment and Student Services. Klockentager departed in January 1998 to accept a position as senior Vice President at Noel Levitz, a premier management consultant firm in Denver, Colorado. Klockentager had worked for Buena Vista since 1978 assuming his vice presidential role in 1986. Klockentager had been active in supporting international programs at Buena Vista and in 1995 had toured three Pacific Rim countries.[136]

Mark Gries, a 1974 Buena Vista graduate and a star pitcher on the Beekmann teams of the early 1970s, left in 1998 to assume the position of Vice President for Institutional Advancement at Sioux Falls University in South Dakota. Gries, a very personable and competitive individual, had worked in admissions and then as assistant director of financial aid and director of annual funds at Buena Vista since 1978.[137]

Jim Daniels, who served as Vice President for Institutional Advancement, also departed the University in 1999 for a similar post at St. Thomas University. Daniels, who held a Ph.D. in philosophy from Duquesne University, had been at Buena Vista for ten years. Under his watch annual giving had jumped from $1 million to $5 million. The number of alumni contributors increased from 739 in 1989 to 2,452 in 1999.[138] He was replaced by Ken Converse, who had served for five years as director of development. Converse would also prove a key figure in the Moore Administration.

By 2004 Moore had established a competent team of new and old administrators. These included the very able Jacqueline Johnson as Vice President for Academic Affairs; Julie Keehner, Vice President for Enrollment and Student Services since 1995 and a Penn State Ph.D.; and the indefatigable Vice President for Business Affairs, Randy Fehr, who since 1989 had continued Buena Vista's long history of balanced budgets, which had reached thirty-one consecutive years in 2005. Keehner had the unenviable task of replacing Ivan Harlan who retired in 1995. She successfully became an integral part of the university's administrative structure. Unfortunately, she decided to leave Buena Vista in September 2005 for West Virginia Wesleyan University. Dr. Jacqueline Johnson came on board in 2002 when Karen Halbersleben accepted a college presidency at Northland College in Wisconsin.[139] Johnson completed her undergraduate work at Macalester and her M.A. and Ph.D. at Purdue. The new VPAA came determined to move Buena Vista onto the national stage as an important academic institution.

Perhaps, most important of all, was the Moore Administration's ability to hire competent young faculty members to bolster departments as older professors retired. The young faculty of the 1980s like Schweller; Jeanne Tinsley, Social Science Religion and Philosophy Chair; Bowers; Jonathan Hutchins; Mary Gill, Associate Dean of the Faculty; Capps; Bochtler; Donath; and Whitlatch were now definitely senior professors and academic leaders. Joining them was a hard core of academically talented and progressive teacher-scholars. Among these were two Wythe Award winners, Dixee Bartholomew-Feis (history), the 2000 winner, and Elizabeth Lamoureux (speech communications), the winner in 2002. Both developed reputations as outstanding teachers. Lamoureux was a 1983 Buena Vista graduate and received her doctorate from the University of Kansas. Dr. Dixee Bartholomew-Feis came out with her first book in 2005 entitled, *The Men on the Ground: The OSS in Vietnam in 1945*, and published by the University of Kansas Press.

Bartholomew-Feis also served as the AEA 5 District Coordinator of National History Day in Iowa.[140] Professor Dixee Bartholomew-Feis was also instrumental in coordinating the 1999–2000 academic year's emphasis on Holocaust Studies, which brought guest speakers, and she organized a series of classes, films, and travel in order to "convey an understanding of the torment, pain and heartache caused by the Nazis."[141]

Historian Dr. Bill Feis was busy proving himself a prolific scholar as well as outstanding classroom teacher. By 2005 he was the author of two books, *Grant's Secret Service: The Intelligence War from Belmont to Appomattox* and *The Worst Angels of Our Nature: Guerrilla Warfare in the American Civil War.* Feis also contributed significant articles to a number of journals, including *Civil War History, North and South,* and *Blue and Gray,* along with being a contributing author to several specialized studies on the Civil War and book reviews in scholarly journals.[142]

Dr. Annamaria Formichella-Elsden quickly established a solid reputation as teacher and scholar in English. Her first book, *Roman Fever,* published in 2005 was highly acclaimed. The volume examined the nineteenth century portrayals of American women traveling abroad.[143] Dr. James Hampton, Professor of Biology, Cornell Ph.D., and strong supporter of broadening stem cell research, has been a distinguished member of the biology department since 1994. Dr. Stan Ullerich, popular economics professor, replaced Houston Polson as Dean of the School of Business in 2005.

Other promising young faculty include Brad Best in political science who has been instrumental in the AHLS, Tim McDaniel in Mathematics who won the 2005 Wythe Award, Robert Dunbar and Brian Lenzmeier in Biology, David Klee and Paula Keeler in Music, and Rita McKenzie in Education. These professors along with others provide Buena Vista with a solid professional faculty, hopefully not only for the present but also for the future.

By the fall of 2005 the Moore Administration had achieved many of its goals. It had modernized the campus with new buildings and intelligent landscaping, it had codified its purpose, it had attracted national attention with technological innovation, it had brought diversity to campus and community, its blend of mature and young faculty added zest to the classroom and a competitive scholarship, its men's and women's basketball teams were consistently among the ranked schools in Division Three. But most of all the Buena Vista University led by President Moore had established among trustees, faculty, staff, students, graduates, and those peering in from the outside, a belief in the institution.

15

The goal of the Founding Fathers of 1891 had been "Education for Service." The motto of that era, however, embraced the traditional liberal arts and education. The main technological apparatus, in that era, was the typewriter invented a half-century earlier. Along with the typewriter, carbon paper was an essential tool for education and business. It is not known whether or not the College had a telephone, but as late as 1958 faculty (because of the expense) did not have phones in individual offices. Calculators were in use by then, and during the 1960s the first somewhat crude and physically imposing computer had been introduced. It was regarded with suspicion and remained dysfunctional until Professor Charles Slagle arrived.

By 1991 it was clear that Buena Vista was destined to become more than a traditional liberal arts college and that its future would be closely related to its innovative spirit. The business department had grown dramatically, education maintained its traditional strong role, and technology was increasingly in command. The College (still a few years from university status), which thirty years earlier had scoffed at the use of computers, now had one on the desk of every administrator and faculty member.

THE UNIVERSITY YEARS

1

2

1 David Gergen, White House advisor and 2004 William W. Siebens American Heritage Laureate, with student panelist Darren Whitfield **2** The Rt. Hon. Sir John Major, former Prime Minister of Great Britain and 2005 William W. Siebens American Heritage Laureate

3

4

3 Bob Woodward, assistant managing editor at *The Washington Post* and 2003 William W. Siebens American Heritage Laureate   **4** Madeleine K. Albright, 64th U.S. Secretary of State and 2001 William W. Siebens American Heritage Laureate

5

6

5 Walter Cronkite, legendary anchorman of the CBS Evening News and 1997 William W. Siebens American Heritage Laureate **6** Five-time Iowa Conference Coach of the Year, Janet Berry (left) instructing player Holly McDonough

7 Adam Jones, Buena Vista's first all-American basketball star, four-time all-conference selection 1998–2002, and second to Jim Ahrens in career points **8** Eric Wiebers, men's basketball star and 2003–04 Iowa Conference most valuable player **9** Men's basketball players Rahn Franklin and Matt Wittry **10** Men's basketball player Eric Wiebers and a Grand View College player **11** Steve Eddie, 2002 Iowa Conference baseball coach of the year

452

12

13

12 Five-time Iowa Conference basketball coach of the year, Brian Van Haaften and his 2003 Iowa Conference championship team   **13** Two champions: Women's basketball coach Janet Berry and Men's basketball coach Brian Van Haaften

14   15

16

14 Women's basketball player Kristina Kapler   **15** Women's basketball player Katie Maguire   **16** Steve Osterberger, Buena Vista football coach and 2004 Iowa Conference coach of the year

17

18

17 Keith and Carmen Briscoe upon Keith receiving the University's Citation of Excellence in 1995 **18** Keith and Carmen Briscoe and Susan and Curt Tideman (Briscoe's daughter and son-in-law) with the bronze bust of Briscoe

19

20

19 The Estelle Siebens Science Center, dedicated on September 17, 2004   **20** Ground-breaking ceremony for the Estelle Siebens Science Center September 30, 2002: Fred Moore, President; Estelle Siebens; Mary Jane Siebens; Donald Lamberti, Chair, Board of Trustees

21

22

21 New laboratory in the Estelle Siebens Science Center **22** Dinner held in conjunction with the dedication of the Estelle Siebens Science Center on September 17, 2004

23   24

25

23 Interior of the Estelle Siebens Science Center   **24** Rotunda of the Estelle Siebens Science Center   **25** Groundbreaking ceremony for the Information Technology Center

458

26

27

28

26 Interior of the Library, part of the Information Technology Center   **27** Ed Bock, 1940 BVU alum and Trustee since 2000   **28** Benjamin Mordecai, 1967 BVU alum and recipient of an honorary Doctor of Fine Arts degree and the John Fisher Alumni Award posthumously at Founders Day 2005

29

30

31

29 Dr. Norm Nielsen, 1961 BVU alum, former President of Kirkwood Community College, and BVU Trustee since 2005 **30** Dennis Young, 1965 BVU alum and Trustee since 1979 **31** Exterior of the Lamberti Recreation Center

32 Dr. Bill Cumberland, BVU Professor Emeritus of History, and President Jimmy Carter, the 1990 William W. Siebens American Heritage Laureate

33

33 Dr. Fred Brown, BVU Provost from 1973 to 1987

34

35

36

37

34 Dr. F. Kline Capps, Dean of the School of Education and Professor of Education
35 Dr. Dixee Bartholomew-Feis, Associate Professor of History and Wythe Award recipient
in 2000 **36** President Frederick V. Moore and his wife, the Rev. Susan Moore
37 Dr. William Feis, Associate Professor of History

38

39

38 President Frederick V. Moore and family   **39** 2005–06 President's Council members Ben Donath (2004 Wythe Award recipient), Ken Converse, Fred Moore, Randy Fehr, Donna Schoneboom, Julie Keehner, and Jacquie Johnson

40   Dr. Kenneth Schweller, Dean of the School of Science and 1996 Wythe Award recipient
41   Dr. Jeanne Tinsley, Dean of the School of Social Science, Philosophy and Religion
42   Dr. Joseph Traylor, Professor of Physics and Computer Science and 1998 Wythe Award recipient   43   Dr. Michael Whitlatch, Professor of Drama and 1994 Wythe Award recipient

44

45

44 Memorial tree in memory of Dr. Marilyn Wikstrom, 1991 Wythe Award recipient and Professor of Education 1972 to 1998   **45** Leon Williams, Director of Intercultural Programs, with student Rolando Zamago

466

46

The new face of the College, in the opinion of some, appeared to diminish the humanities and social sciences. Some majors in these departments occasionally felt they had become second class citizens (in the house that Siebens built), and faculty complained about heavy loads in small departments.[1] Unfortunately, challenges to the historical role of the humanities and social sciences were, desirable or not, a national trend. Newer General Education requirements across the nation meant that from Amherst to Xavier one could graduate with a decreasing number of the traditional liberal arts requirements. A student could escape from the best institutions with a single course in history or literature and sometimes without even a smattering of foreign language. After all what do you do with a major in history or English and how much do liberal arts graduates get paid? One did not have to subscribe to the *Chronicle of Higher Education* to realize that a great disparity existed. Parents who were forced to go to the economic brink in order to educate sons and daughters wanted to see something concrete in economic terms at the end of the journey. Another problem was that the twenty-first century student needed more skills in order to master the explosion of knowledge. How, after all, do you work in all the necessary courses for a well-rounded, liberal education? Still, proponents of the liberal arts did not surrender easily.

Professor Manoocher Aryanpur, a seasoned professor of English, who had contributed books and articles on Persian literature, and who was the author of a widely used Persian-English dictionary, a world traveler, and the master of several languages, endeavored to define the meaning and importance of the humanities. The humanities, Aryanpur explained, and he was speaking for the traditional liberal arts agenda, fostered "an effective and graceful communication in speaking, writing and artistic expression." Beyond that the humanities promoted an "appreciation for the great artistic and literary works that are the common heritage of humankind and provide us with an aesthetic awareness, a shared experience and a common language of discourse across various disciplines." A strong liberal arts education, Aryanpur reasoned, moderated the imbalance between the sciences and the Humane Arts. In the sciences the emphasis is on the "physical truth," in the liberal arts on the "truths of the heart." It is the real world that is dealt with in the sciences. The world of the Humane Arts reaches into the fictive and metaphysical. The goal of the sciences is "well knowing and well-doing." In the liberal arts "it is these as well as enlightenment, values, tolerance, cosmopolitanism, refinement and wisdom." The first—the sciences—gives us "material amenities, leisure time, atomic energy and longer life, the second tells us what to do with these." Aryanpur concluded that without the first, "we would still be the flat-earthians; without the second we would be the Frankensteins, Dr. Jekylls or Dr. Mengeles."[2] Aryanpur, of course, was not trying to build a barricade against new trends in education, but to caution against graduating college students who were still unexposed to the beauty and compassion emanating from the liberal arts.

Dr. Aryanpur penned these words in 1991. The promising 1990s passed quickly and the emerging twenty-first century posed new and sometimes rather terrible challenges. The liberating spirit of the Enlightenment so valued by America's Founding Fathers seemed to be in retreat. The Cold War had given way to an even more menacing terrorism, a restrained containment policy had been blotted out by an aggressive preemptive unilateral approach, corruption raced wildly through both the corporate and government world, hate groups multiplied (some 762 by 2005), and compassion occasionally seemed on the verge of becoming a relic of the past. Religion moved to the right in all three major global religious groups and at times appeared more interested in extremist politics than meaningful faith. Perhaps the humane program of the liberal arts had never taken root or perhaps it had never been sufficiently employed. Was it now in danger of being distorted or even destroyed? However, it was clear as the twenty-first century burst forth that modern learning would go beyond the spiritual and intellectual and embrace more of the technical and the practical aspects of education.

The books and essays by Ernest Boyer and his New American College concepts seemed to support such views, although Boyer's goal was not to limit liberal education but to enlarge its focus as a contributor to the solution of national and international problems.

Could the concepts of the New American College merge the soft aspects of the humanities with the hard practicality of rapidly changing technology? Certainly, a careful reading of Boyer indicates that he was not indifferent to the historic role of the liberal arts, but seeking to harness technology to its spirit for the benefit of the new, often turbulent, process of modern globalization. Globalization, which made the world smaller, made some richer, some poorer, and apparently none more peaceful. Boyer strongly affirmed the importance of both teaching and research along with "the vigorous pursuit of free and open inquiry." Should this be seriously compromised, the nation would lack the capacity to successfully "resolve the huge, almost intractable social, economic, and ecological problems, both national and global."[3] The discovery inherent in scholarship, however, must be related to teaching. It was important that classroom teaching be appreciated and rewarded. Integrative studies in Boyer's opinion were vital in enabling the "work of the academy," to "relate to the world beyond the campus."[4] Boyer also saw that student and faculty diversity on campus was essential in fostering a new relevance to education and in creating a more humane global society.[5] The war in Iraq, the December 2004 tsunami, and the merciless devastation of Katrina all indicated the need for a humane and liberal approach to world problems brought about either by man-made or natural means or a combination of both.

Furthermore, Boyer had no intention of demolishing tenure or the role of faculty in academic governance. He wanted to enlarge the sense of community. Academic pundits across the nation including some at Buena Vista have rightly been concerned about the increasing centralization of the college and university governing structure. Too many decisions appear to come from the top down as corporate management styles increase power in regents and administrators. Boyer noted that increasing centralization "may be causing faculty governance to decline at the very moment higher learning faces the challenge of renewals."[6] Even the most capable and flexible administrations sometimes have difficulty struggling through the democratic process. Buena Vista appears to be capable at every pyramid of government; there is a strong appreciation of academic freedom and the right to dissent, but no matter how paradisiacal the environment, vigilance is always the call of the day.

Buena Vista graduates of the 1960s were now at the peak or in some instances nearing the end of their careers. Steve Smith was president and dean of the California Western School of Law, an independent law school located in San Diego. He continued to do research, writing, and some teaching. In 1997 the ABA honored Smith by electing him to the Council of the Section of Legal Education and Admissions to the Bar. He had also become a public member of the Ethics Committee of the American Psychological Association and the American Board of Professional Psychology.[7] Smith also contributed the seed gift for the Cumberland Writing Award. Rosemary Shaw Sackett continued her always upward bound legal career starting in an era when women had to fight for equality and with some of her law school professors still marching in the army of the chauvinists. Sackett received a Master's in Law from the University of Virginia Law School, served as national president of the Council of Chief Judges of State Court of Appeals, and wrote poetry, children's stories, and three fictional novels with legal themes.[8] Dr. George Christakes neared the end of an outstanding career as Professor of History at City Colleges in Chicago. His long tenure there resulted in the publication of books and articles and the presentation of numerous papers, some of them revolving around ethnicity in American life—a growing topic of interest.[9] Norman Nielsen made Kirkwood College into a nationally known institution and joined the Buena Vista Board of Trustees upon retirement.

The success of the graduates of earlier decades stimulates our expectations as we watch new Buena Vista graduates perform as they move into positions of leadership during the next generation. Some of them will emerge as regional and national leaders. For that matter it will be important to see where globalization has taken the planet and how they wrestle with ever-changing and often dangerous conditions. Will we have healthy societies where basic needs are met and all have an opportunity for work or leisure or a withering planet dominated by tyrants where only a few live in splendor? Will the "life of the mind" remain a major component of the educated person or will humanity become more robotic, easily manipulated by colorful social tyrants and devious advertising?

President Moore had urged his trustees, during their gala Florida get-together in January 2003, not only to perform the usual trustee tasks but to review a small book entitled *Millenials Go To College* by Neil Howe and William Strauss. The book was a marketing device to enable administrators and trustees to better understand the students of the twenty-first century. The first batch of "millennials" would receive their degrees and hit the road in 2004. They would undoubtedly be in positions of leadership by 2020 and beyond. Supposedly, they were smarter and more optimistic, closer to their parents, not interested in protests, more interested in teamwork than in individual accountability, totally comfortable with new and rapidly changing technology (unlike many of their elders), less prone to read, security minded, not as interested in the humanities and the arts (preferring things that can be quantitatively measured), and more racially and ethnically diverse. This is a global generation that has known mostly affluence. It is also a very large group numbering more than 80 million.[10]

If Howe and Strauss are on the correct path then Buena Vista is moving in the right direction by stressing technology, diversity, communications, and computer science, although by no means remaining mute to the historic echoes of the liberal arts. No matter what may be the inherent losses in turning somewhat away from the traditional academic programs, it is the current trend of the twenty-first century. The looming question is how to keep the spirit of the liberal arts alive in an illiberal world that emphasizes the practical, the technical, and above all profits and prestige. After all, it is the spiritual and intellectual qualities within the liberal arts that have instilled in us much of our humanity and our sense of identity. These are elements of our better nature that we dare not lose. Technology, as professor Paul Bowers wisely noted, must remain the servant and not the master.

There is no reason to assume that Buena Vista's historic commitment to "Education for Service" has been diminished by rapidly changing technology and globalization. Rather, one might cautiously assert that it has been enhanced. Students can now reach out to the rest of the world via the Internet, they travel extensively both in the United States and abroad, even their campus experience brings them into contact with new races, new cultures, and a kaleidoscope of ideas that cannot help but broaden understanding and promote tolerance.

The Buena Vista of today is increasingly portrayed as a success story. It is no longer a "well kept secret" among America's colleges and universities. It has attracted national attention and is included in the resumes of America's most prestigious colleges. What are the reasons for the university's rise from the ashes to prominence?

Certainly, the Siebens gift was instrumental in making Buena Vista into more than just another struggling liberal arts college. Without Siebens money there would have been no state-of-the-art School of Business, no Estelle Siebens Science Center, and no $100 million endowment. The Siebens intervention in 1980 changed the momentum and thus the history of the institution. But it has been more than that. Along with the Siebens gift the general prosperity of the 1980s and 1990s helped transform survival instincts into confidence and anticipation. Furthermore, Briscoe and Moore reached out to bring in new and multi-talented trustees. The Lamberti Recreation Center was built without Siebens money, and the trustees were also generous contributors to the $26 million science center. These were trustees who had not only wealth but commitment to higher education and a realization that a sound educational system is paramount if the United States is to maintain its position as a world leader.

The beginning of the Centers in 1974 and their dramatic though gradual expansion greatly expanded the scope and influence of the University. Through the last several decades Buena Vista has had strong humane and entrepreneurial leadership—a leadership that saw great possibilities in international programs, a highly trained faculty and administration, a cosmopolitan governing board, and modern facilities. It has possessed a leadership unafraid to take risks, but at the same time carefully calculating the prospects of success and not engaging in foolish ventures. Furthermore, the Buena Vista leadership, which includes the faculty, has been tolerant of new ideas, it has promoted diversity, and has sought to retain the best of the old while incorporating the possibilities of that which is new. Although Buena Vista retains its important ties to the Presbyterian Church, there are no religious or political hang-ups. All religious faiths are welcomed, and an ecumenical spirit reigns. Ideas compete freely in the marketplace, and the principles of academic freedom remain unchallenged.

The spirit of innovation is an impressive feature of this new generation of Buena Vista leaders. The struggles and endeavors of the passing generation, those who served from the 1930s onward through the preceding century, are still acknowledged and revered. One can say that Olson saved the College, Fisher re-invented it, Halverson steadied it, and Briscoe and Moore moved it dramatically and successfully into the modern era. Now, the Buena Vista millennial generation, more cosmopolitan and more diverse, seeks eagerly to ride the waves of the future. Indeed, its students are much sought after as employees because of their academic excellence and strong work ethic. Buena Vista no longer seeks to catch up—it is now among the leaders.

A relatively young and energetic Buena Vista faculty serves on state and national committees, travels abroad, conducts research, and publishes in a variety of disciplines. President Fred Moore has surrounded himself with a capable and innovative set of administrators who were and are attracted by the fact that Buena Vista does care about its students. Altogether, faculty, administrators, and staff employees number into the hundreds. Student enrollment on the main campus, although down slightly in 2005, will continue to edge toward 1,300, and the total University budget now totals more than $45 million. It was 1936 when Buena Vista proudly boasted, during the Olson Administration, that it now had a budget of $100,000. Trustee Ed Bock has miraculously witnessed the fantastic growth from his days as a student to his present position as a trustee and contributor. Furthermore, for more than three decades Buena Vista has operated on a balanced budget. The institution does not spend money it does not have. Its plans are carefully constructed.

Times do change and they will change more in the future. The legendary personalities at Buena Vista were the great men and women of their time. They nurtured the institution and left something upon which to build. The pyramid is much larger now. A calamity would be more devastating. But for now the view is increasingly magnificent. Never have the waters of the Lake whose billows on a windy day still splash along the campus shoreline been more beautiful, there is now a silhouette of buildings that mark Buena Vista as a center of learning, the campus is richly landscaped for the green of spring and the crisp bronze hue of early autumn, it carries well the windswept white of winter.

The optimism of those who in the 1920s proclaimed that they could hear the footsteps of Buena Vista students for a thousand years now appears justified. The Buena Vista of today possesses the facilities that one-half of a century earlier seemed like an impossible dream, it has a leadership of faculty and administration that is both innovative and efficient. Above all the University is, as always, composed of people who genuinely care for students. As Buena Vista's first woman VPAA, Karen Halbersleben remarked, "This school taught me what a community that is totally devoted to students looks like."[11] But that had always been the case at Buena Vista. Those in the past—the men and women of 1891, of 1941, of 1991, of 2001— all possessed a hope and a vision. Those of us who contributed to those years of building look upon the present architects of the University with admiration. President Moore seeks to ensure a "collaborative culture," with all segments of the community sharing and working together. He speaks of a "new journey," an intellectual journey, a journey of service, a journey that breaks down "walls and silos," a journey of mission and service, "recognizing that the world at large and higher education have changed remarkably in the last ten years." And as Moore reminded the university community, "Buena Vista is much bigger than any one of us."[12] It has now been one-half of a century since Buena Vista, following the great fire, was faced with the challenge of emerging from the ashes. Buena Vista emerged, evolved, triumphed. How far will the winds of progress carry the institution? What is our essential purpose as educators and as human beings? It is a quest that has no end. Ernest Boyer recalls as a young man listening to a distinguished professor proclaim that "humanity has been telling us, love, act, or as a species perish."[13]

It is not too much to ask. Indeed, it is imperative.

APPENDIX

PRESIDENTS

Loyal Y. Hays   Willis Marshall   Harvey Hostetler   Elmer E. Reed

Robert L. Campbell   Edward L. Campbell   James P. Linn   Robert D. Echlin

Stanton Olinger   Arthur M. Boyd   Evert L. Jones   Henry Olson

John A. Fisher   Wendell Q. Halverson   Keith G. Briscoe

PRESIDENTS

Loyal Y. Hays 1891–1892
John M. Linn 1892–1894
Willis Marshall 1895–1897
Harvey Hostetler 1897–1900
Elmer E. Reed 1900–1906
Robert L. Campbell 1906–1908
Edward L. Campbell 1910–1911
James P. Linn 1911–1913
Robert D. Echlin 1913–1917
Stanton Olinger 1917–1920
Arthur M. Boyd 1920–1923
Evert L. Jones 1924–1931
Henry Olson 1931–1953
John A. Fisher 1954–1960
Wendell Q. Halverson 1961–1973
Keith G. Briscoe 1974–1995
Frederick V. Moore 1995–

ACTING PRESIDENTS

John MacAllister 1894–1895
George H. Fracker 1906, 1908–1909
E. F. Blayney 1911
Alfred C. Nielsen 1931
W. D. Wesselink 1953–1954, 1960–1961
Lester E. Williams 1973–1974
J. Robert Siefer 1989–1990

NOTES

Buena Vista College has no central archives. Materials for this volume were scattered among (1) the college library, (2) the public relations office, (3) the president's files, (4) the storage room in the basement of Dixon-Eilers, and (5) those materials collected by and in the personal possession of the author. Most of the *Tacks*, scrapbooks (including those containing newspaper files), catalogues, press releases, yearbooks, and assorted materials including older photos and the Edson file are available in the Buena Vista College library. Some newspaper clippings, recent press releases, sports information, and photos are available in the public relations office. Trustee minutes and recent correspondence are housed in the president's files. The tapes containing interviews; the Drury, E. S. Benjamin, Gladys Kuehl and other correspondence; along with sundry other materials remain, at least temporarily, in the possession of the author. Searches through stored, discarded, forgotten material in the storage room at Dixon-Eilers yielded small but sometimes rewarding tidbits. The public relations staff including Sue Cameron, Nancy Julich, John Cullen, Jay Miller (sports information), and Lori Rohlk were always helpful. The president's assistant, Lynn Harlan, helped in many ways. Librarians Barbara Palling, Jody Morin, and Gail Lind assisted in some of the more desperate searches for material. The author especially thanks Barbara Palling for her interview with Ruth Ann Fisher.

CHAPTER 1. A LAND IS SETTLED

1. Homer L. Calkins, "The Coming of the Foreigners," *Palimpsest*, Apr. 1962, pp. 146–47.

2. C. H. Wegerslev and T. Walpole, *Past and Present of Buena Vista County*, (Chicago, P. J. Clarke Co., 1909), p. 48.

3. Ralph Plagman, Jr., "Storm Lake: The First Decade (1870–1880)" (History thesis, Buena Vista College, n.d.), p. 15.

4. Wegerslev, *Buena Vista County*, p. 44.

5. *History of Western Iowa: Its Settlement and Growth* (Sioux City, Western Publishing Co., 1882), p. 442.

6. Wegerslev, *Buena Vista County*, p. 72.

7. *Storm Lake Pilot-Tribune*, Feb. 26, 1931.

8. Ibid.

9. Wegerslev, *Buena Vista County,* p. 133.

10. Plagman, "Storm Lake," p. 41.

11. *Pilot,* Dec. 2, 1891.

12. *Pilot-Tribune,* Aug. 10, 1900.

13. *Pilot-Tribune,* Sept. 21, 1950.

14. Daniel Williams, *A History of the Lakeside Church,* pamphlet, 1914.

15. Ibid.

16. Plagman, "Storm Lake," pp. 38–39.

17. Wegerslev, *Buena Vista County,* p. 80.

18. Plagman, "Storm Lake," p. 52.

19. W. C. Edson file, Buena Vista College Library, Edson's statement to College Board.

CHAPTER 2.   THE WORK OF SOWING

1. *Rudder,* 1913.

2. Buena Vista College Trustee minutes, 1891, historical note.

3. Ibid.

4. E. A. Ross, *Seventy Years of It* (New York, D. Appleton Century Co., 1936), p. 21.

5. Ibid., p. 22.

6. *Fort Dodge Messenger,* July 17, 1890.

7. Record, Fort Dodge Collegiate Institute, 1889–1891, pp. 1–2.

8. *Storm Lake Pilot,* July 29, 1891.

9. Trustee minutes, 1891, historical note.

10. Sioux City Presbytery minutes, May 18, 1891, p. 21.

11. Trustee minutes, 1891, historical note.

12. *Messenger,* Apr. 30, 1891; May 21, 1891.

13. Ibid., May 14, 1891.

14. Trustee minutes, 1891, historical note; Sioux City Presbytery minutes, May 18, 1891, p. 23.

15. *Messenger,* June 18, 1891; July 23, 1891.

16. *Pilot,* July 29, 1891.

17. Ibid.

18. Buena Vista College Announcement, 1891–92, p. 5.

19. Sioux City Presbytery minutes, May 18, 1891, p. 21.

20. Trustee minutes, 1891, historical note.

21. *Pilot,* July 15, 1891.

22. Trustee minutes, July 24, 1891.

23. Announcement, 1891–92, pp. 17–18.

24. *Buena Vista College Catalogue,* 1891–92, pp. 14–15. The various catalogues of Buena Vista College have been published under several titles. Hereafter referred to as *Catalogue.*

25. Trustee minutes, Sept. 15, 1891.

26. *Tack,* Feb. 1990; March 8, 1923.

27. Trustee minutes, Sept. 15, 1891.

28. *Pilot,* Sept. 14, 1892.

29. *Pilot-Tribune,* June 14, 1928. Mr. Russell had been the engineer of the first steamboat to appear on Storm Lake, the *J. D. Eddy.* He once traded a threshing machine for 400 acres (believed to be swampland at that time) in Maple Valley township and in 1891 turned his attention to the manufacturing of brick and tile. He was one of the great pioneers and builders of Storm Lake.

30. *Tack,* Oct. 8, 1956.

31. Stella Russell Musgrave, "When the Arch of Old Main Was Built." n.d., Buena Vista College Library.

32. E. S. Benjamin, letter to author, Nov. 2, 1963. Mr. Benjamin attended different terms at Buena Vista, 1891–1899. He became a Methodist minister and was still living when the first edition of the *History of Buena Vista College* was published in 1966.

33. *Pilot-Tribune,* May 9, 1929. The writer was Anna von Coelln Stokes. Her father was professor of mathematics, 1891–1896.

34. Ibid., Mar. 24, 1927.

35. *Pilot,* Oct. 28, 1891; *Catalogue,* 1891–92, p. 7.

36. Benjamin letter. Trustee minutes, June 7, 1893, state "Miss Jennie Gordon Hutchison was granted in B.A. as the first graduate of Buena Vista College."

37. *Catalogue,* 1892, p. 22.

38. Benjamin letter, Nov. 22, 1963.

39. Trustee minutes, Oct. 27, 1891.

40. Ibid.

41. *Buena Vista College Bulletin,* Oct. 26, 1893.

42. Trustee minutes, Dec. 24, 1891.

43. *Pilot,* Mar. 19, 1892.

44. *Pilot,* Oct. 21, 1891.

45. Ibid.

46. *College Bulletin,* May, 1892; *Pilot,* May 4, 1892; *Tack,* Oct., 1898.

47. *College Bulletin,* May 1892.

48. *Pilot,* May 18, 1892.

49. Ibid.

50. *College Bulletin,* May, 1892.

51. Benjamin letter, Nov. 2, 1963; *Pilot-Tribune,* May 9, 1929.

52. *Pilot,* May 17, 1893. The remarks were made by President J. M. Linn at a memorial service held in honor of President Loyal Hays.

CHAPTER 3.   THE NOT-SO-GAY NINETIES

1. *Storm Lake Pilot-Tribune,* May 9, 1929.

2. *Tack,* Dec. 14, 1920. Letter of John M. Linn to Elizabeth Ensign. Linn was then residing in Chicago.

3. Trustee minutes, Oct. 6, 1892.

4. Ibid., June 7, 1893.

5. *Who Was Who in America,* vol. I, 1897–1942 (Chicago, A. N. Marquis Co., 1943), p. 733.

6. *Pilot-Tribune,* June 14, 1928.

7. *Tack,* Dec. 14, 1920.

8. *Pilot,* Oct. 5, 1892.

9. Presbyterian Church in the U.S.A., *Minutes of the General Assembly,* "Board of Aid for Colleges," 1894, Part I, p. 322; *Catalogue,* 1895–96.

10. Sioux City Presbytery minutes, Sept., 1892, p. 8.

11. Trustee minutes, June 7, 1893.

12. Jennie G. Hutchison, "The Early Days at Buena Vista," *Tack,* Mar. 15, 1907.

13. Record, Fort Dodge Collegiate Institute, 1889–1891. The volume also contains records of Buena Vista students through 1917–18.

14. Buena Vista College Announcement, 1891–92, p. 25.

15. *Monmouth College Bulletin,* 1951, pp. 187–88.

16. Announcement, 1891–92, p. 25.

17. *Tribune,* Mar. 3, 1894.

18. *Buena Vista College Bulletin,* Oct. 26, 1893; Trustee minutes, Sept., 1893; Presbyterian Church in the U.S.A., Reports of the Board of the General Assembly, 1896, Part II, "Presbyterian Board of Aid for Colleges and Academies," p. 4. The effects of the depression were noted in the reports of the Board of Aid 1894–1896. In view of diminished resources the Board feared to squander its fund on uncertain enterprises.

19. Trustee minutes, Sept. 12, 1893.

20. Ibid.

21. *College Bulletin,* Oct. 26, 1893.

22. Trustee minutes, June 7, 1893.

23. *College Bulletin,* Oct. 26, 1893.

24. Trustee minutes, Dec. 14, 1893.

25. Presbyterian Church report, "Board of Aid," 1896, p. 18.

26. Ibid., pp. 2–3.

27. *Pilot,* Sept. 28, 1892.

28. *Pilot-Tribune,* Apr. 17, 1952.

29. *Pilot-Tribune,* May 19, 1955.

30. *Pilot,* Sept. 28, 1892.

31. *Pilot,* Aug. 1, 1895.

32. E. S. Benjamin, letter to author, Nov. 2, 1963.

33. Trustee minutes, Mar. 17, 1897.

34. Ibid.

35. Trustee minutes, Apr. 23, 1897.

36. Ibid.

37. Trustee minutes, Dec. 14, 1896. A number of creditors dropped the interest and these deductions amounted to $730.10.

38. Trustee minutes, June 17, 1897.

39. Ibid., June 17; June 28, 1897.

40. *Tack,* May 1903.

41. Benjamin letter, Jan. 23, 1965.

42. *College Bulletin,* Oct. 22, 1921.

43. Benjamin letter, Nov. 22, 1963.

44. *Pilot-Tribune,* Sept. 10, 1897.

45. J. F. Hinkhouse, *One Hundred Years of the Iowa Presbyterian Church* (Cedar Rapids, Laurance Press, 1932), p. 508.

46. Benjamin letter, Nov. 2, 1963.

47. W. C. Edson file, letter to Wendell Halverson, Jan. 29, 1963.

48. Trustee minutes, Mar. 24, 1892; June 10, 1895.

49. Benjamin letter, Nov. 2, 1963.

50. John S. Nollen, *Grinnell College* (Iowa City, State Historical Society of Iowa, 1953), p. 61.

51. C. R. Aurner, *History of Education in Iowa* (Iowa City, State Historical Society of Iowa, 1914), p. 406.

52. *Tack,* Apr. 29, 1913.

53. *College Bulletin,* Feb. 22, 1921; *Monmouth College Bulletin,* 1951; *Storm Lake Pilot,* Oct. 28, 1891.

54. Trustee minutes, Sept. 15, 1891; *Tack,* May 23, 1916.

55. *Pilot-Tribune,* Feb., 26, 1931; *Tack,* Mar. 8, 1923.

56. *Tack,* Mar. 5, 1942.

57. *Pilot-Tribune,* Feb. 15, 1951.

58. Ibid.

59. *Tack,* Feb. 1900; Mar. 1898.

60. Trustee minutes, May 30, 1899.

61. *College Bulletin,* Mar. 1899.

62. *Tack,* June-Sept., 1899; *College Bulletin,* 1900–1901, p. 14.

63. C. H. Wegerslev, *A History of Buena Vista County* (Chicago, S. J. Clarke Co., 1909), p. 397.

64. *College Bulletin,* 1900–1901, p. 14.

65. *Pilot,* Mar. 5, 1896.

66. R. E. Flickinger, *The Early History of Iowa and Pioneer History of Pocahontas County* (George Sanborn, *Fonda Times,* 1904), Foreword.

67. *College Bulletin,* May 1898.

68. Ibid.

69. *Catalogue,* 1899–1900, pp. 49–52. Some students were enrolled in more than one department but were counted only once.

CHAPTER 4.   A FIRM FOUNDATION: E. E. REED (1900–1906)

1. *Who Was Who in America,* "Elmer Ellsworth Reed," vol. I, 1897–1942 (Chicago, A. N. Marquis Co., 1943), p. 1016. Mrs. Reed was still living in 1965 at ninety-six years of age. The Reed children were Ellery Francis, Elmer Dodd, Helen A., Gertrude, and Margaret.

2. Parsons College awarded Reed the D.D. degree in 1897 and Emporia, Kansas, awarded the LL.D. degree in 1920.

3. C. F. Lamkin, *A Great Small College* (St. Louis, Horace Barks Press, 1946), p. 478.

4. W. R. Ferguson, "Golden Years," *Palimpsest,* Sept. 1947, p. 281.

5. Trustee minutes, Apr. 23, 1897; *Buena Vista College Bulletin,* 1899–1900.

6. Trustee minutes, Apr. 23, 1897.

7. Trustee minutes, Sept. 11, 1900.

8. *Storm Lake Pilot-Tribune,* Feb. 15, 1901.

9. *Pilot-Tribune,* Feb. 21, 1901.

10. Ibid.

11. *Tack,* Feb. 1901, p. 17.

12. *Pilot-Tribune,* Mar. 22, 1901.

13. Ibid., Mar. 15, 1901.

14. Ibid., Mar. 22, 1901.

15. Ibid., Nov. 1, 1901.

16. Ibid., May 31, 1901.

17. Ibid., Apr. 11, 1902.

18. Ibid., June 6, 1902.

19. Ibid., June 13, 1902.

20. Ibid., Mar. 15, 1902.

21. Ibid., June 13, 1902.

22. Trustee minutes, June 11, 1902.

23. Trustee minutes, Jan. 18, 1904.

24. *Buena Vista College v. Floyd T. Voris,* District Court of Iowa, box 123, no. 4938, Nov. term, 1904.

25. Trustee minutes, Dec. 18, 1903.

26. *Buena Vista v. Voris.*

27. Ibid.

28. Ibid.

29. *Pilot-Tribune,* Jan. 1, 1904.

30. Suggested by E. S. Benjamin in letter to author, Jan. 23, 1965. Mrs. Voris had contributed $1,000 to the endowment fund; see also *Buena Vista College Bulletin,* Mar. 1901, p. 5.

31. *Tack,* June 1899, p. 17.

32. *College Bulletin,* Mar. 1901, p.10.

33. *Tack,* Feb. 1899.

34. Trustee minutes, June 10, 1902.

35. *Pilot-Tribune,* April 16, 1915.

36. *Pilot-Tribune,* Dec. 25, 1914.

37. James Patterson Linn told this story to Prof. George F. Reynolds while Linn was staying at the Reynolds home around 1940. Linn never lost his affection for Buena Vista College and during his later years served as a field agent.

38. Trustee minutes, Apr. 15, 1903.

39. *Buena Vista College Catalogue,* 1904–5, p. 25.

40. Ibid., pp. 25–26.

41. Ibid., p. 21.

42. Trustee minutes, June 1, 1903.

43. *Catalogue,* 1904–5, p. 13.

44. Trustee minutes, July 14, 1903.

45. *Pilot-Tribune,* Mar. 8, 1904; Mar. 15, 1904.

46. *Pilot-Tribune,* Feb. 26, 1931 (historical edition).

47. *College Bulletin,* Mar. 1901.

48. Trustee minutes, Jan. 21, 1901.

49. *College Bulletin,* Mar. 1901, pp. 7–8.

50. Trustee minutes, Jan. 21, 1901.

51. Trustee minutes, Sept. 12, 1903.

52. W. C. Edson file, Edson's statement to the College Board, Nov. 5, 1953.

53. Benjamin letter, Nov. 2, 1963.

54. Trustee minutes, Aug. 8, 1903.

55. C. M. Drury, letter to author, Oct. 19, 1964.

56. *Tack,* Oct. 1900.

57. *Tack*, Mar. 28, 1922.

58. Russell Anderson, interview by Sue Brinkman, May 29, 1985.

59. Drury letter.

60. *Tack,* June 5, 1922.

61. *Pilot-Tribune,* June 16, 1922.

62. Trustee minutes, President's Report, June 1, 1903.

63. *Pilot-Tribune,* May 19, 1911; July 12, 1912; June 20, 1913; *Tack,* Nov. 2, 1920.

64. Trustee minutes, May 21, 1902.

65. *Pilot-Tribune,* July 25, 1902; E. F. Reed, letter to author, Mar. 20, 1965.

66. Edson file, letter to Wendell Halverson, Jan. 29, 1963.

67. Reed letter.

68. Trustee minutes, President's Report, June 8, 1904.

69. Trustee minutes, June 1, 1907.

70. Trustee minutes, June 6, 1906.

71. Trustee minutes, June 9, 1904.

72. Reed letter.

73. *Pilot-Tribune,* May 13, 1904.

74. Trustee minutes, President's Report, June 8, 1904.

75. Ibid., June 6, 1906; *Catalogue,* 1904–5, p. 176; Trustee minutes, Nov. 4, 1908.

76. Trustee minutes, President's Report, June 1, 1903.

77. *Beaver Log,* 1951, p.13.

78. Reed letter.

79. Ferguson, "Golden Years," pp. 277–80; Lamkin, *Small College,* p. 430.

80. Trustee minutes, Sept. 7, 1906. Professor Fracker served as acting president until a successor could be found.

81. *Pilot-Tribune,* Sept. 7, 1906.

CHAPTER 5. BRIGHT PROMISES AND DEEP FRUSTRATIONS

1. *Storm Lake Pilot-Tribune,* Oct. 27, 1938.

2. *History of Western Iowa: Its Settlement and Growth* (Sioux City, Western Publishing Co., 1882), p. 442.

3. Daniel Williams, *A History of the Lakeside Church,* pamphlet, 1914, pp. 2–5.

4. C. H. Wegerslev and T. Walpole, *Past and Present of Buena Vista County* (Chicago, S. J. Clarke Co., 1909), pp. 224–25. The Fiftieth District then included Humboldt, Buena Vista, and Pocahontas counties.

5. *Pilot-Tribune,* Aug. 9, 1918.

6. C. H. Wegerslev, "Buena Vista County," *Who's Who in Iowa* (Iowa Press Association, 1940), p. 154.

7. *Pilot-Tribune,* Sept. 14, 1906.

8. Wegerslev, "Buena Vista County," p. 489.

9. Trustee minutes, Sept. 8, 1906.

10. Trustee minutes, June 1, 1907.

11. *Pilot-Tribune,* May 9, 1907.

12. *Pilot-Tribune,* May 24, 1907.

13. Trustee minutes, June 5, 1907.

14. Ibid.

15. Trustee minutes, June 1, 1908.

16. Ibid.

17. *Pilot-Tribune,* Aug. 28, 1908.

18. *Pilot-Tribune,* Sept. 18, 1908.

19. Trustee minutes, Nov. 4, 1908.

20. *Pilot-Tribune,* Oct. 30, 1908.

21. *Pilot-Tribune,* June 14, 1912.

22. Trustee minutes, June 14, 1910.

23. *Pilot-Tribune,* Nov. 11, 1910.

24. Ibid.

25. *Tack,* May 15, 1910.

26. Trustee minutes, June 14, 1911.

27. Trustee minutes, Aug. 1, 1911. See also *Pilot-Tribune,* May 12 and 19, 1911. The Board of Aid contributed the $5,000 after a stipulated $12,000 was raised in Storm Lake.

28. *Pilot-Tribune,* Dec. 8, 1911.

29. *Pilot-Tribune,* Aug. 4, 1911.

30. Trustee minutes, June 12, 1912.

31. Ibid.

32. Trustee minutes, Oct. 22, 1913.

33. As related by Prof. George F. Reynolds. See Chapter 4.

34. Trustee minutes, Mar. 17, 1914.

35. *Tack,* Oct. 14, 1913.

36. *Pilot-Tribune,* Jan. 30, 1914.

37. Ibid., May 19, 1916.

38. Ibid., June 2, 1916.

39. Ibid., June 16; May 12, 1916.

40. Ibid., July 28; June 30, 1916.

41. Ibid., Aug. 11, 1916.

42. Ibid., Aug. 4, 1916.

43. Ibid., Nov. 17, 1916; Jan. 5, 1917; Trustee minutes, Aug. 28, 1916.

44. *Pilot-Tribune,* June 25, 1915.

45. *Pilot-Tribune,* Jan. 5, 1939. Eastman was a trustee in the 1890s. He was the first male school instructor in Storm Lake, a bank cashier, and businessman. He left Storm Lake in 1926 and died in California in 1939 at the age of ninety-two.

46. *Pilot-Tribune,* Oct. 12; Dec. 7, 1917.

47. C. M. Drury, "Buena Vista College 1914–15," typescript, pp. 22–23.

48. C. M. Drury, letter to author, Feb. 5, 1965.

49. *Pilot-Tribune,* Dec. 17, 1915.

50. *Tack,* Sept. 26, 1917.

51. *Pilot-Tribune,* May 11, 1917; Nov. 22, 1918; *Tack,* Nov. 26, 1918.

52. *Alumni Directory 1893–1951* indicates this.

53. *Tack,* May 1906.

54. *The Beaver Report,* Sept. 1955.

55. *Pilot-Tribune,* Feb. 15, 1951.

56. *Pilot-Tribune,* Aug. 21, 1914.

57. *Jennie G. Hutchison v. Buena Vista College,* District Court of Buena Vista County, Iowa 6507 (1915).

58. *Tack,* Jan. 15, 1910.

59. *Tack,* Nov. 15; Feb. 15, 1911; Dec. 15, 1910.

60. *Buena Vista College Catalogue,* 1916–17, pp. 91–110.

61. *Pilot-Tribune,* Aug. 4, 1916.

62. *Tack,* Apr. 17, 1917.

63. *Tack,* Mar. 22, 1921; *Pilot-Tribune,* Apr. 6, 1917.

CHAPTER 6.   FROM WAR TO DEPRESSION

1. C. M. Drury, "Buena Vista College, 1916–17," typescript, pp. 41–47.

2. C. M. Drury, letter to author, Sept. 7, 1964.

3. *Buena Vista College Catalogue,* 1918–19, pp. 21–24.

4. Drury letter.

5. *Storm Lake Pilot-Tribune,* Nov. 1918.

6. *Pilot-Tribune,* Aug. 1918.

7. *Pilot-Tribune,* Apr. 18, 1918.

8. *Pilot-Tribune,* clipping, n.d.

9. Drury, "Buena Vista College," p. 47.

10. Buena Vista College Chapel Farewell Service, June 4, 1918; *Storm Lake Pilot-Tribune,* June 7, 1918.

11. *Catalogue,* 1918–19, p. 21.

12. *Tack,* June 5; Feb. 14, 1922.

13. *Pilot-Tribune,* June 11, 1920.

14. *Pilot-Tribune,* July 6, 1923.

15. Trustee minutes, Jan. 15, 1924.

16. Trustee minutes, June 10, 1919.

17. *Pilot-Tribune,* June 27, 1919.

18. *Pilot-Tribune,* Nov. 12, 1920; *Tack,* Nov. 30, 1920.

19. Trustee minutes, June 8, 1920.

20. *Buena Vista College Bulletin,* 1921.

21. *Pilot-Tribune,* Nov. 13, 1924.

22. Ibid., June 25, 1925.

23. Ibid., May 27, 1923.

24. Ibid., May 29, 1926.

25. Ibid., July 6, 1923.

26. Ibid., May 31, 1928.

27. *Tack,* Mar. 1, 1932.

28. *Pilot-Tribune,* Sept. 20, 1928; Sept. 22, 1922.

29. *Catalogue,* 1928–29, p. 15.

30. *Tack,* June 3, 1929.

31. *Pilot-Tribune,* July 30, 1925.

32. E. R. Harlan, *History of the People of Iowa,* vol. 3 (Chicago and New York, American Historical Society, 1931), p. 140.

33. *Pilot-Tribune,* Oct. 16, 1930; Aug. 20, 1936.

34. *Pilot-Tribune,* Nov. 9, 1923.

35. *Tack,* Oct. 8, 1929.

36. *Pilot-Tribune,* Mar. 21, 1935.

37. *Tack,* Apr. 8, 1930.

38. *Pilot-Tribune,* Mar. 15, 1928.

39. *Pilot-Tribune,* Jan. 24; Jan. 31, 1929.

40. Ibid., Jan. 31, 1929.

41. Ibid., Feb. 14, 1929.

42. Ibid., Feb. 20, 1930.

43. Trustee minutes, Aug. 10, 1926; *Pilot-Tribune,* Jan. 14, 1932.

44. *Pilot-Tribune,* Jan. 14, 1932.

45. Ibid., Oct. 9, 1930.

46. Ibid., May 12, 1927.

47. Ibid., May 26, 1931.

48. *Tack,* Nov. 12, 1930; *Pilot-Tribune,* Oct. 16, 1930.

49. Trustee minutes, Nov. 29, 1930. The resignation was actually a letter to the president of the Board, Willis C. Edson, and was dated Oct. 18, 1930.

50. *Pilot-Tribune,* Oct. 23, 1930.

51. *Tack,* Nov. 12, 1930.

52. *Pilot-Tribune,* Nov. 13, 1930.

53. *Tack,* Nov. 12, 1930.

54. *Pilot-Tribune,* Nov. 13, 1930.

55. Ibid.

56. *Tack,* May 5, 1931.

57. *Pilot-Tribune,* Dec. 11, 1930.

58. Ibid., Mar. 19, 1931.

59. Ibid., Apr. 23, 1931.

60. Ibid., June 11, 1931.

61. W. C. Edson file, letter to John Fisher, Dec. 30, 1955.

62. Ibid., Jan. 30, 1955.

63. *Pilot-Tribune,* July 16, 1931.

64. Ibid., June 28, 1934.

65. Ibid., Feb. 26, 1931.

CHAPTER 7.   WORK OF SALVATION: HENRY OLSON (1931–1941)

1. W. C. Edson file, letter to John Fisher, Dec. 30, 1955.

2. Edson file, article, Oct. 31, 1944; Lilly Hirsch, "Buena Vista College Profile," Nov. 1966.

3. Edson file, article, Oct. 31, 1944.

4. Ibid.

5. Mrs. Ine Krogstad, letter to Dr. James Zabel, Aug. 23, 1989.

6. *Buena Vista Today,* winter, 1984.

7. Edson file, article, Oct. 21, 1944.

8. Edson file, letter to Fisher.

9. *Tack,* Oct. 1, 1934.

10. Trustee minutes, Apr. 15, 1932.

11. Trustee minutes, Apr. 15, 1932; June 15, 1932; Mar. 31, 1928; Aug. 21, 1931; July 31, 1933; June 2, 1939.

12. Faculty minutes, Sept. 9, 1939.

13. Faculty minutes, Jan. 16, 1941; Mar. 27, 1940.

14. *Storm Lake Pilot-Tribune,* July 28, 1932.

15. *Catalogue,* 1931–32, p. 14.

16. Eleanor Bloom, letter to author, Aug. 19, 1988. Mrs. Bloom is Henry Olson's sister.

17. *Pilot-Tribune,* Nov. 3, 1932.

18. Edson file, letter to Fisher.

19. Edson files, Willis Edson, "Some Facts about Buena Vista College," Oct. 21, 1944.

20. Edson file, letter to Fisher.

21. Trustee minutes, June 2, 1933.

22. *Tack,* Sept. 22, 1933.

23. *Pilot-Tribune,* June 28, 1934.

24. *Pilot-Tribune,* Feb. 28, 1934; June 27, 1934.

25. Steve Smith, letter to author, Jan. 26, 1990.

26. *Tack,* Feb. 18, 1940.

27. George Christakes, letter to author, Apr. 20, 1989.

28. Smith letter.

29. *Tack,* Sept. 28, 1936; Feb. 6, 1936.

30. Trustee minutes, Aug. 2, 1936.

31. *Tack,* May 5, 1933.

32. Ine Krogstad, letter to Dr. James Zabel, Aug. 23, 1989.

33. *Pilot-Tribune,* Dec. 26, 1935.

34. Eleanor Bloom, letter to author, Sept. 14, 1988.

35. *Pilot-Tribune,* June 10, 1937; Trustee minutes, Aug. 9, 1937.

36. *Tack,* May 4, 1936; May 18, 1936.

37. *Pilot-Tribune,* May 14, 1936.

38. *Pilot-Tribune,* July 9, 1936.

39. Trustee minutes, Dec. 21, 1936.

40. *Tack,* July 21, 1941.

41. Edson file, "Incidents as a Trustee of a Denominational College."

42. Ibid.

43. *Pilot-Tribune,* July 31, 1941; *Tack,* Aug. 22, 1941.

44. Paul H. Lahr, letter to Greg Evans, July 3, 1987.

45. *Pilot-Tribune,* June 26, 1941.

46. Ibid., June 13, 1940.

47. Ibid., May 1, 1941; May 29, 1941.

48. Ibid., May 29, 1941.

49. *Tack,* Nov. 24, 1941.

50. *Pilot-Tribune,* June 13, 1940.

51. *Tack,* Dec. 16, 1941.

CHAPTER 8. CONSOLIDATION AND EXPANSION:
HENRY OLSON (1942–1954)

1. *Tack,* Jan. 19, 1942.

2. *Tack,* Dec. 4, 1944.

3. *Storm Lake Pilot-Tribune,* Nov. 2, 1944.

4. Faculty minutes, Jan. 18, 1945.

5. *Tack,* Aug. 20, 1945.

6. *Buena Vista College Press Release,* Aug. 26, 1987.

7. *Buena Vista Today,* spring, 1987.

8. College Press Release, Aug. 26, 1987.

9. *Tack,* Feb. 25, 1946.

10. *Buena Vista County Herald,* Mar. 19, 1936.

11. *Buena Vista College Scrapbook,* (clipping from the *Waukon-Republican Standard,* Sept. 27, 1983.)

12. *Tack,* Feb. 15, 1943; Faculty minutes, Apr. 23, 1942.

13. *Tack,* Sept. 29, 1945.

14. Edson file, "Buena Vista College States Purposes and History," Oct. 31, 1944.

15. Ibid.

16. *Pilot-Tribune,* May 4; Feb. 10, 1944.

17. *Tack,* Aug. 21, 1944.

18. *Pilot-Tribune,* Oct. 24, 1946.

19. *Beaver Log,* 1948, p. 126.

20. Alberta Dwelle, letter to Barbara Palling, Nov. 23, 1985.

21. *Tack,* Apr. 13, 1942.

22. Dr. Clarence Richardson, interview with William H. Cumberland, Oct. 25, 1989.

23. *Pilot-Tribune,* Apr. 7, 1949.

24. *Pilot-Tribune,* May 19, 1949.

25. *Beaver Log,* 1952, p. 31.

26. Louis G. Geiger, *Voluntary Accreditation* (George Banta Co., Menasha, Wisconsin, 1970).

27. Faculty minutes, Feb. 29, 1944.

28. Faculty minutes, Mar. 22, 1945.

29. North Central Association, "Buena Vista College," pamphlet (1950), pp. 2–3.

30. Ibid., p. 3.

31. *Tack,* Sept. 25, 1950.

32. *Tack,* June 26, 1950; Ruth Ann Fisher, interview with Barbara Palling, July 31, 1989.

33. Lilly Hirsch, "Buena Vista College Profile," Nov., 1946.

34. *Pilot-Tribune,* Nov. 14, 1946.

35. Dr. George Christakes, letter to author, Apr. 20, 1989.

36. Gladys Kuehl, letter to author, May 6, 1989.

37. Ibid.

38. Bill Kuehl, letter to author, May 17, 1989.

39. *Tack,* Aug. 18, 1947.

40. *Pilot-Tribune,* July 31, 1947.

41. Faculty minutes, Apr. 9, 1951.

42. Faculty minutes, Oct. 2, 1950; Feb. 21, 1949.

43. C. L. Winters, "Survey Report on Buena Vista College," Oct. 29, 1950.

44. *Tack,* Apr. 7, 1952; *Beaver Log,* 1952, p. 32.

45. *Tack,* Apr. 21, 1952.

46. Edson file, letter to John Fisher, Apr. 30, 1955.

47. *Tack,* Oct. 20, 1952.

48. *Tack,* Oct. 6, 1952.

49. *Pilot-Tribune,* Oct. 30, 1952.

50. Faculty minutes, Oct. 30, 1956.

51. *Buena Vista College Bulletin,* Jan. 1962.

52. Hirsch, "Profile."

53. Bill Kuehl letter.

54. *Pilot-Tribune,* July 9, 1953.

55. Minutes, Synod of Iowa, meeting at Ames, July 6–9, 1953.

56. *Des Moines Register,* Oct. 23, 1953.

57. *Tack,* Oct. 26, 1953.

58. Dr. Clarence Richardson, interview with William Cumberland, Oct. 25, 1989. Dr. Richardson was at that time a young pastor at Lakeside Presbyterian Church and a member of the Board of Trustees.

59. Minutes, Synod of Iowa, meeting at Ames, July 5–8, 1954; July 6–9, 1953.

60. Synod minutes, July 5–8, 1954.

61. Rev. Dr. Hervey Throop, letter to William Cumberland, Oct. 4, 1989.

62. Trustee minutes, Nov. 2, 1953.

63. *Pilot-Tribune,* Oct. 29, 1953.

64. Edson file, letter to John Fisher, Dec. 30, 1955.

65. Trustee minutes, Mar. 14, 1955, "Report of the Finance Committee."

66. *Tack,* Feb. 22, 1954.

67. Richardson interview.

68. Hirsch, "Profile."

69. Faculty minutes, Nov. 23, 1953.

70. Edson file, "Special Meeting of Trustees," Nov. 2, 1953.

71. Trustee minutes, Nov. 10, 1954.

72. Trustee minutes, Nov. 10, 1955. Some of this based on conversation with Kermit L. Buntrock.

73. Mrs. Eleanor Bloom, letter to author, Aug. 19, 1988.

74. Trustee minutes, Nov. 10, 1954.

75. Ibid., the Oct. 25, 1989, interview with Dr. Clarence Richardson is enlightening here.

76. Edson file, Henry Olson, letter to Willis Edson, Jan. 3, 1962.

CHAPTER 9.   THE BEAVER HERITAGE

1. *Tack,* May 1906.
2. *Tack,* Dec. 1902.
3. *Tack,* May 1906.
4. C. M. Drury, letter to William Cumberland, Feb. 5, 1965.
5. *Tack,* Nov. 6, 1902.
6. *Beaver Students' Handbook,* Buena Vista College, 1928.
7. *Tack,* May 1903, p. 8.
8. Johnson Brigham, *Iowa, Its History and Its Foremost Citizens,* vol. 3 (Chicago, S. J. Clarke Co., L915), p. 1247.
9. *Tack,* May 1903, p. 8.
10. Ibid.
11. *Tack,* Oct. 1905.
12. *Tack,* Mar. 15, 1906.
13. *Tack,* Nov. 21, 1917.
14. *Buena Vista County History* (Iowa Writers Project, WPA, 1942), p. 58.
15. *Storm Lake Pilot-Tribune,* Old-Timer's column, July 15, 1954.
16. *Tack,* Jan. 23, 1918.
17. *Tack,* Nov. 21, 1917.
18. E. S. Benjamin, letter to William Cumberland, Aug. 6, 1965.
19. *Tack,* May 2, 1930.
20. *Buena Vista Today,* spring, 1987.
21. *Tack,* May 23, 1962.
22. Translation from an Austrian paper provided by Lilly Hirsch.
23. *Tack,* Apr. 24, 1974.
24. *Buena Vista Today,* winter, 1987.
25. Chuck Offenburger, "Out in Greene County, Iowa," May 22, 200l, Web site.
26. Chuck Offenburger to William Cumberland, July 13, 2005 e-mail.
27. Jamii Claiborne to William Cumberland, July 26, 2005 e-mail.
28. *Tack,* April 20, 2001.
29. *Tack,* Oct. 4, 1996.
30. *Tack,* March 1, 1997.
31. *Tack,* Feb. 12, 1999; *Storm Lake Pilot-Tribune,* November 17, 1997.
32. *Tack,* Feb. 27, 1998.
33. *Rudder,* 1907.
34. *Tack,* Feb. 25, 1930.
35. *Beaver Report,* Apr. 1956.
36. Jay Beekmann, interview with Sue Brinkman, June 13, 1985.
37. *Beaver Log,* 1951.
38. *Beaver Log,* 1947; *Buena Vista Today,* winter, 1981.
39. *Tack,* Jan. 13, 1920.
40. *Beaver Report,* Sept. 1955.
41. *Buena Vista Briefs,* summer, 2002; *Tack,* March 15, 2002.
42. *Pilot-Tribune,* June 8, 1906.
43. Ibid.
44. *Buena Vista College Catalogue,* 1896–97, p. 29.
45. *Rudder,* 1919; 1923.

46. *Tack,* Mar. 1909.
47. Faculty minutes, Apr. 9, 1919; Apr. 13, 1925.
48. Faculty minutes, Sept. 24, 1923.
49. *Tack,* Apr. 27, 1953.
50. *Storm Lake Pilot-Tribune,* May 6, 2003.
51. *Tack,* special edition, Dec. 1972.
52. *Pilot-Tribune,* Dec. 2, 1958.
53. *Rudder,* 1919.
54. *Buena Vista View,* May 5, 1984.
55. *Tack,* Apr. 3, 1987.
56. *Tack,* summer edition, 1972.
57. *Buena Vista Briefs,* summer, 2002.
58. *Tack,* Mar. 29, 1977.
59. *Office of University Communications,* Oct. 22, 2004.
60. *Office of University Communications,* Nov. 1, 2004.
61. *Buena Vista Today,* Feb. 2005.
62. Drury letter, Oct. 19, 1964.
63. *Tack.* March 1895; Dec. 1895.
64. *Pilot-Tribune,* May 21, 1896.
65. *Buena Vista College Songs,* published by Storm Lake Vidette, n.d.
66. *Pilot-Tribune,* May 21, 1896.
67. *Tack,* Mar. 7, 1918.
68. *Buena Vista Today,* fall, 1980.
69. *Tack,* Apr. 2, 1924.
70. *Tack,* Apr. 7, 1924; *Buena Vista College Press Release,* Oct. 26, 1970.
71. *Tack,* Apr. 16, 1929.
72. *Tack,* May 2, 2003.
73. Gladys Kuehl, letter to William Cumberland, Aug. 26, 1989.
74. Gladys Kuehl, letter to William Cumberland, May 6, 1989; Bill Kuehl, letter to William Cumberland, May 19, 1989.
75. Bill Kuehl letter.
76. *Tack,* Apr. 2, 1951.
77. *College Press Release,* Mar. 13, 1962.
78. *Pilot-Tribune,* Dec. 2, 1958.
79. Gladys Kuehl letter.
80. *Buena Vista Today,* fall, 1982.
81. *Tack,* Apr. 5, 1979.
82. *Buena Vista College Catalogue.* 1916–17, pp. 74–80.
83. *Buena Vista College Alumni Directory,* 1935; *Catalogue.* 1920; 1921.
84. *Tack,* Oct. 25, 1966.
85. Information from an interview with Paul Russell on Feb. 8, 1990.
86. *Rudder,* 1909.
87. Ibid., 1924; *Beaver Log,* 1971.
88. *Beaver Log,* 1964; 1971.
89. Ibid., 1974.
90. Research project, Scott Janssen, "Origin of Cottage Names," 1989.
91. *Tack,* Nov. 13, 1981.
92. *Tack,* Dec. 4, 1981; *Vista Vue,* June 15, 1987.

93. *Tack,* April 25, 1987.

94. *Tack,* Oct. 25, 1968; *Press Release,* Nov. 1, 1968.

95. *Tack,* Oct. 10, 1986.

96. *Pilot-Tribune,* Oct. 16, 1969.

97. *Beaver Log,* 1971.

98. *Storm Lake Pilot-Tribune,* Oct. 15, 1970.

99. Travis Lockhart, letter to William Cumberland, Jan. 20, 1990.

100. *Tack,* May 9, 2003.

101. Mike Whitlatch to William Cumberland, July 20, 2005 e-mail.

102. Ibid, July 21, 2005.

103. *Tack,* May 6, 1983.

104. Lockhart letter.

105. Ibid.

106. Mike Whitlatch to William Cumberland, July 20, 2005 e-mail.

107. *Office of University Communications*, Oct. 22, 2005.

108. Mike Whitlatch to William Cumberland, July 20, 2005, e-mail.

109. *Office of University Communications*, April 20, 2005.

110. Mike Whitlatch to William Cumberland, Aug. 1, 2005, e-mail.

111. *Buena Vista Today,* summer, 2003.

112. *Tack,* March 11, 2003.

113. Mike Whitlatch to William Cumberland, July 21, 2005 e-mail.

114. Ibid.

115. *Beaver Log,* 1950.

116. *Tack,* February 2, 2001.

117. *Office of University Communications,* May 2, 2005.

118. Beaver Log, 1964.

119. Benjamin letter, Nov. 22, 1963.

120. *Tack,* Nov. 1903, p. 3, essay by Grace Russell.

121. *Tack,* Oct. 1909.

122. *Tack,* Feb. 16, 1895.

123. *Tack,* Oct. 1902; *College Yell,* Feb. 16, 1895.

124. Drury letter.

125. *Catalogue,* 1909–10, p. 13.

126. *Rules and Regulations Governing Students,* Buena Vista College, June 1, 1911.

127. *Pilot-Tribune,* Jan. 23, 1964.

128. *Sioux City Journal* (clipping from scrapbook), Apr. 22, 24, 1964.

129. *Tack,* May 3, 1977; Feb. 8, 1979.

130. *Beaver Handbook,* 1930.

131. Drury letter.

132. Faculty minutes, Jan. 24, 1918.

133. Faculty minutes, Feb. 12, 1918; Jan. 30, 1919; Sept. 29, 1926.

134. *Tack,* Mar. 25, 1930.

135. Russell Anderson, interview with Sue Brinkman, May 29, 1985.

136. *Tack,* Nov. 15, 1968; Dec. 12, 1969; Nov. 13, 1970; Oct. 3, 1986; Nov. 9, 1979; Faculty minutes, Oct. 16, 1980; Dec. 17, 1985.

137. *Buena Vista University Catalog,* 2004–05.

138. Steve Smith, letter to William Cumberland, Jan. 26, 1990.

139. Trustee minutes, Oct. 20, 1972.

140. *Tack,* Sept. 10, 1982.

141. *Pilot-Tribune,* Sept. 14, 2002.

142. Ibid.

143. Ibid.

144. *Tack,* Sept. 21, 2001; Sept. 20, 2002.

145. *Tack,* April 30, 2004.

146. *Tack,* May 2005.

147. *Interview with Fred Moore,* June 6, 2005.

148. *Iowa Press Clipping,* April 11, 1998. *University Communications,* Sept. 15, 2005.

149. Ibid, Aug. 27, 1996.

150. Ibid., May 9, 1980.

151. Ibid., Dec. 11, 1981.

152. Ibid., Feb. 29, 1984; Apr. 4, 1984; Mar. 14, 1986; Oct. 10, 1986.

153. *Catalogue,* 1913–14, p. 31.

154. *Des Moines Register,* n.d. but assume 1933; Beekmann interview, June 13, 1985.

155. *Buena Vista Today,* spring, 1987; Beekmann interview, June 13, 1985.

156. *Buena Vista Today,* spring, 1987.

157. *Office of University Communications,* Jan. 19, 2005.

158. Drury letter; *Storm Lake Register,* May 21, 1968.

159. *Sioux City Journal* (scrapbook clipping), Oct. 29, 1968.

160. Drury letter; typescript, "Summer, 1916," p. 38.

161. Drury letter.

162. *Tack,* May 10, 1966.

163. Ibid., Sept. 21, 1979.

164. Ibid., Nov. 20, 1981.

165. Ibid., Feb. 24, 1964.

166. Ibid., Nov. 15, 1966.

167. Smith letter.

168. *Tack,* Feb. 10; Feb. 24, 1964.

169. Trustee minutes, executive committee, Dec. 13, 1983.

170. *Tack,* May 6, 1988.

171. *Pilot-Tribune,* March 14, 2001.

172. *Tack,* April 30, 1999.

173. Ibid., May 1, 1987.

174. Ibid., May 27, 1913; May 15, 1910; June 24, 1913.

175. Ibid., Apr. 15, 1913; Apr. 29, 1913.

176. Ibid., May 15, 1910; Oct. 1909.

177. *Pilot-Tribune,* Jan. 22, 1998.

178. *Tack,* Oct. 7, 1994.

179. *Buena Vista Today,* spring, 1995. *Office of University Communications,* Sept. 15, 2005.

180. Ibid., Feb. 24, 1964.

181. Ibid., Apr. 27, 1966.

182. Ibid., Apr. 3, 1987.

183. *Buena Vista Today,* spring, 1983.

184. *Tack,* Mar. 8, 1923.

185. Trustee minutes, special meeting, June 6, 1955.

186. *Tack,* Mar. 6, 1970.

187. Briscoe memo to faculty on covenant relationship.

188. "A Covenant Between Buena Vista College and the Synod of Lake and Prairies of The Presbyterian Church (U.S.A.)."

189. *Buena Vista Today,* spring, 1984.

190. *Tack,* Oct. 2, 1987.

191. *Tack,* Oct. 21, 1963; *Bulletin,* Jan. 1960.

192. "The Order of the Arch" pamphlet, Buena Vista College.

193. Trustee minutes, Oct. 26–27, 1996.

CHAPTER 10.   AN ATHLETIC TRADITION

1. *Tack*, letter from J. Weber Linn, Nov. 4, 1919.

2. *Tack*, Oct. 15, 1907.

3. Ibid.

4. W. C. Edson file, "Story Told at Alumni Banquet" pamphlet.

5. *Tack*, Nov. 4, 1919.

6. Ibid.

7. Edson file, football record, 1894–1905.

8. *Storm Lake Pilot-Tribune*, Jan. 4, 1901.

9. Nick Huber to William Cumberland, June 15, 2005 e-mail.

10. *Tack*, Dec. 3, 1951, recollections by W. C. Edson.

11. Ibid.

12. *Tack*, Oct. 15, 1909.

13. *Tack*, Oct. 14, 1913.

14. Dr. C. M. Drury, letter to author, Feb. 5, 1965.

15. Ibid.

16. Ibid.

17. *Pilot-Tribune*, Dec. 10, 1959; *Buena Vista College Catalogue*, 1924–25, pp. 22–23; *Pilot-Tribune*, July 19, 1972.

18. *Pilot-Tribune*, Dec. 10, 1959; *Tack*, summer, 1969 (article by Maury White, reprinted from *Des Moines Register*).

19. *Tack*, Oct. 16, 1981; Nov. 21, 1921.

20. *Pilot-Tribune*, Feb. 28, 1935.

21. J. E. Turnbull, *The Iowa Conference Story* (Iowa City, State Historical Society, 1961), p. 66.

22. Ibid., p. 24.

23. *Buena Vista College Press Release*, June 2, 1958; Jan. 24, 1961.

24. John Naughton, interview with Sue Brinkman, June 3, 1985; *Pilot-Tribune*, Dec. 18, 1969.

25. *Pilot-Tribune*, Oct. 23, 1980.

26. *Sioux City Journal*, Nov. 12, 1972 (scrapbook clippings).

27. *Pilot-Tribune*, Oct. 17, 1973; *Des Moines Register*, Nov. 11, 1973.

28. Jay Miller, "Buena Vista College Athletic Records."

29. *Pilot-Tribune,* Jan. 25, 2002.

30. Ibid., Oct. 21, 2003.

31. *Buena Vista News Release*, Nov. 19, 2004.

32. *Storm Lake Register*, Nov. 11, 1978.

33. Miller, "Athletic Records."

34. *College Press Release*, Nov. 14, 1989.

35. *Buena Vista Today*, fall, 1994; fall, 1998.

36. *Buena Vista Athletic Records,* Internet.

37. *Tack*, Jan. 28, 1913.

38. *Tack*, Apr. 18, 1922.

39. *Buena Vista Athletic Records,* Internet.

40. Ibid.

41. Van Haaften, Brian, *A Look from Within,* N & K Publishing Co., Virginia, 2003.

42. *Rudder*, 1927.

43. *Tack*, Apr. 9, 1928.

44. Ibid.

45. *Pilot-Tribune*, Mar. 26, 1942.

46. *Tack*, Feb. 17, 1941.

47. Gerald Wood, interview with William H. Cumberland, July 1988.

48. Glenn Theulen, interview with William Cumberland, July 1988.

49. *Pilot-Tribune*, Dec. 11, 1962 (scrapbook clippings).

50. *Des Moines Register*, Jan. 27; Feb. 2, 1964 (scrapbook clippings).

51. *Sioux City Journal*, Mar. 18, 1973 (scrapbook clippings).

52. *Tack,* May 5, 2005.

53. *Pilot-Tribune,* June 15, 1998, Van Haaften, *A Look from Within.*

54. *Tack,* March 7, 1997.

55. Ibid., March 5, 2005.

56. *Buena Vista Briefs,* summer, 2002.

57. *Buena Vista Briefs,* spring, 2002.

58. *Tack*, Oct. 19, 1979.

59. *Pilot-Tribune*, May 7, 1980.

60. Jay Beekmann, interview with Sue Brinkman, June 13, 1985.

61. Ibid.; *Tack*, Oct. 19, 1979.

62. *Buena Vista Athletic Records,* Internet.

63. *Des Moines Register*, Oct. 31, 1978.

64. *Buena Vista Today*, winter, 1988.

65. *Buena Vista Briefs,* summer, 2002, *Buena Vista Athletic Records,* Internet.

66. Al Baxter to William Cumberland, April 21, 2004 e-mail.

67. *Buena Vista Athletic Records,* Internet.

68. *Rudder*, 1913.

69. *Tack,* March 3, 1995.

70. *Buena Vista Today,* Feb. 2000.

71. *Tack,* May 12, 1995.

72. *Buena Vista Today,* Feb. 2000.

73. *Pilot-Tribune*, Feb. 11, 1987.

74. *Buena Vista Today,* spring, 1995.

75. *Buena Vista Athletic Records,* Internet.

76. *Buena Vista Athletic Headlines,* Jan. 13, 2005.

77. *Pilot-Tribune*, May 4, 1983; *Tack*, Feb. 27, 1987. Demers's record was broken by Briar Cliff's Cheryl Dreckmann in 1990.

78. *College Press* (Sports) Releases, Jan. 21; Feb. 25; Apr. 22, 1987.
79. *Tack*, May 8, 1987.
80. *Buena Vista Athletics,* Internet.
81. Material taken from *Iowa Conference Yearbooks*, 1982–1990.
82. *Catalogue*, 1924–25, p. 23.
83. Turnbull, *Iowa Conference*, p. 130.
84. Carl Adkins to William Cumberland, July 21, 22, 2005 e-mail.
85. *Buena Vista Athletic News,* Internet.
86. *Pilot-Tribune*, Oct. 16, 2001.
87. *Buena Vista Athletic Records,* Internet.
88. *Tack,* April 16, 2004.
89. *College Press Release*, Oct. 6, 1969.
90. *Buena Vista News Release,* March 6, 2002.
91. *Buena Vista Today,* winter, 2002.
92. *Fort Dodge Messenger*, May 1, 1964 (scrapbook clippings).
93. Marge Willadsen to William Cumberland, Aug. 13, 2005 e-mail.
94. From Internet athletic records and Beaver football program 2001.
95. Charles Slagle, interview with Sue Brinkman, June 11, 1985.

CHAPTER 11.   THE FISHER INTERLUDE

1. *Storm Lake Pilot-Tribune*, May 6, 1954.
2. Ruth Ann Fisher, interview with Barbara Palling, July 25 and 26, 1989.
3. *John Albert Fischer,* public relations pamphlet, Buena Vista College; *Storm Lake Register*, Apr. 26, 1960; Lester and Edith Williams, interview with William H. Cumberland, July 7, 1989.
4. *Storm Lake Register*, Apr. 26, 1960
5. Fisher Interview.
6. Trustee minutes, report of the finance committee, Mar. 14; May 9, 1955; Nov. 10, 1958.
7. *Beaver Report,* Sept. 1954.
8. Ibid.
9. Trustee minutes, June 10, 1955; Feb. 13, 1956.
10. *Beaver Report,* Jan. 1956.
11. *Tack,* Sept. 19, 1955.
12. *Tack,* Sept. 28; Oct. 4, 1954.
13. *Buena Vista Today,* winter, 1981.
14. *Tack,* Oct. 29, 1974.
15. *Pilot-Tribune,* Oct. 5, 1965.
16. Williams interview.
17. *Pilot-Tribune,* Sept. 22, 1977.
18. *Tack*, Nov. 23, 1959.
19. *Tack,* May 28, 1956; *Beaver Report,* Apr. 1956; *College Press Release,* "Ambler Address," May 8, 1956.
20. *Tack,* Sept. 24, 1956.
21. *Buena Vista Today,* summer, 1987; *Storm Lake Register,* Oct. 2, 1956.
22. Fisher interview.

23. *Buena Vista Today,* winter, 1983.

24. Fisher interview.

25. Williams interview.

26. Gladys Kuehl, letter to author, May 6, 1989.

27. Bill Kuehl, letter to author, May 17, 1989.

28. *Tack,* May 4, 1976.

29. Recollections of Phoebe La Foy, Ruth Ann Fisher, and the Williamses in *Tack,* May 4, 1976, and interviews cited.

30. *Tack,* Oct. 8, 1956; May 4, 1976.

31. *Pilot-Tribune,* Oct. 2, 1956.

32. Ibid.; *Buena Vista Today,* summer, 1987.

33. *Beaver Report,* Jan. 1957.

34. *Storm Lake Register,* Oct. 2, 1956

35. Gladys Kuehl letter.

36. *Beaver Report.* Jan. 1957.

37. Trustee minutes, special report, Oct. 5, 1956.

38. *Buena Vista Today,* winter, 1983; Fisher interview.

39. *Beaver Report,* Sept. 1958.

40. *Beaver Report,* Jan. 1959.

41. *Pilot-Tribune,* Mar. 10, 1922.

42. *Dedication of Schaller Memorial Chapel,* pamphlet, Buena Vista College, May 12, 1963.

43. Ibid.

44. *Pilot-Tribune,* July 28, 1971.

45. *Storm Lake Register,* June 28, 1959.

46. *Tack,* Dec. 14, 1959.

47. *Tack,* Sept. 28, 1959.

48. *Storm Lake Register,* Jan. 27, 1959.

49. *Sac Sun,* Jan. 13, 1960 (Scrapbook).

50. *Tack,* Feb. 8, 1960.

CHAPTER 12.   HOLDING THE LINE WITH HALVERSON

1. The author's recollection; *Tack,* Oct. 16, 1961.

2. *Storm Lake Pilot-Tribune,* Dec. 8, 1960.

3. *Tack,* Dec. 12, 1960.

4. *Des Moines Sunday Register,* Oct. 8, 1961.

5. *Sioux City Journal,* Sept. 22; Oct. 7, 1961; *Storm Lake Register,* Oct. 10; 19, 1961.

6. *Tack,* Oct. 16, 1961.

7. Faculty minutes, Apr. 19, 1973.

8. Faculty minutes, Oct. 7, 1970.

9. Trustee minutes, Oct. 9, 1962.

10. *Pilot-Tribune,* May 15, 1969.

11. *Buena Vista Today,* Oct, 1973.

12. *Buena Vista College Press Release,* June 4, 1961.

13. Ibid., May 1, 1963.

14. *Tack,* Oct. 2, 1981.

15. *Buena Vista Today,* Apr. 1979.

16. *College Press Release,* Oct. 15, 1964.

17. Wendell Q. Halverson, interview with William H. Cumberland, Oct. 7, 1988.

18. *College Press Release,* Oct. 15, 1964.

19. Robert J. Siefer, letters to Harold Walter Siebens, Oct. 23; Nov. 16, 1970.

20. Harold W. Siebens, letters to Robert Siefer, Dec. 5, 1970; Sept. 10, 1971.

21. Ibid., May 1, 1972.

22. Wendell Halverson, letter to Harold Siebens, May 8, 1972; Harold Siebens, letter to Roberts Siefer, May 9, 1972.

23. Harold Siebens, letter to Robert Siefer, May 30, 1972.

24. *College Press Release,* Apr. 30, 1972.

25. Halverson interview; *Tack,* Feb. 21, 1969.

26. Faculty Senate minutes, Oct. 18, 1966.

27. *Tack,* Oct. 22, 1982.

28. Trustee minutes, Mar. 21, 1969; *College Press Release,* Aug. 5, 1971.

29. Trustee minutes, Jan. 15, 1971.

30. *College Press Release,* Sept. 24; Nov. 3, 1964.

31. Board of Visitors Report, 1968.

32. *College Press Release,* Mar. 5, 1971.

33. Ibid., Jan. 20, 1969.

34. Ibid., Nov. 16, 1967.

35. *Buena Vista College Scrapbook,* clippings from *Des Moines Register,* Jan. 24, 1967; and *Sioux City Journal,* Feb. 9, 1967.

36. Long Range Planning Document, 1970-71; John P. Williams, memo to faculty, Jan. 28, 1972.

37. Trustee minutes, Oct. 20, 1972.

38. *Pilot-Tribune,* June 9, 1966.

39. *College Press Release,* May 2; 10, 1967.

40. *College Scrapbook,* clippings, *Fort Dodge Messenger,* Jan. 25, 1966, *Storm Lake Register,* Jan 25, 1966.

41. Trustee minutes, June 4, 1966.

42. *Pilot-Tribune,* May 20, 1969.

43. *Fort Dodge Messenger,* Nov. 24, 1966.

44. *Des Moines Register,* May 19, 1970.

45. *Pilot-Tribune,* Apr. 26, 1972.

46. *College Scrapbook,* clippings, *Sioux City Journal,* May 27, 1968; *Storm Lake Register,* May 28, 1968.

47. Trustee minutes, May 30, 1970.

48. *Pilot-Tribune,* Oct. 16, 1969.

49. *Pilot-Tribune,* Sept. 19, 1973.

50. Trustee minutes, Jan. 21, 1972.

51. Halverson interview.

52. *College Press Release,* Oct. 29, 1968.

53. *Pilot-Tribune,* Jan. 26, 1972.

54. David Lampe, letter to author, Sept. 28, 1989.

55. Halverson interview.

56. *Buena Vista Today,* Oct. 1973.

CHAPTER 13.   BURGEONING WITH BRISCOE

1. Fred Brown, interview with William H. Cumberland, June 1, 1987.

2. *Sioux City Journal*, June 15, 1974 (scrapbook clipping); *Tack*, Oct. 22, 1974.

3. *Buena Vista Today*, fall, 1982; *Tack*, May 2, 1986.

4. *Des Moines Register*, June 26, 1977 (scrapbook clippings).

5. *Tack*, Oct. 21, 1975.

6. *Buena Vista Today*, winter, 1987.

7. *Storm Lake Pilot-Tribune*, Aug. 15, 1979; Mar. 2, 1988; *Vista Vue*, Oct. 1, 1987.

8. Keith G. Briscoe, "Covenant Relationship to Presbyterian Church," memo to faculty, Apr. 20, 1984.

9. See Chapter 9. The new relationship is clarified in the document "A Covenant Between Buena Vista College and the Synod of Lakes and Prairies of the Presbyterian Church (U.S.A.)."

10. Trustee minutes, Oct. 18, 1974.

11. *Buena Vista College Press Release*, Oct. 14, 1987.

12. *Tack*, Sept. 10, 1974.

13. Committee on the Future, Report, 1975.

14. Ibid.

15. Keith Briscoe, interview with William Cumberland, Sept. 29, 1989.

16. *College Press Release*, Dec. 23, 1982.

17. Henry Wilder Foote, *The Religion of Thomas Jefferson* (Beacon Press, Boston, 1960), p. 11; Dumas Malone, *Jefferson and the Ordeal of Liberty* (Little, Brown & Co., Boston, 1962), p. 253.

18. William Cumberland, Wythe Committee Notes (n.d.).

19. *Storm Lake Register*, Apr. 5, 1980; *Vista Vue*, Sept. 14, 1987.

20. *Buena Vista Today*, summer, 2000.

21. *College Press Release*, Sept. 8, 1987.

22. Darrell Peck, interview with Sue Brinkman, June 6, 1985; William Cumberland, Notes, faculty recognition dinner, May 1988.

23. *Sioux City Journal*, Nov. 26, 1988 (scrapbook clipping); Charles Slagle, oral interview with Sue Brinkman, June 11, 1985.

24. *Storm Lake Times*, Dec. 27, 1997.

25. Sandra Madsen to William Cumberland, April 22, 2005 e-mail.

26. *College Press Release*, Aug. 28, 1986.

27. *Buena Vista Today*, autumn, 1986.

28. *Tack*, Oct. 7, 1975.

29. *Tack*, Mar. 6, 1987.

30. Baccalaureate and Commencement Program, 1989.

31. *Tack*, April 24, 1997.

32. *Buena Vista News Release*, May 18, 2005.

33. *Storm Lake Register*, Mar. 8, 1980.

34. *Pilot-Tribune*, May 31, 1989.

35. *Buena Vista Today*, spring, 1982; *College Press Release*, Oct. 13, 1982; *Tack*, Sept. 13, 1985.

36. *Tack*, Oct. 11, 1996.

37. *Des Moines Register*, Nov. 14, 1986.

38. *Tack,* Mar. 29; Nov. 15, 1977; Mar. 6, 1987.

39. *Pilot-Tribune,* Feb. 20, 1986.

40. *Buena Vista Today,* Spring, 1987.

41. *Tack,* Feb. 12, 2002.

42. *Fort Dodge Messenger,* June 11, 1988 (scrapbook clipping); *Pilot-Tribune,* Oct. 19, 1988.

43. *Pilot-Tribune,* Sept. 26, 1998. *Tack,* Sept. 23, 1998.

44. *Rembrance,* sent to William Cumberland by Gunnar Wikstrom.

45. *Tack,* Mar. 29, 1985.

46. *Des Moines Register,* May 14, 1989.

47. Manoocher Aryanpur, interview with William Cumberland, May 25, 1988; interview with Sue Brinkman, April 17, 1986.

48. *Sioux City Journal,* Aug. 28, 1986 (scrapbook clipping); *Tack,* May 8, 1981; *Buena Vista Today,* autumn, 1986.

49. *College Press Release,* Apr. 24; May 16, 1979.

50. Harold Walter Siebens, interview with William Cumberland and Sue Brinkman, July 1985.

51. Ibid.

52. *Des Moines Register,* Jan. 31, 1989.

53. Ibid.; Siebens interview.

54. *Album 62,* Siebens Den.

55. *Fort Dodge Messenger, Oct.* 6, 1985 (scrapbook clipping).

56. *Des Moines Register,* Jan. 31, 1989.

57. Harold Walter Siebens Memorial Service, I, Buena Vista College chapel, Feb. 16, 1989.

58. Harold Walter Siebens Memorial Service, II, Buena Vista College chapel, May 24, 1989.

59. Keith Briscoe address at Siebens Memorial Service, I, Feb. 16, 1989.

60. Briscoe interview.

61. Faculty minutes, Apr. 17, 1980.

62. *Buena Vista Today,* spring, 1995.

63. Siebens Memorial Service, 1, Feb. 16, 1989.

64. Siebens Memorial Service, 11, May 24, 1989.

65. *College Press Release,* Feb. 21, 1985.

66. *Odebolt Chronicle,* July 15, 1982 (scrapbook clipping).

67. *College Press Release,* Feb. 21, 1985.

68. Tack, Sept. 26, 1980.

69. *Des Moines Register,* Jan. 31, 1989.

70. *Tack,* Feb. 20, 2004.

71. *Oskaloosa Daily Herald,* Dec. 1, 1980 (scrapbook clippings); *College Press Release,* May 19, 1981.

72. *Buena Vista Today,* winter, 1986.

73. *Tack,* Sept. 27, 1985; *Buena Vista Today,* winter, 1986.

74. *Des Moines Register,* Oct. 4, 1985.

75. *Sioux City Journal,* Oct. 3, 1984 (scrapbook clipping); *Pilot-Tribune,* Feb. 12, 1986.

76. Trustee minutes, Oct. 8, 1987.

77. *Album 62,* Siebens Den.

78. Chuck Offenburger to William Cumberland, June 15, 2005 e-mail. See Teri Kramer's article in *Tack,* Sept. 22, 2000.

79. *Tack,* May 7, 1993.

80. *Sioux* City Journal, Mar. 15, 1986 (scrapbook clipping); *Tack,* Oct. 10, 1986; *Buena Vista Today,* fall, 1985.

81. *College Press Release,* Oct, 19, 1987.

82. *Des Moines Register,* July 8, 1988; *Tack,* Oct. 9, 1987; *Buena Vista Today,* autumn, 1987.

83. *College Press Release,* Aug. 2, 1978.

84. Ibid., May 17, 1973.

85. Brown interview.

86. *Buena Vista Today,* Jan. 1982.

87. Brown interview.

88. *College Press Release,* May 8, 1979.

89. *Buena Vista Today,* winter, 1980; *Storm Lake Register,* Sept. 13, 1980.

90. *Tack,* Oct. 23, 1987.

91. *Tack,* Feb. 8, 1985.

92. Keith Briscoe, "Address," faculty recognition dinner, May 21, 1988.

93. Trustee minutes, Oct. 22, 1976.

94. *Des Moines Tribune,* Feb. 18, 1981 (scrapbook clipping).

95. *Pilot-Tribune,* June 7, 1989.

96. James Zabel, memo to faculty, Nov. 16, 1989.

97. *Pilot-Tribune,* June 28, 1978.

98. William Cumberland, personal notes from trustee meeting, Oct. 24, 1986.

99. Trustee minutes, Aug. 23, 1976.

100. Trustee minutes, Executive Committee meeting, Feb. 27, 1979.

101. *Buena Vista Today,* fall, 1983.

102. *Pilot-Tribune,* Sept. 2, 1984; The Irons Document.

103. *Buena Vista Today,* fall, 1984.

104. Ibid., Jan. 1982; *College Press Release,* Feb. 10; Mar. 19, 1982.

105. *College Press Release,* Mar. 19, 1982.

106. Uwe Kitzinger, Commencement address at Buena Vista College, May 18, 1986.

107. *Worthington Daily Globe,* Nov. 26, 1982 (scrapbook clipping).

108. *Buena Vista Today,* winter, 1983; *Seventeen Magazine,* Nov., 1983.

109. *Sioux City Journal,* Feb. 2, 1986 (scrapbook clipping); *U.S. News and World Report,* Nov. 25, 1985.

110. *Pilot-Tribune,* Mar. 30, 1983.

111. President's Report, 1984.

112. *Tack,* Feb. 8, 1991.

113. Ibid., March 1, 1991.

114. Ibid., Feb. 8, 1991.

115. John Madsen to William Cumberland, August 1, 2005 e-mail.

116. *Tack,* May 3, 1995.

117. *Buena Vista Today,* July 1992.

118. Ibid., Nov. 1990.

119. *Tack,* Oct. 21, 1994.

120. *Buena Vista Today,* Nov. 1992.

121. Ibid., spring, 1995.

122. Ibid.

123. *Tack,* April 21, 1995.

124. Ibid., Nov. 11, 1994.

125. Ibid.

126. Ibid., Oct. 21, 1994.

127. *Buena Vista Today,* fall, 1994.

128. *Tack,* Oct. 21, 1994.

129. Ibid.

130. J. L. Fisher and M. W. Tack (eds.), *Leaders on Leadership: The College Presidency*, Keith G. Briscoe, "Interiors of the Presidency," pp. 43–46.

131. *Board of Trustees,* April 29, 1995.

CHAPTER 14.   MORE WITH MOORE

1. *Tack,* April 28, 1995.

2. Chuck Offenburger to William Cumberland, June 13, 2005, e-mail. Also the opinion of the author.

3. *Sioux City Journal,* Aug. 1, 1996.

4. *Iowa Press Clipping,* Nov. 10, 1996.

5. Interview with Fred Moore, June 6, 2005.

6. *Buena Vista Today,* fall, 1996.

7. Sandra Madsen to William Cumberland, April 26, 2005, e-mail.

8. Carl Adkins to William Cumberland, March 27, 2004, e-mail. Jeanne Tinsley to William Cumberland, Sept. 13, 2005, e-mail.

9. *Buena Vista Today,* winter, 1998.

10. Buena Vista University, *NCA Self Study,* p. 5.

11. Ernest Boyer, *Scholarship Reconsidered,* pp. 77–78.

12. *Sioux City Journal,* Aug. 1, 1996.

13. *Storm Lake Pilot-Tribune,* April 23, 1996.

14. *Buena Vista Today,* Inaugural Address, fall, 1996.

15. *Pilot-Tribune,* Feb. 18, 1997.

16. *Tack,* Sept. 26, 1997.

17. Ibid.

18. Buena Vista University, *NCA Self Study,* p. 20.

19. Ibid.

20. *Buena Vista Today,* Feb. 2005.

21. Ibid., winter, 2000.

22. Ibid.

23. *Cedar Rapids Gazette,* Nov. 28, 2004.

24. *Buena Vista Briefs,* spring, 2002.

25. *Tack,* Sept. 3, 1999.

26. Interview with Fred Moore, June 6, 2005.

27. Ibid.

28. *Tack,* Sept. 3, 1999.

29. *Tack,* March 8, 1996.

30. Buena Vista University, *NCA Self Study*, p. 35.

31. *Buena Vista University College Catalogue* 2004–05, pp. 8–12.
32. *Tack,* Oct. 29, 1999.
33. Ibid., March 2, 2001.
34. *Tack,* Oct. 29, 1999.
35. *Campus Technology,* March 23, 2005.
36. William Feis to William Cumberland, July 6, 2004, e-mail.
37. *Buena Vista Today,* winter, 1997.
38. *Tack,* May 3, 1996.
39. *Tack,* Sept. 26, 1997.
40. *Campus Ministry and Spiritual Life Pamphlet,* 2003.
41. Interview with Fred Moore, June 6, 2005.
42. *Buena Vista Today,* winter, 2004.
43. *Campus Technology,* March 23, 2005.
44. Interview with Fred Moore, June 6, 2005.
45. *Tack,* Feb. 18, 2000.
46. *Storm Lake Times,* March 24, 2001.
47. *Cedar Rapids Gazette,* May 20, 2001.
48. Ibid.
49. *Pilot-Tribune,* Oct. 17, 2000.
50. *Tack,* Oct. 13, Oct. 20, 2000.
51. *Sioux City Journal,* Oct. 6, 2001.
52. *Tack,* Dec. 1, 2000.
53. *Pilot-Tribune,* Feb. 14, 1996.
54. *Storm Lake Times,* April 18, 2001.
55. *Campus Technology,* March 23, 2005.
56. *Pilot-Tribune,* April 25, 2001.
57. Interview with Fred Moore, June 6 2005.
58. *Buena Vista Today,* summer, 2003.
59. William Feis to William Cumberland, March 18, 2005, e-mail.
60. *Campus Technology,* March 23, 2005.
61. Ibid.
62. Ibid.
63. Interview with Fred Moore, June 6, 2005.
64. Paul Bowers to William Cumberland, April 15, 2005, e-mail.
65. *Tack,* May 13, 2005.
66. Ibid.
67. *Buena Vista Today,* winter, 1998.
68. *Tack,* May 9, 1997.
69. *Buena Vista Today,* winter, 1997.
70. *Sioux City Journal,* Sept. 18, 2000.
71. *Buena Vista Web Site,* March 2005.
72. *Buena Vista Today,* winter, 2002.
73. *Tack,* May 4, 2001.
74. *Buena Vista Today,* winter, 2002.
75. Ibid., *Buena Vista University College Catalogue* 2004–05.
76. *Tack,* Sept. 8, 2000.
77. *Pilot-Tribune,* March 9, 2002.
78. Ibid.

79. Ibid.
80. Ibid.
81. Ibid.
82. *Pilot-Tribune*, Sept. 22, 2004.
83. *Storm Lake Times,* Sept. 15, 2004.
84. *Pilot-Tribune*, Sept. 22, 2004.
85. *Storm Lake Times,* Sept. 22, 2004.
86. *Pilot-Tribune*, Sept. 11, 2004.
87. *Buena Vista University, President's Report,* 2000–01.
88. Ibid.
89. *Tack*, Sept. 14, 2001.
90. *Tack*, Sept. 28, 2001.
91. *Tack*, Nov. 21, 2003.
92. Interview with Fred Moore, June 6, 2005.
93. *Tack*, Feb. 28, 1992.
94. *Buena Vista Today*, winter, 2004.
95. *Tack*, Oct. 8, 1998.
96. *Tack,* Oct. 13, 1995.
97. *Tack,* Sept. 25, 1992.
98. *Tack,* April 19, 1996.
99. *Tack,* Oct. 4, 1996.
100. *Storm Lake Times,* Jan. 22, 1997.
101. *Tack*, Nov. 3, 1995.
102. *Buena Vista Today*, winter, 2004.
103. Ibid.
104. *Pilot-Tribune,* Feb. 2, 2002.
105. *Buena Vista Today,* winter, 2004.
106. *Tack,* Feb. 21, 2003.
107. *Tack,* April 11, 2003.
108. *Tack,* Sept. 5, 2003.
109. *Tack,* Oct. 29, 2004.
110. *Buena Vista Today,* winter, 2004.
111. *Pilot-Tribune,* Feb. 2, 2002.
112. Mike Whitlatch to William Cumberland, July 20, 2005, e-mail.
113. *Tack,* Oct. 26, 1996.
114. *Buena Vista Today,* winter, 1997.
115. *Tack,* Oct. 8, 1998.
116. *Pilot-Tribune,* Sept. 12, 2004.
117. Buena Vista University, *NCA Self Study,* p. 49.
118. *Pilot-Tribune,* June 14, 2001.
119. Ibid.
120. Buena Vista University, *NCA Self Study,* pp. 15–16.
121. Ibid., p. 19.
122. *Storm Lake Times,* Oct. 20, 2001.
123. Interview with Fred Moore, June 6, 2005.
124. *Tack,* March 7, 2003.
125. *Tack,* Nov. 17, 2000.
126. *Pilot-Tribune,* Dec. 21, 2002.

127. Sandra Madsen to William Cumberland, April 26, 2005, e-mail.

128. *Tack,* Nov. 17, 2000.

129. *Tack,* April 16, 2004.

130. Buena Vista University, *NCA Self Study,* p. 42.

131. *Tack,* April 16, 2004.

132. *Academe,* March–April 2005, July–Aug. 2005.

133. Gubanc left for a faculty position at Simpson College and as previously noted, Inglis died an untimely and tragic death as a cancer victim.

134. Buena Vista University, *NCA Self Study,* pp. 51–52.

135. Ibid., p. 52.

136. *Tack,* Nov. 10, 1995.

137. *Tack,* Nov. 21, 1997.

138. *Tack,* Oct. 8, 1999.

139. *Tack,* Feb. 15, 2002.

140. William Feis to William Cumberland, July 7, 2004, e-mail.

141. *Buena Vista University News Release,* May 20, 2000.

142. William Feis to William Cumberland, July 7, 2004, e-mail.

143. *Buena Vista University Announcement,* May 2005.

CHAPTER 15.   EPILOGUE

1. *Tack,* May 3, 1996.

2. Ibid., Oct. 25, 1991.

3. Ernest Boyer, *Scholarship Reconsidered,* p. 75.

4. Ibid., p. 75.

5. Ibid., p. 76.

6. Ibid., pp. 79–80.

7. Steve Smith to William Cumberland, Oct. 6, 1997,

8. *Buena Vista Today,* winter 2005.

9. George Christakes to William Cumberland, Resume, spring, 2005.

10. Howe & Strauss. *Millennials Go to College.*

11. *Tack,* Feb. 15, 2002.

12. *Office of the President,* Aug. 9, 2005.

13. Ernest Boyer, *Scholarship Reconsidered,* p. 73.

BIBLIOGRAPHY

Academe, March–April, July–August 2005.

Alumni Directory, 1893–1991.

Anderson, Russell. Interview with Sue Brinkman, May 13, 1985.

Articles of Incorporation. Buena Vista College, 1899.

Aryanpur, Manoocher. Interview with Sue Brinkman, April 17, 1986.

Athletic Files, Buena Vista College 1897–1990. Compiled by Jay Miller.

Athletic Records, Buena Vista Internet 1990–2005.

Aurner, C. R. *History of Education in Iowa.* 4 vols. Iowa City: State Historical Society of Iowa, 1914.

Beaver Log. Buena Vista College 1947–78.

The Beaver Report. Buena Vista College 1955–59.

Beekmann, Jay. Interview with Sue Brinkman, June 13, 1985.

Benjamin, E. S. Letters to author, 1963–65.

Bloom, Esther. Letters to author, 1988.

Board of Trustees. Minutes, 1891–1988, 1995–96.

Boyer, Ernest. *Scholarship Reconsidered.* The Carnegie Foundation: New
York, 1990.

Brigham, Johnson. *Iowa, Its History and Its Foremost Citizens.* 3 vols.
Chicago; S. J. Clarke Co., 1915.

Briscoe, Keith G. "Address." Siebens Memorial Service I. February 16,
1989.

———. "Interiors of the Presidency," J. L. Fisher and M. W. Tack (eds.).
Leaders on Leadership: The College Presidency. San Francisco:
Jossdey-Bass, Spring 1988.

———. Interview with author, September 29, 1989.

———. Memo on Covenant Relationship to Presbyterian Church, April
20, 1984.

Brown, Fred G. Interview with author, June 1, 1987.

Buena Vista College. *Announcement,* 1891–92.

———. *Baccalaureate and Commencement Program,* 1989.

———. *Buena Vista Today,* 1973–2005.

———. *Buena Vista View,* 1984.

———. *Buena Vista Bulletin,* 1891–1965.

———. *Catalogue,* 1891–1961.

———. Chapel Farewell Service, June 4, 1918.

———. *The College World,* 1892–93.

_____. *The College Yell,* 1895.

_____. Committee on the Future, report, 1975.

_____. Long–range planning document, John Williams to faculty, January 28, 1972.

_____. *Newsletter,* 1891–1991.

_____. *President's Report,* 1984.

_____. Press Releases, 1954–90.

_____. *Scrapbook.* 1954–2005 (contains clippings pertaining to Buena Vista from newspapers throughout Iowa).

_____. *Students' Handbook,* 1928–30.

_____. *Vista Vue,* 1986–90.

_____. *Buena Vista College v. Floyd T. Voris.* District Court of Iowa, Box. No. 123, No. 4938, November Term, 1904.

_____. *Buena Vista County Herald,* 1936.

_____. *Buena Vista County History.* WPA, Iowa Writers Project, 1942.

_____. *Buena Vista University Announcement,* May 2005.

_____. *Briefs,* 2000–05.

_____. *Catalogue,* 2004–05.

_____. *News Release,* 2000–05.

_____. *NCA Self Study Report,* 2000.

_____. *Office of University Communications,* 2003–05.

_____. *President's Reports,* 1996–2005.

_____. *Progress Report on the Assessment of Student Academic Achievement at Buena Vista University.* Storm Lake, Iowa, 2004.

Calkins, Homer L. "From Many Lands." *The Palimpsest* (April 1962).

Campus Technology, 2005.

Cedar Rapids Gazette, May 20, 2001, November 28, 2004.

Christakes, George. Letter to author, 1989.

Chronicle of Higher Education, October 13, 2000.

Cooke, Edith. "A Scrapbook for Our Soldiers and Sailors." College Library.

Cumberland, William H. "Notes from Briscoe Address." Faculty recognition dinner, May 21, 1988.

_____. "Notes from Board of Trustees Meeting," October 24, 1986.

_____. "Notes from Faculty Recognition Dinner, May 21, 1988.

_____. "Notes from the Wythe Committee."

Dedication of the Schaller Memorial Chapel, May 12, 1963. Pamphlet. Buena Vista College, 1963.

Design for Learning. Pamphlet. Buena Vista College, 1960.

Des Moines Register. 1933, 1954–89.

Drury, C. M. "Buena Vista College 1914–18." Typescript, n.d.

_____. Letters to author. 1964–65. These cover the period when Drury was a student, 1914–18.

Dwelle, Alberta. Letters to Barbara Palling, 1985.

Edson, W. C. File containing notes, letters, and statements covering Edson's long career as student and trustee, 1893–1961.

Eilers, T. D., ed. *Buena Vista's Part in the World War.* Cedar Rapids: Torch Press, 1920.

e-mail respondents:
> Carl Adkins
> Al Baxter
> Paul Bowers
> George Christakes
> Jamii Claiborne
> Nassar Dastrange
> William Feis
> Nick Huber
> John Madsen
> Sandra Madsen
> Chuck Offenburger ("Iowa Boy")
> Donna Schoneboom
> Steve Smith
> Jeanne Tinsley
> Mike Whitlach
> Marge Willadsen
> Leon Williams

Faculty Minutes, Buena Vista College, 1920–90.

Ferguson, W. R. "Golden Years." *The Palimpsest* (September 1947).

Fisher, John Albert. Public Relations Pamphlet, 1950.

Fisher, Ruth Ann. Interview with Barbara Palling, July 25, 26, 31, 1989.

Flickinger, R. E. *The Early Years of Iowa and Pioneer History of Pocahontas County.* George Sandborn, *Fonda Times,* 1904.

Foote, Henry Wilder. *The Religion of Thomas Jefferson.* Boston: Beacon Press, 1947.

Fort Dodge Messenger, June 20, 1889–July 23, 1891.

Geiger, Louis G. *Voluntary Accreditation.* Menosha, Wisconsin: George Banta Co., 1970.

Glass, R. J. *Iowa and Counties of Iowa.* Mason City: Klipto Loose Leaf Co., 1940.

Halverson, Wendell Q. Interview with author, October 1989.

Harlan, E. R. *A Narrative History of the People of Iowa.* 3 vols. Chicago and New York: American Historical Society, 1931.

Hinkhouse, J. F. *One Hundred Years of the Iowa Presbyterian Church.* Cedar Rapids: Laurance Press Co., 1932.

Hirsch, Lilly. *Profile of Buena Vista College,* 1966.

Howe, Neil, and Strauss, William. *Millennials Go to College.* AACRAO, 2003.

The Inauguration of Wendell Quelprud Halverson. Pamphlet. Buena Vista College, 1961.

Iowa Press Clippings (state newspaper files from BVU Communications Center).

Irons, William. *Document,* 1985.

Irvine, Reed. "*A Tribute to Harold W. Siebens,*" May 24, 1989.

Janssen, Scott. Research Project, 1989.

Jennie G. Hutchison v. Buena Vista College, District Court of Iowa, 1915.

Krogstad, Inc. Letter to Jim Zabel, 1989.

Kuehl, Gladys. Letters to author, 1989.

Kuehl, William. Letter to author, 1990.

Lahr, Paul H. Letter to Greg Evans, 1987.

Lakeside Church. Historical Materials.

Lamkin, C. F. *A Great Small College.* St. Louis: Horace Barks Press, 1946.

Lampe, David. Letter to author, 1989.

Malone, Dumas. *Jefferson and the Ordeal of Liberty.* Boston: Little, Brown & Co., 1962.

Marple, Alice. *Iowa Authors and Their Works.* Des Moines: Historical Department of Iowa, 1918.

Meissner, Rev. Kenneth D., *Campus Ministry and Spiritual Life.* 2002–03 Annual Report.

Monmouth College. *Bulletin,* 1951.

Moore, Fred. Interview with author, June 6, 2005.

Musgrave, Stella Russell. "When the Arch of Old Main Was Built." Buena Vista College, n.d.

Nollen, John S. *Grinnell College.* Iowa City: State Historical Society of Iowa, 1953.

North Central Association. *Report.* Pamphlet, 1950.

_____. "Report of Visit to Buena Vista College." Pamphlet. May 11–13, 1971.

North Central Association of Schools and Colleges. "Report of A Comprehensive Visit to Buena Vista University." November 13–15, 2000.

Offenburger.com. *Out in Greene County, Iowa.* Web site.

Office of the President, August 9, 2005.

Patillo, Manning M., Jr. (associate secretary NCA). Letter to Henry Olson, May 9, 1952.

Peck, Darrell, G. Interview with Sue Brinkman, June 6, 1985.

Plagman, Ralph Jr. *Storm Lake: The First Decade (1870–1880).* History Project. Buena Vista College, n.d.

Presbyterian Church in the U.S.A. Boards of the General Assembly Reports, 1893–1912.

Presbyterian Church in the U.S.A. Boards of Visitors Report, 1968.

Reed, Ellery F. Letters to author, 1965.

Richardson, Clarence. Interview with author, October 25, 1989.

Riegel, R. E. *America Moves West.* New York: Holt, Rinehart & Winston, 1960.

Ross, E. A. *Seventy Years of It.* New York: Appleton Century Co., 1936.

Rudder. 1907, 1909–33, 1937.

Rules and Regulations Governing Students. Buena Vista College, June 1, 1911.

Siebens Den. Album 62. A collection of articles and photos covering the life of the Philanthropist.

Siebens, Harold W. Interview with Sue Brinkman and William Cumberland, July 1985.

_____. Letters to Robert J. Siefer, 1970–72.

_____. Memorial Service I. Schaller Chapel, February 16, 1989.

_____, Memorial Service II. Schaller Chapel, May 24, 1989.

Siefer, Robert J. Letters to Harold W. Siebens, 1970–72.

Sioux City Journal, August 1, 1996, April 18, 2000, October 6, 2001.

Sioux City Presbytery Minutes, 1891–1900.

Slagle, Charles. Interview with Sue Brinkman, June 11, 1985.

Smith, Steve. Letter to author, October 6, 1997.

Storm Lake Pilot, 1890–96.

Storm Lake Pilot-Tribune, 1896–2005.

Storm Lake Times, December 22, 1997, March 24, 2001, April 18, 2001, October 20, 2001, September 15, 2004.

Storm Lake Tribune, 1892–94.

Storm Lake Vidette. Buena Vista College Songs, n.d.

Synod of Iowa, Presbyterian Church in the U.S.A. Minutes, seventy-second annual meeting, Ames: July 6–9, 1953.

Synod of Iowa, Presbyterian Church in the U.S.A. Minutes, seventy-third annual meeting, Ames: July 5–8, 1954.

Tack, 1895–2005 (some issues missing).

Theulen, Glenn. Interview with author, Summer, 1988.

Throop, the Rev. Mr. Hervey. Letter to author, 1989.

Turnbull, J. E. *The Iowa Conference Story.* Iowa City: State Historical Society of Iowa, 1961.

U.S. News & World Report, November 25, 1985.

Van Haaften, Brian. *A Look from Within.* N & K Publishing, Virginia, 2003.

Williams, Daniel. *A History of Lakeside Church.* Pamphlet, 1914.

Wegerslev, C. H. "Buena Vista County," *Who's Who in Iowa.* Iowa Press Association, 1940.

_____. *Past and Present of Buena Vista County.* Chicago: S. J. Clarke Co., 1909.

Who Was Who in America. Vol. I, 1897–1942. Chicago: A. N. Marquis Co., 1943.

Wikstrom, Gunnar, "Remembrance," Fall, 1999.

Williams, Les and Edith. Interview with author, July 7, 1989.

Winters, C. L. *Survey Report of Buena Vista College,* October 29, 1950.

Wood, Gerald. Interview with author, Summer, 1988.

INDEX